Making a Living
in
France

A Survival Handbook

by
Joe Laredo

SURVIVAL BOOKS • LONDON • ENGLAND

First published 2005

Survival Books Limited,
26 York Street, London W1U 6PZ, United Kingdom
☎ +44 (0)20-7788 7644, ▤ +44 0870-762 3212
✉ info@survivalbooks.net
🖥 www.survivalbooks.net
To order books, please refer to page 419.

British Library Cataloguing in Publication Data.
A CIP record for this book is available
from the British Library.
ISBN 1 901130 78 9

Printed and bound in Finland by WS Bookwell Ltd.

ACKNOWLEDGEMENTS

I would like to thank Adam Dakin of Vignobles Investissement, who provided information about buying a vineyard, David Franks of Blevins Franks for explaining the vagaries of commercial transfer tax, Wanda Glowinska-Rizzi for investigating the ins and outs of being self-employed in France, Annie Graf for information about working as a ski instructor, Micky Kay of Waterside Properties for information about buying a lake for fishing, Bev Laflamme for delving into the labyrinthine world of business set-up and its financial implications, Pascal Martory for information about working as a sports and dance instructor, Jo Whelan for unravelling the legal complications of self-employment and running a business in France, Martin Hills for tracking down and interviewing the 39 expatriates who have contributed their experiences to **Part Two**, and, of course, the interviewees themselves (listed in **Appendix A**). I would also like to thank Catherine Wakelin for proofreading the text and pointing out inconsistencies and omissions, and my wife Kerry for producing the index and laying out the book for printing. Last but not least, a big thank-you to Jim Watson for his inimitable illustrations and the stylish cover design and pages of photographs.

TITLES BY SURVIVAL BOOKS

Alien's Guides
Britain; France

The Best Places To Buy A Home
France; Spain

Buying A Home
Abroad; Cyprus; Florida;
France; Greece; Ireland; Italy;
Portugal; South Africa; Spain;
Buying, Selling & Letting
Property (UK)

Foreigners Abroad: Triumphs & Disasters
France; Spain

Lifeline Regional Guides
Costa Blanca; Costa del Sol;
Dordogne/Lot; Normandy;
Poitou-Charentes

Living And Working
Abroad; America;
Australia; Britain; Canada;
The European Union;
The Far East; France; Germany;
The Gulf States & Saudi Arabia;
Holland, Belgium & Luxembourg;
Ireland; Italy; London;
New Zealand; Spain;
Switzerland

Making A Living
France; Spain

Other Titles
Renovating & Maintaining
Your French Home;
Retiring Abroad

Order forms are on page 419.

What Readers & Reviewers

When you buy a model plane for your child, a video recorder, or some new computer gizmo, you get with it a leaflet or booklet pleading 'Read Me First', or bearing large friendly letters or bold type saying 'IMPORTANT – follow the instructions carefully'. This book should be similarly supplied to all those entering France with anything more durable than a 5-day return ticket. It is worth reading even if you are just visiting briefly, or if you have lived here for years and feel totally knowledgeable and secure. But if you need to find out how France works then it is indispensable. Native French people probably have a less thorough understanding of how their country functions. – Where it is most essential, the book is most up to the minute.

LIVING FRANCE

Rarely has a 'survival guide' contained such useful advice. This book dispels doubts for first-time travellers, yet is also useful for seasoned globetrotters – In a word, if you're planning to move to the USA or go there for a long-term stay, then buy this book both for general reading and as a ready-reference.

AMERICAN CITIZENS ABROAD

It is everything you always wanted to ask but didn't for fear of the contemptuous put down – The best English-language guide – Its pages are stuffed with practical information on everyday subjects and are designed to complement the traditional guidebook.

SWISS NEWS

A complete revelation to me – I found it both enlightening and interesting, not to mention amusing.

CAROLE CLARK

Let's say it at once. David Hampshire's *Living and Working in France* is the best handbook ever produced for visitors and foreign residents in this country; indeed, my discussion with locals showed that it has much to teach even those born and bred in l'Hexagone. – It is Hampshire's meticulous detail which lifts his work way beyond the range of other books with similar titles. Often you think of a supplementary question and search for the answer in vain. With Hampshire this is rarely the case. – He writes with great clarity (and gives French equivalents of all key terms), a touch of humour and a ready eye for the odd (and often illuminating) fact. – This book is absolutely indispensable.

THE RIVIERA REPORTER

A mine of information – I may have avoided some embarrassments and frights if I had read it prior to my first Swiss encounters – Deserves an honoured place on any newcomer's bookshelf.

ENGLISH TEACHERS ASSOCIATION, SWITZERLAND

HAVE SAID ABOUT SURVIVAL BOOKS

What a great work, wealth of useful information, well-balanced wording and accuracy in details. My compliments!

THOMAS MÜLLER

This handbook has all the practical information one needs to set up home in the UK – The sheer volume of information is almost daunting – Highly recommended for anyone moving to the UK.

AMERICAN CITIZENS ABROAD

A very good book which has answered so many questions and even some I hadn't thought of – I would certainly recommend it.

BRIAN FAIRMAN

We would like to congratulate you on this work: it is really super! We hand it out to our expatriates and they read it with great interest and pleasure.

ICI (SWITZERLAND) AG

Covers just about all the things you want to know on the subject – In answer to the desert island question about the one how-to book on France, this book would be it – Almost 500 pages of solid accurate reading – This book is about enjoyment as much as survival.

THE RECORDER

It's so funny – I love it and definitely need a copy of my own – Thanks very much for having written such a humorous and helpful book.

HEIDI GUILIANI

A must for all foreigners coming to Switzerland.

ANTOINETTE O'DONOGHUE

A comprehensive guide to all things French, written in a highly readable and amusing style, for anyone planning to live, work or retire in France.

THE TIMES

A concise, thorough account of the DOs and DON'Ts for a foreigner in Switzerland – Crammed with useful information and lightened with humorous quips which make the facts more readable.

AMERICAN CITIZENS ABROAD

Covers every conceivable question that may be asked concerning everyday life – I know of no other book that could take the place of this one.

FRANCE IN PRINT

Hats off to *Living and Working in Switzerland*!

RONNIE ALMEIDA

CONTENTS

Part One

THE AUTHOR

Having obtained a Modern Languages degree and worked for a number of years in the marine industry, Joe Laredo became a freelance translator, proofreader and writer in 1996. A year later, he began working for Survival Books, for whom he has written two books – *Buying a Home in Ireland* and *Living and Working in Ireland* – and compiled the *The Best Places to Buy a Home in France*.

Joe and his wife, Kerry, moved to Normandy in 2001 and together they're now responsible for regularly updating Survival Books' popular titles *Buying a Home in France* and *Living and Working in France* as well as editing, proofreading and typesetting other Survival Books publications.

Joe has also contributed to *French* magazine, *French News*, *The Connexion*, *The Squash Player* magazine and *International Piano* magazine.

Important Note

France is a large country with myriad faces and many ethnic groups, religions and customs. Although ostensibly the same throughout the country, many laws, rules and regulations, especially those associated with doing business, are open to local interpretation and are occasionally even formulated on the spot! The laws and regulations relating to business also change frequently as France grapples with European Union strictures.

I cannot recommend too strongly that you check with an official and reliable source (not always the same) before making any major decisions or undertaking an irreversible course of action. However, don't believe everything you're told or have read, even – dare I say it? – in this book! Always check and double check things for yourself.

To help you obtain further information and verify data with official sources, useful addresses and references to other sources of information have been included in all chapters and in **Appendices A to C**. Important points have been emphasised throughout the book in bold print, some of which it would be expensive or foolish to disregard. **Ignore them at your peril or cost.** Unless specifically stated, the reference to any company, organisation, product or publication in this book doesn't constitute an endorsement or recommendation.

Author's Notes

- Frequent references are made throughout this book to the European Union (EU), which comprises 25 countries, and to the European Economic Area (EEA), which comprises the EU countries plus Iceland, Liechtenstein and Norway.

- Times are shown using the 24-hour clock; for example, two o'clock in the afternoon is written as 14.00.

- His/he/him/man/men (etc.) also mean her/she/her/woman/women (no offence ladies!). This is done simply to make life easier for both the reader and, in particular, the author, and isn't intended to be sexist.

- British English is used throughout, but American English equivalents are given where appropriate.

- Warnings and important points are shown in **bold type**.

- French words and phrases are given in brackets in *italics*.

- The following symbols are used in this book: ☎ (telephone), 🖷 (fax), 🖳 (internet) and ✉ (email).

- Lists of useful addresses, further reading and useful websites are contained in **Appendices A, B** and **C** respectively.

- For those unfamiliar with the metric system of weights and measures, conversion tables are included in **Appendix D**.

- A map of France showing the departments and regions is in **Appendix E**.

INTRODUCTION

France continues to hold a fascination for millions of tourists every year, many of whom decide to buy holiday homes or retire to France. The last few years have seen a significant change in expatriate demographics, a growing number of younger people, many with families, selling up in their home countries and coming to France in search of a new life, and more immigrants than ever wanting (or needing) to make a living in France.

The purpose of *Making a Living in France* is to provide you with the information necessary to help you to do just that. One of the most common mistakes people make when coming to work or start a business in France is to assume that they can continue working as they did in their home country, especially if they had a successful business. **Don't assume anything!** France is a large and immensely varied country, with 22 regions, 96 departments and over 35,000 communes. Each area has its own culture and, inevitably, its own way of doing business, and the one thing you can be sure of is that it won't be the same as in your home country! You will be far more successful if you learn to adapt and be flexible than if you try to fight the system, as most of the contributors to this book have discovered.

Making a Living in France contains practical advice to help you find work in France, whether you wish to be self-employed or plan to start a business, as well as the experiences of people from all walks of life who have already taken the plunge and are successfully making a living in France. They explain how they've overcome the notorious French bureaucracy and achieved (more or less!) what they set out to do. Their hard work, perseverance and sense of humour should inspire you to follow in their footsteps.

A love affair with France is all very well, but if you want to do business there you cannot afford to view the country through rose-tinted spectacles, but must take a long, hard look at the realities of French life and give it your long-term commitment. It may be less romantic, but you're more likely to succeed if you accept that life in France, as in any country, has its bad days as well as its good. Making a living in France will change your life for ever and, if you approach it in the right way, open your mind, broaden your horizons, win you new friends, improve your language skills . . . and hopefully make you some money along the way!

Bon courage!

Joe Laredo
May 2005

1.

WHY FRANCE?

If you've only ever visited France on holiday, you may have unrealistic expectations about living and working there, especially if you have to earn a living. It's hard not to be seduced by the relaxed lifestyle and, in the south of the country at least, those endless sunny days. Perhaps that's why you began to think about settling in France in the first place. **It may sound obvious, but spending a holiday and earning a living are two completely different things and confusing the two is a fundamental mistake many people make when they come to work in France.**

Being attracted to France by its weather, cuisine, wine and lifestyle is understandable, but doesn't rate highly as a qualification or a motivation for working there. You should have a positive reason for living and working in France; simply being fed up with your job or the weather isn't the best motive for moving to France. It's extremely difficult to find work in rural areas and isn't easy in cities and large towns (even Paris), especially if your French isn't fluent. You shouldn't plan on obtaining employment in France unless you have a firm job offer and special qualifications or experience for which there's a strong demand. If you want a good job, you must usually be extremely well qualified and speak fluent French. If you intend to come to France without a job, you should have a plan for finding employment on arrival and try to make some contacts before you arrive. If you have a job offer, you should ensure that it's in writing (preferably in French) and check that it isn't likely to be revoked soon after you arrive.

If you're intending to be self-employed or set up a business in France (with which this book is primarily concerned), you should be aware that the French aren't 'natural' entrepreneurs and that support for private enterprise is usually scant and often non-existent. Indeed, as many of our contributors have discovered, you may have the impression that French bank managers and administrators are going out of their way to obstruct your best-laid plans. This isn't usually the case, but is merely symptomatic of a fundamentally non-creative, non-inventive and risk-averse mentality and culture. While such attitudes can be frustrating, they can ultimately be to your advantage: as an entrepreneur, you will generally have less competition from the natives in France than in many other foreign countries. If you can grin and bear the bureaucracy (see page 25), you will have a head start in your aim to make a living in France.

There's no question of simply starting to trade and then paying your taxes at the end of the year – even if you're just a lone freelancer working from your spare bedroom. It's an offence to carry out any sort of economic activity without registering with the appropriate official bodies, even if your clients or customers are outside France. If you're resident in France, having your earnings paid into a foreign bank account doesn't allow you to remain outside the system either. Penalties for illegal working can be steep, and on top of that you are made to pay backdated tax and social security contributions, plus penalties for late payment (see Working Illegally on page 33).

SEEING PAST THE SUNSHINE

It isn't easy to stay focused when you're surrounded by holiday-makers enjoying a long, lazy lunch and your own, seemingly endless, stream of visitors keep urging you to join them on the patio or the beach. You have to be very strong-willed not to take the day off or shut up shop and join them. In this sense, France can be a difficult place to work (especially in the tourist areas) but, unless you have large financial reserves, you cannot afford to play at earning a living there, any more than you can in your own country. You must be professional, hard-working, determined to keep bouncing back after the inevitable knocks, and willing to leave the sunbathing for the weekends!

The people who make a success of making a living in France have usually done exhaustive research and spent a lot of time in the country (other than on holiday). Begin your research by thinking hard about why you've chosen France to work in, rather than any other country. Can you speak any French? This book looks in detail at language learning options, in your home country and in France because, even if you only plan to live and work in the expatriate community, **you must be able to speak at least basic French**. How well do you know the area you're planning to settle in? France is a **big** country – the largest in Europe – and encompasses a surprising variety of accents, attitudes and lifestyles, as well as landscapes. Buy yourself a large map and read as much as you can about the areas you're interested in (a good book is *The Best Places to Buy a Home in France* – see page 419). Find out about France's economy in general and especially the economy of your chosen area. This book contains economic guides to the regions of France that attract the most foreigners. How well do you know the French people and understand their history and culture? It's important to have a little background knowledge before you launch yourself into their world.

Most importantly, are you prepared to forget everything you've learned in your own country and begin again with none of the support networks you used to take for granted? Are you strong enough to deal with feeling like the new boy in school not just for a few months, but for longer than you can imagine? Finally, take a long hard look at France's unemployment figures, which are among the highest in Europe at almost 10 per cent (9.9 per cent in February 2005), compared with UK figures of around 4.5 per cent, for example.

All this may seem daunting, but these are the questions it's vital to research and think about before you make any other decisions. Make yourself answer them honestly at an early stage and you will save yourself time, money and endless heartache in an unfamiliar country. If, after that, you're still feeling strong and determined to try to make a living in France, then you can start to consider how exactly you're going to do so. There's no doubt that it's a long and difficult road; as you struggle to make your way, you will hear plenty of hair-raising stories about people who have lost everything. Learn from them, but don't allow yourself to be thrown off balance by their misfortune. There are many foreigners who have successful businesses and good jobs in France. They're usually the ones who have done, and continue to do, their homework and who are willing to adapt and keep an open mind. Above all, they're prepared to work long and hard to create their own 'luck', rather than sit in a bar talking enviously about other people's 'luck'.

Before moving to France to work, you should dispassionately examine your motives and credentials, and ask yourself the following questions:

- What kind of work can I realistically expect to do?
- What are my qualifications and experience? Are they recognised in France?
- How old am I? (Although discrimination on the basis of your age, physical appearance, name and sexual preference is illegal, age discrimination is rife in France, where only 38 per cent of men aged 55 to 64 work – the lowest percentage in Europe.)
- How good is my French? Unless your French is fluent, you won't be competing on equal terms with the French (you won't anyway, but that's a different matter!). Most French employers aren't interested in employing anyone without, at the very least, an adequate working knowledge of French and to set up almost any business, even if most of your customers are English-speakers, you must be able to speak the language.
- Are there any jobs or opportunities in my profession or trade in the area where I wish to live?
- Do I have what it takes to be self-employed or start my own business – anywhere, let alone in France?
- What are my strengths and weaknesses and does the business I have in mind play to my strengths?
- Am I prepared to go it alone or am I better off going into partnership, bearing in mind that it's difficult to change from being a sole trader to being a partner and vice versa?

The answers to these questions can be disheartening, but it's better to ask them before moving to France than afterwards.

Self-employment and starting a business are strewn with pitfalls for the newcomer. **Most foreigners hoping to earn a living in France don't do sufficient homework before moving.** While hoping for the best, you should anticipate the worst and have a contingency plan and sufficient funds to last until you're established, which can take three years or more. You must also be prepared to do battle with French bureaucracy (see page 25), which is notorious for its intricacy, long-windedness and sheer obstructiveness – *bon courage!*

THE FRENCH ECONOMY

France is one of the wealthiest countries in the world, with one of the highest per capita Gross Domestic Products (GDP) in the European Union (EU) (currently just under US$26,000), although GDP growth in 2003 fell to 0.5 per cent – its slowest rate since 1993 – and overall, the French labour market is stagnant or even in decline. The number of job-seekers is on the increase and is nearing 10 per cent of the workforce.

The country has experienced an economic transformation in the last few decades, during which its traditional industries have been thoroughly modernised and a wealth of new high-tech industries have been created, although increasing competition, particularly from Far Eastern countries (known collectively as *le low-cost!*), has meant that traditional industries such as steel, clothing and textile production have become less competitive. Investment in these areas fell by 0.2 per cent and exports by 2.5 per cent in 2003. On the other hand, the manufacture of ships, cars, aeroplanes and defence equipment remains significant.

Other sectors currently in decline include chemicals (including rubber and plastic products), the electrical and electronic equipment industries, mechanical engineering, metalworking, and the component and household equipment industries. Surprisingly, unemployment is increasing in the computing sector, with the exception of management and engineering jobs. Other sectors affected by increased unemployment are tourism and transport, due largely to the increase in worldwide terrorist activity since September 2001 and the resulting liquidation and failure of a number of airlines, including AirLib recently. In the building sector, only unskilled workers are having difficulty finding jobs (see below). There are also very few secretarial jobs and general unskilled or low-skilled jobs (e.g. cash desk operators, supermarket workers, domestic staff, and caretaking, maintenance and security staff). Would-be artists, writers and performing artists should note that these sectors are traditionally affected by high unemployment. Since the start of the new millennium, inflation has been at just under 2 per cent (it's expected to fall to around 1.5 per cent in 2005), but the government's budget deficit rose to 4.1 per cent of GDP in 2003, when the national debt was estimated at €840 billion – over €2,700 for every man, woman and child!

France has the highest proportion of public sector workers in the EU (around 25 per cent) and they enjoy long holidays, a 35-hour week and often early retirement, with the result that most French people don't dream of becoming businessmen, but of being *fonctionnaires*. Indeed, although the word entrepreneur is of French origin, the concept is alien to French culture in general – only just over 6 per cent of France's workforce is self-employed – so foreigners setting up a business in France often have a head start over the natives.

Business Sectors

Before deciding on a business sector, you must examine the market – nationally, regionally and locally, as appropriate.

Generally, less labour and capital intensive industries such as electronics, food processing, pharmaceuticals and communications have flourished since the '80s, although the largest growth in recent years has been in service industries, e.g. banking, insurance and advertising, which now account for over 70 per cent of GDP compared with industry at around 26 per cent and agriculture at a mere 3 per cent. (France is, nevertheless, Europe's largest agricultural producer with 23 per cent of total EU production.) Other growth areas include construction, retailing (in particular property sales), the consultancy and assistance sectors, the hotel and restaurant sector, and the IT industry.

Nationally, there's currently a shortage of workers in the following areas:

● **Catering** – Bakers, butchers (especially pork butchers), although this is largely due to often difficult working conditions and low wages, which dissuade many potential applicants;

- **Construction** – Skilled building workers and construction managers;
- **Financial Services** – Particularly banking and insurance workers at all levels (from bank managers to bookkeepers and tellers), business management and administration staff;
- **Health Services** – Midwives, nurses and personal care workers, largely as a result of the increased demand for hospital staff following the introduction of the 35-hour week;
- **Industry** – Technicians and managers, particularly in electrical, mechanical and process engineering;
- **Personal Services** – Including hairdressers;
- **Retailing** – Particularly shop managers and sales representatives;
- **Other** – Lorry and taxi drivers, salespeople and stonemasons. There's also a lack of staff in the renewable energy industries (estimated to need over 100,000 extra workers in the next few years).

The following categories of worker are expected to be in demand in the coming years: pastry-cooks and confectionery makers, chemical and physical science technicians, civil engineers, electrical engineering technicians, fishmongers and related food processing staff, institution-based personal care workers, insurance representatives, mechanical engineering technicians, production and operations department managers in the wholesale and retail trades, statistical and finance clerks, and technical and commercial sales representatives.

These shortages may not exist in all areas, of course, so you must check the local situation before settling in a particular place. For details of opportunities in the areas of France most popular with foreigners, see **Chapter 2**.

Female entreneurs should note that male chauvinism is alive and well in France, and women must generally work twice as hard as men to be taken seriously in business. Career women are generally more readily accepted in Paris, which has a more progressive outlook than the provinces (particularly the south, where opinions and attitudes lag behind the north). (See **Business Practice** on page 39.)

Information about specific business sectors can be obtained from the relevant trade journals, which are listed in *L'Annuaire de la Presse, de la Publicité et de la Consommation* (Editions Ecran Publicité) and the MediaSig service (☎ 01 42 75 80 00, 🖳 www.premier-ministre.gouv.fr). For statistics and other information about almost every conceivable occupation in France, go to 🖳 www.patrimoine.com and click on '*Profession*'.

EARNINGS

How much you are able to earn from your employment or business activity obviously depends on a multitude of factors. As an employee, your wages are known in advance, are more or less guaranteed and, at least in theory, can only increase. As a self-employed worker or business owner, you have the potential to earn millions, but also risk bankruptcy and destitution!

French salaries are similar to those in Germany, but generally lower than those in the UK. Most salaries are around the same or slightly lower than in the US, except those of senior management staff, which tend to be higher in France. The average gross annual salary in 2003 was around €16,000; the average manager earned around €40,000, although the average for the Managing Director of a small company was less: around €30,000 for men and €23,000 for women. Trends in earnings are monitored by the Fédération des Centres de Gestion Agréés (🖳 www. fcga.fr – click on 'Etudes économiques'), but published figures are usually at least a year out of date. **When assessing likely earnings, you should take into account that social security contributions are higher in France than in most other western countries (see Chapter 5).**

For many employees, particularly executives and senior managers, their remuneration is much more than what they receive in their monthly pay packets. Many companies offer a range of benefits for executives and managers that may include a company car, private health insurance and health screening, expenses-paid holidays, private school fees, inexpensive or interest-free home and other loans, rent-free accommodation, free or subsidised public transport tickets, free or subsidised company restaurant, sports or country club membership, non-contributory company pension, stock options, bonuses and profit-sharing schemes, tickets for sports events and shows, and 'business' conferences in exotic places. Most employees in France also receive an extra month's salary at Christmas, known as the 13th month's salary, and some companies also pay a 14th month's salary before the summer holiday period.

At the other end of the wage scale, the statutory minimum wage (*salaire minimum de croissance/SMIC*) is currently €7.61 per hour, equal to €1,154.21 per month for 151.67 hours (the new standard under terms of the 35-hour working week), but the *SMIC* obviously doesn't apply to the self-employed, who, for all the government cares, can earn nothing at all! If you employ staff, you must pay them at least the minimum wage, plus social security contributions (see page 210). Many employees, particularly seasonal workers in the farming and tourist industries, are traditionally paid below the minimum wage (although the French government is increasingly clamping down and forcing employers to comply with the law).

Salaries in many industries are decided by collective bargaining between employers and unions, regionally or nationally. When there's a collective agreement, employers must offer at least the minimum wage agreed, although this is exceeded by most major companies. Agreements specify minimum wage levels for each position within main employment categories in a particular industry or company and often require bonus payments related to the age or qualifications of the employee or the length of time he has been with the company (*prime d'ancienneté*). This means that wage levels are effectively fixed. Cost of living increases for salaries above the *SMIC* aren't regulated by the government, although the collective agreement may provide for annual increases based on cost of living figures.

The introduction of the 35-hour week included guarantees that salaries could not be reduced from the levels paid on a 39-hour week basis. Government incentives available to employers for hiring additional workers did little to reduce the overall cost of reducing the working week, and it's likely most salaries will remain static and pay rises will be few and far between for the next several years.

Salaries in France must be reviewed once a year (usually at the end of the year), although employers aren't required by law to increase salaries which are above the minimum wage, even when the cost of living has increased. Salary increases usually take effect on 1st January.

Self-employed

It's obviously almost impossible to give an indication of likely earnings for the self-employed, which could be anything from zero to riches, depending on your success (or luck). The only guide is average earnings, which in recent years, according to INSEE, the national statistics office, have been as follows:

- **Business Consulting** (legal services, accountancy, etc.) – €38,100;
- **Business Services** (security, cleaning, etc.) – €23,000;
- **Car Sales & Repair** – €21,700;
- **Construction** – €24,100;
- **General Sales, Wholesale & Distribution** – €20,400;
- **Hospitality Services** (including hotels, cafes, restaurants and hairdressers) – €16,700;
- **Industry** (other than the commercial tradesmen and those in the energy industry) – €19,800;
- **Non-scholastic Education** (training, driving instruction, etc.) – €14,800;
- **Pharmacy** – €100,800 (being a pharmacist is a licence to print money in France!);
- **Property Sales & Management** – €24,100;
- **Recreational, Cultural & Sports Activities** – €15,600;
- **Retail Sales** (other than pharmacy and cars) – €19,100;
- **Transport** – €17,000.

⚠ **The large majority of self-employed people are married or living with a partner and depend in some way on their spouse or partner for 'support' (i.e. unpaid help) in getting the business started (usually to assist with paperwork). Only 57 per cent of new businesses survive the first three years; only 45 per cent survive five years (roughly one in two tradespeople and one in three people working in commerce or a *profession libérale*).**

For more information on self-employment, see **Chapter 3**.

COST OF LIVING

No doubt you would like to try to estimate how far your euros will stretch if you live and work in France. If you're coming from the UK, you will generally find property prices considerably lower, and food and (especially) drink relatively cheap; Americans won't be so pleasantly surprised. Tools and building materials tend to be slightly more expensive and most household and hygiene products cost considerably more. The cost of transport (i.e. fuel and public transport tickets) is similar to the UK; car insurance is expensive and there are motorway tolls to pay, but parking is often free. The price of entertainment is comparable and there are many subsidised clubs and societies. Communications (e.g. telephone and internet connections) are competitive and constantly being reduced. Income tax is lower than in the UK, but social security costs are much higher, particularly for the self-employed, and the combined burden of social security, income tax and indirect taxes make French taxes among the highest in the EU.

Anyone planning to live in France, particularly retirees, should take care not to underestimate the cost of living, which has increased considerably in the last decade. In recent years, many US visitors have found it difficult or impossible to remain within their budgets. (Americans will be particularly shocked by the price of fuel, electricity, clothing, paper products and English-language books.)

It's difficult to calculate an average cost of living in France, as it depends on each individual's circumstances and lifestyle and varies according to where you live: in the major cities, the higher cost of living is usually offset by higher wages.

If you insist on eating and drinking as you did in your previous country of residence, your shopping bills will inevitably be high. If, on the other hand, you adopt French ways and buy local produce, when it's in season, you can live relatively cheaply (and well).

Shopping abroad for selected items can result in significant savings, although you should take into account transport or shipping costs and, if you're buying outside the EU, import duties.

BUREAUCRACY

French bureaucracy (euphemistically called *l'administration*) is legendary and, when applying for documentation, you should be prepared for frustration caused by overefficiency, inefficiency and various kinds of deficiency on the part of officials (properly known as *fonctionnaires*, but sometimes referred to as *cravattés*, meaning 'tie-wearers'). This isn't necessarily xenophobia – they treat their fellow countrymen in the same way! – and whether you speak perfect French or no French at all often makes no difference. Often you may wonder whether the right hand knows what any other part of the body is up to and you should expect to receive conflicting information from consulates, government departments, *préfectures* and town halls.

Red tape (*paperasse*) is a way of life in France, where every encounter with officialdom requires the production of a *dossier* as thick as your arm. In order to obtain a permit you must complete numerous forms, answer dozens of seemingly irrelevant questions and provide mountains of documents with official translations (a paperchase designed to keep as many civil servants in 'employment' as possible). As one of our contributors (a fluent French-speaker, incidentally) wryly put it: "At the time of the Revolution, the French people cut off the king's head but, since then, the administration has generated many little 'kings', each of whom needs to have some power ..."

Never take anything for granted where French administration is concerned and make sure you have copies of **everything** to hand, just in case. When dealing with officialdom in France, you must persevere, as the first answer is almost always '*Non!*' Bear in mind also that French administrators (and others) are essentially passive rather than active ('proactive' is a term they would scarcely comprehend) and you must invariably prompt them in order to obtain the advice or help you need, which will rarely be proffered. The French are masters of the art of responding to questions, but generally incompetent at anticipating them, let alone assessing your needs, pre-empting your concerns and allaying your fears (although they will frequently exhort you not to worry – "*Ne vous inquiétez pas*"!).

All our contributors are agreed on one thing: that perseverance, persistence, patience and politeness are essential, as you won't get far without plenty of all four. And if *l'administration* ever threatens to get the better of you, treat yourself to a leisurely French meal and your tribulations will pale into insignificance!

PERMITS & VISAS

Before making any plans to live and work in France, you must ensure that you have the necessary identity card or passport (with a visa if necessary) and, if you're planning to stay long-term, the appropriate documentation to obtain a residence and/or work permit. There are different requirements for different nationalities and circumstances, as detailed below.

Immigration is a complex and ever-changing subject and the information in this chapter is intended only as a general guide. You shouldn't base any decisions or actions on the information contained herein without confirming it with an official and reliable source, such as a French consulate.

Visas

Visitors from European Union (EU) countries plus Andorra, Canada, Iceland, Japan, Monaco, New Zealand, Norway, Singapore, South Korea, Switzerland and the US don't require a visa to enter France. Non-EU nationals may need a visa to enter the country, either as visitors or for any other purpose. Some countries (e.g. Ireland and Italy) allow foreigners with close ancestors (e.g. a grandfather) who were born there to apply for a passport for that country, which can allow non-EU citizens to become 'members' of the EU. Visas may be valid for a single entry only or for multiple entries within a limited period. A visa is stamped in your passport, which must be valid for at least 60 days **after** the date you intend to leave France.

There are three main types of visa:

Short-stay Visa

A short-stay visa (*visa de court séjour*, sometimes referred to as a 'Schengen Visa') is valid for 90 days and is usually valid for multiple entries as well as for free circulation within the group of EU nations that are signatories to the Schengen agreement (i.e. Austria, Belgium, Denmark, Finland, France, Germany, Greece, Italy,

Luxembourg, the Netherlands, Portugal, Spain and Sweden). A short-stay visa costs from €25 to €50, depending on the type.

Long-stay Visa

A national of any country other than those listed above intending to remain in France for more than 90 days, whether to work, study or merely holiday, must obtain a long-stay visa (*visa de long séjour*) **before** arriving in France and must apply for a residence permit within a week of arrival. **If you arrive in France without a long-stay visa, it's almost impossible to change your status after arrival and, if you wish to remain for longer than 90 days, you must return to your country of residence and apply for a long-stay visa.** Parents requiring a visa who have children under 18 must also obtain long-stay visas for their children.

Au Pairs: To obtain a long-stay visa for an au pair position, you must usually have an agreement (*déclaration d'engagement*) with a family, a certificate of registration for French-language classes and medical insurance. The family or au pair agency must complete the application forms (*accord de placement au pair d'un stagiaire aide-familial*) available from the office of the Direction Départementale du Travail et de la Main d'Oeuvre in the department where you will be resident. Two copies of the form are returned to the family or agency, one of which is forwarded to you so that you can apply for a visa. An au pair's residence permit (*permis de stagiaire aide-familiale*) is valid for six months and renewable for up to 18 months.

Applications

Applications for visas must be made to the French embassy or consulate in your country of residence. Applicants for long-stay visas living in a country other than their country of nationality must apply in their country of nationality unless they've been resident abroad for at least a year. You can usually apply for a visa in person or by post. If you apply in person, you should bear in mind that there are long queues at consulates in major cities (take a big book to read).

The documentation required for a visa application depends on the purpose of your visit to France. All applicants require:

- A passport valid for at least three months beyond the last day of your intended stay in France;
- A ticket (or evidence of having booked a ticket) for your outward and return journey;
- The official visa application form(s), obtainable from a French consulate or via the internet (🖳 www.service-public.fr and follow the links to 'Etrangers en France' and then 'Entrée en France');
- A number of passport-size photographs on a white background (usually one for each application form, of which there may be up to eight!);
- A stamped-addressed envelope.

Depending on the purpose of your stay, you may require some or all of the following:

- A 'validated' copy or official translation of your birth certificate or an extract from your civil status record dated within the last three months, as well as those of your spouse and other members of your family;

- An affidavit stating that you've never been convicted of a criminal offence or declared bankrupt;

- Evidence of accommodation: e.g. the title deeds to a property, a rental agreement or a 'certificate of accommodation' (*attestation d'accueil*) from a French family or friends with whom you will be staying in France;

- Evidence of financial independence, which may take the form of bank statements, letters from banks confirming arrangements for regular transfers of funds from abroad, letters from family or friends guaranteeing regular support. Letters should be notarised (witnessed by a public notary). Evidence of financial independence isn't required by someone coming to France to take up paid employment, who must,of course, be able to supply an employment contract or equivalent.

- If you're taking up employment in France, a work contract (*certificat d'emploi*) approved by the French Ministry of Labour or the District Labour Department where the business is registered if you're a non-EU national. This must be obtained by the prospective employer in France. It's sent to the Office des Migrations Internationales (OMI, 44, rue Bargue, 75732 Paris Cedex 15, 🖳 www. omi.social.fr) for transmission to the appropriate French consulate abroad.

- An undertaking not to engage in any occupation without authorisation (on plain, unheaded paper and signed by you);

- A medical certificate by an OMI-approved doctor, which is necessary for most long-term visa applicants, including employees and their family members, and au pairs. It must be carried out during the three months before taking up residence in France. Applicants must pay a fixed fee.

- A health insurance certificate if you aren't eligible for health treatment under French social security and your stay is for less than six months. Some foreign insurance companies don't provide sufficient cover to satisfy French regulations, and you should check the minimum cover necessary with a French consulate in your country of residence and obtain a letter from your insurance company confirming that your policy is valid in France. (If you intend to stay longer than six months and you're under 28, you must join the French social security system, which must be done when applying for your residence permit – see page 30.)

- A marriage certificate if you're a non-EU national married to a French citizen or to a foreigner who's resident in France.

- An agreement (*déclaration d'engagement*) with a French family and a certificate of registration for French-language classes if you're an au pair (see page 347).

Documents should be translated into French, and translations must be made by a translator approved by your local consulate, a list of whom (*liste de traducteurs*) is provided on request by French consulates.

If you require a visa to enter France and attempt to enter without one, you will be refused entry. If you're in doubt as to whether you require a visa to enter France, enquire at a French consulate before making travel plans or go to the French Ministry of Foreign Affairs website (Ministère des Affaires Etrangères, 🖳 www.diplomatie. fr/venir/visas/index.htm), where you can enter information about your situation to find the visa you require.

Visa applications usually take six to eight weeks to be approved, although they can take much longer and you should allow at least three months.

A number of websites provide further details about visas and work permits in France, including the following:

🖳 www.diplomatie.fr (in English) – includes a useful device for finding out which type of visa you need;

🖳 www.afii.fr (in English) – the Invest in France website, which has general information on settling in France, as well as details about visas;

🖳 www.edufrance.fr – contains general information about studying in France, including visa requirements for students.

Work Permits

Whether or not you require a permit to work in France depends on your nationality (see below). For further information about work permits, contact your country's embassy in France or the commercial attaché at a French consulate.

EU Nationals

Under EU law, EU nationals have the right to carry out self-employment or start a business in another member country and therefore don't require a foreign trader's permit (see page 30). Nationals of Norway, Liechtenstein, Monaco, Andorra and Algeria are also exempt, although they require a residence permit (see page 30).

Non-EU Nationals

A combined residence and work permit (*carte unique de séjour et de travail* or *carte de séjour salarié*) is issued to non-EU nationals coming to France to take up permanent employment. To obtain this, you must present the following:

● A completed long-stay visa (*visa de long séjour*) application form (see page 27);

● An 'introductory' employment contract (a contract submitted by the employer stating that the position has been registered with the national employment agency and other relevant authorities);

● A medical certificate (from an examination carried out by an OMI-approved doctor).

When you arrive in France, you have two months in which to apply for a temporary residence permit (*carte de séjour temporaire salarié* – see below) while your application for a *carte unique de séjour et de travail* or *carte de séjour salarié* is being processed (French bureaucracy at its inimitable best).

Carte de Commerçant Etranger: Non-EU nationals other than citizens of Norway, Liechtenstein, Monaco, Andorra and Algeria wishing to start or run a business or any commercial activity in France must obtain a foreign trader's permit (*carte de commerçant étranger*). This applies whether you wish to carry out a self-employed industrial, commercial or artesian profession, or whether you're to be the manager or director of a limited company (e.g. an *SA* or *SARL*) or the French-based manager of any establishment through which a foreign company carries out a commercial, industrial or artesian activity in France (e.g. an agency or branch office). **Conducting any of these activities without this permit is punishable by a fine of up to €3,750 and up to six months' imprisonment.** Permits aren't required by self-employed workers performing a service (rather than a commercial activity).

, A foreign trader's permit cannot be issued for a period longer than that for which your residence permit is valid. You can submit a request for a permit at the same time as you apply for your long-stay visa, and the consulate forwards it directly to France. Your residence permit is stamped *non-salarié, profession libérale* and you aren't permitted to work as a salaried employee in France. Alternatively, you can apply for one in France at the *préfecture* of the department in which you will be carrying out your business. If you're already resident in France, you can apply for a permit at your local town hall or *préfecture*. You must provide the following:

- Details relating to the incorporation of the prospective business;
- A detailed description of the proposed business activity;
- Proof of adequate financial resources, which must take the form of a letter from a financial institution offering enough credit to cover all the financial needs in starting up the proposed activity or a certificate from a banking institution or La Poste declaring that you have an account holding enough money to cover these needs;
- Evidence that the proposed business has a provisional budget for more than a year;
- An affidavit stating that you've never been convicted of a criminal offence or declared bankrupt.

It may take up to six months to obtain a permit, although a temporary permit can be issued within a shorter period.

Switzerland and the US have special arrangements with France, under which nationals cannot be refused a foreign trader's permit unless they're unqualified to carry out their chosen activity in France (or if they pose a threat to public order!).

Residence Permits

In general, foreigners remaining in France for longer than 90 days in succession (for any reason) require a residence permit (*titre de séjour*). EU nationals aren't obliged to obtain a residence permit, but must meet the criteria for a permit and are recommended to obtain one in any case. Where applicable, a residence permit holder's dependants are also granted a permit. Children can be listed on a parent's permit until the age of 18, although they require their own residence permit at the age of 16 if they're working. Different types of residence permit are issued depending on your status, including long-stay visitors (*visiteur*), salaried employees (*salarié*), transferees (*détaché*), family members (*membre de famille*) and traders (*commerçant*). A combined residence and work permit (*carte unique de séjour et de travail* or *carte de séjour salarié*) is issued to non-EU nationals taking up permanent employment in France.

There are two main categories of residence permit in France: a *carte de séjour* and a *carte de résident*. To avoid confusion, the *carte de séjour* is referred to below as a temporary residence permit and the *carte de résident* as a permanent residence permit.

Temporary Residence Permit

A temporary residence permit (*carte de séjour*) is issued to foreigners aged 18 and above who are to remain in France for more than 90 days. The period of validity of a temporary residence permit varies according to your circumstances, as follows:

- Non-EU employees must apply for a temporary residence permit (*carte de séjour temporaire salarié*) within two months of arrival. This is valid for a maximum of a year and can be renewed two months before its expiry date, upon presentation of a new employment contract or verification of your continued employment. Employees transferred to a French company for a limited period (*statut détaché*) may not stay longer than 18 months initially with a possible extension to 27 months. If you're taking up employment for less than a year, your permit is valid only for the period of employment. The permit has the annotation *salarié* or the professional activity for which the contract was approved and lists the department(s) where the holder can be employed. Dependent family members are entitled to a temporary residence permit with the annotation *vie privée et familiale*, which prohibits the holder from working in France. Exceptions are foreigners with a permanent residence permit (see page 30) and spouses of French citizens. If you're taking up long-term employment, you must apply for a *carte unique de séjour et de travail* or a *carte de séjour salarié* (see page 29).

- EU nationals who are or will be working in France can obtain a temporary residence permit (*carte de séjour de ressortissant d'un état membre de l'UE*) valid for ten years and automatically renewable for further ten-year periods, although this is no longer mandatory.

- EU nationals who are unemployed and have no proof of income may be issued with a one-year temporary residence permit.

- Non-EU spouses of EU nationals are granted a temporary five-year residence permit (*carte de séjour*) permitting them to live and work in France.

A residence permit automatically becomes invalid if you spend over six months outside France and it can be revoked at any time if you no longer meet the conditions for which it was issued (or if you obtained a permit fraudulently). After three years of continuous residence in France, the holder of a temporary residence permit can obtain a permanent residence permit (see below). You can be fined up to €1,500 for failing to apply for a *carte de séjour* if you require one.

Permanent Residence Permit

A permanent residence permit (*carte de résident*) is usually issued to foreigners who have lived in France for three consecutive years (the exception is the foreign spouse of a French citizen, who's automatically granted a permanent residence permit after one year of marriage) and speak fluent French. It's valid for ten years and renewable provided the holder can furnish proof that he's practising a profession in France or has sufficient financial resources to maintain himself and his dependants. A permanent residence permit authorises the holder to undertake any professional activity (subject to qualifications and registration) in any French department, even if employment was previously forbidden.

Applications & Renewals

An application for a residence permit must be made to the *préfecture de police* in towns that have them and otherwise to your local town hall (*mairie*) in small towns or the police (*gendarmerie/commissariat de police*) in large towns and cities. If permits aren't issued locally, you will be referred to the *Direction de la Réglementation* of your department's *préfecture* or the nearest *sous-préfecture*. In large towns and cities, many police stations have a foreigners' office (*bureau des étrangers*). In Paris, applications must be made to the appropriate police centre (*centre d'accueil des étrangers*) for the area (*arrondissement*) where you live. Centres are open from 08.45 to 16.30 Mondays to Fridays.

If you arrive in France with a long-stay visa, you must apply for a residence permit within a week. EU nationals who visit France with the intention of finding employment or starting a business have 90 days in which to find a job and, if they wish to obtain one, apply for a residence permit. **Failure to apply for a residence permit within the specified period is a serious offence and can result in a fine.** It isn't possible to obtain a residence permit while living in temporary accommodation such as a hotel or caravan site.

You will be notified of the documentation required to apply for a residence permit, which depends on your situation and nationality (and on the issuing office and possibly even officer!). The following documents are required by all applicants, including those from EU countries:

● A valid passport, with a long-stay visa if necessary, or a national identity card (neighbouring EU countries only)*;

● A 'validated' copy or official translation of your birth certificate or an extract from your civil status record dated within the last three months*;

● A number (usually three) of black and white (white background) or colour passport-size photographs*;

● Proof of residence, which may consist of a copy of a lease or purchase contract or an electricity bill (*facture EDF*). If you're a lodger, the owner must provide an *attestation d'accueil* confirming that you're resident in his home.

● Two stamped and self-addressed envelopes;

● Evidence of financial independence (see page 28);

- Details of your French bank account;

- Evidence of health insurance or a medical certificate from an OMI-approved doctor if you aren't covered under French social security. If you're covered by French social security, you must produce your social security number.

* **If you're accompanied by any dependants, they also require a passport, birth certificate and photographs. British dependants under 16 must have their own passport.**

In addition to the above, you are required to produce the following, as appropriate:

- A marriage or divorce certificate or other papers relating to your marital status (this isn't usually required by EU nationals, but British applicants require a copy of their marriage certificate because the maiden name of a married woman isn't included in a British passport). The spouse of a French citizen or of a foreigner resident in France must produce his or her marriage certificate and proof of nationality or legal residence of the spouse when applying for a residence permit.

- An employment contract or letter of employment if you're taking up employment in France.

If you don't have the required documents, you will be sent away to obtain them. If you're applying for a renewal of your residence permit and don't have all the necessary documents, you can apply for an extension (*prolongation*). Certain documents must be translated by a notarised translator (listed under *Traducteurs – Traductions Officielles Certifiées* in the yellow pages), but you shouldn't have documents translated in advance, as the requirements often vary depending on the area or office and your nationality and you might be wasting your time and money. There's no fee for residence permit applications, but you must pay to renew a permit.

You are given a date (usually from 2 to 12 weeks after your application) when you can collect your permit (usually from the *préfecture de police*). In the meantime, or if it isn't possible to issue a residence permit immediately, you're given a temporary authorisation (*récipissé de demande de carte de séjour* or an *attestation d'application de résidence*) valid for up to three months and renewable. You should keep this as evidence that you've applied for your residence permit. You're notified by post or by telephone when your residence permit is ready for collection.

There's a fee for the renewal of a residence permit (which varies according to the type of permit), paid in the form of tax stamps (*timbres fiscaux*), which you purchase at a tobacconist's (*tabac*).

WORKING ILLEGALLY

Illegal working (*travail au noir* or *travail clandestin*) thrives in France, particularly among sections of the expatriate community and immigrants from North Africa and other non-EU countries, for whom it's illegal to work in France without a work permit. It has been conservatively estimated that the loss of tax revenue due to the 'black' or 'underground' economy (*l'économie souterraine*) totals around €5 billion a year, with up to a million people regularly doing 'odd jobs' (*petit boulot*), i.e. working illegally. Even among those with legal businesses, it's estimated that some 30 per cent of all work in France isn't declared to the tax authorities – i.e. is paid for in cash.

Many unscrupulous employers use illegal labour in order to pay low wages (below the minimum wage) for long hours and poor working conditions. Abuse is common in industries that traditionally employ casual labour, such as building, farming, service and textile industries.

In recent years there has been a clamp-down on 'black' labour with greater powers given to the police, gendarmerie, courts and work inspectors (*inspecteurs de travail*), and increased penalties. Illegal working is punishable by up to two years in prison and fines of between €300 and €30,000 (which are doubled for a second offence). If you employ someone who's an illegal immigrant, you can be fined €500 to €5,000 and can be imprisoned for up to three years.

If you use illegal labour or avoid paying VAT (*TVA*), you have no official redress if goods or services are substandard. If you work illegally, you have no entitlement to social security benefits such as insurance against work injuries, public health care, unemployment pay and a state pension.

QUALIFICATIONS & EXPERIENCE

The most important qualification for working (and living) in France is the ability to speak French fluently (see page 36). Once you've overcome this hurdle, you should establish whether your trade or professional qualifications and experience are recognised in France. If you're seeking employment but aren't experienced, French employers expect studies to be in a relevant discipline and to have included work experience (*stage*). Professional or trade qualifications are required to work in most fields in France, where qualifications are also often necessary to be self-employed or start a business. It isn't just a matter of hanging up a sign and waiting for the stampede of customers to your door.

Before starting a business or self-employment, you must make sure that you're legally qualified to carry out your chosen activity in France. The labour market is highly regulated, and restrictions apply to many occupations, not only to 'professional' activities such as being a doctor or lawyer. For example, you must provide proof of qualifications or experience to work as an estate agent, a travel agent, a food producer, a builder or in any of the manual trades or crafts. Depending on your occupation, you may have to obtain authorisation from your *préfecture*, or a *carte professionnelle* (card showing your membership of a profession), a licence to operate, or you may have to register with the appropriate professional body. Many foreign traders are also required to undergo a 'business' course before they can start work in France (see pages 106 and 146).

It isn't possible to detail the requirements of every profession here; for information on your particular activity, consult your local *centre de formalités des entreprises* (see pages 103 and 137) or the appropriate French professional body or trade organisation. You will find their addresses and contact numbers in the directory of the Mouvement des Entreprises de France

(MEDEF); for a list of offices where you can consult this directory, go to the MEDEF website (🖳 www.medef.fr/staging/site/page/php?pag_id+2003).

Theoretically, qualifications recognised by professional and trade bodies in one EU country should be recognised in France. However, recognition varies from country to country and in some cases foreign qualifications aren't recognised by French employers or professional and trade associations. All academic qualifications should also be recognised, although they may be given less prominence than equivalent French qualifications, depending on the country and the educational establishment. A ruling by the European Court in 1992 declared that where EU examinations are of a similar standard with just certain areas of difference, individuals should be required to take exams only in those areas.

Certain professions are 'regulated', which means that qualifications obtained in one EU country are valid in another, but you must check that you satisfy the required conditions in terms of qualifications and experience to carry out the activity you've chosen. Regulated professions are broadly those in the fields of architecture, law, medicine and transport. Some are covered by what's called a 'sectoral directive', which means that those with the relevant qualification can exercise their profession freely in any EU state. These include architects, dentists, doctors, midwives, nurses, pharmacists, surgeons and veterinary surgeons. Other regulated professions are covered by a 'general directive' (including most recognised trades), which means that you must check with the relevant French government department or professional body (e.g. the Conseil National de l'Ordre des Architectes, 🖳 www. architectes.org, for architects) that your qualifications are acceptable.

Other occupations are unregulated ('non-regulated' in EU-speak), but you must still register your occupation and be assigned an official status (*statut* or *régime*) , e.g. itinerant tradesmen, estate agent, driving instructor; it's illegal simply to hang up a sign and start business. Acceptance of your status may depend on the assessment of your qualifications and training by individual employers or trade associations. In such cases, you must contact the Chambre de Métiers, the Chambre d'Agriculture or the Chambre de Commerce in the department where you plan to work. You can obtain the address of the relevant body from your local town hall. For information about French Chambers of Commerce contact the Assemblée des Chambres Françaises de Commerce et d'Industrie/APCFCI, 45 avenue d'Iéna, Paris 75016 (☎ 01 53 57 17 00, 🖳 www.acfci.cci.fr – available in English). All EU member states issue occupation information sheets containing a common job description with a table of qualifications. These cover a large number of trades and are intended to help someone with the relevant qualifications look for a job in another EU country.

British craftspeople wishing to practise in France can apply to have their experience certificated under the UK Certificate of Experience scheme. Contact the Certification Unit, Department of Trade and Industry Trade Policy Europe Branch, Second Floor, 212 Kingsgate House, 66–74 Victoria Street, London SW1E 6SW (☎ 020-7215 4454/4648). Applicants are charged a non-refundable processing fee of around £105 and £45 for a certified translation.

For further information about equivalent qualifications you can contact the Centre d'Études et de Recherche sur les Qualifications (CEREQ), 11 rue Vauquelin,

75005 Paris (☎ 01 44 08 69 10, 💻 www.cereq.fr) or ENIC-NARIC, run by the European Network of Information Centres and the National Academic Recognition Information Centre (💻 www.enic-naric.net). NARIC in the UK doesn't deal directly with individuals, although its website (💻 www.naric.org.uk) will provide you with most of the basic information.

Another source of information about qualifications is the EU website (💻 http:// europa.eu.int/eures). Choose 'en' for English and click on 'Living and Working', choose 'France', then 'Living and Working Conditions' and finally, under 'Working Conditions', 'Recognition of Diplomas and Qualifications'.

Further information about qualifications can be obtained from the Bureau de l'Information sur les Systèmes Educatifs et de la Reconnaissance de Diplômes of the Ministère de la Jeunesse, de l'Education Nationale et de la Recherche, 110 rue de Grenelle, 75357 Paris Cedex 07 (☎ 01 40 65 65 90) and from the Département des Affaires Internationales de l'Enseignement Supérieure, 61–65 rue Dutot, 75015 Paris (☎ 01 40 65 66 19).

A useful booklet, *Europe Open for Professionals*, is available from the UK Department for Education and Skills (☎ 0114-259 4151).

Language

Although English is the *lingua franca* of international commerce and may help you to secure a job in France, **the most important qualification for anyone seeking employment is the ability to speak fluent French**. While it's a myth that the French don't speak English (most French children learn English at school and the majority of educated French people speak some English), many French people have an ingrained fear of appearing foolish and are reluctant to speak any foreign language. (In a recent survey, 66 per cent of French people claimed to speak only French and a mere 22 per cent admitted to speaking English 'well'.) The French are also extremely proud of their language (to the point of hubris) and – quite rightly – expect everyone living or working in France to speak it (even though they daily borrow or invent new Anglicisms to make French more 'modern'!).

If necessary, you should have French lessons before arriving in France. A sound knowledge of French won't just help you find a job or perform your job better, but will make everyday life much simpler and more enjoyable. If you come to France without being able to speak French, you will be excluded from everyday life and will feel uncomfortable until you can understand what's going on around you. **The most common reason for negative experiences among foreigners in France, visitors and residents alike, is that they cannot (or won't) speak French.** However bad your grammar, poor your vocabulary and terrible your accent, an attempt to speak French will be much better appreciated than your fluent English. Don't, however, be surprised when the French wince at your torture of their beloved tongue or correct you in public for minor grammatical or pronunciation errors! The French honestly believe they're doing you a favour by pointing out your mistakes to you while they're fresh in your mind. (This also explains much of their hesitance to use English in public – for fear of being corrected themselves.)

Learning French

If you don't already speak good French, don't expect to learn it quickly, even if you already have a basic knowledge and take intensive lessons. It's common for foreigners not to be fluent after a year or more of intensive lessons in France. If your expectations are unrealistic, you will become frustrated, which can affect your confidence. **It takes a long time to reach the level of fluency needed to be able to work in French.** If you don't speak French fluently, you should consider taking a menial or even an unpaid voluntary job on arrival in France, as this is one of the quickest ways of improving your French.

Although it isn't easy, even the most non-linguistic person can acquire a working knowledge of French. All that's required is a little hard work, some help and perseverance, particularly if you have only English-speaking colleagues and friends. **Your business and social enjoyment and success in France will be directly related to the degree to which you master French.**

Most people can teach themselves a great deal through the use of books, tapes, videos and even computer and internet-based courses.

A good place to start, and a resource you can continue to use wherever you are, is the impressive languages section of the BBC website (💻 www.bbc.co.uk/languages/french), which is comprehensive and informative. You can test your ability to find out which level is best for you and learn French online at your own pace. The site also contains news and features about France, to help you get a feel for the country and its people, and there's a fascinating section entitled 'French for Work'. Here, you can find out what it's like working in a French business environment and get help with specialist language practice for a variety of business situations. Particularly valuable are the experiences of those who have already taken the plunge and the expert tips from those who have been in the world of work in France for some time.

Other websites offering free tutorials include 💻 www.frenchlesson.org and 💻 www.frenchtutorial.com. There are also self-study French courses you can buy – if you've paid money for a course, you're more likely to see it through! – including those offered by Eurotalk (💻 www.eurotalk.co.uk) and Linguaphone (💻 www.linguaphone.co.uk). A quarterly publication, *Bien-dire* (sic), is aimed at adult learners (💻 www.learningfrench.com).

There are several things you can do to speed up your language learning before and after your arrival in France, including watching television (particularly quiz shows where the words appear on the screen as they're spoken) and DVDs (where you can select French or English subtitles), reading (especially children's books and product catalogues, where the words are accompanied by pictures), joining a club or association, and (most enjoyable) making French friends!

Lessons: However, even the best students require some professional help. Teaching French is big business in France, with classes offered by language schools, French and foreign colleges and universities, private and international schools, foreign and international organisations (such as the British Institute in Paris), local associations and clubs, and private teachers. There are many language schools (*école de langues*) in cities and large towns, most universities provide language courses, and many organisations offer holiday courses year-round, particularly for children and young adults (it's best to stay with a local French family). Tuition ranges from courses for complete beginners, through specialised business or cultural courses to university-level courses leading to recognised diplomas. If you already speak French but need conversational practice, you may prefer to enrol in an art or craft course at a local institute or club. You can also learn French via a telephone language course, which is particularly practical for busy executives and those who don't live near a language school.

In some areas the *Centre Culturel* provides free French lessons to foreigners. If you're officially registered as unemployed and have a residence permit (*carte de séjour*), you can obtain free lessons (*perfectionnement de la langue française*), although complete beginners don't qualify (contact your local ANPE office for information).

One of the most famous French language teaching organisations is the Alliance Française (AF), 101 boulevard Raspail, 75270 Paris Cedex 06 (☎ 01 42 84 90 00, 🖳 www.alliancefr.org), a state-approved, non-profit organisation with over 1,000 centres in 138 countries, including 32 centres in France, mainly in large towns and cities. The AF runs general, special and intensive courses, and can also arrange a homestay in France with a host family.

Another non-profit organisation is Centre d'Échanges Internationaux, 1 rue Gozlin, 75006 Paris (☎ 01 43 29 60 20), offering intensive French language courses for juniors (13 to 18 years) and adults throughout France. Courses include accommodation in their own international centres, with a French family, or in a hotel, bed and breakfast, or self-catering studio. Junior courses can be combined with tuition in a variety of sports and other activities, including horse riding, tennis, windsurfing, canoeing, diving and dancing.

Another well known school is Berlitz (☎ 01 40 74 00 17, 🖳 www.berlitz.com) with around 16 schools in France, including five in Paris. The British organisation CESA Languages Abroad (☎ 01209-2211800, 🖳 www.cesalanguages.com) offers advice and arranges language courses.

Most language schools run various classes depending on your language ability, how many hours you wish to study a week, how much money you want to spend and how quickly you wish to learn. Language classes generally fall into the following categories: Extensive (4 to 10 hours per week); Intensive (15 to 20 hours); Total Immersion (20 to 40 or more).

Don't expect to become fluent in a short time unless you have a particular flair for languages or already have a good command of French. Unless you desperately need to learn French quickly, it's better to arrange your lessons over a long period. However, don't commit yourself to a long course of study, particularly an expensive one, before ensuring that it's the right course. The cost for a one-week total immersion course is usually between €2,500 and €3,000! Most schools offer free tests to help you find your appropriate level and a free introductory lesson.

You may prefer to have private lessons, which are a quicker, although more expensive way of learning a language. The main advantage of private lessons is that you learn at your own speed and aren't held back by slow learners or left floundering in the wake of the class genius. You can advertise for a teacher in your local newspapers, on shopping centre/supermarket bulletin boards and university notice boards, and through your or your spouse's employer. Otherwise, look for advertisements in the English-language press (see **Appendix B**). Don't forget to ask your friends, neighbours and colleagues if they can recommend a private teacher. Private lessons by the hour cost from around €50 at a school or €15 to €35 with a private tutor, although you may find someone willing to trade French lessons for English lessons. In some areas (particularly in Paris), there are discussion groups which meet regularly to talk in French and other languages; these are usually advertised in the English-language press (see **Appendix B**).

Our sister-publication, *The Best Places to Buy a Home in France* (see page 419) includes lists of language schools in the most popular regions of France. A comprehensive list of schools, institutions and organisations providing French language courses throughout France is contained in a booklet, *Cours de Français Langue Étrangère et Stages Pédagogie de Français Langue Étrangère en France*. It includes information about the type of course, organisation, dates, costs and other practical information, and is available from French consulates or from the Association pour la Diffusion de la Pensée Française (ADPF), 6 rue Ferrus, 75683 Paris Cedex 14 (☎ 01 43 13 11 00, 🖳 www.adpf.asso.fr).

Regional Languages & Dialects

As well as French, there are a number of regional languages in France, including Alsatian (spoken in Alsace), Basque (Pyrénées), Breton (Brittany), Catalan (Roussillon), Corsican (Corsica) and Occitan (Languedoc). Although you're unlikely to have to deal with anyone who speaks **only** a regional language, you should bear in mind that your linguistic life will be even more complicated if you decide to live and work in any of these areas. If you have school-age children, you should note that in some areas, schools teach in the regional language as well as in French.

As well as regional languages, France has a plethora of local dialects (*patois*), which are often incomprehensible even to native French speakers! Add to all this the various accents of 'standard' French, particularly the typical twang of southerners (who pronounce the word *accent* 'aksang') and you will appreciate the importance of mastering the language before you even **think** about working in France!

BUSINESS PRACTICE

Working or running a business in a foreign country isn't only a matter of learning the language and abiding by the local laws and regulations; you must also conform to local business practices – or your business won't go far. Particularly if you come from a neighbouring country, such as the UK, you might think that the way the French do business cannot be very different from they way things are done in your home country. You would be wrong. The French have particular – and in some cases peculiar – ways of doing things in all areas of life, and business practice is no exception.

Many foreigners, particularly Americans, find that they need to adjust to a slower pace of working life. Most French managers and executives rarely take work home and they **never** work at weekends, which are sacrosanct. However, don't be misled by French people's apparent lack of urgency and casual approach to business – they can be just as hard-headed as any other people.

Company Hierarchy

Experience, maturity and loyalty are highly valued (although qualifications are even more valuable) in French business, and newcomers generally find it difficult to secure a senior position with a French company. In particular, the French 'old boy' network is still alive and well and can militate against foreigners achieving the promotion they deserve. When it comes to hiring new employees (particularly managers and executives), the process is slower in France than in many other western countries. If you do obtain a job with a French company, you are expected to make your way within the company; 'job hopping' as a way of increasing your salary or promotion prospects is rare.

The French business world is largely a 'technocracy', in that company directors and managers are obsessed with technical and organisational detail and generally unconcered with the emotional aspects of running a business, such as motivating, understanding or *sympathiser* (meaning to fraternise as well as sympathise) with their staff. Company structures tend to be rigidly hierarchical, and the head of a company, who has the imposing title of *Président Directeur Général* (*PDG*), has absolute control and can be autocratic and aloof. As in the US, French employers tend to expect high standards and are intolerant of mistakes or inefficiency. Unlike the US, however, there's generally little contact between management and workers, both of whom are reluctant to take on responsibilities outside their immediate duties. There's a widespread reluctance to delegate, discuss or consult; employees are simply given instructions and expected to get on with their job.

It isn't a case of ends justifying means, however; in fact, processes often matter more than results, with lengthy debates over how best to organise certain functions and apparently arbitrary postponement of 'deadlines'.

Meetings

Face-to-face meetings are still the preferred method of doing business in France. The French are generally telephone-phobic, and the use of email for communication has been slow to catch on. Meetings are rarely held outside office hours or even at lunchtime, however, and you're expected to give up part of your working day for routine meetings with an accountant, for example. What's more, meeting times are 'flexible', i.e. the person you're meeting may turn up late or not at all, without warning you or even contacting you afterwards to explain why. (Don't expect an apology from a French person under **any** circumstances!)

Even trying to arrange a meeting can be a frustrating task, unless you're fortunate enough to be able to contact the person concerned directly: colleagues or receptionists often won't have access to his diary or know his whereabouts, and leaving a message for him to phone you back is usually a waste of time (indeed, you are generally asked to call again, even if you're the customer).

Before you even arrange a meeting, however, check that you're in contact with the right person. If you go to the trouble of meeting someone who cannot make the decisions you require (e.g. whether or not to purchase your products or appoint you as an agent or distributor), you're wasting your time. Don't expect to arrange meetings in August, when most French people are on holiday, or at Christmas, or of course on any public holiday (see page 167).

Lunch meetings are unusual in France, where business and pleasure are strictly separated (and there are few greater pleasures for the French than eating!). Similarly, it isn't usual to invite business acquaintances (or colleagues) out to dinner, let alone to any other sort of entertainment. If you do so, make it clear that you're paying – and don't expect the treat to have any bearing on the person's decision whether or not to buy your products or use your services.

Meetings should always be begun with 'small talk', and you shouldn't be in too much of a hurry to 'get down to business'. The French value relationships in business and like to feel that they know you before buying from or even selling to you. It's therefore important to make general conversation. Don't, however, ask personal questions – avoid asking about a person's family, age, political or religious beliefs or 'status' – or try to tell jokes; you should discuss topical subjects in order to demonstrate that you're a cultured and educated person and therefore deserving of respect (the ultimate insult in French is *abruti*, which means ignorant and brutish) and avoid potentially sensitive topics, such as religion, the French Occupation and immigration. Under no circumstances extol the virtues of your native country of compare anything French unfavourably with anything non-French. Wait until the meal is almost over before broaching any business-related subject.

The French are easily bored. If you're giving a presentation, make it short and to the point; and make sure you have all the facts at your fingertips to deal with any questions that might be fired at you. Expect interruptions and even arguments. In fact, these are a sign of attention and interest and should encourage you. If you're trying to sell a product of service, avoid the 'hard sell'; the French don't respond to this approach and your effort will be counter-productive. Subtelty and indirectness, although slower and more difficult, will, eventually, achieve better results.

Don't expect to achieve anything at a first (or even second) meeting. Be patient and aim first to establish that all-important rapport. Write a follow-up letter (see **Formality** below), thanking the person for seeing you and suggesting a date for a further meeting.

Don't be afraid to disagree, but avoid arguing and, above all, never lose your temper with a French person: he will either ignore you or dig his heels in and become even less cooperative.

Formality

The French are a formal people, in all aspects of life and not least in business. You should therefore observe the required formalities in your appearance, speech, bearing and behaviour. It's almost impossible to be too formal – at least on first acquaintance – but all too easy to be unacceptably casual and 'familiar'.

Even among colleagues, business relations tend to be formal. As in personal relationships, you should always use the formal *vous* until the person you're dealing with switches to *tu*.

Always dress smartly for work – especially if you're meeting customers, clients or suppliers; appearances are important, and you should show by the clothes you wear that you're serious about your job.

Written communication in French is highly formalised and stylised (the French for 'yours sincerely' generally runs to at least a dozen words), which may be why the casual use of email is unpopular. If you need to write letters in French, you should have them checked by a native speaker, as it's easy to use the wrong tone and therefore fail to achieve the desired communication. Job applications (*lettres de motivation*) in particular should follow an accepted pattern (there are numerous books on the subject); they should also be handwritten, as the French set great store by the analysis of handwriting, which they believe reveals a person's character.

Although the French love to create elaborate business structures, rules and procedures, however, they're equally eager to bend the rules or short-cut systems (a favourite phrase is *passer à côté*, meaning literally to 'bypass') in order to achieve the desired result. In France, the old adage 'It isn't what you know, it's who you know' applies in many areas of life, including the business world. Nevertheless, as a foreigner, you should never take the lead in this process, but allow your 'host' to suggest that there might be an alternative approach . . .

CASE STUDIES

As this chapter has outlined, several qualifications and qualities are required to make a living in France: not only academic and technical qualifications and the ability to speak and understand French, but also perseverance, adaptability, opportunism, patience and a willingness to accept French ways of doing things – frustrating as these can be. The second part of this book (**Chapters 7 to 14**) contains summaries of the experiences of expatriates who have become self-employed or started businesses in France – referred to as **Case Studies**. These are invariably success stories, although not without their ups and downs. However, not everyone who attempts to make a living in France succeeds in doing so, and it's also worthwhile considering the experiences of those who have failed – for one reason or another. Here, by way of a cautionary tale, is the story of such a failure.

Tom Taylor-Duxbury owned and ran a television equipment distributorship in Herefordshire before leaving for France in 2002 to follow "the *gîte* dream route". He purchased several properties in Dordogne, "some with potential, others already improved", but found the business "fatuous" and sold all but one of the properties. A qualified engineer and a fellow of the Institute of Marketing, and self-employed since 1980, Tom was nevertheless "moderately adept at opportunism and listening for openings" and soon found another avenue to explore.

"After listening to complaints about French paint, and experiencing the dire stuff myself, I started a paint import business," explains Tom. "It took me 18 months to find a *notaire* who understands Anglo-Saxons and our quirky ways of thinking outside their box. She's good and trusty and offers sound advice. I then went to KPMG and discovered that France was a bundle of red tape. I attended local 'start-up enterprise' lectures, which were a joke:

mostly about grants and how to make a business plan. A lawyer at FIDAL, a large legal group, was so exasperated when trying to find insurance for a company we thought of starting that he suggested we write to the EU, as it seemed that the French refusal to accept UK and Swedish qualifications was a non-tariff barrier.

"After several months of research, I established my new company as a UK exporter. I used sterling and invoiced from the UK. I held no stock in France, so I couldn't be deemed to be trading. I didn't pay myself a salary so I had no 'income' if I made a profit, as these are regarded as dividends in the UK. I hoped this would keep me legal here, although no one could advise me with certainty. I cannot find advice I believe in 100 per cent; nor do I know anyone who has found consistent advice which is never contradicted during the next meeting or by some other official.

"Shipping paint around France seemed easy. SERNAM [a national distributor] said the prices seemed OK, but since I had a UK company and no *SIRET* number, they couldn't offer an account. The British consulate managed to move them to open a personal account but they wanted a €2,000 deposit – another non-tariff barrier?"

Tom's conclusion is that "there's no market in France for British labour, skills or products, regardless of how much lower priced or superior the products may be." And his advice for anyone attempting to start a business in France is simple: "Don't. If you want to do business, if you enjoy work, if you enjoy trading, if you enjoy enterprise, don't come here. Any enterprise is seen as a crime; regulations and protectionism abound – and that's not to mention fear of strangers and their practices, most of which are proscribed. See if you can't get into the US or Canada."

Nevertheless, Tom hasn't given up on the dream of making a living in France. Whatever becomes of the paint operation, he's now looking to property development and building and has already built his first property in Brittany. Whether his attitude towards doing business in France will change is another matter.

2.

CHOOSING THE AREA

You may already have decided on the area of France you want to work in, you may have a shortlist of possible locations or you may have little idea of where the best place for you to live is. In any case, you should consider the alternatives, taking into account linguistic factors (see page 36) as well as the cost of living, the infrastructure and the labour market.

France is divided into 22 regions, each of which has its attractions, limitations, advantages and disadvantages – with regard to working and to living there. A description of the geographical and cultural features of each region and a detailed breakdown of residential property prices are included in *The Best Places to Buy a Home in France* (Survival Books – see page 419); the alphabetical guide to the regions in this chapter (Normandy is treated as one region, although it's officially two) focuses on population, including the number of foreign residents, employment prospects, and the cost of commercial property, although there's also a guide to residential property prices.

More detail is given for the regions most popular with expatriates. Note, however, that these aren't necessarily those in which your business is most likely to flourish. The regions in which there was the biggest growth in new business creation in 2004 were Limousin, Corsica, Centre, Franche-Comté, Lorraine, Nord-Pas-de-Calais, Pays-de-la-Loire and Poitou-Charentes. Further information and statistics regarding employment can be found on the following websites:

- The relevant regional office of the state employment agency, Agence Nationale Pour l'Emploi (ANPE, 💻 www.anpe.fr – go to 'anpe.fr en région', select your region then click on 'points de repère').

- Assurance Chômage (ASSEDIC, 💻 www.assedic.fr);

- The Ministry of Employment's Direction de l'Animation de la Recherche, des Études et des Statistiques (DARES, 💻 www.dares.fr);

- Institut National de la Statistique et des Études Économiques (💻 www.insee.fr).

It's also worth contacting the Conseil Général of the region you're interested in, as well as departmental Chambres de Commerce and Chambres des Métiers and local town halls and *mairies*. Further sources of regional information are given in each section and a map of the regions and departments can be found in **Appendix E**.

This chapter includes information about private property prices, but not about commercial property prices, as these vary enormously, not only according to the size, condition and (above all) location of the premises, but also according to whether you're buying or renting only the premises (unusual), whether you're buying an existing business (*fonds de commerce*) plus the premises or buying a business and renting the premises, or buying a lease (*bail*) and renting a premises. For details of the different ways of obtaining business premises and examples of the costs of each option, see **Premises** on page 148.

ALSACE

France's smallest and most easterly region has much in common with neighbouring Germany and contains one of the country's most important cities in Strasbourg.

Population & Employment Prospects

Alsace has a population of 1.7 million, which is the second-fastest growing in France (after Languedoc-Roussillon). The global economic slow-down in 2002 and the weakness of the German economy hit Alsace particularly hard, and the region began losing jobs in the commercial sector (excluding temporary staff) for the first time in nine years. The unemployment rate in Alsace is rising faster than the national average, although it's still well below the national average; men are worst affected as a result of cutbacks in the industrial workforce. The only sector which has escaped

the general trend is the hotel trade, where employment rates are high. Further information can be found on the website of the Observatoire Régional Emploi Formation (🖥 www.oref-alsace.org).

Property

Strasbourg has some of the most expensive property in France, which affects average property prices for the region. These are as follows:

Type of Property	Average Price Range (€)
New 2- or 3-bedroom apartment	105,000 – 120,000
Older 2- or 3-bedroom apartment	75,000 – 90,000
New 3- or 4-bedroom house	125,000 – 160,000
Older 3- or 4-bedroom house	110,000 – 140,000

Rented accommodation starts at around €400 per month for a two-bedroom apartment, rising to €1,000 or more for a four-bedroom house.

AQUITAINE

Aquitaine includes one of the most and one of the least popular departments with expatriates: Dordogne and Landes respectively. Property prices and employment opportunities therefore vary widely with the area and detailed research is essential if you're considering trying to make a living in south-west France.

Population

The population of Aquitaine is around 2.9 million and grew faster than the national average between 1990 and

1999 (the dates of the last national censuses): 4 per cent compared with 3.5 per cent. The department of Gironde (33), which has 47 per cent of Aquitaine's population, attracts two-thirds of its population growth. There are around 107,000 foreign residents (including 42,500 North Africans) in Aquitaine. The highest concentration of North Africans is in Gironde – primarily in and around Bordeaux. Gironde also has the highest concentration of Spanish and Portuguese with around 18,000 out of a total of 40,000 in the region. Other non-French European Union (EU) nationals living in Aquitaine are mainly British, Dutch, German and Belgian, although they account only 0.5 per cent of the population. There are around 7,000 Britons in the region, although a major proportion of them live in Dordogne. Although it's generally thought that the British are the most numerous immigrants in Dordogne, in fact Portuguese and Moroccans outnumber them by far; there are over 2,300 Portuguese and almost 1,300 Moroccans, compared with a total of 4,435 other EU nationals (including British) and 1,380 other non-EU nationals. (Of the British population in Aquitaine, around two-thirds are retired or otherwise non-working, but the proportion varies between less than 50 per cent in Gironde to around 80 per cent in Dordogne). Gironde has the next largest number of British residents.

Employment Prospects

The region is noted for economic dynamism and a rapid increase in employment, but a continuing high level of unemployment. It's home to some 1,158,300 jobs, of which 1,022,600 are salaried.

The region is characterised by the importance of its agricultural sector and the weakness of its industrial sector, in spite of its particularly dynamic aeronautics and timber industries. Services account for 65 per cent of employment, industry 20 per cent and agriculture 15 per cent.

Major service sectors (824,500 jobs) include call centres, logistics and tourism. The fifth biggest tourist region in France, Aquitaine is the country's leader in spa cures (Dax) and pilgrimages (Lourdes). Tourism brings in approximately €2.3 billion each year and employs between 30,000 and 55,000 people, depending on the season. There are also 150,000 jobs in commerce, which is another thriving sector. A number of companies advertise in French and English on their websites. There's a variety of seasonal work in the area, for which no particular skills or qualifications are required, ranging from fruit and grape picking in the summer/autumn to bar and other ski resort work in the winter, but you must apply several months in advance to secure a position.

The main industry sectors are aerospace, chemicals, electronics, energy, oil (Elf), paper, pharmaceuticals and wine-making. There are around 172,000 jobs in 16,500 companies, almost 85 per cent of which have fewer than ten staff. The agro-food industry is the region's largest employer, with 30,000 staff. Wood and paper are a traditional sector (16,000 jobs in 1,200 companies) with a number of major groups, including the British conglomerate Smurfit. Chemicals employs over 12,000 people in just under 400 companies, and aeronautics is a thriving sector, with 25,000 jobs in 250 specialised firms and 200 small and medium-size enterprises (SME) acting as subcontractors. There are over 3,500 jobs in pharmaceuticals and 2,500 in the medical and surgical industry.

Agricultural land and forest cover 90 per cent of the regional territory. Almost 2 million hectares are covered by trees (mostly in Landes), and timber production is a major industry. The production of high-quality wine (the Bordeaux area produces almost a third of France's AOC wine), sweetcorn (Aquitaine is France's largest corn-growing region) and goose and duck products (especially the famous *foie gras*) have gained international fame, although the last are threatened by impending EU legislation. This sector accounts for 84,000 jobs, less than half of which are salaried.

Aquitaine's level of unemployment (particularly among women) is higher than the national average (10.2 compared with 9.9 per cent), although the region has been creating more new jobs than the national average for the past 25 years. Current large-scale projects include the 'Laser Mégajoule' (LMJ) and the Centre d'Études Atomiques (CEA) at Barp (Gironde), where almost 1,000 people are employed. Salaries are slightly lower than the French average, with a gap of over 10 per cent for managerial staff.

Property

The south-west has been steadily increasing in popularity over the past 15 years or so. On the coast, Gironde is particularly popular, especially among the British, although (relative) bargains can still be found on the Garonne estuary north of Bordeaux (beyond commuting distance), including large properties with vineyards. There are fewer properties available in Landes, and these tend to be snapped up by the French. Typical half-timbered *landais* houses near the coast can fetch high prices. The extreme south-west is perhaps France's best-kept secret, although prices are beginning to shoot up here too and a lot of new properties are being built in and around Pau (64).

Inland, Dordogne has become one of the most sought-after areas among expatriates, particularly British, and it's difficult to find houses to renovate for the simple reason that there are very few properties left in need of renovation. It's easier to find properties that have been renovated, but of course, the price is much higher. Many people want a house within 15km (11mi), north or south, of the river Dordogne, or within the triangle Souillac/Sarlat/Gourdon, where prices are highest, although it's possible to find reasonably priced property in other parts of the departments.

Those unable to find a suitable property in Dordogne (or Lot in Midi-Pyrénées) look mainly to Lot-et-Garonne, and the area between Albi, Cordes-sur-Ciel and Gaillac in Tarn has become known among estate agents as the 'Golden Triangle' (prices can safely be left to the imagination!). Lot-et-Garonne is now so popular with tourists that there's a shortage of almost 1,000 beds each year to accommodate them, and grants of up to 50 per cent are available to those wanting to renovate properties in order to provide tourist accommodation. Therefore, there's considerable demand for such properties and generally for habitable stone houses with plenty of land which are secluded but not isolated, and consequently there's a shortage of this type of property around Agen, Villeneuve and other main towns in the department. Properties are easier to come by in more rural areas, mainly to the north-west of Agen and north of Villeneuve.

Generally, prices have been rising sharply in the last five years or so, and it's predicted that they will continue to do so in the coming years. Cheaper areas can be found in Pyrénées-Atlantiques, where prices generally drop the higher you go; on the other hand, the region's highest average prices are to be found in Bayonne. The table below gives average prices per m² for older properties in major towns in the area:

Town	Average Price per m² (€)
Bordeaux (33)	1,005
Périgueux (46)	1,024
Bayonne (64)	1,085
Pau (64)	850

Average property prices aren't always a reliable indication of the relative price of similar properties in different towns, as one town may have a preponderance of cheaper or more expensive properties and, as elsewhere, location has a significant effect on the value of property; a home with a sea-view, for example, can command a 100 per cent premium.

By far the greatest number of available houses is in Gironde. There are also plenty of houses for sale in Lot-et-Garonne and Pyrénées-Atlantiques. Prices range from as little as €50,000 for a small house high in the Pyrenees to €500,000 or more for a substantial property in Dordogne or popular parts of the coast. There are few properties available for restoration in any department.

Rented Accommodation

There's a fair number of apartments available for long-term rent in Gironde and Pyrénées-Atlantiques. Most apartments are in the main towns in each department (i.e. Périgueux in Dordogne, Bordeaux in Gironde, Dax and Mont-de-Marsan in Landes, Agen in Lot-et-Garonne, and Bayonne and Pau in Pyrénées-Atlantiques), and few are available elsewhere. Price ranges for each department (except Hautes-Pyrénées) are shown below.

Town/Department	No. of Bedrooms	Monthly Rental (€)
Gironde	Studio	225 – 375
	1	350 – 550
	2	600 – 650
	3	600 – 1,250
Landes	Studio	190 – 255
	1	370 – 520
	2	400 – 600
	3	450 – 575

Lot-et-Garonne	Studio	275
	1	400
	2	550
	3	750
Pyrénées-Atlantiques	Studio	200 – 400
	1	200 – 460
	2	400 – 650
	3	400 – 500

Rented houses are less common than apartments, and very few are to be found in most departments. Gironde has the largest number of houses for rent; prices range from €400 per month for a two-bedroom house to €1,200 or more for a five-bedroom property.

AUVERGNE

Increasingly popular with expatriates seeking to 'get away from it all', the beautiful Auvergne is a challenging region in which to find work or start a business, although there are several government incentives to do so.

Population

With a population of 1.3 million, Auvergne has one of the lowest population densities in France – 51 people per km^2 (132 per mi^2) compared with the national average of 100 – and few large towns; only Clermont-Ferrand (population 261,000) has over 50,000 inhabitants. The population is in decline (Champagne-Ardenne was the only other French region to decrease in population between the national censuses of 1990 and 1999, but at a much slower rate). Vichy (03) has the fastest-ageing population of any major town in France.

Of the 23,375 official non-French EU residents of Auvergne, 16,450 are Portuguese and the remaining 7,000 or so include all other EU nationalities. Haute-Vienne (87) is home to half of the foreigners living in the region, of which more than a third come from the EU. The capital, Clermont-Ferrand, boasts two universities and six engineering colleges and so has a young population.

Employment Prospects

Around two-thirds of jobs are in services, while industry provides 22 per cent, agriculture 7.5 per cent and construction 6 per cent. Although the rate of unemployment in the region is lower than the national average (7.8 per cent compared with 9.9 per cent – the number of retired people probably distorts the figures), there are few large companies and finding employment isn't easy. Until recently, the economy was based on small (40 to 200ha/100 to 500 acre) family farms passed down through generations. However, farming is becoming less profitable, and small farms are unable to compete with the big concerns and foreign prices. Fewer people want the hard work of running a farm for little return; they prefer to look for other work, which usually means moving out of the area. The advantage of this situation is that, if you have some agricultural experience, farming is a strong option, and the French government offers substantial subsidies to farmers. Departmental chambers of commerce (CCI) can help you to set up a farming business (see page 371).

In fact, a number of initiatives have been created at departmental, regional and national level to encourage companies and individuals to settle in the area, and there's financial and educational assistance for those wishing to become self-employed. Several departments offer training and grants (amounts vary from department to department) for those wanting to create a business or take over an existing company. For example, the Haute-Loire CCI has a monthly meeting for people wishing to create a *gîte* or a B&B to advise them on applying for assistance. The Conseil Régional d'Auvergne (🖥 www.cr-auvergne.fr) provides assistance to creators and developers of companies and can help you to obtain assistance from the national government or from the European Union. According to a recent survey by *Le Point* magazine, Montluçon (03) is a particularly good place to start a business, as it enjoys one of the highest rates of new business success in France.

The region is seventh in the national research league table, and home to businesses which are leaders in their sector, including Michelin (tyre production), Limagrain (agri-industry). There are also strong specialist industries, such as cutlery in the Thiers region and mineral water, headed by Volvic. The presence of the agri-food and pharmaceuticals industries has led to the creation of a national centre of excellence.

The services sector is growing strongly, an increasing number of jobs being taken by women, while agriculture, industry and construction are shedding workers. Metalworking, mineral water and the meat and dairy industries are stable, while the buildings and public works sector has faced difficulties in recent months. In the services sector, IT is declining, but personal services are making progress.

In the last few years, there has been an increase in British-owned or British-run companies. These are mostly in the service industry (e.g. tourism, estate agency) or the building trade. It's possible to set up and run a tea room or a *gîte* or offer *chambres d'hôtes*, although competition in many areas is intense. A certain number of jobs are available in the tourist industry during the summer and winter (skiing) seasons, but there's a tendency for these to go to French nationals, whatever their English-language ability, rather than to foreigners.

Long-distance working using computers is possible in some parts, but outside the main towns cable and broadband internet connections are unlikely to be available for a few years.

Further information can be found on the websites of the Auvergne regional institute for statistics and economic studies (go to 🖥 www.insee.fr and click on '*Le Portrait de Votre Région*').

Property

There are few apartments and housing estates outside the large towns, and most people moving to this area are looking for houses or farms to renovate with at least 1,000m^2 (a quarter of an acre) of land. It's also becoming difficult to find a typical stone house with a large plot. Often, when a farm is sold, a local farmer buys the land and perhaps a barn, leaving the house with a small garden or, in some cases, virtually no land at all. It's worth bearing in mind that in rural areas of Auvergne, 10 to 15 per cent of houses have no septic tank or sanitation, and when a property is described as 'for renovation' this usually means 'requiring drainage, electricity and other basic amenities'; even when a house is lived in, it isn't necessarily habitable!

New houses are generally bought (or built) by French people and tend to be in or near a town, although there are some new housing estates that may appeal to foreigners, especially those looking to let a property to holidaymakers.

In general, property prices in the region have risen around 10 to 20 per cent in the last two years. Among major towns, Montluçon (03) boasts the lowest average prices for older properties, not only in Auvergne, but in the whole of France. The table below gives average prices per m^2 for older properties in major towns in the area:

Town	Average Price per m^2 (€)
Montluçon (03)	570
Vichy (03)	730
Clermont-Ferrand (63)	910

Average property prices aren't always a reliable indication of the relative price of similar properties in different towns, as one town may have a preponderance of cheaper or more expensive properties.

A small, isolated house or farm for renovation (if you can still find one) costs from as little as €20,000 in the wilds of Allier to €40,000 in Puy-de-Dôme, a small renovated house a similar price, and a four or five-bedroom property between €100,000 and €200,000 or more depending on location.

Rented Accommodation

Rented accommodation is easiest to find in Clermont-Ferrand (63), where there are apartments from studios to five-bedrooms, although smaller apartments are in demand from students. Outside the main towns, rented accommodation tends to be limited to *gîtes*, which can be expensive for a long period. It's possible to find rural houses for rent from around €400 per month for a two-bedroom property.

BRITTANY

Brittany has long been popular with expatriates, particularly the British, owing to its proximity to the UK and many shared cultural values resulting from a common

Celtic heritage. Popularity has its price, however, as can be witnessed in the recent increases in property values. Predominantly rural, Brittany has few large cities, little major industry and a relatively poor transport network.

Population

Around 2.9 million people live in Brittany, whose population is growing at slightly above the national average rate (Vannes in Morbihan has the fastest growing population of any major town in France). The department of Ille-et-Vilaine attracts half of Brittany's immigrants. Over two-thirds of the population live in urban areas (an increase of 20 per cent in the last decade), and the capital Rennes (35) and its surrounding area, the country's third-fastest growing urban area, has over half a million inhabitants. Brest (29) is the only other town in Brittany with more than 67,000 inhabitants. Brittany has a generally young population, 35 per cent of people being under 25. Rennes (35) has a very high proportion of students (around 25 per cent) among its population, whereas the percentage of students in other towns is low, e.g. 6 per cent in Quimper (29) and a mere 2 per cent in Saint-Malo (35). It's predicted that the population of Brittany will continue to increase over the coming decades, although at a slower rate.

Côtes-d'Armor is the least densely populated department in Brittany and the one with the lowest proportion of foreign residents and the highest average age (over 40), with a high proportion of retired people, especially in rural areas along the coast. Saint-Brieuc has the department's youngest population. Finistère has the most static population in Brittany: over one in three people were born in the department, although three-quarters of immigrants to the department in the last decade have come from outside Brittany. Brest and the surrounding area has the youngest population. Ille-et-Vilaine is the most densely populated department in Brittany and includes the regional capital, Rennes, which has 212,500 inhabitants and attracts a large mobile population, mainly because of its university. The population of Ille-et-Vilaine is the youngest in Brittany, averaging under 37. Morbihan has the most rapidly ageing population of the four Breton departments, as many young people leave the department to study or work.

Employment Prospects

Overall, 65 per cent of employment in Brittany is service-related, 15 per cent in industry and 20 per cent in agriculture. The service sector is the only one of the three to have created jobs since 1990 and it employs almost 700,000 people. The principal service industries are research and tourism.

Brittany is particularly noted for technological innovation, with 12 technology transfer centres and around 6,000 full-time researchers in a variety of fields, including telecommunications, electronics, medical imaging, materials chemistry and marine technologies. Some 60 per cent of French oceanographic research is carried out in Brest.

The second most important tourist region in France, Brittany has a very high seasonal demand for labour in the hotel and restaurant sector, although several years of growth have been followed by a fall in employment since 2001.

Brittany is the most important region in France for fishing, pig rearing, poultry production and vegetable production. The food-processing industry is still the spearhead of the Breton economy (30 per cent of industrial employment in the region), with some powerful agricultural cooperatives: meat, canning and salting industries, including fish products; dairy industries (producing a third of France's production of butter and powder); biscuit and ready-made meal factories.

There are more than 60,000 farms in Brittany, employing over 100,000 people (10 per cent of the working population) and the region produces over half of French pork, half the country's poultry consumption and 20 per cent of its milk, as well as vast quantities of vegetables (over 90 per cent of French production of cauliflowers, 75 per cent of its artichokes and a high proportion of its beans, Brussels sprouts, cabbages, chicory, lettuces, peas, spinach and tomatoes) and fruit (apples, apricots, cherries, grapes, peaches, pears and plums). Fishing employs around 5,000 in Brittany, where over 50 per cent of France's fish are caught and 75 per cent of its shellfish produced, including up to 4,000 tonnes of *coquilles St-Jacques* per year. (The French hypermarket chain Intermarché even has its own fishing fleet in Lorient!) Brittany is also a major source of seaweed (over 650 species!), of which almost 100,000 tonnes are harvested annually for use in food additives, fertilisers and cosmetics, but also in balneology.

The home of a number of major distribution groups (Leclerc, Les Comptoirs Modernes), the region has diversified its activities to embrace the electronics industry and telecommunications (concentrated in Rennes, Lannion, Brest), armaments and ship building (Brest, Lorient, Saint-Nazaire) and the car industry (Citroën in Rennes).

Brittany has less industry than Normandy. Fewer than 200,000 people work in the manufacturing industry (18 per cent of regional employment), the major sectors being cars, electronics, ship building, armaments and communications, and a further 70,000 in the construction industry and 60,000 in food production. There are over 40,000 small craft and cottage businesses in Brittany, employing more than 80,000 people. There has recently been a downturn in the industrial sector, particularly in the field of electrical and electronic equipment, and in ship building. In agriculture, the animal sector is undergoing a crisis. By contrast, the construction sector is continuing to create new jobs and to experience recruitment problems. The services sector is also continuing to grow, especially in the retail trade, personal and domestic services, social work, health and the hotel and restaurant trade.

During the second quarter of 2004, the unemployment rate stood at 8 per cent, compared with 9.9 per cent for the whole of metropolitan France (source: Ministry of Employment). However, it has been rising for the past two years.

Brittany has recently enjoyed a surge in job creation and new business success; Saint-Malo (35) has by far the country's highest new business success rate. In a comparative survey of 100 major towns in France published in January 2002 by *Le Point* magazine, Rennes (35) was rated in second place behind Paris in terms of its attractiveness to workers, and Vannes (56) came eighth.

Until a decade ago, there was little in the way of employment prospects in Brittany outside the towns, but there are now opportunities throughout the region, especially in the building industry (including renovation work), but also in the tourist trade, which is enjoying an upturn, particularly in coastal areas. However, salaries tend to be low and many immigrants (especially Britons) are tempted to work 'on the black', which is of course illegal and punishable by large fines and even imprisonment.

There are also offices of the international employment agencies ADECCO, ADIA and Manpower France in most major towns, and jobseekers should consult the two regional newspapers, *Ouest France* and *Le Télégramme* as well as local publications.

Further information can be found on the website of the Observatoire Régional Emploi-Formation (🖳 www.oref-bretagne.org).

Property

The popularity of Brittany, particularly among British buyers, means that the demand for properties exceeds the supply. House building in Brittany enjoyed a boom in 1999 and 2000, when the number of houses increased by around 5 per cent per year, but the rate has since slowed to around 1 per cent. However, the demand for new properties in Brittany is still high, especially in coastal areas, where second homes represent almost 10 per cent of the property market. (In some communes, there are over 100 second homes per km^2.)

The most popular areas in Brittany is the area around Dinan, Dinard and Saint-Malo. This is reflected in relatively high prices, which have caused buyers to look further west along the coast of the Côtes-d'Armor and into Finistère. If there are bargains to be found, they're in central Brittany and the extreme west of Finistère. The demand for holiday accommodation in Brittany in particular is as great as anywhere in France, so second homebuyers have little difficulty in letting their properties and can usually cover their mortgage payments through rental income.

Brittany has experienced steep price rises, especially on islands, where property has increased in value by 300 per cent in 15 years. A 100m^2 house with a sea view on the island of Bréhat off Paimpol, for example, can cost up to €500,000, and similar properties on islands such as Moines and Arz in the Golfe de Morbihan can fetch up to €750,000. (Houses in need of renovation are cheaper, but restoration costs on islands can be 30 per cent higher than on the mainland.) Elsewhere, prices are more reasonable, although the days when you could pick up a habitable farmhouse for €30,000 are gone.

Of the major towns in the area, Brest (29) boasts the lowest average prices for older properties, while the highest average prices are to be found in Saint-Malo (35). The table below gives average prices per m^2 for older properties in the major towns in Brittany:

Town	Average Price per m^2 (€)
Saint-Brieuc (22)	920
Brest (29)	760

Quimper (29)	885
Rennes (35)	1,190
Saint-Malo (35)	1,425
Vannes (56)	1,215

Average property prices aren't always a reliable indication of the relative price of similar properties in different towns, as one town may have a preponderance of cheaper or more expensive properties. Location has a significant effect on the value of property; a home with a sea-view, for example, can command a 100 per cent premium.

Residential property prices range from €50,000 for a two-bedroom house in inland Côtes-d'Armor or Morbihan to €500,000 or more for a five-bedroom property in a popular area.

Despite what estate agents might tell you, there are still plenty of properties to restore in Brittany, although you should always check whether there are problems associated with a property (e.g. whether it's in an area liable to flooding or has no proper sanitation). Prices start at around €30,000 for a small house, but restoration costs can double or triple the purchase price.

Rented Accommodation

Apartments are available for long-term rent in all departments, although few have more than three bedrooms (in Rennes, there are few with more than two). The majority of rental apartments are to be found in the principal towns in each department (except in Côtes-d'Armor, where the few available apartments are spread among several towns, and Morbihan, where the majority are in Lorient), and few are available elsewhere. Price ranges for these towns (and the department of Côtes-d'Armor) are shown below.

Town/Department	Apartments No. of Bedrooms	Monthly Rental (€)
Côtes-d'Armor	Studio	250 – 400
	1	300 – 500
	2	400 – 550
	3	500 – 600
Brest (29)	Studio	250 – 350
	1	300 – 500
	2	350 – 550
	3	500 – 650
Rennes (35)	1	325 – 450
	2	450 – 600
Lorient (56)	Studio	250 – 300

	1	300 – 400
	2	400 – 550
	3	400 – 650

Rented houses are less common than apartments, and very few are to be found in or near the main towns. The table below gives an indication of the rental prices for houses in each department.

Town/Department	Houses No. of Bedrooms	Monthly Rental (€)
Côtes-d'Armor	2	300 – 500
	3	400 – 600
	4	600 – 650
Finistère	3	550 – 800
	4	650+
	5	700+
Ille-et-Vilaine	3	700 – 1,000
	4	700 – 1,100
	5	750 – 1,100
Morbihan	3	500 – 650
	4	600 – 950

BURGUNDY

Known to the French as *Bourgogne*, as is the wine for which it's famous, Burgundy is largely unspoiled; it has even been dubbed the 'rural soul' of France). Surprisingly unpopular with foreign buyers (although this is changing), it remains an enigmatic part of the country.

Population & Employment Prospects

Burgundy's population is 1.62 million and is neither growing nor in decline. The economic situation varies from one department to another; while Yonne is the most buoyant, Saône-et-Loire still faces considerable difficulties. The economic weakness of Germany, Burgundy's main trading partner, hasn't helped the development of the regional economy. Nevertheless, Burgundy's exports are holding up, and the number of salaried staff has remained stable for the past few years. The manufacturing sector accounts for more jobs than it does at national level: it employs 129,000 people and represents 23 per cent of the regional workforce, although industrial employment has continued to fall since mid-2001. Metalworking, engineering, chemicals, rubber and plastics, and agri-food industries are the principal sectors of economic activity in the region. There's a high level of industrial employment in Saône-et-Loire, in the south of Nièvre and in the north of Yonne.

Some other sectors, such as building, civil engineering and public works, have recently carried out recruitment drives, while others, such as the hotel and catering trade, still lack attractiveness, particularly among young people, whose regional unemployment level is almost 23 per cent compared to the national average of 20 per cent.

Property

Property prices tend to be above the national average, although inexpensive, habitable village houses and farmhouses in need of restoration can be found in most areas. Average property prices for the region are as follows:

Type of Property	Average Price Range (€)
New 2- or 3-bedroom apartment	95,000 – 110,000
Older 2- or 3-bedroom apartment	65,000 – 75,000
New 3- or 4-bedroom house	95,000 – 115,000
Older 3- or 4-bedroom house	75,000 – 95,000

Rented accommodation starts at around €250 per month for a two-bedroom apartment, rising to €800 or more for a four-bedroom house.

CENTRE-VAL-DE-LOIRE

Split across the middle by the Loire, which is reckoned to be the dividing line between the colder north and the warmer south of France, the central region (in name and location) is famous for its châteaux (the best known are in Loir-et-Cher and Indre-et-Loire) and is largely unspoiled by industry, mass tourism or a surfeit of holiday homes, although it's popular with Parisians and other second-homeowners.

Population & Employment Prospects

The region has 2.45 million inhabitants, including some 1,300 Britons, and is growing at just below the national average rate. Employment in Centre-Val-de-Loire accounts for just under 1 million jobs, but the population is growing faster than the job base, so unemployment in the region is expected to rise. The northern part of the region is more industrialised, whereas the southern part of the region is more agricultural. Overall, around 20 per cent of the population is in manufacturing, 5 per cent in agriculture, 6.4 per cent in construction and 66 per cent in the service sector.

Property

Property prices vary considerably – mainly according to proximity to Paris – and are generally above the French average; bargains are rare. Average property prices for the region are as follows:

Type of Property	Average Price Range (€)
New 2- or 3-bedroom apartment	105,000 – 125,000
Older 2- or 3-bedroom apartment	65,000 – 75,000
New 3- or 4-bedroom house	90,000 – 115,000
Older 3- or 4-bedroom house	80,000 – 100,000

Rented accommodation starts at around €300 per month for a two-bedroom apartment, rising to €900 or more for a four-bedroom house.

CHAMPAGNE-ARDENNE

Often called simply Champagne, after the famous sparkling wine, whose production dominates life in the region, Champagne-Ardenne may not be the prettiest part of France and isn't popular with expatriates, but it has many attractions – not least the Ardennes mountain range in the north of the region.

Population & Employment Prospects

The population is 1.4 million, and Champagne-Ardenne is one of only three regions in France where the population is in decline (the others being Auvergne and Limousin). Located at the heart of the major trading route from the North Sea to Italy, Champagne-Ardenne has long been a transit region and has excellent transport links, with the recent opening of an ultra-modern international freight airport at Vatry. Renowned for its champagne, Champagne-Ardenne is also the fifth industrial region of France. Industry (not including public works) employs 22 per cent of the regional salaried population, i.e. 117,000 employees in 6,500 companies. Its industry is diverse. The major sector is metallurgy (800 companies employing almost 30,000 people, making them France's principal producers of metal products), followed by textiles and clothing (14,000 workers, mainly concentrated in Aube) and agri-food production (18,500 people in 2,000 companies, only 180 of which have more than ten employees, and representing 35 per cent of exports from the region, mainly due to champagne). Other industries include consumer goods, logistics, packaging (for which Champagne-Ardenne is the second-most important region in France), plastics and smelting. Only ten companies employ more than 1,000 people. Further information can be found on the website of the Chambre Régionale de Commerce et d'Industrie (🖳 www.champagne-ardenne.cci.fr).

Property

Average property prices for the region are as follows:

Type of Property	Average Price Range (€)
New 2- or 3-bedroom apartment	100,000 – 115,000
Older 2- or 3-bedroom apartment	70,000 – 80,000
New 3- or 4-bedroom house	100,000 – 120,000
Older 3- or 4-bedroom house	80,000 – 100,000

Rented accommodation starts at around €300 per month for a two-bedroom apartment, rising to €900 or more for a four-bedroom house.

CORSICA

The island of Corsica, 160km (100mi) to the south-east of mainland France, has strong historical links with Italy, which is twice as close. Its culture is quite different from that of the rest of France (Corsican men are reputed to be among the country's most chauvinistic – which is saying something!), and it even has its own language, spoken regularly by around 60 per cent of the population.

Population & Employment Prospects

Corsica's population numbers just 260,000 and is growing at just above the national average rate, although the population of Ajaccio is declining faster than that of any other major town in France. The island's major 'industry' is tourism (many mainland French people holiday there). There are just under 100,000 people in employment, 78,500 in the service sector (including restaurants and hotels), 8,600 in construction, 6,300 in manufacturing and around 4,000 in agriculture.

Property

Two-bedroom apartments (both new and older) by the sea vary between 40 and 80m^2 and prices range from under €60,000 to over €100,000. Older two-bedroom apartments in a historic town measure between 60 and 75m^2 and cost from around €75,000 to €130,000. Three-bedroom apartments (both categories) tend to be much larger, from 90 to 105m^2, and cost from around €140,000 to €200,000. Most houses on the island have three or four bedrooms and prices start at around €200,000, with average plots around 1,500m^2. A small two-bedroom house near the sea in Corsica can cost €120,000. Rental prices are somewhere between those of Alsace and those of the Côte d'Azur.

FRANCHE-COMTE

Bordering Switzerland, with which it shares much of its architecture, cuisine and culture, Franche-Comté (literally 'free country') is largely unspoiled and reputed to be France's greenest region.

Population & Employment Prospects

The population of France-Comté is around 1.15 million and is growing at below the national average rate. Employment totals around 454,000 and is declining, particularly in some of the traditional areas: manufacturing (eyeglass and clock-making) and car manufacture. One of the few industries still prospering is the chemicals-rubber-plastics industry. Construction is also doing well thanks to various local and national subsidies. The tourist trade is strong in the region, and jobs are being created in the recreation, cultural and sports sectors.

As in other parts of France, there are shortages of personnel in health and social services. The temporary employment business has slumped in recent years and long-term unemployment has been rising. As the local population isn't increasing, it's expected that some professions will be in short supply as the older generation retires over the next few years. The main shortages are expected to include teachers, child care workers and after-sales service staff.

Property

Franche-Comté is largely ignored by foreign homebuyers. Property prices are higher than the French average, although bargains can be found, particularly if you're seeking a winter holiday home. Besançon is served by the A36 motorway and has good connections with the centre and south of France, Germany and Switzerland via TGV. Average property prices for the region are as follows:

Type of Property	Average Price Range (€)
New 2- or 3-bedroom apartment	85,000 – 100,000
Older 2- or 3-bedroom apartment	60,000 – 70,000
New 3- or 4-bedroom house	95,000 – 120,000
Older 3- or 4-bedroom house	80,000 – 100,000

Rented accommodation starts at around €200 per month for a two-bedroom apartment, rising to €700 or more for a four-bedroom house.

ILE-DE-FRANCE

The so-called 'Island of France' is dominated by the capital, the surrounding departments being largely suburban, although there are rural parts to be found in the outer reaches of Essonne, Seine-et-Marne, Seine-St-Denis, Val-d'Oise and Yvelines.

Population

According to the latest census (taken in 1999), the population of the Ile-de-France is almost exactly 11 million, over a sixth of the population of France, including almost 40 per cent of all foreigners living in France. In all, there are around 1.3 million foreigners, accounting for almost 12 per cent of the region's population, more than double the overall average for France (5.6 per cent), although there has been a gradual decline in the number of foreigners over the last decade, due both to the naturalisation of older immigrants and to migration away from the Paris area into other regions of France.

Traditionally, Paris and the Ile-de-France region have been a magnet for young French people, drawing population from the countryside. This is still true in some towns surrounding Paris, particularly Rueil-Malmaison (92) and Evry (91), the latter also boasting the lowest population ageing rate of any major town in France. In recent years, however, this trend seems to have reversed, thanks largely to government-sponsored development of industry and employment in the regions. More and more *Franciliens* are moving elsewhere to escape crowded living conditions, traffic congestion, pollution and the high cost of living in and around Paris. Saint-Germain-en-Laye and Versailles (78), Corbeil-Essonnes (91), Saint-Denis (93) and Paris itself are all decreasing in population. Although the latest census figures showed a slight increase in overall population since the previous count (in 1990), the Ile-de-France is growing much more slowly than most other parts of France. Even foreigners coming to France to join family members now have a greater tendency to settle in other regions. The populations of Créteil (94) and Evry (91) comprise a high proportion of students (around 20 per cent), compared with 3 per cent in Neuilly-sur-Seine (92) and a mere 1 per cent in Corbeil-Essonnes (91), Rueil-Malmaison (92) and Sarcelles (95).

By far the most numerous foreign nationals in the Ile-de-France are the Portuguese, with over 270,000 official residents. Algerians and Moroccans number 190,000 and 145,000 respectively. Completing the top ten foreign nationalities are (in order): Tunisians, Turks, Spanish, Italians, Malians, Yugoslavians and Congolese, accounting in total for a further 285,000 people. Contrary to the fears of those on the political far right, the 1999 census showed that percentage increases in the foreign population were virtually identical to those in the native population, although there have been some shifts in the immigrants' countries of origin over the past decade (notably increases in immigrants from the former Yugoslavia and other conflict-torn regions of the world).

The greatest concentration of foreigners is in Seine-Saint-Denis, where there are many immigrants of Algerian, North African and sub-Saharan African origin. *Immigrés* make up almost 20 per cent of the population in this department, often living in high-rise *HLM* (council flats or subsidised housing blocks). Yvelines and Hauts-de-Seine to the west contain concentrations of Moroccans, particularly in the towns of Mantes-la-Jolie, Canteloup-les-Vignes and Les Mureaux (in Yvelines) and Gennevilliers, Clichy and Villeneuve-la-Garenne in Hauts-de-Seine. Val-de-Marne is home to many Portuguese immigrants and is increasingly popular with Asians seeking to move out of Paris. The departments of the *grand couronne* generally have much lower proportions of foreigners, except for Val-d'Oise, whose foreign population of around 11 per cent includes many Turkish immigrants. Within Paris, the proportion of foreigners is around 15 per cent, with distinct communities of Asians in the 1st, 2nd and 10th *arrondissements* and a concentration of African immigrants in the 18th and 19th.

There are relatively few Britons and Americans living in the Ile-de-France, and their numbers tend to rise and fall according to the needs of the multinational corporations headquartered in the Paris area. It's estimated that there are between 5,000 and 10,000 Britons and 5,000 to 8,000 Americans living in and around Paris (the French statistical institute, INSEE, doesn't publish these figures). Paris is hardly a popular retirement destination, and many English-speaking expatriates in the area are 'transient' executive families making a two to five-year tour of duty with an international company or students enjoying a 'Paris experience' as part of their studies. The few permanent residents of British or American background include those married to French nationals.

Employment Prospects

The Ile-de-France has a special position in the French labour market. Although one of France's smallest regions, it represents 28 per cent of the country's gross domestic product (GDP) and 5 per cent of Europe's and is the third most important economic region in the world after New York and Tokyo. The Paris region provides over 20 per cent of all employment in France and thus is usually the first destination for most newcomers seeking employment. The office complex at La Défense, on the western edge of Paris, provides employment for 140,000 people and houses the headquarters of many of the largest international companies doing business in France. There are also a number of sites near the *villes nouvelles* outside Paris where large office parks are being or have been developed. In spite of decentralisation efforts, Paris and the department of Yvelines to the west are home to a large number of public administrations (the state remains the leading employer in the capital with 200,000 employees) and private companies (one in three French companies has its headquarters in Paris). Almost a third of the Ile-de-France's workers are employed by foreign companies.

Although industry remains an important sector, employing almost 700,000 people (agri-industry, aeronautics, car manufacturing, chemicals, construction, electronics and metallurgy), the Ile-de-France is characterised by its buoyant services sector, with a workforce of over 3.8 million, i.e. almost 80 per cent of the total. This is mainly accounted for by property, finance (the third European stock market after London and Frankfurt) and company services (880,000 workers). Research is also an important international activity and accounts for 45 per cent of those working in this sector.

France's grey matter is heavily concentrated in and around Paris, accounting for 40 per cent of executive employees and 30 per cent of university staff.

The Ile-de-France has excellent infrastructure (road, air and rail transport) making it a commercial communications centre of worldwide importance. It's of little surprise that the Ile de France is the leading European venue for trade shows, with 360 national or international shows each year, attracting 90,000 exhibitors and 9 million visitors.

Paris is a popular location for expatriate executives, and in many companies transfers or secondments to Paris are eagerly sought-after and generally reserved for upper level managers deserving of 'rewards'. Most employers in the Ile-de-France expect job candidates to speak and understand French well enough to function on a day-to-day basis with colleagues, even in offices or companies where English is commonly used. While some executive-level employees in international companies can function with minimal French, it can be almost impossible to find work in the area if you cannot carry on a conversation (or employment interview) in French. Many large employers provide language training as part of their required 'continuing education' – English lessons for French staff and French lessons for foreign staff.

For English speakers there are usually plenty of jobs on offer, including temporary or permanent bilingual secretaries and administrative or personal assistants. English-language teachers are also in high demand, although the best jobs in this field usually require a qualification such as a TEFL or TESOL certificate. In the business world, bookkeepers and accountants are often required to have knowledge or experience of what the French call 'Anglo-Saxon' accounting (*la comptabilité anglo-saxonne*), although you must also have some basic understanding of some of the peculiarities of the French system.

There's a shortage of experienced high-tech workers in many fields (notably computer-related areas) to the extent that the government has created a special exemption in the work permit process, although the exemption doesn't automatically apply to anyone with computer experience. It helps greatly if you're a qualified engineer (*ingénieur*), as the French have high respect for technical and scientific qualifications.

The Paris area offers greater potential than other parts of France for those willing to work 'under the table' in unskilled and unregistered jobs, although competition for the available 'jobs' can be fierce because of the large number of illegal foreigners (*les sans papiers*). Be aware, however, that controls are also more frequent in and around Paris than in other regions and the penalties are severe if you're caught.

Further information can be found on the website of the Conseil Régional de l'Ile de France (🖥 www.iledefrance.fr)

Property

Residential property in the Ile-de-France is automatically considered to be a 'primary residence' (*résidence principale*). You're also far less likely than in almost any other area of France to find a tumble-down farm or *château* going for a song that you can 'fix up' as a second home. Even virtual ruins can command top prices, in accordance with the property value mantra: 'location, location, location'.

Not surprisingly, the rate of new building in Paris and the major surrounding towns is low or – in the case of Evry (91), Rueil-Malmaison (92) and Sarcelles (95) – virtually non-existent. However, many areas on the edges of the Ile-de-France are undergoing something of a construction boom, as land previously held for agriculture is gradually being converted to housing estates. Along the *routes nationales* of Seine-et-Marne, Essonne, Yvelines, and at the outer limits of Val-d'Oise, you're likely to see signs directing you to housing estates in the process of construction, with countdowns of the number of homes or plots left to sell.

There are at least half a dozen weekly publications, costing between €2 and €5 and available at newsstands throughout the region, which are dedicated to property advertisements, for rent and for sale. *De Particulier à Particulier*, one such journal that carries only direct ads (i.e. where sellers are trying to avoid an estate agent's hefty commission), devotes almost half of its 300 to 400 pages each week to properties in the Ile-de-France region. Other property advertising journals concentrate on new properties or focus on 'luxury' properties. There are also many estate agents throughout the region, including the American franchise, Century 21, which handles purchases and rentals as well as land, commercial property and property management, although most estate agents cover limited areas of the city and it can be worthwhile using a foreign-based buying agent, who deals with several local agencies to find suitable properties for you to view. Many estate agencies and property publications have websites, with search functions to help you narrow your choice by specifying a price range, size, location or other criteria (see also **Appendix C**).

Not surprisingly, property prices in the Ile-de-France are the highest in France and form the basis of comparison for prices in the rest of the country. The five French towns and cities with the highest average property prices are all in the Ile-de-France, the average home in Neuilly-sur-Seine (92) costing on average almost ten times as much as in Montluçon in Auvergne, five times as much as in Toulouse, twice as much than in Cannes and Antibes and over 60 per cent more even than in Paris. (Small consolation is that property taxes in Neuilly are the lowest in France!) The Ile-de-France's lowest average property prices are to be found in Sarcelles (95), where property taxes are also relatively low. The table below gives average prices per m^2 of older properties in major towns in the Ile-de-France.

Town	Average Price per m^2 (€)
Paris (75)	2,975
Saint-Germain-en-Laye (78)	3,355
Versailles (78)	3,355
Corbeil-Essonnes (91)	1,100
Evry (91)	1,100
Boulogne-Billancourt (92)	2,440
Neuilly-sur-Seine (92)	5,030
Rueil-Malmaison (92)	3,050
Saint-Denis (93)	1,370
Créteil (94)	1,675
Sarcelles (95)	990

Average property prices aren't always a reliable indication of the relative price of similar properties in different towns, as one town may have a preponderance of cheaper or more expensive properties. In the city of Paris you can expect to pay up to €100,000 for a tiny studio. The smallest *studettes* (estate agent terminology for a studio of 20m^2 or less) start at around €50,000 and can cost €80,000 to €90,000 in a desirable area or if they include special features (e.g. a lift!). Standard one-bedroom apartments range from 25 to 40m^2 and cost between €100,000 and €200,000, depending on the location. A standard three-room (i.e. two-bedroom) flat can cost from €200,000 to €300,000. A penthouse near the Place Charles de Gaulle (Étoile) will set you back at least €1 million.

Features and factors that increase prices include proximity to shops and restaurants, nearby access to public transport, a quiet neighbourhood or nearby parks, availability of parking, a terrace, balcony or courtyard, a lift, and location in a building of *grand standing* (which can mean either a luxury building or one of established reputation).

Most apartments are part of a community property (*co-propriété*) arrangement, where residents share common costs (e.g. lighting in hallways, maintenance of lifts, *gardien*'s salary) and building maintenance charges. When it's time to paint or sandblast the exterior of the building, mend the roof or substitute a digi-code system for the *gardien* who's retiring, you will be summoned to a meeting to vote on the work, and then be assessed your share of the costs. *Co-propriété* meetings can become very heated and 'political', and of course the proceedings are governed by an entire body of rules and regulations decreed by the state.

If a Parisian house comes onto the market, you should expect to pay €250,000 to €300,000 for a mere 60 or 70m^2 in an outer *arrondissement* (e.g. the 18th and 19th). In more desirable districts (e.g. the 12th, 13th and 17th), a house priced under €500,000 is liable to need 'some work' (i.e. will probably be virtually uninhabitable without major renovation!).

Outside Paris, there's a wide range of apartments and houses on offer, with prices in the €100,000 to €250,000 range depending on factors such as location and ease of access to Paris (by motorway or public transport), as well as size and amount of land, restrictions on building or renovation, and general condition of the property. Prices for properties just outside the city limits are often virtually identical to those in Paris itself, particularly in upmarket parts of Neuilly-sur-Seine, Boulogne-Billancourt and Issy-les-Moulineaux. Generally speaking, the farther away from Paris, the lower the prices, except for homes in and around Versailles, a highly desirable residential area having large homes with spacious grounds. To a lesser extent, residential property in or very close to a town centre with shops and access to public transport and other services is more expensive than property in the countryside, some distance from town services and conveniences.

If you have money to burn, you can always splash out on a *château*, *manoir*, or other *propriété de caractère*, complete with extensive grounds, woods, equestrian facilities or other special features, starting at around €500,000. This sort of property is generally to be found in the outer reaches of the region, although now and then a spectacular *maison de ville* or other unusual residence comes up for sale in the *petit couronne*. There are entire publications dedicated to larger and more elegant residences, such as *Demeures de Charme*, produced by the publishers of *De Particulier à Particulier* (see **Appendix B**).

Rented Accommodation

In Paris itself, monthly rents start at around €500 for a studio apartment (which can be as small as 20m^2), to which you must normally add 10 to 20 per cent for charges such as water, rubbish collection and communal costs (e.g. maintenance of common areas or the services of a *gardien*). Even smaller flats (called *studettes* in the adverts) can be found for as 'little' as €350 per month, fully furnished (how much furniture can you fit in a 10m^2 room?). These tiny units, often converted maid's quarters in older buildings and sometimes with shared bathrooms or toilets, are highly sought-after by students and others on a limited budget.

Three-room apartments (i.e. two bedrooms and a living room) are the standard rental accommodation, prices ranging from around €900 per month to €1,500 or more, depending on the size of the apartment, equipment included and, of course, location. Charges are sometimes included in the quoted price, but you should usually allow an additional €50 to €150 per month if they aren't part of the basic rent. Apartments in older buildings (sometimes centuries old) are highly sought-after and rents can be sky high (as much as €8,000 per month) in buildings of 'character' in desirable districts, such as along the Champs-Elysées (where there are still a few private apartments), in certain neighbourhoods in the 16th and nestled among the designer shops in parts of the 8th.

Outside Paris, you can find apartments and houses for rent, costs generally declining as you move away from the city. It's possible to rent a three-room apartment with 75m^2 of living space for less than €1,000 per month in many areas of the *grand couronne*. There's a premium to be paid, of course, for flats that include parking space and those located close to shopping, public transport and other amenities. Monthly rents for detached houses start at around €1,000 for a house of around 70 to 85m² with a small garden (e.g. 300 to 500m²), prices varying according to similar factors as for an apartment (see above).

For an overview of rents throughout the Ile-de-France region, consult the publication *De Particulier à Particulier* (see **Appendix B**), which is also available online in searchable form and in English (🖳 www.pap.fr).

LANGUEDOC-ROUSSILLON

For a long time Provence's poor relation, neighbouring Languedoc-Roussillon, has become almost as sought-after among expatriates seeking a life in the sun, with four of its five departments being on the Mediterranean coast. Prices have escalated accordingly and some parts, particularly around Carcassonne (11), have become almost foreign enclaves, many immigrants needing to make a living.

Population

The population of Languedoc-Roussillon is around 2.3 million and has almost doubled in the last 40 years – the fastest-growing population of any region in France – and by 8.5 per cent between 1990 and 1999, although the inland department of Lozère remains one of France's most sparsely populated and 'remote'. The town of Montpellier (34) is among the fastest-growing in France. However, these increases have been largely due to migration rather than a high birth rate, and population ageing is a significant factor in many towns. There's a high British population: it's estimated that there are 700 Britons living in Aude, 650 in Gard, 1,800 in Hérault, 700 in Pyrénées-Orientales and 600 in Vaucluse.

Language

Languedoc-Roussillon is the homeland of France's second language, the *langue d'Oc* (also known as *Occitan*), which was once spoken throughout southern France, while those in the north spoke the *langue d'Oïl* (*oc* and *oïl* are the two medieval words for 'yes' in the respective areas). (The language is sometimes called Provençal, but in fact this was just one of the dialects of *Occitan* and is now spoken only in Italy.)

Although the *langue d'Oïl* has become the national *lingua franca*, *Occitan* was the everyday language of most of the rural population of the south until well into the 20th century and still survives in most of southern France (as many as 31 departments, according to some surveys), where it's estimated that there are around 3 million speakers of *Occitan* (around a third of whom use the language daily) and a further 1.5 million who can read or understand it. (It's also spoken in parts of Spain and Italy.)

Although most speakers are older people, there has recently been an attempt to revive the language, for example through *Occitan*-language pre-schools (*calandretas*), where there are around 1,500 pupils at any time, and it's taught as an optional subject in some state schools. The language has no official status, although around 40 minutes of *Occitan* programmes are broadcast every week by France 3 and there's a number of local radio programmes in the language, as well as articles in local newspapers and a number of *Occitan* magazines.

Related to *Occitan* (and to French) is Catalan (also known as Castillian), which is spoken by around 6 million people, mostly in Spain, but also in Andorra (where it's the official language) and parts of Pyrénées-Orientales in France (as well as in a single village in Sardinia!) – a region known as Catalonia.

Although it isn't necessary to learn *Occitan* or Catalan in order to be accepted by the local community, if you can master a few words and phrases it will probably improve your chances. French is spoken with a pronounced 'twang' in southern France (not at all like the pronunciation you learned at school), which may take a while to get used to.

Employment Prospects

Total employment in the region totals 794,000, with nearly 75 of those working in service industries and only 15 per cent in manufacturing and 10 per cent in agriculture. Job growth in the region is better than the national average, particularly in consumer services, education and health. On the other hand, shortages are expected in the coming years in traditional sectors, including maintenance and construction. Thanks to an active tourist trade, which includes foreign tourists, there are many new jobs being created in the hotel and restaurant industries, as well as in the cultural and sport trades. Specialist opportunities include wool weaving in Lodève (34) and silk working in the Cévennes area.

Languedoc-Roussillon holds the record for unemployment in France at around 4 per cent above the national average. Particularly badly affected are Béziers, Montpellier and Sète (34), and Perpignan (66), where there are large numbers of long-term unemployed. Sète suffers the country's highest rate of unemployment at over 25 per cent, although it also enjoys a high rate of new business success. The area also has some of the lowest average annual salaries in France, at below €17,000. The best executive appointment prospects are in Montpellier (34).

Casual, high season jobs in the tourist trade will always exist (you should apply in good time), but the peak of the high season is short – July and August – when almost 50 per cent of the annual visitors to the region flock there.

Property

Most properties in the Mediterranean coastal area are purchased by French people (around 25 per cent of French executives have a second home), and permanent foreign residents account for only 6 to 7 per cent of the total population. Following a long period of stagnation, and at times regression, in the early and middle '90s, property prices on the Mediterranean coast escalated towards the end of the decade. There was a slow-down at the beginning of the new century, but since then prices have begun to rise again.

In Languedoc-Roussillon, Montpellier and the Hérault department account for approximately 50 per cent of all property sales and developments. There have been steep price rises in one or two parts of the region, notably in and around Nîmes (30), where prices rose by up to 30 per cent in the year following the arrival of the *TGV*, and in Uzès (30), where 100 per cent increases were recorded between 2001 and 2002, thanks largely to an influx of British buyers taking advantage of new low-cost flights. Cheaper (but not cheap) properties are to be found in Gard.

A number of purpose-built resorts have been created on the *Côte Vermeille* (Vermillion Coast) in the last few decades, including Argelès-sur-Mer, Gruissan, St Cyprien, Port Bacarès, Port Leucate and Cap d'Agde, where apartment blocks are mostly unattractive if you're looking for a home with character. Collioure, on the other hand, known as the 'jewel of the Vermillion Coast', is a most attractive (and expensive) port.

Languedoc-Roussillon is popular with second homeowners, property being much cheaper here than in the Provence-Alpes-Côte d'Azur region (see page 89). Prices in Languedoc-Roussillon are around average for France and comparable with those in neighbouring Midi-Pyrénées (see page 75) and in Brittany and Upper Normandy (see pages 53 and 78). Average property prices for all categories of property combined in Languedoc-Roussillon are around €1,100 per m^2, although prices in Montpellier (34) are generally well above the region's average. Béziers (34) boasts the lowest average prices for older properties in the area (and the third-lowest in France). The table below gives average prices per m^2 for older properties in major towns in the area:

Town	Average Price per m^2 (€)
Carcassonne (11)	685
Nîmes (30)	795
Béziers (34)	625
Montpellier (34)	980
Sète (34)	1,035
Perpignan (66)	695

Average property prices aren't always a reliable indication of the relative price of similar properties in different towns, as one town may have a preponderance of cheaper or more expensive properties. Location has a significant effect on the value of property; a home with a sea-view, for example, can command a 100 per cent premium. Prices on the coast start at around €50,000 for a small apartment, rising to €300,000 or more for a large house; inland prices are generally lower, although not around Carcassonne. Prices for single private parking spaces start around €4,000, garages twice as much!

Rented Accommodation

There's a shortage of properties for rent in the Mediterranean coastal area generally, where it's almost impossible to find a furnished (*meublé*) apartment or house. In Languedoc-Roussillon, rental properties are particularly scarce in Aude and Pyrénées-Orientales. The rates listed below are approximate average monthly rates, exclusive of maintenance and standing charges, for long-term lets. You may find quite respectable properties below these figures and there are certainly luxury properties far above them. Holiday or short-term lets, for one to four-week periods, particularly at the peak of high season, i.e. July to mid-August, can cost three or four times these rates or even more in the purpose-built coastal resorts of Argelès-sur-Mer, Gruissan, Saint-Cyprien, Port-Bacarès, Port-Leucate and Cap-d'Agde.

Town	Monthly Rental (€)	
	One-bed. Apartment	Three-bed. House
Carcassonne (11)	350	700
Nîmes (30)	350	700
Montpellier (34)	450	770
Perpignan (66)	325	700

LIMOUSIN

Like that of neighbouring Auvergne (see page 51), the population of Limousin is in decline. Limousin has just 710,000 inhabitants with an average density of 42 people per km^2 (109 per mi^2) and one of the oldest populations in France (the department of Creuse holds the record); at the last census there were 247 people over the age of 100 in the region!

A quarter of the 20,000 or so foreign residents of Limousin are Portuguese, only 5.2 per cent British; all other nationalities represent less than 5 per cent of the foreign population. Haute-Vienne (87) is home to half of the foreigners living in the region, of which more than a third come from the EU. More than 75 per cent of Limousin's foreign residents live in urban areas.

Employment Prospects

Employment is 55 per cent in services, 30 per cent in industry and 15 per cent in agriculture. Although the rate of unemployment in the area is lower than the national average (the number of retired people probably distorts the figures), there are few large companies and finding employment isn't easy. As in Auvergne, the economy was, until recently based, on small family farms passed down through generations. However, farming is becoming less profitable, and small farms are unable to compete with the big concerns and foreign prices. The advantage of this situation is that, if you have some agricultural experience, farming is a strong option, and the French government offers substantial subsidies to farmers. Departmental Chambers of Commerce (CCI) can help you to set up a farming business.

In fact, a number of initiatives have been created at departmental, regional and national level to encourage companies and individuals to settle in the area, and there's financial and educational assistance for those wishing to become self-employed. Several departments offer training and grants (amounts vary from department to department) for those wanting to create a business or take over an existing company.

In the last few years, there has been an increase in British-owned or British-run companies. These are mostly in the service industry (e.g. tourism, estate agency) or the building trade. A certain number of jobs are available in the tourist industry during the summer and winter (skiing) seasons, but there's a tendency for these to go to French nationals, whatever their English-language ability, rather than to foreigners. Long-distance working using computers is possible in some parts, but outside the main towns cable and broadband internet connections are unlikely to be available for a few years.

As in the country as a whole, unemployment in the Limousin region has been increasing since early 2003, although overall it's still below the national average (6.8 per cent compared with 9.1 per cent). Industrial activity is remaining steady, but forecasts are on the cautious side, and there's still a reasonable level of employment in construction, although job vacancies are becoming fewer. In the services market, there are a number of vacancies in the hotel sector, although temporary employment is suffering badly from the downturn in economic activity.

Property

There are few apartments and housing estates outside the large towns, and most people moving to this area are looking for houses or farms to renovate with at least 1,000m^2 (a quarter of an acre) of land. As in Auvergne, it's also becoming difficult to find a typical stone house with a large plot. New houses are generally bought (or built) by French people and tend to be in or near a town, although there are some new housing estates that may appeal to foreigners, especially those looking to let a property to holidaymakers.

In general, property prices in the region have risen around 10 to 20 per cent in the last two years. The average prices per m^2 for older properties in Brive-la-Gaillarde (19) is around €760 and in Limoges (87) around €860. Average property prices aren't always a reliable indication of the relative price of similar properties in different towns, as one town may have a preponderance of cheaper or more expensive properties. A small, isolated house or farm for renovation (if you can still find one) costs from as little as €20,000 in the wilds of Creuse to €40,000 in Haute-Vienne, a small renovated house a similar price, and a four or five-bedroom property between €100,000 and €200,000 or more depending on location.

Rented Accommodation

Rented accommodation is easiest to find in Limoges (87), where there are apartments from studios to five-bedrooms, although smaller apartments are in demand from students. Outside the main towns, rented accommodation tends to be limited to *gîtes*, which can be expensive for a long period. It's possible to find rural houses for rent from around €400 per month for a two-bedroom property.

LORRAINE

Lorraine (also called Lorraine-Vosges) is a mainly industrial region, although much of it is unspoiled. It has relatively few foreign residents and is largely ignored by tourists and second-homebuyers despite the relatively low cost of living and reasonable property prices.

Population & Employment Prospects

The population of Lorraine is 2.3 million and is neither growing nor declining. The eastern and western areas are vast and sparsely populated, in contrast to the highly-urbanised central part running from Nancy to the three nearby frontiers (Luxembourg, Germany and Belgium). The region's unemployment rate is around the national average.

Lorraine was for a long time dominated by heavy industry (iron and steel, iron mines, coal mines, the chemical and textile industries). Changes in the global economy triggered major industrial restructuring and employment has since diversified, industry now employing only 23 per cent of workers compared with the services sector at 67 per cent. Industry is still dominated by iron and steel, with car manufacture and electronics major sectors. The agri-food sector includes cheese-production, for which Lorraine is France's third-largest region, rapeseed oil production and mineral water packaging. Around 35 per cent of the region is wooded, and in the timber and paper sector, Lorraine is the country's leading producer (by value). Other important industrial sectors include chemicals, glass and crystal (two-thirds of France's hand-made crystal is produced here). Metz (57) is home to Europe's largest river port for handling cereals.

The largest workforces in the service sector are in companies offering business services (59,000), the retail trade (51,000), personal services (42,000) and logistics (40,000). A large number of call centres have recently been opened in Metz, Nancy, Forbach and Saint-Avold, and IKEA has an operation in Metz.

The Metz Technopolis has also attracted many firms in the IT and communications sector. A high-speed train link from Paris to Strasbourg, due to open in 2007, will prove a further boost to this already high level of activity.

Further information is to be found on the website of the Direction Régionale du Travail et de la Formation Professionnelle (🖳 www.sdtefp-lorraine.travail.gouv.fr).

Property

Average property prices for the region are as follows:

Type of Property	Average Price Range (€)
New 2- or 3-bedroom apartment	95,000 – 110,000
Older 2- or 3-bedroom apartment	60,000 – 70,000
New 3- or 4-bedroom house	100,000 – 125,000
Older 3- or 4-bedroom house	80,000 – 100,000

Rented accommodation starts at around €300 per month for a two-bedroom apartment, rising to €700 or more for a four-bedroom house.

MIDI-PYRENEES

The same size as Denmark and larger than Belgium, this is the biggest region in France (45,348 km², or 8.3 per cent of the country) with eight departments and 3,020 communes. Midi-Pyrénées is also the only one of the four southern regions with no coast. It contains the highly sought-after departments of Lot and Tarn-et-Garonne in the north and one of the country's most out-of-the way, Ariège, in the south. Not the most popular tourist destination, Midi-Pyrénées nevertheless has a vibrant economy.

Population

The population of Midi-Pyrénées is just over 2.5 million and grew by 5 per cent per between 1990 and 1999. This vast, formerly agricultural, area has a low population density – 55 people per km² compared with the national average of just over 100 – while only six towns have more than 50,000 inhabitants: Albi, Castres Montauban, Rodez, Tarbes and the capital Toulouse. The focus is firmly on the regional capital, Toulouse (31), which is among France's fastest-growing towns. Over 40 per cent of the region's population, 44 per cent of jobs and 32 per cent of companies are located in Haute-Garonne. Lot has a population of only just over 160,000, which makes it one of the most sparsely populated departments in France, with a density of just 31 people per km² (80 per mi²).

There are around 100,500 foreign residents (including over 33,000 North Africans) in Midi-Pyrénées. Around 13,500 Spanish and Portuguese and 8,370 other non-French EU nationals (including around 1,700 Britons) live in Haute-Garonne, mainly in and around Toulouse. The second-largest contingent of British people is to be found in Gers (over 1,000) followed by Tarn-et-Garonne (around 600). In Hautes-Pyrénées, there are almost 13,500 Spanish and Portuguese, but fewer than 800 English, Dutch, Germans and Belgians.

Employment Prospects

Services account for 60 per cent of employment in Midi-Pyrénées, industry 25 per cent and agriculture 15 per cent. The economy is dominated by high-tech industries, although industrial activity has slowed in recent years and the region has retained its vitality thanks largely to the strength of the job-creating services sector. Jobs have been shed in the textile, clothing and leather industries, and hundreds of people working in the chemical industry are now being laid off. On the other hand, the region's core industries, such as aerospace, agri-food and electronics systems, chemicals, electronics, energy, oil, paper, pharmaceuticals and wine-making continue to prosper.

Demand is also high for all building and public works trades. Midi-Pyrénées is home to three of the largest European construction projects of recent years: Aéroconstellation in Blagnac (31), the B line of the Toulouse metro and the Millau viaduct in Aveyron. Aéroconstellation, where the new 550-seat Airbus A380 is being built, will, directly and indirectly, employ some 9,000 people. Biotechnology is gradually expanding, and the health industry offers favourable prospects.

Major service sectors include call centres, logistics and tourism. Public and private-sector research is another growth area, and Toulouse has joined Paris and Grenoble at the head of the French 'grey matter' league table. According to a recent survey by Le Point magazine, Albi (81) is a particularly good place to start a business, as it enjoys one of the highest rates of new business success in France. There's a variety of seasonal work in the area, for which no particular skills or qualifications are required, ranging from fruit and grape picking in the summer/autumn to bar and other ski resort work in the winter, but you must apply several months in advance to secure a position.

In the last few years, there has been an increase in British-owned or British-run companies. These are mostly in the service industry (e.g. tourism, estate agency) or the building trade. For example, in Lot, where agriculture was for a long time the primary economic resource, there are now more service businesses than agricultural concerns. The Lot chamber of commerce offers courses in selling, tourism and language-teaching. Further information can be found on the website of Midi-Pyrénées Expansion (⌨ www.midipyrenees-expansion-fr).

Property

Property prices are highest in Lot, where many people want a house within 15km (11mi), north or south, of the river Dordogne, or within the triangle Souillac/Sarlat/Gourdon; a recent survey concluded that properties for sale in Lot were on average the second-most expensive in the country after Paris.

Tarn-et-Garonne is also becoming sought-after (and consequently expensive). Cheaper properties can be found in Ariège, Aveyron and Hautes-Pyrénées and generally on higher ground. In fact, prices tend to drop the higher you go, as areas below around 500m (1,600ft) enjoy better weather. Above this height, tiles give way to slate roofs to keep out the rain and snow. There are also fewer properties generally on higher ground, where they tend to be dotted around and many are isolated.

Castres (81) boasts the lowest average prices for older properties in the south-west and the second-lowest in France (after Montluçon in Allier). The table below gives average prices per m² for older properties in major towns in the area:

Town	Average Price per m² (€)
Toulouse (31)	1,010
Albi (81)	805
Castres (81)	595
Montauban (82)	915

Average property prices aren't always a reliable indication of the relative price of similar properties in different towns, as one town may have a preponderance of cheaper or more expensive properties.

Most apartments are, of course, to be found in the main cities and towns, particularly Toulouse, whereas there are few apartments in Ariège, Aveyron, Gers or Tarn. Prices range from €25,000 for a studio to €300,000 for a plush suite in Toulouse. House prices are similarly varied, ranging from €50,000 or €60,000 for a cottage in the mountains to €500,000 or more for a five-bedroom property in a popular area. There are plenty of properties available for restoration in Aveyron and a number in Gers, Tarn and Tarn-et-Garonne, although bargain ruins without hidden problems (e.g. liable to flooding or the subject of lengthy inheritance battles) are hard to find.

Rented Accommodation

Most apartments are in the main towns (i.e. Toulouse in Haute-Garonne, Castres in Tarn, and Montauban in Tarn-et-Garonne), and few are available elsewhere. Prices range from €125 per month for a studio to €1,000 or more per month for a three or four-bedroom apartment in Toulouse. Rented houses are less common than apartments, and very few are to be found in most departments. Prices start at around €400 per month for a two-bedroom village house (if you can find one) and can reach €3,000 for large properties in sought-after areas.

NORD-PAS-DE-CALAIS

France's most northerly region, bordering Belgium, which lends it its Flemish influence, was the birthplace of French manufacturing industry in the 19th century and is still heavily industrialised. Nevertheless, it has attractive parts, including an impressive coastline, and is within sight of the UK for easy commuting.

Population & Employment Prospects

Although one of France's smallest regions, Nord-Pas-de-Calais has a population of 4 million, including around 2,000 Britons. It's also popular with Belgians and Dutch. The region's population is growing at well below the national average rate. There are

around 1.4 million working people, of whom almost half are involved in manufacturing industrial products – specifically consumer goods, metal and chemical products, mechanical and industrial equipment, printing and publishing, railway equipment, and textiles and clothing (especially leather products). Most of this sector is shedding jobs, although the mineral products and the railway sectors have managed to maintain steady levels of employment in recent years, and the car industry (including automotive services) and the construction industry have shown a slight increase in workforce, although it's the smaller companies rather than the larger ones that have taken on more staff. The automobile industry is particularly strong in the Douai area.

Sales and services jobs increased by over 3,000 in 2003 (0.6 per cent), although this was limited to specific areas – mostly business consultancy. The temporary services industry is slowing down and employment in commerce is flat, although there has been some hiring in retail sales. Other service industries in the region (transportation, financial services and property services) lost a total of 1,200 positions in 2003. The one growth area (as in many regions of France) is that of health and social services.

Property

Average property prices for the region are as follows:

Type of Property	Average Price Range (€)
New 2- or 3-bedroom apartment	120,000 – 135,000
Older 2- or 3-bedroom apartment	75,000 – 90,000
New 3- or 4-bedroom house	105,000 – 130,000
Older 3- or 4-bedroom house	75,000 – 95,000

Rented accommodation starts at around €300 per month for a two-bedroom apartment, rising to €800 or more for a four-bedroom house.

NORMANDY

Normandy is officially two regions (see maps below), although there's a strong reunification movement. The population of Normandy is around 3.1 million (1.7 million in Upper Normandy, 1.4 million in Lower Normandy). The population of Normandy is growing at above the average rate for France. Caen (14) has a high proportion of students (around 25 per cent) among its population, whereas the percentage of students in other towns is low, e.g. 5 per cent in Le Havre (76).

Upper Normandy is one of the most densely populated areas of France with 140 people per km^2 (55 per mi^2) compared with the national average of just over 100 (40 per mi2). It has a relatively young population (over 30 per cent are under 20) and a higher than average birth rate, although the population is growing more slowly and, therefore, ageing more rapidly than the national average. Paris is gradually 'overflowing' along the Seine valley, and Eure is the fastest growing department (at 0.57 per cent or around 3,000 people per annum). Around 30 per cent of the population of Upper Normandy lives within 25km (15mi) of the centre of Rouen.

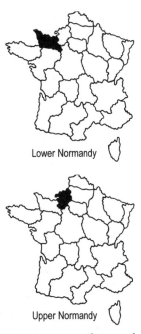

Lower Normandy

Upper Normandy

Some 45 per cent of the population of Lower Normandy is concentrated around the towns of Alençon, Argentan, Caen, Cherbourg-Octeville, Flers, Lisieux and Saint-Lô, and the region's population is expected to rise by around 45,000 in the next 20 years before beginning to decline. The population of Orne is already in gradual decline (30 per cent of the population is over 60), whereas that of Calvados, which is attracting people, particularly those in their early 20s, from neighbouring departments, is expected to continue to increase until around 2030. The population of Manche is fairly stable, although it has lost around 16,000 people between the ages of 20 and 30 and gained half as many elderly people in the last decade.

Some 60 per cent of Calvados's population live in or near the capital of Lower Normandy, Caen and nearby Hérouville-Saint-Clair. Almost 30 per cent of Calvados's population is under 19. The second-least densely populated department in Normandy is Manche, whose largest town (and the second-largest urban area in Lower Normandy after Caen) is Cherbourg-Octeville with a total population of around 120,000. Orne is the most sparsely populated department in Normandy and has few large towns; the capital Alençon has just 31,000 inhabitants.

Eure, in Upper Normandy, has no large town either: Evreux, the capital, has only 54,000 inhabitants. By contrast, Seine-Maritime – by far the most densely populated department in either region – includes the city of Rouen, the capital of Upper Normandy. Over 40 per cent of the department's population of 1.24 million lives in and around Rouen, which has seen an influx of students since the opening of the new university science faculty in 2001.

Employment Prospects

Employment across the two regions of Normandy is varied, with 55 per cent of jobs service-related, 40 per cent in industry and 5 per cent in agriculture in Upper Normandy, and 50 per cent services, 30 per cent industry and 20 per cent agriculture in Lower Normandy. Upper Normandy is more industrialised than Lower

Normandy. It enjoys an excellent transport network (thanks to its ports, rivers, motorways and rail link with Paris) although it's strongly dependent on Paris, which lies only 120km (80mi) from Rouen, the regional capital.

The service sector is the only one of the three to have created jobs since 1990. The principal service industries are tourism, which employs 36,000 in Lower Normandy, mostly in the Pays d'Auge, and 18,000 in Upper Normandy, and research.

Industry in Normandy is centred around cars and accessories (employing over 30,000 people with major Renault and Peugeot/Citroën factories in Calvados and Seine-Maritime), petrochemical and chemical products (employing around 30,000 people); the region is France's leading area for refining, oils and additives, as well as a European leader in the manufacture of fertilizers and polymer production, especially in 'Chemical Valley' along the Seine near Le Havre), and electrical and electronic goods (employing around 20,000).

Other important industries in Normandy include aeronautical and aerospace (the engines for the Ariane rocket are manufactured in Eure), ship building (especially in Le Havre and Cherbourg-Octeville, where nuclear submarines are constructed), mechanical and metallurgy (especially in Eure), printing (Herissey in Evreux is one of the five biggest printing companies in France), paper and paper products (especially along the Seine), IT and telecommunications (international companies include Hewlett Packard, IBM, Oracle and Rank Xerox, and Caen has a high-tech research centre), pharmaceuticals (especially in Eure, where companies include Aventis Pasteur and GlaxoSmithKline), plastics (Alençon is second-largest plastics industry centre in France), glass making and textiles.

Transport is big business in Upper Normandy, where it employs over 6 per cent of the workforce (compared with 4.5 per cent nationally) and the ports of Le Havre (Europe's second-largest port after Antwerp, it handles all the coffee consumed in France!) and Rouen (although inland, Europe's largest grain port) directly or indirectly employ over 3,000 people. Ports are very important to the region, as shown by an ambitious development programme, 'Port 2000', concentrating on the Seine estuary and the port of Le Havre.

The main agricultural product in Upper Normandy is grain, followed by meat and milk, which account for only 20 per cent of output compared with 75 per cent in Lower Normandy, where agriculture is less diversified. The agri-food industry is also important – particularly in coffee, bread and pastry goods, ready prepared fish products, frozen foods, and mass catering.

In general, industrial activity is remaining stable: company managers are retaining their workforce, but are using temporary staff or people on non-permanent contracts. But the situation varies from one sector to the next. Agri-food industries are seeing an upturn in activity, except for the meat industry, which is suffering from falling consumption. Production remains high in the car industry, but overall car sales are falling sharply; this is reflected by people being hired on fixed-term contracts. In consumer goods, overall activity appears stable, although with a rise in pharmaceuticals.

Activity in the Upper Normandy building sector is moderate, although there are ambitious construction projects under way in Rouen and Le Havre. SMEs in the building finishing sector are currently prospering.

Service companies and design offices are expanding in the light of new information and communications technology and company attitudes to organising work, focusing on quality, commercial strategy, exports and human resources management; a major element in this is the creation of strategies to replace staff due to retire within the next ten years or so.

Sales in the three main wholesale sectors (food, non-food and inter-industry) are rising, and more staff are being taken on in the food sector. The situation is tighter in the retail sector. All the major French chains are present in the region, offering good job prospects, particularly for young people.

The best prospects for expansion and job creation lie in personal services, healthcare and social work, following the introduction of new working hours regulations and financial aid packages for the elderly.

The largest number of jobs in Upper Normandy are in the Rouen area (there's a large industrial zone to the west of the city), followed by Le Havre (one of Europe's largest petrol refining centres), Evreux, Vernon/Gaillon and Louviers in that order (the last three forming an employment triangle). Almost 30,000 people in Upper Normandy commute to work in the Ile-de-France. In Lower Normandy, jobs are centred around the towns of Alençon, Argentan, Caen, Cherbourg-Octeville, Flers, Lisieux and Saint-Lô.

Job seekers in Normandy should contact Emploi Conseil in Rouen (☎ 02 35 07 52 95), the Fédération Nationale des Associations d'Accueil et de Réinsertion Sociale (FNARS) in Rouen (☎ 02 35 07 41 50), and Retravailler (which has offices in Caen, Evreux, Flers and Rouen). There are also offices of the international employment agencies Adecco, ADIA and Manpower France in Normandy.

Property

The popularity of Normandy, particularly among British buyers, means that the demand for properties exceeds the supply. There was a spate of house building in the '80s in Upper Normandy, when the number of houses grew three times as fast as the population, mainly on account of Parisians (and others) building and buying second homes in the area, particularly in Eure. The rate of increase slowed in the '90s, to around 1 per cent per year. The most popular areas in Normandy are those within a short drive of the Channel ports (i.e. Caen, Cherbourg, Dieppe and Saint-Malo), particularly the southern half of the Cherbourg peninsula and the coast of Calvados near Deauville and Honfleur. If there are bargains to be found, they're in the department of Orne, which is the least popular (and least known) of the five departments. Demand has led to a steady overall increase in prices in recent decades, with sharp rises in certain parts. The table below gives average prices per m² for older properties in all the major towns in Normandy and Brittany:

Town	Average Price per m² (€)
Caen (14)	955
Le Havre (76)	975
Rouen (76)	1,075

Average property prices aren't always a reliable indication of the relative price of similar properties in different towns, as one town may have a preponderance of cheaper or more expensive properties than another. Location has a significant effect on the value of property; a home with a sea-view, for example, can command a 100 per cent premium.

Property prices vary between €50,000 for a two-bedroom house inland in Calvados or Manche to €500,000 or more for a five-bedroom property in a desirable area. There are still plenty of properties to restore in Normandy, with prices starting as low as €30,000, but restoration costs can easily triple the purchase price.

Rented Accommodation

Apartments: Apartments are available for long-term rent in all departments, although few have more than three bedrooms (in Cherbourg, there are few with more than two). The majority of rental apartments are to be found in the principal towns in each department, and few are available elsewhere. Price ranges for these towns are shown below.

Town/Department	No. of Bedrooms	Monthly Rental (€)
Caen (14)	Studio	225 – 350
	1	300 – 400
	2	375 – 600
	3	450 – 800
Evreux (27)	Studio	300 – 400
	1	300 – 500
	2	500 – 700
	3	700 – 1,100
Cherbourg-Octeville (50)	Studio	125 – 200
	1	225 – 400
	2	350 – 450
Alençon (61)	Studio	200
	1	225 – 350
	2	350 – 500
	3	400 – 700
Rouen (76)	Studio	150 – 350
	1	200 – 500
	2	350 – 650
	3	600 – 1,000

Houses: Rented houses are less common than apartments, and very few are to be found in or near the main towns. The table below gives an indication of the rental prices for houses in each department.

Town/Department	No. of Bedrooms	Monthly Rental (€)
Calvados	2	350+
	3	400 – 750
	4	500 – 900
	5	600 – 1,000
Eure	2	400 – 550
	3	650 – 800
	4	700 – 1,250
Manche	2	450 – 550
	3	500 – 800
	4	550+
Orne	2	300 – 550
	3	400 – 600
	4	500 – 700
	5	700+
Seine-Maritime	2	350 – 500
	3	400 – 750
	4	650 – 1,200
	5	900 – 1,500

PAYS-DE-LA-LOIRE

Sandwiched between the popular regions of Brittany and Poitou-Charentes, Pays-de-la-Loire is a varied region – from the industrial St Nazaire in the west to the wilds of Vendée in the south and the inland charm of the eastern departments.

Population

The Pays-de-la-Loire has 3.2 million inhabitants (over 100 people per km^2) and its population is growing faster than the average for France, especially in the two coastal departments of Loire-Atlantique and Vendée. Nantes (44) has the second-fastest-growing population of any major town in France (after Vannes in Brittany), and that of La Roche-sur-Yon (85) is also growing rapidly. The big centres of population are Nantes (44) with 270,000 people, Saint-Nazaire (44) with 66,000 – both on the coast – and inland, Angers (49) with 156,000 and Le Mans (72) with 146,000.

The population of the Pays-de-la-Loire includes 56,000 foreigners; there were sufficient British residents in Mayenne (460) and Vendée (310) for their numbers to appear in the official analysis of the 1999 census – and there are undoubtedly many more today.

Employment Prospects

Employment in the Pays-de-la-Loire is 55 per cent in the service sector, 30 per cent in industry and 15 per cent in agriculture, and the area is currently enjoying a surge in employment prospects, with a high rate of new business success, particularly in Saint-Nazaire (44). One in four employees is expected to retire by 2010. More than a third of the jobs thus vacated will be in the services/public sector (principally health and social work). A third of staff in the capital goods industries will have retired by 2010, accounting for a third of workers in the car-manufacturing sector and over 16,000 people in the capital goods sector. Between 5,000 and 7,000 people are expected to retire from each of the following sectors: metal industry, household goods, metalworking and chemistry. Other sectors in which workers are expected to be required include the construction and transport industries.

The coastal region, in particular, attracts engineering businesses, with the shipyards at Saint-Nazaire (44) and the Michelin tyre factory at Cholet (49). Major local activities by department include the following:

- **Loire-Atlantique** – Ship building, boiler-making, aircraft manufacture, wine-making;
- **Maine-et-Loire** – Slate quarrying, market gardening, vegetable and flower seed growing, poultry farming, wine-making, confectionery and tyres manufacture, food processing;
- **Mayenne** – Cereal and pig farming, cattle breeding, market gardening;
- **Sarthe** – Cattle breeding, forestry, dairy farming, cereal growing, agricultural machinery construction (in Le Mans), insurance, electronics;
- **Vendée** – Tourism, forestry, market gardening, fishing, boat building.

Further information can be found on the website of the Pays-de-la-Loire regional council (🖥 www.paysdelaloire.fr).

Property

After a relatively stagnant period at the end of the '90s, property prices in the region have been rising by around 20 per cent per year (more in Vendée) and, where three or four years ago buyers were slow to commit themselves, they're now snapping up available homes – particularly the British, many of whom are moving away from Dordogne, for example, to the coast. House-hunters are advised to visit the area between mid-October and mid-February, when agents are less busy, but you shouldn't expect a house that you saw in November still to be available in March. On the other hand, it doesn't pay to be too hasty, and British buyers in particular should be wary of buying from other Britons, who often inflate the price of a property, knowing that prices in the UK are generally far higher. Cheaper properties requiring renovation or modernisation with a reasonable plot on the outskirts of a small town or village (the foreign buyer's dream) are becoming extremely scarce in all areas.

Cholet (49), where the average property costs around €75,000, has the highest proportion of property owners (56 per cent) of any major town in France, as well as the second-highest percentage (63 per cent) of large properties (i.e. four rooms or more) and the lowest percentage (5 per cent) of vacant properties. However, the rate of new building is only average, whereas Saint-Nazaire (44) has the second-highest rate of new building (2 per cent) in France, after Bastia in Corsica.

Average prices in the area are rising by around 20 per cent per year, and in some parts (especially Vendée) increases are even higher. Coastal areas are naturally more expensive than inland parts. However, there's also considerable demand for properties close to airports offering low-price flights (particularly to the UK) and to main railway stations. The table below gives average prices per m^2 for older properties in major towns in the area:

Town	Average Price per m^2 (€)
Nantes (44)	1,160
Saint-Nazaire (44)	995
Angers (49)	1,025
Cholet (49)	760
Laval (53)	880

Average property prices aren't always a reliable indication of the relative price of similar properties in different towns, as one town may have a preponderance of cheaper or more expensive properties. A small, isolated house or farm for renovation (if you can still find one) costs from around €30,000 in Mayenne to €60,000 in Loire-Atlantique, a small renovated house between €50,000 and €70,000, and a four or five-bedroom property from €150,000 to €300,000 or more.

Rented Accommodation

There's a fair amount of long-term rental accommodation available in all departments: most in Loire-Atlantique and Sarthe, and least in Laval and Vendée. There are few houses available in coastal areas, as their owners can earn more by offering holiday lets in the summer. Where available, unfurnished houses with two or three bedrooms are offered for rents ranging from €350 to €600 per month. Apartments are more plentiful. Rents range from around €300 for a one-bedroom apartment to around €800 for three bedrooms.

PICARDY

One of the least known regions of France, and among the least popular with expatriates, Picardy is most famous for its First World War battlegrounds and the cathedrals of Amiens and Beauvais. It has only a short coastline, but some attractive areas inland and is within easy travelling distance of the UK.

Population & Employment Prospects

Picardy's population of 1.9 million, including over 1,000 Britons, is growing at just below the national average rate. The services sector is the region's largest employer, and the four main industrial activities are (in order of importance) metallurgy; chemicals, rubber and plastics; agri-food products; and mechanical engineering.

Property

Average property prices for the region are as follows:

Type of Property	Average Price Range (€)
New 2- or 3-bedroom apartment	105,000 – 120,000
Older 2- or 3-bedroom apartment	75,000 – 85,000
New 3- or 4-bedroom house	85,000 – 110,000
Older 3- or 4-bedroom house	80,000 – 100,000

Rented accommodation starts at around €550 per month for a two-bedroom apartment, rising to €1,000 or more for a four-bedroom house.

POITOU-CHARENTES

The Poitou-Charentes region, on the central west coast of France, is one of the most popular with expatriates, particularly British, on account of its excellent (if windy) climate and relative proximity to the UK (compared with the south coast). Property prices reflect this popularity, particularly near the coast. Employment prospects, however, are generally poor.

Population

Poitou-Charentes has a population of just over 1.6 million (population density is just 63.5 people per km²) and it's growing at slightly below the national average rate. The departments of Charente and Deux-Sèvres have declining populations, while that of Vienne is increasing. The population of Charente-Maritime is also growing, but growth is concentrated in the coastal area; inland, the department is in decline, both in population and in its economy. Poitiers (86) has a higher proportion of students among its population (32 per cent) than any town in France. The big centres of population are La Rochelle (17), on the coast, with 80,000 and inland, Poitiers (86) with 83,000. The population of Poitou-Charentes includes around 25,000 foreign nationals.

Employment Prospects

The region has an active population of under half a million, including over 100,000 employed in industry and under 15,000 in agriculture, and the job market is relatively stagnant. Overall, unemployment is just below the national average at 9.1 per cent, although it varies across the four departments: Charente 9.6 per cent; Charente-Maritime 10.9 per cent; Deux-Sèvres 7 per cent; Vienne 8 per cent. Gross annual product is less than €18,500 per head, among the lowest in France and only around half that of the Paris region. Except in coastal areas, the population is slowly diminishing and, as a result, employment prospects are generally poor.

Exceptions are the building trade, which is particularly busy in coastal areas, where there's a continuous demand for new homes, and the tourist industry, although most jobs in this sector are seasonal. The region boasts over 7,000 hotel beds, 1,500 beds in self-catering accommodation, over 1,000 *gîtes* and 1,000 *chambres d'hôtes*, 15,000 camp-site pitches, and almost 100,000 second homes. One of the region's major employers is the *pôle image* (image centre) called Magelis on the banks of the Charente in Angoulême (16), incorporating the Centre National de la Bande Dessinée et de l'Image and the École Supérieure de l'Image and 30 businesses. The centre's annual international cartoon show is the fifth largest show of any kind in France.

Britons looking for work in the region should note that a small number of local factories in the region have been bought up by British companies, only for them to close down within three or four years. In some cases, British management seems unable to acclimatise to French conditions, particularly in the field of human resources. However attractive the idea may seem to work for a British company in France, care is needed to be sure that the management really knows what it's doing and has a good track record.

Property

After a relatively stagnant period at the end of the '90s, property prices in Poitou-Charentes have been rising by around 20 per cent per year and buyers are now snapping up available homes – particularly the British, many of whom are moving away from Dordogne, for example, to the coast. House-hunters are advised to visit the area between mid-October and mid-February, when agents are less busy, but you shouldn't expect a house that you saw in November still to be available in March. On the other hand, it doesn't pay to be too hasty, and British buyers in particular should be wary of buying from other Britons, who often inflate the price of a property, knowing that prices in the UK are generally far higher. Cheaper properties requiring renovation or modernisation with a reasonable plot on the outskirts of a small town or village (the foreign buyer's dream) are becoming extremely scarce in all areas.

Coastal areas, particularly in Charente-Maritime, are naturally more expensive than inland parts, and the area around La Rochelle and Royan has become something of a summer 'playground' for Parisians, with an inevitable effect on prices. However, there's also considerable demand for properties close to airports offering low-price flights and to main railway stations.

Angoulême (16) boasts the lowest average prices for older properties of any main town in the west, the average price of older properties generally being €650 per m^2, although this rises to between €800 and €1,200 per m^2 in the town centre. On the other hand, the town imposes the second-highest rates of *taxe foncière* in France (after Périgueux in Dordogne). The region's highest average property prices are to be found in La Rochelle (17). The table below gives average prices per m^2 for older properties in major towns in the region:

Town	Average Price per m^2 (€)
Angoulême (16)	650
La Rochelle (17)	1,405
Niort (79)	780
Poitiers (86)	900

Average property prices aren't always a reliable indication of the relative price of similar properties in different towns, as one town may have a preponderance of cheaper or more expensive properties. A small, isolated house or farm for renovation (if you can still find one) costs from around €30,000 in Deux-Sèvres to €75,000 in Charente-Maritime, a small renovated house between €45,000 and €90,000, and a four or five-bedroom property from €200,000 to €400,000 or more.

Rented Accommodation

There's a fair amount of long-term rental accommodation available in all departments, although less in Charente-Maritime and Deux-Sèvres. There are few houses available in coastal areas, as their owners can earn more by offering holiday lets in the summer. Where available, unfurnished houses with two or three bedrooms are offered for rents ranging from €350 to €600 per month. Apartments are more plentiful, especially in the main towns, although there are few in La Rochelle (17). Rents range from around €300 for a one-bedroom apartment to around €800 for three bedrooms.

PROVENCE-ALPES-COTE-D'AZUR

The 'original' destination of dream-seeking expatriates, the PACA region, as it's known, is now beyond the reach of most, although it retains a unique appeal and offers opportunities for a variety of business activities.

Population

The population of Provence-Alpes-Côte-d'Azur is around 4.6 million and is concentrated along the coast, where most of the major towns and cities are. PACA is the country's third-fastest growing region, the department of Var being among the fastest growing in France. However, this increase has been largely due to migration rather than a high birth rate, and population ageing is a significant factor in many towns, especially Cannes. Aix-en-Provence (13) has a very young population, over 30 per cent of whom are students – the second-highest proportion of any town in France.

Employment Prospects

Considerable numbers of migrants arrived when the region's economy was buoyant, with employment increasing steadily until 2002. In 2003, the trend in the region's economy was similar to that of France as a whole. Having enjoyed a more favourable economic climate, however, it was less badly hit by the general slow-down, and there are now signs of improvement in the region's economy, although unemployment is still high at almost 12 per cent.

The region's industrial fabric has been transformed over the past two decades, with traditional industries in decline. On the other hand, PACA has benefited from transfers and start-ups. Hi-tech companies have sprung up, taking advantage of the presence of high-quality, efficient universities and research centres. The region is in third place nationally when it comes to public and private research, boasting six technology parks: Aix Europôle, Avignon-Agroparc, Manosque-Cadarache, Marseille-Provence-Technopole, Sophia-Antipolis and Toulon-Var-Technopole.

PACA's attractive environment means more new companies are setting up there than in any other region of France. In 2003, some 200,000 companies were created from scratch in the south of France, up 12 per cent on 2002. All sectors saw an increase, above all property and commerce. In 2003, the PACA region saw 13,000 new jobs created, against a national average of 7,000. This represented an increase of 85 per cent.

The decline of traditional industry and the boom in new technologies and research activities, combined with dynamic employment policies, have increased the share of the services sector in the region's economy. Over 50 per cent of companies operate in the service sector, industry accounting for only 8 per cent of the total number of companies.

Those considering setting up a business in Marseilles should investigate a recent scheme called Capital Local Marseille, which helped over 120 new business ventures in the two years following its introduction in 1999 and has recently launched a second programme (see 💻 www.marseille-msd.org/dispositifclm.html).

Property

Most properties in the Mediterranean coastal area are purchased by French people (around 25 per cent of French executives have a second home), and permanent foreign residents account for only 6 to 7 per cent of the total population, although in some parts (e.g. Cannes) British buyers make up a significant proportion of homebuyers. Following a long period of stagnation, and at times regression, in the early and middle '90s, property prices on the Mediterranean coast escalated towards the end of the decade. There was a slow-down at the beginning of the new century, but since then prices have begun to rise again. Marseille (13) is enjoying something of a property boom, with luxury, two or three-bedroom waterfront apartments selling for over €200,000 and any good quality properties being snapped up within a day or two of coming on the market.

The PACA region is the second-most expensive for property in France, marginally behind the Ile-de-France, with average property prices for all categories combined (i.e. new, recent and old properties, apartments and houses) around €1,700 per m². Not surprisingly, the region's highest average prices are to be found in Cannes and Antibes (06), where the average home is more expensive than anywhere else in the country outside the Ile-de-France and where prices for waterfront properties have doubled in the last few years. However, away from the coastal strip, prices fall dramatically, although there are other expensive pockets, such as the area around the Gorges du Verdon. The table below gives average prices per m² for older properties in major towns in the area:

Town	Average Price per m² (€)
Antibes (06)	2,540
Cannes (06)	2,345
Nice (06)	1,525
Aix-en-Provence (13)	1,565
Arles (13)	760
Marseille (13)	1,090
Toulon (83)	965
Avignon (84)	830

Average property prices aren't always a reliable indication of the relative price of similar properties in different towns, as one town may have a preponderance of cheaper or more expensive properties and, particularly on the Côte d'Azur, location is everything. While you may be able to find a small village house inland for as little as €50,000, the sky's the **lower** limit (you may have to throw in a few stars as well) for a seafront villa in Juan les Pins or Saint-Tropez. Prices for single private parking spaces start at around €5,000, and garages cost twice as much!

Rented Accommodation

There's a shortage of properties for rent in the Mediterranean coastal area generally, where it's almost impossible to find a furnished (*meublé*) apartment or house. The rates listed below are approximate average monthly rates, exclusive of maintenance and standing charges, for long-term lets. You may find quite respectable properties below these figures and there are certainly luxury properties far above them. Holiday or short-term lets, for one to four-week periods, particularly at the peak of high season, i.e. July to mid-August, can cost three or four times these rates or even more in Saint-Tropez and other exclusive spots on the Riviera. An apartment in Cannes, for example, can cost up to €3,000 per week (more during the Film Festival), which means of course that, if you own a property there, you can let it for that amount.

Town	Monthly Rental (€)	
	One-bed. Apartment	Three-bed. House
Cannes (06)	450	1,200
Nice (06)	450	1,100
Aix-en-Provence (13)	450	1,000
Marseille (13)	450	900
Montpellier (34)	450	770
Hyères (83)	450	900
Toulon (83)	400	900
Avignon (84)	400	900

RHONE-ALPES

Rhône-Alpes, comprising the departments of Ain, Ardèche, Drôme, Isère, Loire, Rhône, Savoie and Haute-Savoie, is another highly varied region, with mountains and valleys, sprawling towns and tiny villages. Renowned for its skiing, the region is also home to France's second city.

Population

Rhône-Alpes region has a population of 5.6 million, of whom 1.6 million live in the department of Rhône – the great majority in an around Lyon. The population has increased by around 6 per cent over the last decade or so, compared with the national average of 4 per cent. Isère is one of the most densely populated departments in France, while Hautes-Alpes, with under eight people per km^2 (20 people per mi^2), is one of the least. The proportion of students among the population of the major towns is generally low; Grenoble (38) has the highest proportion of students (12 per cent).

Employment Prospects

The Rhône-Alpes region has a highly diversified economy. It has the highest number of seasonal jobs (primarily winter sports and summer fruit picking) on offer in the whole of France. In industry, the predominant sector is that of intermediate goods, namely chemicals and electrical and electronic components. Within the industrial sector, the setting-up of major businesses in the Grenoble area has allowed the number of jobs on offer in the fields of electronics and automation to remain constant. In the service industry, the main sectors represented are hotels and catering, business services, transport and property.

The working population of Rhône-Alpes is 2.6 million. The unemployment rate stands at 8.8 per cent, just below the national average rate, and most of the region's eight departments are experiencing a fall in the number of job seekers and a corresponding increase in economic activity, with growth in all economic sectors, particularly in industry and capital goods. There's also growth in market services. On the other hand, there has recently been a slowdown in retail activity. The slight upturn in the Rhône-Alpes economy has led to greater demand for workers. Most of the vacancies are for casual and/or part-time staff, but the recovery has benefited all categories of job seeker, although there's little demand for managers and technicians.

Job prospects are considerably higher in the northern Alps, where the rate of unemployment is around 10 per cent, than in the southern Alps, where the rate is around 14 per cent. Additionally, Valence and Grenoble are, with the *TGV* and motorway links, within commuting distance of Lyon. Grenoble is an important industrial town and is classed among the top five towns in France for scientific research centres. The Isère department is the seventh-biggest exporting department in France. Geneva, which is the headquarters of several international companies and institutions, has dormitory areas spilling over into Haute-Savoie. The major industries and companies in the principal towns in the Alps are:

- **Annecy** – Alcatel (telephone equipment), Salomon (golf and ski equipment) and Sopra (computers);
- **Chambéry** – Dressmaking, chemical, glass and metallurgical works;
- **Gap** – craftwork, printing and textiles;
- **Grenoble** – Computer, electrical, electronic and mechanical goods; chemical and metallurgical works. There's also a nuclear research centre.
- **La Tour du Pin** – Shoe manufacturing and textiles;
- **Valence** – Electronic, mechanical and textiles.

Property

Property prices are above the national average in the Alpine (i.e. eastern) departments, with especially high prices in and around tourist towns such as Annecy (74), although even here prices are well below those of Paris and top resorts on the Riviera. Typical village houses are much sought after and are rarely for sale in or near ski resorts. Properties in or near ski resorts are expensive but usually an excellent investment. Demand for new property is particularly strong in Isère and the two Savoy departments.

Valence (26) boasts the lowest average prices (around €750 per m^2) for older properties in Rhône-Alpes, while the area's highest average prices are to be found in Annecy (74) at €1,835 per m^2. Generally, the higher you live, the higher the prices. Haute-Savoie is the most expensive department for older property (houses and flats), but slightly cheaper than Savoie for new apartments. New houses in Savoie are considerably more expensive than in Haute-Savoie, particularly in the Albertville area. Drôme is the cheapest department. Luxury properties, with two to five rooms (i.e. one to three or four bedrooms), cost from €1,500 to €2,000 per m^2.

Ski Resorts

Not surprisingly, ski resorts generally command higher property prices, and prices vary according to the prestige of the resort, situation within the resort, construction quality and finish, floor area (for apartments), aspect and outlook, balcony size, etc. Most of the top resorts are in the Tarentaise valley in Savoie, where Méribel is particularly popular with the British (there are around 75 chalets owned by Britons). Courchevel and Val d'Isère, which have more 'cachet' than Méribel and are correspondingly more expensive (and have fewer available properties), are the next most popular. In fact, Courchevel is one of the most expensive resorts anywhere in the Alps; every barn and cowshed is eagerly eyed by property developers and you must be quick, in the know or plain lucky (as well as rich!) to secure a property. Méribel-les-Allues, the 'real' village below the ski resort, is somewhat cheaper, but has poorer access to the slopes; two-bedroom apartments can be had for as 'little' as €200,000. If you're looking to buy a three or four-bedroom chalet to turn into accommodation for holidaymakers, you can expect to pay around €1.5 million. (In fact, such properties rarely even appear on the market!)

Rented Accommodation

Unfurnished property for rent is difficult to find outside the major towns, where prices range from around €300 per month for a studio flat to €1,000 or more for a four-bedroom house. Holiday apartments and flatlets are usually let on a weekly basis. The two weeks just before, during and after Christmas are the most expensive, with another peak in February. For example, a 30m^2 apartment in Chamonix (not the cheapest of ski resorts) sleeping up to four people costs between €300 and €400 per week in the summer months, between €300 and €500 per week in the period January to March, and around €700 per week over Christmas.

3.

SELF-EMPLOYMENT

Many foreigners come to France to escape the daily grind of a nine-to-five job and throw off the millstone of being answerable to a boss. If you want more freedom, but still need to make a living, registering as self-employed could be the answer. It means that you can work when you like and for whom you like. Most importantly, it means that you can start your new venture on a small scale until you see how much demand there is for your services. The disadvantage is that self-employment carries certain risks and you have none of the extensive protection that an employed person enjoys. You may also need to work all hours of the day and night to get your business going – and keep it going. So, before you take the plunge, look carefully at the cost implications in terms of tax and social security and also consider the extent (and risk) of your personal liability if you're self-employed.

The French notion of self-employment differs from that of most English-speakers (see **Status** below). Many types of worker considered to be self-employed in the UK or the US, for example, are officially regarded as salaried employees in France. The distinction is largely a matter of how you decide that your business should be taxed (see **Tax Regimes** on page 192), which is something you should sort out at an early stage.

An important rule governing self-employment in France is that **you may practise as many professions as you wish, but each profession must be registered separately unless they're related**. You cannot register as a gardener and practise as a builder. This is the same as working illegally, even though you may be paying your social charges. If, for example, you first registered as a property developer and you wish to add a hand-holding service, you must notify the chamber of commerce, which will register this change – for a fee, of course! If, however, you want to add translating services, this constitutes a new activity which depends, not on the chamber of commerce, but on URSSAF. You will be given a separate status and company registration number. You will also be obliged to pay social charges separately for each activity, thus incurring extra costs: you will be required to pay at least the minimum amount twice (or more, if you want to exercise further activities). If you have one activity that's more important than the other in terms of income, this activity may be considered the principal activity and you may be allowed to pay the social charges relating to this activity only; you should check whether this is the case before starting or registering a secondary activity.

In financial terms, there are a usually few advantages to self-employment over salaried employment. Social security contributions for the self-employed are much higher than for salaried employees. During your first years in business, your social security contributions may be based on a flat minimum charge of several hundred euros per month, irrespective of your turnover or business results. As a self-employed person in France you aren't entitled to unemployment benefit should your business fail and there are no benefits for accidents at work (except for artisans), although you're insured against invalidity. There's no sick pay for those in *professions libérales* (see **Status** below), although *artisans* and *commerçants* are covered provided they've been paying their social security charges for at least a year (see **Social Security** on page 210).As a self-employed person you risk bankruptcy and ruin if your business fails, and it may be advantageous to operate as a limited company (see **Chapter 4**), although the government has recently changed the law to offer better protection for those in a *profession libérale* (see **Protection** on page 108). **Always obtain professional advice before deciding**

whether to be self-employed or to form a company in France, as it has far-reaching social security, tax and other consequences.

On the other hand, there's one major advantage to being self-employed over that of creating a company. If your activity doesn't involve dealing directly with the public (i.e. face to face), you may use your home as your business premises – provided your lease allows you to in the case of rented accommodation or a communal property, such as an apartment (see **Working from Home** on page 109). Conversely, companies may use a private residence only for the first two years, after which they must find separate commercial premises (see **Chapter 4**).

Despite the disadvantages, people of all ages, economic statuses and educational levels become self-employed or create companies in France, and for a myriad of reasons. However, there are certain trends that can be observed. For example: the majority of them are male (although this is slowly changing); 40 per cent are former executives between the ages of 40 and 55 with a degree or higher qualification who have lost their jobs for one reason or another; 42 per cent leave salaried jobs and change profession; 75 per cent have no employees and initially work from home; and – perhaps the most important statistic of all – 87 per cent don't regret having taken the plunge!

> ⚠️ **Many expatriates assume (or hope) that they can earn money for 'odd jobs' without needing to register in the tax and social security system. This isn't true. As soon as you spend more than half the year in France and earn money there, you must declare your activity to the French authorities, pay French taxes and contribute to French social security.**

For information about being employed in France, which may be a necessary prelude to becoming self-employed or starting a business, refer to *Living and Working in France* (Survival Books – see page 419).

STATUS

There are a number of types of self-employment in France and it's important to select the status that applies to your line of work and that best suits your situation. The most common status is that of 'independent worker' (*travailleur indépendant* – see below), but there are a number of other options, including a *contrat de collaboration libérale* (see page 99) and working under the *portage salariale* system (see page 99). It's also possible to work as a self-employed person using the *chèque emploi service* system (see page 195). For details of running a franchise, see page 127.

You're free to change your status according to your needs. For example, you can start as a *profession libérale* and change to an *EURL* and from an *EURL* to a *SARL* (see page 125).

Travailleur Indépendant & Entreprise Individuelle

There are essentially two names for a self-employed person in France: *travailleur indépendant* (independent worker) and *entrepreneur individuel* (individual business person); the work they do is referred to as *travail indépendant* and the business entity as an *entreprise individuelle* (similar to a sole proprietorship in the UK or the US). This isn't, however, a company or corporation (these are dealt with in **Chapter 4** – see page 123), as the businessman (or woman) is registered personally (*en nom personnel*) in the Registre de Commerce or the Registre des Métiers, whereas with an *EURL* (see page 125) or any other form of company, it's the business itself (as a legal entity) that's registered. If you're an 'independent worker', your business has no legal identity or substance of its own.

As with a sole proprietorship in the UK or US, if the individual fails to pay a bill, the creditor can come after his house, his car and anything else he owns. But, whereas in the US, for example, it's possible to put all your personal assets in your spouse's name to protect them from creditors, French marital regimes (see page 133) limit the extent to which you can do so (or at least make it extremely expensive to do so). In practice, an *entreprise individuelle* is limited to the *micro-BIC* or *micro-BNC* regime (see **Financial Regimes** on page 192). In order to borrow money, get credit terms from a vendor or protect any of your personal assets, you must usually set up some sort of company (see **Business Entities** on page 123).

There are three main categories of 'independent worker' (*travailleur indépendant*): *profession libérale* (e.g. accountants, doctors, lawyers), *commerçant* (traders and shopkeepers) and *artisan* (craftsmen).

Professions Libérales

Around 60 per cent of all registered companies in France fall into the *profession libérale* category. The reason for this is that registering as *profession libérale* is the cheapest – at around €150 (or even free for some categories) – and the quickest option. It's ideal for activities demanding little or no investment, such as teaching English, writing, translating, tour guiding and representing a foreign company in France. If you aren't sure which category you come under, you can visit the website of Agence Pour la Création d'Entreprises (🖳 www.apce.com), which is dedicated to the self-employed and those starting a business in France and has a wealth of information as well as a simple yes/no questionnaire that tells you the status that applies to your particular situation (parts of the site are in English, Spanish and German).

The professions that come under the status *profession libérale* can be split into three main groups (see below); a complete list of *professions libérales* (in French) can be found on the website of the Chambre de Commerce et d'Industrie de Paris (🖳 www.inforeg.ccip.fr/formsoc/liberal/listepro.htm).

● **Legal** – This group includes lawyers, bailiffs, court assessors and industrial assessors. Needless to say, these professions require a perfect command of French and, in most cases, training in France; they're therefore unlikely to be relevant to many English-speaking expatriates and aren't considered in this book.

● **Medical & Para-medical** – Includes dieticians, midwives, nurses, orthopaedists and pedicurists. Some of these professions would be difficult for most Anglophones to undertake for the same reasons as noted above. However, under EU law, many UK qualifications are recognised in France.

- **Technical** – This is the group that covers the professions in which foreigners have the most opportunities to work in France, as the vast majority of service jobs fall into this category: i.e. architects, astrologists, decorators, genealogists, guides, interpreters and translators, and landscape gardeners.

Contrat de Collaboration Libérale

A way of easing your way into self-employment in France and getting started without high risk and with 'free' help and advice is to enter into a 'collaborative contract' (*contrat de collaboration libérale*) with an established professional in the same field. This is rather like entering into a 'practice'. The contract allows you to use the premises and professional equipment of one or more practising colleagues in exchange for dues, which are normally a percentage of the fees received. You may usually deal with existing clients of the practice, but are expected to bring in new clients as well. You must register for self-employment in the normal way (see page 102) and remain self-employed and not an employee of the practice. You're responsible for your own actions and aren't subordinate to your colleagues. You're also responsible for paying all social charges and becoming a member of the relevant professional organisation (which may be obligatory).

At the end of the contract period, which is determined by the parties concerned, you have the following options:

- To replace a colleague who's retiring and take over his clients;
- To become an associate of the practice;
- To set yourself up on your own, taking the clients you brought into the practice while respecting the non-competition clause that was in the contract signed with the practice.

This method of working is used by certain professions, such as dentists, doctors, lawyers and some para-medical professions (physiotherapists, home carers, etc.), but there's no reason why other professions, such as teachers and IT specialists, couldn't do the same. For example, a language school might take on an IT trainer on this basis in order to broaden its range of services.

The drawback of this system is its legal insecurity. Collaborative contracts are often regarded as employment contracts by URSSAF, which demands that the practice pays the social charges of the 'employee', for example. However, the Union Nationale des Professions Libérales (UNAPL) is currently lobbying the government to change this situation and make a collaboration contract a legally recognised self-employment status.

Portage Salarial

If you want to be self-employed, but dread the idea of affronting French administration (which even the French acknowledge is enough to make the most strong-hearted quail!), a *portage salarial* could be exactly what you're looking for. This involves signing a working contract with a company (known as the *entreprise de portage*) and becoming in effect a teleworker. The company banks any payments you receive and pays you a salary minus a management fee. They take charge of all administrative formalities and you also have social security protection, including unemployment benefit in the case of the business going bust.

The main disadvantage of this arrangement from the company's point of view is that, although it employs you, it has no authority over you; your only obligation to the company is to pay the agreed fees. From your point of view, the contract may not take into account the peaks and troughs of the job and you may have to pay a set monthly fee irrespective of your earnings. The company's management fee can be high and, coupled with the social charges you must pay, this may mean that you receive only around 50 per cent of what you invoice.

It's best to shop around to find the company that offers the best contract for your type of work and the best support. For example, there are companies that offer business cards, headed letter paper, professional meetings and a sliding scale of fees according to the amount of your turnover, taking into account seasonal variations, for example. With some companies, you can choose between a contract that assures you a fixed monthly salary and one that applies to individual 'jobs'. It's best to contact companies that are members of the Syndicat des Entreprises de Portage Salarial (🖳 www.portagesalarial.org) or the Fédération Nationale du Portage Salarial (🖳 www.fenps.org). Further information in French about the *portage salarial* system can be found on 🖳 www.guideduportage.com. The site of New Freelance (🖳 www. newfreelance.com) provides some information in English, but it applies specifically to this company.

Chèque Emploi Service

To combat illegal working the government introduced a scheme called *chèque emploi service*. Available only to private individuals, it allows them to legally employ someone to carry out 'odd jobs' around the home: cleaning, gardening, babysitting or even help with homework and provides them with insurance in the case of an accident (e.g. if the employee cuts off a finger when pruning roses). The employer also benefits from an income tax reduction.

From the worker's point of view, the system is ideal if you want only a few hours' work per week or like working for several people rather than just one or two. Technically, you aren't self-employed, as the person for whom you do the work pays your social charges. However, you don't have to sign a contract (although it's recommended) unless you do more than eight hours per week for one employer or you work the same number of hours every week. The main disadvantage is that you cannot work full-time for one person or for a company. Further information about the system can be found on 🖳 www.ces.urssaf.fr.

TYPES OF WORK

There are hundreds of self-employment options, a few of which are listed below. Types of work in each category most commonly undertaken by foreigners in France are discussed in greater detail in **Part Two**. Certain professions, such as lawyer and doctor, aren't covered in this book, as they require highly specialised knowledge and qualifications – not to mention perfect French – and are therefore practised by very few expatriates.

- **Property Services** – Includes estate agents and *marchands de biens*, letting agents, re-location services, 'property-sitting', cleaning, property maintenance, renovation, surveying, building and specialist trades, such as carpenter, electrician, plumber, stonemason (see **Chapter 8**);

- **Teaching** – Includes teaching English or other languages, arts and crafts, and information technology (see **Chapter 10**);

- **Publishing** – Includes writing, translating, editing, proofreading, indexing, graphic design and desktop publishing (see **Chapter 11**);

- **Health Services** – Includes acupuncture, chiropractic, fitness training, holistic medicine, massage, osteopathy, physiotherapy and yoga (see **Chapter 12**);

- **Leisure Services** – Includes holiday representatives, travel agents and tour operators (see **Chapter 13**);

- **Financial Services** – Includes insurance sales, mortgage brokering and portfolio management (see **Chapter 14**);

- **Catering Services** (see **Chapter 14**);

- **Arts & Crafts** – Includes painting, sculpture, pottery, and jewellery and model making (see **Chapter 14**);

- **Miscellaneous Services** – Includes satellite television installation; IT services; washing and ironing services; piano tuning; child and pet minding (see **Chapters 11 & 14**).

REQUIREMENTS

If you're an EU-national, you're free to work on a self-employed basis, although you cannot simply hang up a sign and start trading, but must have appropriate qualifications, if required (see page 34), and register with the relevant authorities (see page 102). A non-EU national with a long-term residence permit (*carte de résident*) is entitled to be self-employed. However, this is something of a Catch 22 situation, as it's difficult for non-EU nationals to obtain a residence permit if they intend to be self-employed.

In most cases, to work as a self-employed person in France, you need the following:

- Qualifications and diplomas that are recognised in France for professions and trades requiring certification (see page 34) or membership of the appropriate organisation;

- A residence permit (no longer required for EU nationals);

- A foreign trader's permit (see page 30);

- Contracts or letters of intent from prospective clients (for those in some service industries only);

- A social security number (see page 210).

Before being permitted to register as self-employed, you may also be required to attend a business course (*cours/stage de gestion*) run by the relevant local organisation for your trade or profession, covering all aspects of business administration. Courses last from four to nine days and cost around €125. At the end of the course you're issued with a certificate (whether you understood anything or not!), which must be presented to your local chamber of commerce when registering your business. Most courses are held only in French, although some departments are now offering the course in English. In certain cases, you may also need to pass an exam (in French).

If your profession requires you to register with the Registre du Commerce et des Sociétés, you must sign a declaration that you've never had a criminal, civil or administrative judgement against you prohibiting your right to undertake a commercial activity or to manage, administer or direct a company.

RESEARCH

It should go without saying that you must thoroughly research the market you intend to work in before setting up as a self-employed person. It's worth repeating that the people who make a success of making a living in France have usually done exhaustive research and spent a lot of time in the country (other than on holiday). The importance of research is emphasised by almost all those who have contributed to this book (see **Case Studies** in **Part Two**). Details of how to research your market are given in **Chapter 4** (see **Research** on page 116); although this deals with starting a business, most of the information is also relevant to self-employment and need not be repeated here.

REGISTRATION

Whatever kind of self-employment you're starting, you must register your business. Don't be in too much of a hurry to register as self-employed, as from the date of registration you must pay hefty social security, pension and health insurance payments, and are also liable for income tax and VAT (see **Chapter 5**). If you're an *entreprise individuelle* (see page 96), you don't need to register until you contract your first paid job. It's legal to prepare your business and prospect for clients without being registered, provided you aren't earning money. Registration is free for the self-employed, although *centres de formalités des entreprises* (see below) make a charge of around €50 for helping you with the formalities (see **Centres de Formalités des Entreprises** below).

As soon as you register, you begin receiving quarterly bills from the various social security agencies, amounting to over €6,000 for the first year (see page 210), whether you're earning or not, so unless you need immediate social security cover, it's unwise to register too soon. As an independent, your first two years' social insurance payments are based on assumed earnings of around €6,000 the first year and €9,000 the second. At the end of the second year, you must make up any difference according to your actual earnings for the first year, and again at the end of the third year for the second. (There's no refund if your earnings were less than the assumed figure.) However, in certain professions, you must have the required insurance and accreditation in place **before** undertaking work.

Your local *centre de formalités des entreprises* (see below) is a good source of information regarding when you must register, which varies according to your activity. To register as legally self-employed in France, you must do the following.

- Register with your local social security (URSSAF) office and obtain a social security number;

- Register for value added tax (*TVA*) at the tax office nearest to your business location if your turnover is over a certain limit (see page 208);

- Register with the appropriate *centre de formalités des entreprises* (CFE) for your profession or trade within 15 days of starting a business (see below).

It's also wise to join a professional association, as they provide valuable information and assistance and may also offer insurance and even tax discounts. Most professional associations are organised locally. Check with your departmental chamber of commerce or with the local town hall for information about groups active in your area and profession.

Centres de Formalités des Entreprises

Registration is administered by local *centres de formalités des entreprises* (CFE), which checks your application and submits details to the relevant agencies (for a small fee). The CFE you should use depends on your activity; in fact, the term CFE is used to denote any of several organisations responsible for registering business activities, which include the following, and there's no such thing as a *centre de formalités des entreprises*! Local addresses of the relevant organisations can be found in the telephone directory.

- **Chambre d'Agriculture** – if your business involves farming ;

- **Chambre de Commerce et d'Industrie** – if your business involves trading, retailing or industry, i.e. you're a *commerçant* (equivalent to a chamber of commerce in the UK);

- **Chambre des Métiers** – for manual trades, including arts and crafts (equivalent to a chamber of guilds);

- **Tax Collection Office** (Centre des Impôts or Hôtel des Impôts) – for other categories of self-employment, e.g. artists and writers;

- **Tribunal de Commerce** (equivalent to the Commercial Court Clerk's Office in the UK) – if you want to act as a sales representative;

- **URSSAF** (the office responsible for the collection of social security contributions) – for a professional activity (i.e. a *profession libérale*).

The CFE sends you form P0 if you intend to operate as a sole trader (*entreprise individuelle*). Among other things, form P0 asks you to list your intended activity or activities (your *métier*), from which information the authorities allocate to you financial regimes under which you must operate (see **Financial Regimes** on page

192). **It's essential to take professional advice (e.g. from an accountant) and to make sure you know the implications of your choice of *métier* before completing form P0.** Giving yourself a particular 'label' can also cause unexpected complications; for example, some professionals, such as journalists, aren't recognised as self-employed. You have three months in which to change your mind (by notifying your tax office); thereafter you're stuck with your nominated regimes until the end of the year that follows your year of registration.

Staff at the *CFE* will help you with the paperwork for a small fee. They charge €40 simply to review the *dossier* and make sure everything is complete and correct before they file and distribute it. For €60 you can have a personalised consultation regarding your project and its registration. These services are excellent value, as they ensure that your registration is done properly (and that *CFE* takes the blame if it isn't!).

You can obtain the address of the relevant *CFE* from your local town hall. For information about French chambers of commerce contact the Assemblée des Chambres Françaises de Commerces et d'Industrie (APCFCI), 45 avenue d'Iéna, Paris 75016 (☎ 01 53 57 17 00, 🖳 www.acfci.cci.fr – available in English). For information about the appropriate Chambre des Métiers for your profession, contact the Assemblée Permanente de Chambres des Métiers, 12 avenue Marceau 75008 Paris (☎ 01 44 43 10 00, 🖳 www.apcm.com).

When the *CFE* receives your completed dossier and form P0, it issues you with a receipt (*récépissé de dépôt du dossier de création d'entreprise*). This may take the form of a computerised printout of your P0 form and should include a dossier number to quote if you need to contact the *CFE* concerning your application. **The receipt itself doesn't mean that you're registered and doesn't allow you to begin trading.** However, it does allow you to set up utility accounts in the name of your business, to take an entry in the telephone book, and to notify the post office of your business address.

The *CFE* sends your details to the following organisations:

- The Institut National de la Statistique et des Etudes Economiques (INSEE), France's national statistics office, which enters your company on the national register of businesses and issues your *SIREN*, *SIRET* and *NAF* code (see below);

- The tax authorities;

- The social security agencies – URSSAF (for family allowances), the CAM (for medical cover) and the relevant *caisse de retraite* (for pensions) – which will send you demands for contributions (see page 210);

- The Greffe du Tribunal de Commerce (applies only to individuals classed as commercial or industrial), which enters you on the Registre National du Commerce et des Sociétés (RNCS). You must tick the box at the bottom of form P0 to request this registration.

- The Répertoire des Métiers if you're an artisan (tick the appropriate box at the bottom of form P0).

Certification

When you've been entered in the appropriate register, you receive confirmation, which takes the form of a certificate issued by the relevant authority. For commercial and industrial activities, entry on the RNCS is confirmed by an *extrait Kbis* (literally 'extract KB'), issued by the Greffe du Tribunal de Commerce. Tradesmen receive an *extrait d'immatriculation* from the Répertoire des Métiers. Those in a *profession libérale* receive a *certificat d'identification au Repertoire National des Entreprises* from INSEE. You need copies of your certificate to establish credit with suppliers.

SIREN

Your *SIREN* (pronounced 'seeren') is the official number that proves you're legally registered to do business in France. **It's illegal for anyone to pay invoices from individuals who are based in France, but don't provide (or don't have) a *SIREN*.** A *SIREN* is a unique identification number given to each business or sole trader and used by all public administrative bodies. It's issued by INSEE when your business activity is entered on the Répertoire National des Entreprises et des Etablissements (RNE). It has nine digits, which derive simply from the order in which registrations are entered.

Alongside the *SIREN* goes information about the body with which you're registered. For example, a trader or shopkeeper (*commerçant*) registered with the RNCS in Paris might be identified as RNCS PARIS A 123 456 789 (the letter A denotes a *commerçant*; companies are designated B). An artisan registered on the Répertoire des Métiers might have the number 123 456 789 RM 012 (RM is for Répertoire des Métiers; the number identifies the local Chambre des Métiers). Those in a *profession libérale* have just a nine-digit *SIREN*.

Your *SIREN* must be quoted, in full, on your business stationery. This includes invoices, orders, tariff cards, marketing documents, receipts and any correspondence.

SIRET

The *SIRET* identifies individual establishments within a company and is composed of 14 digits, namely the *SIREN* followed by a five-digit establishment-specific number called the NIC. It's demanded only by certain administrations, such as the social security and tax authorities. It must be quoted on employees' pay slips, for example.

NAF

In addition to a *SIREN* or *SIRET*, your business is allocated a code relating to the *nomenclature d'activité française* (*NAF*), which is sometimes referred to as an *APE* code. Like the *SIREN* and *SIRET*, the *NAF* is issued by the national statistical office, INSEE, and it defines your main activity (your *métier*). The mind-numbingly complex classification system gives rise to a code with three numbers and a letter, e.g. 72.2Z, which is assigned based on the activities you list on your P0 (see page 103. A list of codes is included on the website of the Greffe du Tribunal de Commerce in Paris (🖳 www.greffe-tc-paris.fr/code_NAF.htm).

Your *NAF* code determines which social security regime (see **Financial Regimes** on page 192) you fall under, whether or not you must charge VAT, and your insurance premiums, which is why you should take professional advice when completing your P0 form. The *NAF* code also determines the continuing education taxes you must pay (as some industries impose a special tax in addition to the standard one). Some vendors sell or extend credit only to customers with certain *NAF* codes.

The code must be printed on business documents along with your *SIREN*. Fortunately, changing *NAF* codes isn't difficult. You write to INSEE requesting a change in code (it's usually safest to tell them which one you want) and they will ask you for documents backing up your description of your business activities.

SOCIAL SECURITY

If you're registering as a self-employed worker, you must apply to join the non-salaried social security regime (*régime social des travailleurs non-salariés* or *TNS*). You must complete a *TNS* form, also available from the *CFE*, on which you must give details of the health insurance and pension organisations you wish to join. These depend on your profession; the names are given to you by the *CFE*. The *TNS* form is submitted by the *CFE* to the appropriate agencies, who then contact you directly about registering with them or sometimes simply send you a bill!

OTHER REQUIREMENTS

Before you can start trading, you may need to fulfil other requirements or undertake other procedures, such as the following.

Management Courses

Before being permitted to register as self-employed, you may be required to attend a business course (*cours/stage de gestion*) run by the relevant local organisation for your trade or profession, covering all aspects of business administration. Courses last from four to nine days and cost between around €125 and €250. For example, certain tradesmen (*artisans*) must take a four-day management course (*stage de préparation à l'installation*) costing around €200; details of providers are available from your local Chambre des Métiers. This might seem like a bureaucratic nuisance if you've run a similar business for years in your home country, but it's essential to understand the French system and the courses offer useful training at a reasonable price. The snag is that most courses are held only in French and you may understand little, although some departments are now offering courses in English. In certain cases you may also need to pass an exam (in French). At the end of the course you're issued with a certificate (whether you understood anything or not!), which must be presented to your local chamber of commerce when registering your business.

Accounting

There are strict laws regarding accounting records, which, along with all marketing material, must be in French (mostly for the convenience of VAT auditors). It's therefore highly recommended to use a French accountant – who, if he's worth his salt, can also save you money. See **Accounting** on page 221.

INSURANCE

It's essential that your business activity is properly insured. This section covers the compulsory insurances for various professions, and also looks at other insurances relevant to the self-employed, including the following:

- **Car Insurance** – Make sure that your car insurance covers business use if you will be using your car for business purposes. Basic car insurance is, of course, compulsory.

- **Premises** – If you work from home, make sure your household insurer is notified and that the policy has sufficient cover for your computers, etc.

- **Professional Indemnity** – If you're practising a regulated profession (e.g. medical or legal), you must have appropriate insurance against accidents and mistakes. For details of what's required, consult your professional association or look for policies tailored to your particular activity.

- **Public Liability** – Everyone living in France must be insured for public liability (*responsabilité civile*). This is often included in household insurance policies, but if you're taking up self-employment, you must insure your business activity separately, as business activities aren't covered by personal policies.

- **Health Insurance** – Although your social security contributions (see page 210) cover you for a proportion of treatment in the case of illness or accident, they won't always cover all your costs and won't normally compensate you for loss of earnings resulting from incapacity. There are various policies that will do so, known as *assurance complémentaire maladie* or, more commonly, *une mutuelle*. (For details of these, refer to *Living and Working in France* – see page 419). You may also wish to take out life assurance or insurance (see page 220).

Other compulsory insurance includes a ten-year guarantee (*garantie décennale*) on all building work if your business is involved in construction or renovation. Other optional insurance includes the following:

- Policies called *assurance de matériel professionnel* are available to cover tools and machinery.

- *Assurance perte d'exploitation* covers your business if you're prevented from operating, for example by a fire or an equipment breakdown.

- *Protection juridique* covers legal costs.

Insurers have networks of branch offices in every town, and arranging insurance is easier face to face than by telephone, even if your French is fluent. You can also arrange insurance over the internet. Many insurers offer 'multi-risk' (*multirisques*) policies aimed at various types of self-employed person (e.g. tradesmen or professionals) which cover all the relevant risks. Insurance premiums are generally reasonable, but as always, it pays to shop around. See also **Pensions** on page 218. **As**

with all optional insurance, you should carefully consider the cost of cover in relation to your likelihood of requiring it.

PROTECTION

As a self-employed person, you have no protection if your business fails, if you have an accident or fall ill, as you would if you were an employee; obviously, you are entitled to medical treatment through social security, but you won't have any income while you're incapacitated. If you wish to protect yourself against these eventualities, you must take out insurance, which is an additional cost to your business. Another risk of self-employment is that, if a customer or client sues you for malpractice or negligence, for example, you could lose not only your business, but also your livelihood in France, as you're personally liable for any 'damages' caused by your activity. These issues are discussed below.

Further information about insurance and other legal protection is available from the Association pour la Promotion des Entrepreneurs et de leur Protection Sociale (🖳 www.apeps.com) and the Fédération Française des Associés d'Assurance (🖳 www.ffsa.fr).

Liability

If you register as self-employed rather than a company, your liability is unlimited and your private assets, including your home, could, in theory, be seized to pay business debts or in the event of your being sued. However, the French government has recently changed the law to offer better protection to those in a *profession libérale* (see page 98), who can now separate business from private assets. This means that, even if your office is in your home, it cannot be repossessed to pay off business debts. This applies even if your home has been used as collateral for a business loan. However, anything that's used for professional purposes, e.g. stock, car and computers, can be seized. To separate business from private assets, you must make a declaration (*déclaration d'insaisissabilité*) before a *notaire*, which is then lodged at the Bureau des Hypothèques (equivalent to the Land Registry in the UK) and with other organisations depending on your status. Whereas previously a spouse had no legal or financial status even if he worked alongside his self-employed partner, he or she is now recognised under this declaration in terms of social security cover, retirement benefits, etc. The cost of a declaration depends on the value of your property, but for an average property is in the region of €500 to €600 plus a charge of €150 for the publication of a legal announcement (everyone cashes in on bureaucratic procedures in France!).

If you aren't in a *profession libérale*, you can take out insurance against being sued for damages and the cost of legal advice, as well as against loss of work due to sickness, invalidity, death and other risks. Costs vary greatly according to the cover you want, your legal status, etc. April Assurances (🖳 www.april.fr) is a company offering a range of such insurances, including *responsabilité personnelle des dirigeants*.

Unemployment

As a self-employed person you aren't entitled to unemployment benefit if your business fails, as you make no unemployment contributions, although the government is considering implementing a scheme for a 'loss of work' insurance. However, you can insure yourself privately against this eventuality. There are two main insurance providers, for different types of worker:

- **Garantie Sociale des Chefs et Dirigeants d'Entreprise (GSC)** – for all types of business;

- **Association pour la Protection des Patrons Indépendants (APPI)** – not for registered companies.

The cover offered by both organisations is similar. Minimum payments are around 2 to 3 per cent of your annual income plus an annual payment to the relevant professional body or the insurance organisation itself; you can pay more to qualify for higher benefits. There are six levels of cover according to the amount you pay into the fund. Payment is made only in the case of bankruptcy or official receivership. There's a delay of between 12 and 24 months before payments are made, and benefits are paid for 12, 18 or 24 months depending on the type of cover chosen.

WORKING FROM HOME

Some of the above can be practised from home (known as *télétravail*), which is a dream for many: no more traffic jams, no more finding someone to look after the children, the freedom to organise your work the way you want (in theory) . . . However, there are also disadvantages to working from home, such as giving up part of your living space to create an office, finding a place to work free of interruptions, little contact with the 'outside world', separating 'home work' and even leisure time from office work, and calculating business expenses and claiming VAT or tax allowances. Conversely, you don't have to find and pay for business premises and can deduct even part of the cost of running and paying for your home as expenses (unless you're a *micro-entreprise* – see page 197).

Computers and the internet have made the process of working from home vastly more realisable and interesting. Work can be ordered, carried out and supplied without the provider ever leaving his home or, with a portable computer, wherever he chooses or happens to be. With broadband (*haut-débit*), you can transfer even large files in seconds, although it isn't yet available in all areas of France (see page 230). As with any technology, however, there are disadvantages as well as advantages. The other side of the coin is that customers often expect the work to be done 'immediately' and at all times of the day and night. Bear in mind also that the vast majority of French business people expect to meet their suppliers regularly (unless, of course, the work is typing letters, translating, etc.) so you may have to do some travelling – for which you won't be paid, although you may be able to claim travelling expenses – and must be prepared to work on site.

You may exercise a business activity from your home provided there isn't a continual stream of clients or customers coming and going. If that's the case, the law states that you must find commercial premises. You may get round this by registering part of your home that's separate (e.g. a garage or outbuilding) or has a separate entrance as 'commercial'. This can only be done if you own the buildings or if your lease allows you to do so (which in most cases it won't!).

With the above proviso, if your home is rented or leased, you can run your business from it for two years without the permission of the owner or management committee, provided that you notify them of your activity by registered letter (*lettre recommandée*). After the two years, the contract may require you to obtain the owner's or committee's permission to continue. If you own your home, you can run the business or company from there indefinitely, although in some cases it may be necessary to apply for a change of use for your building under local planning rules. You should consult your town hall or *mairie* to check whether this is the case.

Further information about working from home is available from Télétravail, 45 avenue du Bac, 94210 La Varenne Saint-Hilaire - Saint Maur des Fossés (☎ 01 49 76 07 74, 🖥 www.teletravail.net) and the website of Virtu@ (🖥 www.virtua.fr).

4.

RUNNING A BUSINESS

An increasing number of people are starting businesses (*démarrer une entreprise*) in France, although the bureaucracy associated with it is frightening and rates among the most pernicious in the world. France is a red tape jungle and civil servants (*fonctionnaires*) can be inordinately obstructive (endlessly recycling bits of paper to create 'employment' for themselves). For foreigners, the wall of paper is almost impenetrable, especially if you don't speak French (it's bad enough for the natives!), as you will be inundated with official documents and must be able to understand them. It's only when you come up against the full force of French bureaucracy that you understand what it **really** means to be a foreigner!

Nevertheless, France is a nation of small (and predominantly family-owned) businesses: of the 2.5 million French companies, almost 95 per cent have fewer than ten employees and an annual turnover of less than €1 million, and there are fewer medium-size businesses than in most other European countries. Three-quarters of new companies have no employees and less than a third opt for corporate status.

At least in theory, the economic philosophy of France encourages and even nurtures the creation of small businesses. (Keep reminding yourself of this when you're submitting your dossier for approval for the nth time!) Thanks to a raft of measures designed to encourage enterprise, setting up a business in France is simpler now than ever before . . . However, the improvement is relative, and to those used to the Anglo-Saxon model the process will still seem a quagmire of bureaucracy, as most of the expatriates who contributed to this book (see **Part Two**) testify.

The rate of new business creation in France is on the increase: some 320,000 businesses were started in 2004 – an increase of 9 per cent over the previous year. The biggest increases were in IT businesses (up 28 per cent), construction (23 per cent), property (21 per cent) and 'personal' services (20 per cent). It should also be noted, however, that one in two new businesses ceases trading or undergoes a change of status or owner within five years.

As in most other countries, of course, many small businesses in France exist on a shoe string and certainly aren't what would be considered thriving enterprises. Most people run their own businesses for the freedom it affords (no boss to tell you what to do) rather than for the financial reward.

⚠ **Working for yourself or being the 'boss' (*dirigeant*) of a French company means that you lose all the rights of an employee – which is why so many French people are reluctant to be self-employed or start a business. These include the right to work a 35-hour week, the right to national holidays and paid (e.g. summer) holidays, the right to earn at least the statutory minimum wage, the right to days off for births, deaths, marriages, etc. and, most importantly, the right to unemployment benefit if your business fails.**

Generally speaking, you shouldn't consider running a business in France in a field where you don't have experience (even activities such as bed and breakfast and *gîtes*, where you may think that experience isn't necessary – see *Earning Money From Your French Home*, Survival Books). It's often wise to work for someone else in the same line of business in order to gain experience, rather than jump in at the deep end. Always thoroughly investigate an existing or proposed business before investing any money.

When you do take the plunge, it's important to keep your plans small and manageable and work well within your budget, rather than undertaking some grandiose scheme. **Most people are far too optimistic about the prospects for a new business in France and over-estimate income levels (it often takes years to make a profit).** Be realistic, or even pessimistic, when estimating your income and overestimate the costs and underestimate the revenue (then reduce it by 50 per cent!). While hoping for the best, you should plan for the worst and have sufficient funds to last until you're established (under-funding is the major cause of business failures, of which there are thousands every year). New projects are rarely, if ever, completed within a set budget, and you must ensure that you have sufficient working capital and can survive until a business takes off. French banks are extremely wary of lending to new businesses, especially businesses run by foreigners (see **Financing Your Business** on page 178). As any expert can tell you, France isn't a country for amateur entrepreneurs, particularly amateurs who don't speak fluent French!

A fundamental decision to be made is whether to take over or buy an existing business (see **Taking Over a Business** on page 142) or to start one completely from scratch. Your choice may be partly dictated by the premises you intend to run the business from, which may be available only with an existing business infrastructure or with a lease that restricts the activity you may carry out (see **Premises** on page 148). In some ways (not least the paperwork involved), it's much easier to take over an existing business and it may be less of a risk, although there are possible disadvantages as well. You must pay for the business in addition to the premises and you may also be liable for taxes and transfer fees. Most significantly, of course, you can never be sure that the business is really a 'going concern' and not a 'dead duck' and you may have less control over its fortunes than over those of a new business.

This chapter provides you with the information necessary for you to make a reasoned decision (although it won't make the decision for you!) and will guide you through the steps necessary to ensure that, whether you start a business or take one over, your activity in France is carried out legally. But it isn't a substitute for professional advice. **The decisions you make at the beginning, especially regarding business structure and the definition of your activity (*métier*), but also in some cases regarding marital regime, can have a big influence on the way you must run your business, your entitlement to social security benefits and, most importantly, the amount of money that ends up in your pocket.** The registration process is when these decisions are made concrete, and mistakes made at this stage may be difficult to rectify (see **Example** below). So be clear about what business structure, *métier* and, if applicable, marital regime are right for you before you start.

EXAMPLE

Mr and Mrs L. ran a company which, until the end of 2002, was organised as a SARL with three shareholders. They had set up a silent partner (in their case, Mr L.'s sister) with 51 per cent of the ownership interest to allow Mr L. to be a *gérant minoritaire* (see page 124). After 2002, however, the silent partner decided to relinquish her share in the company, so Mr and Mrs L. bought out her share (a purely paper transaction) and set Mr L. up as a *gérant majoritaire* – a process which it took them over a year to sort out. He was, from that point, considered to be an artisan (his job was repair work) and, as such, had a choice between basing his declared income on (a) the results of the company or (b) on what he actually took out of the company each year (plus all contributions paid by the company) or (c) declaring a fixed salary (plus all the contributions paid on his behalf), whether or not he was actually paid the 'salary'. (The form for the transfer of shares didn't require him to declare which option he was using, even though each option requires different accounting procedures and has different tax and social security implications.)

Meanwhile, Mrs L. was still considered to be an 'employee' of the company, although she now had the option of declaring herself an unpaid working spouse shareholder, in which case she was obliged only to make social security contributions (which would be paid by the company), although this would also involve a change of regime and consequently a change of caisse to which she must send her contributions . . .

A consultation with a French accountant (*expert comptable*) – the first meeting is usually free – can be invaluable. Don't hesitate to seek advice from organisations such as the local chamber of commerce (*chambre de commerce et d'industrie/CCI*), 'chamber of guilds' (*chambre des métiers*) and URSSAF, as well as small business associations, usually supported by local town halls and cantonal or regional governments. These often have libraries with information (mostly in French) on running a business in France, as well as all the forms you could ever need. Some offer personalised assistance with the business set-up process. Staff may be helpful, although unfortunately this cannot be guaranteed. However, beware of consultants, French or foreign, who offer to help you set up your business. You may end up paying handsomely for information that's available free of charge from the authorities (or indeed in books such as this one!).

RESEARCH

As with self-employment, it's imperative to conduct exhaustive research before starting a business. In fact, it's even more important, as the cost and complexity of setting up a business, particularly if you need to buy or rent premises, are usually far greater than for registering as self-employed. Research enables you to:

- Check that the market (i.e. customers) for your product or service actually (or potentially) exists and is sufficiently numerous, accessible and willing to part with money to sustain your proposed business;
- Define your marketing strategy – i.e. how best to promote and sell your product or service to your target market;
- Establish a price or rate for your product(s) or service(s) in relation to what your customers are prepared to pay and/or what your competitors are charging;
- Assess your business objectives and estimate your turnover and profit.

The information you require includes the following:

- **Market** – A definition of your customers, e.g. individuals or companies, men or women, old or young people, their location, 'socio-economic' status, lifestyle and habits;

- **Competition** – The extent and nature of actual, likely and potential competitors, including details of rival products or services offered or available and their market share;

- **Influences** – Information about any and all political, economic, scientific and sociological factors that could affect your business, such as developments in infrastructure, changes in legislation and social trends.

The first decision to make is whether to use the services of a professional market research company or other agency or to carry out your own research. Using a professional company (*cabinet de conseil*) is usually expensive: a bespoke market study can cost at least €8,000. A list of agencies registered with the Fédération des Syndicats de Cabinets de Conseil can be obtained from Syntec Conseil (☎ 01 44 30 49 20, 🖳 www.syntec.fr). A cheaper option (usually around €3,500) is to use what is known as a *junior entreprise*, which is a group of business students, whose work is supervised by a tutor. There are around 100 *juniors entreprises* in France; to find your nearest group, contact the Confédération Nationale des Juniors Entreprises (CNJE, 48 rue Montmartre, 75002 Paris, ☎ 01 40 28 48 68, 🖳 www.cnje.org).

If you decide to do your own research, there are numerous resources available to you, including the following:

Specialist Organisations

There are various organsations that exist specifically to assist entrepreneurs to set up businesses in France. These include the following:

- **Agence pour la Création d'Entreprise** – APCE operates at all levels, from European to local, and coordinates the Entreprendre en France network (see below). It doesn't provide an individual consultation service but publishes a number of information packs (*dossiers*), including *Artisanat, Commerce, Industrie* and *Services*, costing €8 each and posts information on its website; contact APCE, 14 rue Delambre, 75014 Paris (☎ 01 42 18 58 58, 🖳 www.apce.com).

- **Association pour le Conseil à la Création d'Entreprise et à la Coopération Internationale** – An association comprising four delegations (in Ile-de-France, PACA and Rhône-Alpes) of retired business managers who offer their expertise free to those setting up small businesses in 'sensitive' urban areas; contact 3CI, 14 rue des Dominicaines, 13001 Marseille (☎ 04 91 15 17 17, 🖳 www.3ci.asso.fr).

- **Boutiques de Gestion** – A network of around 100 offices providing information and advice to entrepreneurs. The first consultation is free but thereafter you must pay. For details of your nearest office contact the Comité de Liaison des Boutiques de Gestion, 14 rue Delambre, 75014 Paris (☎ 01 40 64 10 20, 🖳 www. boutiques-de-gestion.com).

- **Entente des Générations pour l'Emploi et l'Entreprise** – An association of retired business managers who offer advice at reasonable rates to budding entrepreneurs; contact EGEE, 15–17 avenue de Ségur, 75007 Paris (☎ 01 47 05 57 71, 💻 www.egee.asso.fr).

- **Entreprendre en France** – This is a network of information points coordinated by APCE (see above) in conjunction with chambers of commerce and industry and the association of French banks. Information points (*espaces entreprendre*) are located in chambers of commerce; for details contact Entreprendre en France 45 avenue d'Iéna, 75016 Paris (☎ 01 40 69 38 37, 💻 www.entreprendre-en-france.fr).

- **Femmes et Entreprises** – A support network for female entrepreneurs; contact Femmes et Entreprises, Préfecture des Hauts-de-Seine, 167 avenue Joloiot-Curie, 92000 Nanterre (☎ 01 40 97 21 92).

- **Fédération Française des Clubs de Créateurs et de Repreneurs d'Entreprise** – Around 50 'clubs' of new business organisers, who share ideas and information through a 'godfathering' system; contact the FFCCRE, CCI de Nantes, 16 quai Ernest-Renaud, 44100 Nantes (☎ 02 40 44 60 68).

- **France Initiative Réseau** – FIR is a network of local 'platforms' providing advice and information to entrepreneurs; for details of your nearest platform contact FIR, 14 rue Delambre, 75014 Paris (☎ 01 40 64 10 20, 💻 www.fir.asso.fr).

- **Prospective, Innovation, Valorisation, Opportunité, Disponibilité** – An association of retired volunteers who make their skills and experience available to entrepreneurs. PIVOD is active in Ile-de-France, Lorraine and Nord-Pas-de-Calais; contact PIVOD, 30 rue Brey, 75017 Paris (☎ 01 56 68 07 00, 💻 www. pivod.org).

- **Réseau Entreprendre** – A federation of business owners (over 2,500 of them in 31 'regional' groups) offering free advice (as well as loans see page 182) to entrepreneurs; addresses of all 31 groups can be found on 💻 www.reseau-entreprendre.org.

- **Service des Droits des Femmes** – A branch of the Ministry of Work, offering assistance to female entrepreneurs; contact the Centre National d'Information et de Documentation des Femmes et de la Famille (CNIDFF), 7 rue du Jura, 75013 Paris (☎ 01 42 17 12 34, 💻 www.infofemmes.com).

Chambers of Commerce

Among the best sources of help and information is your local chamber of commerce (*CCI*), of which there are over 160 and at least one in each department (listed on 💻 www.cci.fr). The website includes a long list of schemes designed to help in the creation or development of a business activity. Most *CCIs* have good libraries of books, magazines and documents relevant to businesses and setting up small businesses in France, all of which can be consulted free of charge. Most publications are in French, but some *CCIs* have information in English. Many *CCIs* organise regular conferences (e.g. once a month) and training programmes on starting a business, business practices, financing small businesses etc., free of charge or for a nominal fee (e.g. €10). The *CCI* can also advise you where to find the relevant *centre de formalités des entreprises* – see pages 103 and 137). However, chambers of commerce aren't professional associations made up of businesses and business owners in France, as chambers of commerce are in the UK and US, but departmental government offices. For further information contact the Assemblée des Chambres Françaises de Commerce et d'Industrie, 45 avenue d'Iéna, 75116 Paris (☎ 01 40 69 37 00, 💻 www.acfci.cci.fr).

Chambres des Métiers

Another good source of information is the relevant *chambre des métiers* (some are called *chambre de métiers*). These serve a similar function to the *CCI*, but for occupations that are regarded as 'trades', e.g. butchers, bakers and candlestick makers. The *chambres des métiers* are, therefore, able to advise you on the specific rules and regulations covering each trade. Each department has a *chambre des métiers*, and the contact details of all 96 are listed on 💻 www.artisans-de-france.com/f_chambres.html. Further information can be obtained from the Assemblée Permanente des Chambres de Métiers, 12 avenue Marceau, 75008 Paris (☎ 01 44 42 10 00, 💻 www.apcm.com).

Government Agencies

Information about industry and trade sectors can be found on the websites of the relevant government ministries: enter 💻 www.[name of ministry].gouv.fr (e.g. 💻 www.agriculture.gouv.fr). The website of the Agence Pour la Création d'Entreprises (💻 www.apce.com – see also below) contains a wealth of information (in French) about all the major business areas (e.g. agriculture, construction, health, hospitality, industry, leisure and transport); click 'Informations Sectorielles' for lists of relevant organisations, publications and exhibitions and links to related sites.

Specific market studies are undertaken by the Centre de Recherche pour l'Etude et l'Observation des Conditions de Vie (CREDOC), 142 rue du Chevaleret, 75013 Paris (☎ 01 40 77 85 06, 💻 www.credoc.asso.fr). The website lists the studies available, which can be purchased or consulted at CREDOC's offices, although you must make an appointment, as only a few people are admitted at a time; waiting lists are long. More general economic and demographic studies are available from La Documentation Française, 29 quai Voltaire, 750007 Paris (☎ 01 40 15 70 00, 💻 www.ladocfrancaise.gouv.fr).

Statistical information is available from the The Institut National de la Statistique et des Etudes Economiques (INSEE, ☎ 08 25 88 94 52, 💻 www.insee.fr – the site is available in English and lists INSEE's regional offices), the Association Française de Recherches et d'Etudes Statistiques Commerciale (AFRESCO), 46 rue de Clchy, 75009 Paris (☎ 01 48 74 32 80), and the Documentation d'Analyse Financière (Dafsa), 117 quai de Valmy, 75010 Paris (☎ 01 55 45 26 00, 💻 www.dafsa.fr). The 25 Agences Régionales d'Information Scientifique et Technique (ARIST) are 'regional' agencies providing scientific and technical information; contact details are listed on 💻 www.arist.tm.fr. There's also a network of Centres Techniques Industriels; contact CTI Réseau, 41 boulevard des Capucines, 75002 Paris (☎ 01 42 97 10 88, 💻 www.reseau-cti.com).

For information about French and European standards, contact the Association Française de Normalisation (AFNOR), 11 avenue Francis de Pressensé, 93571 Saint-Denis La Plaine Cedex (☎ 01 41 62 80 00, 💻 www.afnor.fr).

Trade Associations

There are a number of trade associations for artisans, shopkeepers and other businesspeople, including the following:

- Association pour la Promotion et le Développement Industriel, 17 rue Hamelin, 75783 Paris Cedex 16 (☎ 01 47 27 51 49, 💻 www.aprodi.com) – industrial businesses;

- Confédération de l'Artisanat et des Petites Entreprises du Bâtiment, 46 avenue d'Ivry, 75625 Paris Cedex 13 (☎ 01 53 60 50 00) – building trades;

- Confédération Française du Commerce de Gros et du Commerce International, 18 rue des Pyramides, 75001 Paris (☎ 01 44 55 35 00, 💻 www.cgi-cf.com) – wholesale and international commerce;

- Confédération Générale l'Artisanat, Français, 30 rue des Vinaigriers, 75010 Paris (☎ 01 40 38 06 67) – general trades;

- Confédération Nationale de l'Artisanat, des Métiers et des Services, 8 impasse Daunay, 75011 Paris (☎ 01 44 93 20 44) – general trades;

- Fédération Française de la Franchise, 60 rue de la Boétie, 75008 Paris (☎ 01 53 75 22 25, 💻 www.franchise-fff.com) – franchises;

- Union Fédérale des Coopératives de Commerçants, 77 rue de Lourmel, 75015 Paris (☎ 01 44 37 02 00) – shopkeepers and cooperatives;

- Union Professionnelle Artisanale, 79 avenue de Villiers, 75017 Paris (☎ 01 47 63 31 31) – general trades.

Companies

A number of major companies in France offer support to young entrepreneurs, whose business activity doesn't necessarily need to relate to that of the supporting company. The type and extent of support offered varies considerably, e.g. from advice and technical or marketing services to loans and grants (see page 182). Companies include the following:

- Aérospatiale Développement, 12 rue Pasteur/BP76, 92152 Suresnes Cedex (☎ 01 46 97 43 15).

- Alcatel CIT, 10 rue Latécoère, 78141 Vélizy Cedex (☎ 01 30 77 30 77).

- Charbonnages de France, 100 avenue Albert 1er/BP220, 92503 Rueil-Malmaison Cedex (☎ 01 47 52 35 00).

- Danone Initiative, 7 rue de Téhéran, 75381 Paris Cedex 08 (☎ 01 44 35 23 05).

- EDF, 91 rue du Faubourg Saint-Honoré, 75384 Paris Cedex 08 (☎ 01 40 42 22 22).

- Geris Thomson, 18 rue de la Pépinière, 75008 Paris (☎ 01 44 13 69 00).
- Giat-Sofred, 13 route de la Minière, 78034 Versailles Cedex (☎ 01 30 97 38 31).
- Michelin, 23 place des Carmes, 63040 Clermont-Ferrands Cedex 01 (☎ 04 73 32 66 20).
- Rhône-Poulenc-Sopran, 55 avenue René-Cassin, CP310, 69337 Lyon Cedex 09 (☎ 04 72 85 43 43).

Magazines & Exhibitions

There are numerous business magazines in France, available from newsagents' (see **Appendix B**). There are also specialist exhibitions aimed at entrepreneurs, the two largest being the Salon des Entrepreneurs in Paris (in January) and Lyon (in June). Details can be found on the exhibition website (🖳 www.salondes entrepreneurs.com). To find out about smaller shows in your area, contact the Fédération des Foires et Salons de France, 11 rue Friant, 75014 Paris (☎ 01 53 90 20 00, 🖳 www.foiresalon.com). Another useful website is 🖳 www.salons-online.com.

Other

A list of businesses in France can be found in *Le Kompass France* (Editions Kompass France), which is available for consultation in most libraries and information centres or via the internet (🖳 www.kompass.fr). A register of commercial businesses can be found on the website of the Greffes Tribunaux (🖳 www.infogreffe.fr), and legal and financial details of French companies are accessible via 🖳 www.societe.com.

If you intend your business to export products, you should contact some or all of the following agencies: Centre Français du Commerce Extérieure (CFCE, 🖳 www. cfce.fr); Compagnie Française d'Assurances pour le Commerce Extérieur (COFACE, 🖳 www.coface.fr); Direction des Relations Economiques Extérieures (DREE, 🖳 www.missioneco.org); Echanges et Consultations Techniques Internationaux (ECTI, 🖳 www.ecri-vsf.org); Syndicat des Sociétés Françaises de Conseil de d'Assistance au Développement International (SYCADI, ☎ 01 44 69 44 43). For information about export/import partnerships and international distribution arrangements, go to 🖳 www.informactis.com.

Don't forget to make contact with your local town hall or *mairie*. Even if they cannot provide you with the information you need, they will almost certainly be able to point you in the right direction. In any case, it's imperative to establish a good relationship with the mayor (if possible) and his staff, not only in the interest of your business but also to hasten your integration into the local community.

An essential part of your research should be to find the best location for your business (see below).

Research Grants

Innovative new businesses (or businesses with an innovative new product) can apply for grants to cover up to 70 per cent of the cost of research, as well as zero-

and low-interest loans, from the Agence Nationale pour la Valorisation de la Recherche (ANVAR, 43 rue de Caumartin, 75436 Paris Cedex 09, ☎ 01 40 17 83 00, 🖳 www.anvar.fr). There's also a European initiative called Eureka, which offers research grants of up to around €90,000 to around 50 French companies per year provided the research is carried out in more than one EU country. You should allow a year between application and receipt of funds. For details contact ANVAR (see above).

LOCATION

The location for a business is even more important than the location for a home. For example, you may need access to the motorway or *TGV* network, or to be located in a popular tourist area or near local attractions. Local plans regarding communications, industry and major building developments, e.g. housing complexes and new shopping centres, may also be important. Plans regarding new motorways and rail links are normally available from local town halls.

However, town halls and *mairies* aren't always willing to give information about local plans to 'strangers', and local small business associations (run by the town, canton or department) are generally a better source. If your French is up to it, you can simply attend town council meetings to find out what issues are being discussed or even ask questions!

If your business will rely on passing trade (e.g. a restaurant or shop), it's obviously imperative to assess the suitability of the location before buying or renting premises. You should visit the location at different times of day and, if not at different times of year (which may not be possible), at least in different weather. Are enough of the right type of people passing the premises to provide a clientele. Obviously, if the business is highly specialised (e.g. a shop selling foreign food), location may be less critical, although you may have to work harder to develop a clientele.

A business that doesn't rely on passing trade (e.g. a language school or manufacturing unit) can, in theory, be anywhere and it may be pleasant to work out in the country or halfway up a mountain, but it must still be easily accessible (for customers, deliveries, etc.) and preferably near to amenities such as banks and post offices – after all, you don't want to have a 20-minute drive every time you must send a parcel or withdraw money!

A recent law allows entrepreneurs to run a business for up to two years in their home (see **Premises** on page 148).

BUSINESS PLAN

Whether you're starting a business or 'simply' becoming self-employed, it's imperative to draw up a detailed business plan. This isn't only a requirement if you need finance or other types of support; if nothing else, it defines on your aims and focuses your attention on your strengths, weaknesses, opportunities and threats (known as a 'SWOT' analysis). A business plan should include the following:

- An outline or overview of your business;

- A description of the person or people who are to run the business, including their qualifications, skills, experience and goals;

- A description of your product(s) or service(s) and how they're to be provided (e.g. method of manufacture or means of distribution);

- A market study, including relevant trends, actual or potential demand, current or possible future opportunities and a description of existing and potential competition;

- Your commercial strategy, i.e. your intended market positioning, pricing policy, marketing plan, methods of communication, etc.

- A financial statement including initial capital, sources of additional funding, likely profit margins, break-even point and a three-year cash-flow forecast (see **Financing Your Business** on page 178);

Attached to the plan should be all relevant documentation, such as written confirmation of financial support, letters of recommendation, expert opinions and necessary permissions or licences.

BUSINESS ENTITIES

A crucial decision to be made before you can register your business and start trading is the type of structure or entity that will best suit your business and help you to realise your aims. There are around 13 different types of business entity (*statut*) in France. The most important ones are described below. Note that *une entreprise individuelle* isn't a company, but similar to a sole proprietorship in the UK and is dealt with in **Chapter 3**.

It's essential to obtain professional advice regarding the best method of establishing and registering a business, which can dramatically affect your liability in the event of incurring debts or being sued, as well as your tax position, and you must never use a non-trading company (e.g. a *société civile* or association) to trade.

Companies cannot be purchased 'off the shelf' in France, and incorporating a company in France takes longer and is more expensive and more complicated than in most other European countries, although it's possible to buy an existing business, which is simpler (see page 142).

The Agence Pour la Création d'Entreprises (APCE, 14 rue Delambre, 75014 Paris, ☎ 01 42 18 58 58, 💻 www.apce.com) publishes a book entitled *Quel Statut pour mon Entreprise?*. Further information is available on the website of the Chambre de Commerce et d'Industrie (💻 www.cci.fr). For details of the business registration procedure, see page 136.

Officially, the director of an *SC*, *SARL* or *SCA* is a *gérant*, and the managing director of an *SA* is a *président-directeur général* (*PDG*). The general word for the manager of a company is *dirigeant* or *chef d'entreprise*.

Corporations

A corporation has one or more directors and shareholders. A corporation can be foreign-owned. Corporations are subject to corporation tax as well as other taxes. The most common type of corporation is a *SARL* (see below).

Société à Responsabilité Limitée

A *SARL* must have between 2 and 50 shareholders and a managing director (*gérant*), who's usually paid a salary. You can start a *SARL* with a capital of just €1, although it's recommended to invest a 'sensible' amount – not least because any losses of half or more of the stated capital must be formally acknowledged by a special shareholders meeting and resolution, which is registered with the Registre National du Commerce et des Sociétés (RNCS – see page 138) and then the information appears on your *Kbis* (see page 139), which doesn't do a thing for your ability to get bank or any other sort of credit! Whatever amount of capital you choose to start with, this figure must be included on all your official documentation, e.g. letterhead, invoices and orders.

The managing director (MD) of a *SARL* can be a salaried employee of the company (but isn't eligible for unemployment benefit unless he buys private insurance). If, as MD, you're also a shareholder, your status is determined by whether or not you have 'effective control' of over 50 per cent of the shares (*actions*) in the company. You're deemed to control any stock owned by your spouse (no matter what regime you're married under) and any minor children who own stock in the company. If you don't have control over more than 50 per cent of the shares, you're considered a *gérant minoritaire* and can be treated like an employee for social insurance purposes, which means that you have around 20 per cent deducted from your pay and the company must pay 40 to 50 per cent of your gross salary in social charges.

If you have effective control of over 50 per cent (50 per cent isn't enough), you're considered a *travailleur indépendent* (see page 97) for social security purposes, which means that you must enrol in the appropriate *caisses* (for *commerçants*, *artisans* or *professions libérales*). URSSAF continues to collect for family allowance and the CSG/CRDS (see **Chapter 5**). Contributions vary slightly between *caisses*, but are generally around 40 to 45 per cent of 'remuneration'.

A *SARL* can elect, under certain circumstances, to pay corporation tax (*impôts sur les sociétés*) rather than having its net income included on the *gérant*'s personal income tax declaration (i.e. *impôts sur le revenu*).

There are certain optional benefits available to a *gérant majoritaire*, including *prévoyance* (a sort of life and accident insurance – see page 220), a complementary insurance fund (*mutuelle* – see page 214) and extra (i.e. adequate!) retirement funds. If the company pays these for a *gérant majoritaire*, the amounts paid must be added back to the base used to calculate his social insurance contributions, but they aren't counted in his personal income for income tax purposes.

A legal 'dodge' is to set up a 'silent' partner (often a spouse) with 51 per cent of the ownership interest to allow the MD to be a *gérant minoritaire* and thus qualify for all the benefits of being an employee of the company (except for unemployment insurance) – see **Example** above. If you do this, you must consider the effect on the spouse (see **Couples Working Together** on page 132).

A *SARL* must hold an annual general meeting (AGM), although many merely produce the paperwork required to 'prove' that a meeting has been held!

Entreprise Unipersonelle à Responsabilité Limitée

An *EURL* is a type of *SARL* formed by a sole trader and has only one shareholder; otherwise it operates like a *SARL* and can be set up with a capital of just €1. Although it's operated by one person, an *EURL* is **not** an *entreprise individuelle* and the owner-operator of an *EURL* is considered a *gérant* rather than *travailleur indépendant* (see page 97).

Société Anonyme

An *SA* is similar to a plc in the UK and must have a minimum of seven shareholders (there's no maximum). It must be run by a board of directors (*conseil d'administration*) and have a *président directeur-général/PDG*, roughly equivalent to a chief executive. To start an *SA* you must invest a minimum of €37,000. An *SA* is probably the most difficult sort of company to start; the registration requirements are elaborate (because an *SA* can sell shares on the public stock exchange) and you must have a *commissaire aux comptes* to audit your accounts every year. The biggest advantage of an *SA* over a *SARL* is that all risk is limited to the extent of the investment and all executives can be regular salaried employees of the company, with rights to holidays, redundancy pay and other 'perks'. The *PDG* can also be fired at any time by the board (which isn't the case in some of the other types of business).

Société par Actions Simplifiées

An *SAS* is a simplified form of *SA* (see above), with at least two shareholders and a minimum capital of €23,000. An *SAS* isn't allowed to trade shares publicly. The form of the corporation is much more flexible than that of a *SARL*; for example, you can hold annual general meetings by email or telephone, which is strictly forbidden in a *SARL* (provided you allow for this in the articles of incorporation), and the MD can be given the power to do almost anything by edict or by telephone or email consultation with the shareholders.

The major disadvantage of an *SAS* is that you must have a *commissaire de comptes* to audit your accounts every year; he must also be present at your AGMs – for a fee, of course.

Société par Actions Simplifiées Unipersonnelle

A *SASU* is a simplified version of an *SAS*, which can be set up by a single person. The minimum capital is €37,000 or €225,000 if you want your stock to be publicly traded. You still need a *commissaire aux comptes*, who must attend your AGM. An *SAS* is subject to corporation tax (*impôts sur les sociétés*) and the President (*dirigeant*) is considered an employee of the company and so pays normal social security contributions for an employee (except for unemployment insurance). Although it's operated by one person, a *SASU* is **not** an *entreprise individuelle* and the owner-operator of a *SASU* is considered a *dirigeant* rather than a *travailleur indépendant* (see page 97).

Société Civile Professionelle

An *SCP* is limited to certain regulated professions, such as medical personnel (doctors, nurses, physiotherapists, etc.), lawyers, certain types of 'expert' (agricultural, forestry, etc.) providing a consultancy service, *commissaires aux comptes*, and industrial property consultants. Precise requirements are controlled by the various professions.

Société d'Exercice Libérale

There are several types of *SEL*, which mimic the *SARL*, *SAS*, *SA* and *SCA*, for specific professions where practitioners are allowed to incorporate their practice; these include architects, dentists and accountants.

Partnerships

Certain business entities have some things in common with what are known as partnerships (in the UK, for example), although they're technically forms of incorporation. These include the following.

Société Civile

An *SC* is a non-commercial partnership, commonly formed by members of the *professions libérales*, e.g. farmers and those engaged in what are called 'intellectual activities', including writers, researchers and some types of consultant. Shareholders of an *SC* (known as *associés*) may not be engaged in any trading activity (*commerce*). An *SC* can elect to pay corporation tax or not; if not, each shareholder includes his portion of the partnership's profit or loss on his personal income tax declaration. The *gérant* pays contributions to the appropriate *caisse*, depending on the activity of the *SC*.

A *société civile immobilière* (*SCI*) is a special type of *SC* used to hold property (buildings and land). It's widely used to separate the ownership of a building from other personal assets (the individual then holds shares in the company rather than title to the building itself), although it can also be used by companies (e.g. a *SARL* or *SAS*) to hold property. It keeps the financing for the property off the books, while allowing the company to deduct a theoretical 'rent' paid for the use of the building it occupies (see **Société Civile Immobilière** on page 150). An *SCI* is also often used to avoid inheritance problems, e.g. when several children inherit the family home or a building used to generate revenue.

Société en Nom Collectif

An *SNC* is a general partnership. There's no capital requirement, but there must be at least two partners/shareholders. Profits and losses are passed on to the partners, who are liable for unlimited debts. All partners are considered to be traders (*commerçants*). All changes in partner shares must be unanimously approved and all decisions must be made collectively and documented (through minutes, which must be kept on file). Social security contributions are based on each partner's total revenue 'not otherwise subject to salary taxes' (i.e. not just their share of earnings from the *SNC*).

Société en Commandité par Actions

An *SCA* is a limited liability partnership – similar to an *SNC*, but a joint-stock company whose partners have unlimited liability. You need a minimum of four partners/shareholders, of whom one or more is the *commandité* and the others *commanditaires*. The *commandité* runs the company on a day-to-day basis. His financial liability is unlimited and he's considered a *commerçant* (i.e. not an employee; he must have something invested in the company). He also pays personal income tax on his portion of the earnings of the company, and he makes contributions as a *commerçant*. The *commanditaires* are the shareholders and their financial responsibility is limited to the amount they've invested. Their portion of the company's income is subject to corporation tax. The minimum investment capital is €37,000 or €225,000 if the *commanditaires* want to be able to publicly trade their shares.

This form of business used to be very popular in France, but since other business structures (e.g. *SARL* and *SAS*) have been simplified, it has become less so. One disadvantage is that the accounting procedures (dividing the net income between the two categories of shareholder and calculating who's taxed in what way for how much) are far more complicated than for other forms of business entity. Another major disadvantage is the unlimited liability for shareholders/partners.

Société en Commandité Simple

An *SCS* is a limited liability partnership. It's a simplified form of the *SCA* (see above). It has two categories of shareholder, but no minimum capital requirement and the liability of each *commanditaire* is limited to his original investment, although the *commandité* has unlimited liability. It isn't possible to sell shares publicly.

FRANCHISES, PARTNERSHIPS & AGENCIES

If you want to minimise the risk involved in starting a business, you may wish to consider taking on a franchise (see below) or partnership (see page 129) or acting as an agent for an existing business (see **Agencies** on page 127). In all three cases you must register with the appropriate authorities before you can begin trading: to run a franchise or set up a partnership, you must register a business entity (see above); to act as a *locataire-gérant*, you must declare yourself as self-employed (see **Chapter 3**).

Franchises and partnerships are subject to the Loi Doubin, which applies to the use of trademarks and brands.

Other types of joint-business arrangement include the *chaîne, commission-affiliation, dépôt-vente, distribution sélective, groupement d'intérêt économique, licence de marque* and *relais-vente*, all of which are explained in the book *Franchise et Partnariat* by Michel Kahn (Dunod). Further information about franchises and partnerships can be obtained from the Fédération des Réseaux Européens de Partenariat et de Franchise, 15 boulevard Richard-Lenoir, 75011 Paris (☎ 01 54 44 19 90). The magazine *Bureaux & Commerces* (see page 144) includes an occasional supplement entitled *Franchise et Partenariat*, which contains details of franchise opportunities throughout France as well as articles on related subjects.

Franchises

As in other countries, it's possible to set up a franchise (*franchise*), of which there are several thousand in France, or to act as a distributor, agent or representative. However, you must still set up a business (whatever entity best suits your circumstances) and then enter into a contract with the franchiser, which provides product, services, logos, marketing services, advertising material, etc. to help you run your business. The contract specifies what each business is going to do, pay for and provide for the other. You agree to buy certain products and services from the franchiser and to run your business according to the standards it sets. In return, the franchiser agrees to undertake promotions for you, list you on its website or in its directories or catalogues, provide training and advertising material, etc. Contracts run for a number of years – usually five or ten initially.

Normally, there's an initial 'buy-in' fee (*redevance initiale forfaitaire* or commonly *droit d'entrée*), which varies with the franchiser and according to whether you choose the location and premises (which the franchiser must approve) or these are found for you. The big name franchises, such as McDonald's, require huge up-front payments – up to €500,000, although the fee varies according to location, size of premises and other criteria. Smaller, less well known businesses may charge only €10,000 or €20,000. There's often also a franchise fee based on your turnover or profits.

Expected income depends on the business, the location and your own ability to run a business. **Franchisees can, and do, go broke, and franchisers can, and will, take the franchise away if they find you breaking any of the terms of the contract or failing to meet their standards**, e.g. not buying the specified amounts of their products from them or providing an inadequate service.

The main advantage of running a franchise is that you have an 'instant' business, with virtually guaranteed custom and support from the 'parent' company. Depending on the business and the level of support provided, a franchise can be almost a licence to print money, e.g. a *McDos* (as the French call them) just opposite a *lycée* (at least until government legislation prohibits children from eating hamburgers!).

Disadvantages can include a large set-up cost, a fly-by-night franchiser going bust (just after cashing your cheque), or a well established franchiser making inordinate demands and forcing you to run your business in a way that's against your inclinations. As with any business, location is everything and a poor location (whether chosen by you or the franchiser) can make it impossible for you to cover your initial outlay and continuing obligations towards the franchiser.

The best franchisers investigate carefully the people they take on and usually require experience that's at least vaguely related to the business. In France, this means someone who has significant experience dealing with French business practices and who speaks fluent French. Others will take anyone prepared to make the required initial payment and then, when you fail to make the business work the way they promised it would, tell you that it's because you lack relevant experience . . .

Before taking on a franchise, research the franchisers and the types of business you're considering. A respectable franchiser should be a member of the Fédération Française de la Franchise (☎ 01 53 75 22 25, 🖳 www.franchise-fff.com). Talk to other franchisees – especially those closest to you (some franchisers have no qualms about setting up competing franchises a few streets apart; others are careful to protect each operator's territory) and find out what they're unhappy about.

A list of available franchises can be found on the website of AC Franchise (🖳 www.ac-franchise.com – it claims to list all the franchises available in France), which includes descriptions of the franchisers, the type of contract they offer, and the average size of facility they expect, in terms of floor space and number of employees. Franchisers include hotels, estate agencies, DIY stores, hairdressers', lingerie shops and every sort of fast food operation – even something called the Belgian Beer Café. Franchises are listed by the amount required to buy in – from less than €40,000 to over €150,000. Further information (in French) can be found on the OBS Emploi portal (🖳 www.obs-emploi.com) and in the periodical L'Officiel de la Franchise (🖳 www.lentreprise.com) and the bimonthly Franchise Magazine (in French).

Partnerships

Like a franchise, a partnership (partenariat) entitles you to use an established brand, but it allows you greater autonomy. For example, you may sell products other than branded goods, provided these remain a sideline. You aren't obliged to follow strict procedures, but can benefit from the knowledge and experience of other partners in order to adapt guidelines to personal and local needs. As with a franchise, there's an 'entry fee', but it's usually lower, as it pays only for the services of existing partners, who will help you to find premises and finance, train staff, run a publicity campaign, etc. Business decisions are generally made on a democratic basis rather than simply being imposed upon you, as with a franchise operation. A partnership contract is similar to a franchise contract, except that it isn't standardised, but can vary from case to case. In theory, you can start a franchise with no experience, as you're in a sense following a formula; to enter into a partnership, you are usually expected to have relevant experience.

Agencies

If you already have a business in another country and wish to extend its activities to France, you can set up a bureau de liaison, branch or subsidiary. A further option open to budding entrepreneurs is that of a *location gérance*. These possibilities are discussed below.

Bureau de Liaison

A *bureau de liaison* ('liaison office') or *représentation* ('representative office') is essentially a 'shop window' set up by a foreign company. It's regarded as a non-commercial entity and may therefore handle only activities such as information gathering and marketing. Being non-commercial, it isn't liable for tax or VAT in France. To set up a *bureau de liaison* you must employ a French resident and register with URSSAF in order to obtain a *SIREN* (see **Registration** on page 136). Registration is free and involves completion of a simple form. However, you must ensure that the office doesn't engage in any commercial activity, e.g. advertising and contracting, which limits its usefulness. A *bureau de liaison* isn't an option as far as choosing a business entity is concerned, unless you have a foreign business and want to expand its activity into France; it's usually a temporary solution to the set-up of a branch office or subsidiary in France (see below).

Branch

A branch office (*succursale*) of a larger company, e.g. a French branch of a foreign publishing or software company, isn't strictly a business entity, and the branch must register as one of the main French business entities. Like a *bureau de liaison*, a branch office is legally part of the foreign company and has no separate assets or liabilities, but it has greater autonomy: it can engage in advertising and contracting on behalf of the parent company (*société mère*) and is therefore liable for tax in France on the business it generates there. A branch office must be registered with the local Greffe du Tribunal de Commerce (see page 137) within two weeks of commencing activity, and obtaining a *SIREN* is more complicated than for a *bureau de liaison*. The administration costs are a few hundred euros. To convert a branch office into a full-blown subsidiary (see below) can be extremely complicated and costly, however, and it may be advantageous in the long run to set up a subsidiary from the start.

Subsidiary

A subsidiary (*filiale*) is, to all intents and purposes, an independent French company and must be set up as such, using one of the standard business entities (see page 123), irrespective of the extent to which it's controlled by the parent company.

Location Gérance

This is officially defined as making an agreement with a liquidator to manage a company in liquidation, although this is misleading, as the company need not be in liquidation. The owner must, however, have been running the business for at least two years and a similar business for at least seven. The arrangement is designed for business owners who no longer want to run their business (e.g. to retire), but who still want to draw income from it and for people who have inherited a business they don't want to run (or aren't qualified to run) themselves.

In a *location gérance*, the owner of a business (which can be a sole proprietorship or an *EURL* or *SASU*) 'rents' his business to you and you run it for him. The owner retains the *fonds de commerce* (see **Fonds de Commerce & Cession de Bail** on page 142) and, in the case of rented property, remains responsible for extending the lease if necessary. In return, he's paid an agreed fee (*redevance*), quarterly or monthly, which can be a fixed sum or a percentage of the turnover or earnings of the business. As the renter (*locataire-gérant*), you must be qualified to run the business and must run it as it is (i.e. you cannot change the nature of the business at all). You must register yourself in the Registre National du Commerce et des Sociétés (🖥 www.euridile.inpi.fr), e.g. as a *commerçant* or *artisan* as appropriate (see page 98), and advertise the fact that you're managing the business in the relevant publication(s).

The agreement can be limited or open-ended, but is usually an annual contract. At the end of the agreed period, the owner must take back the business as it is. He cannot claim compensation if the business is 'worth' less than it was at the beginning of the contract, but neither can you claim benefit from any 'improvement' you made while you were running it. The agreement should specify who's responsible for capital and other expenditure (repairs, improvements, etc.) during the contract period.

A *location gérance* agreement cannot be used to sell or buy a business and you cannot have any part of the *redevance* credited against the selling price if you do eventually buy the business. Nor should the agreement mention any rights or intention to purchase the business during the term of the contract; otherwise, the owner can lose his exemption from capital gains tax (see **Capital Gains Tax** on page 207) when he does sell the business.

There are tax advantages on both sides, and a *location gérance* gives you the chance to 'test-drive' a business before deciding whether or not to buy it. If the business is sold within five years of the original *location gérance* agreement, there are further tax advantages for the seller of the business, e.g. not having to pay part or all of any capital gains accrued provided the rent was less than a certain amount (currently around €54,000).

There are usually advertisements in business publications for *location gérance* arrangements, but the same rules apply as to the purchase of a business: research the market, check the viability and reputation of the business, and seek professional advice before committing yourself to a contract.

ASSOCIATIONS

It's possible to set up a business as an association, known as an *association de la loi de 1901* after a law of that date governing their formation. Technically, an association of the law of 1901 is a not-for-profit association, and there are many restrictions on the types of activity they can undertake, whether and when they're subject to taxes and/or VAT, etc. Broadly, an association's intentions must be social, cultural or informative and beneficial in a non-financial sense to its members and others. It may receive funds provided that the money is used for running the association and furthering its aims.

An association must have at least two founding members. It may employ people, including the founding members, but there's a restriction on an association's 'managers' (*dirigeants*) drawing a salary. In theory, elected officials of an association may not draw payment for their elected duties, but may be paid by the association for other work done for the association. For example, the elected treasurer cannot be paid anything for keeping the books of the association, but he can be paid – as an employee or as a *travailleur indépendant* – to run the computer system or conduct training classes that are part of the association's function. All payments made to elected officers must be vetted and approved by the association's annual meeting (attended by the membership). There are limits to how much an association can pay to any one officer, as well as overall limits to how much can be paid to all officers, though these limits are pretty generous (up to €84,000 to any one officer in a year!).

It's the nature of these payments that determines how the recipients must pay taxes and social charges. If the work being done is subject to an employment contract, they're considered as employees of the association and subject to the general regime for social security. If the payments fall under contract work or any other type of casual or self-employment heading, it's up to the individual to register himself as self-employed with the appropriate agencies (i.e. as an *artisan*, *commerçant* or *profession libérale*).

However, as so often happens in France, there's an exemption under which an association can pay salaries to certain officers – usually an executive director and an office manager or secretary – which creates a loophole that's exploited by certain organisations. There are also subsidies of up to 66 per cent of salary for associations which employ people between 18 and 25, those who have been unemployed or the disabled or 'disadvantaged' and a monthly allowance for those that employ people under a *contrat initiative emploi* (see page 155).

You must create and file association articles, and there are reporting requirements that are similar to those for businesses if you engage in certain kinds of fund raising activity (charging entrance fees, selling merchandise, etc.) and your turnover is above a certain level. You must also hold an annual general meeting to allow the membership to approve the financial statements and the expenditure of their dues. Your town hall or *mairie* must approve the setting up of the association and may make an annual contribution to the funds or offer assistance in kind (e.g. photocopying).

An association is usually an inappropriate vehicle for setting up a business – particularly one from which you want to make a living – and you can be heavily fined if you break the conditions relating to associations, although many expatriates (and French people) run business operations as associations and few are penalised. If you think your business idea could (legally) take the form of an association, consult a French lawyer or accountant.

COUPLES WORKING TOGETHER

If you're setting up your business as a couple, it's important to think about how the various financial rights and responsibilities are to be shared. One option is to set up a company in which each partner has a specified share (see **Business Entities** on page 123). Alternatively, one partner can own the business and take on the other as an employee. This is only allowed if the 'employee' has a proper contract of employment and receives a salary commensurate with his or her duties and isn't involved in the management of the business.

Whether or not your spouse is going to work with you in the business, you must know what your marital regime is and how this affects your various choices regarding the type of business you set up (see below).

Marital Regimes

In France, a couple isn't simply married: there are some half dozen different marital regimes. However, for purposes of setting up a business, the only significant factor is whether you have a communal regime (*communauté universelle*) or have elected to keep your respective assets separate (*séparation de biens*).

If you marry in France, it's assumed that you jointly own all assets acquired after your marriage (e.g. furniture and property, and including debts) unless you've been to a *notaire* before the wedding and drafted a different agreement. Anything each partner brings into the marriage belongs to him, and there's no joint ownership of inheritances you each receive during the marriage; anything you receive from your parents, for example, remains yours and yours alone. If you divorce, the property acquired during the marriage must be divided equally between husband and wife before the divorce can be finalised. If one of you dies, the heirs (usually your children) will become owners of their parents' property – including a business.

For couples married outside France, a *notaire* or attorney may be required to determine what marital regime was in effect when and where you were married. Sometimes, this information can be obtained from your country's embassy or consulate in France; in the US, it varies by state.

To set up most types of business, you must identify your spouse and specify the regime you were married under. Most business registrations also require a sworn statement by your spouse that he's aware of the business activity, his spouse's role in it and his own rights regarding ownership interest in the company. If the spouse is buying into the business as well, you don't need this statement, but in some situations (such as determining whether the *gérant* of a *SARL* is *majoritaire* or *minoritaire* – see page 124) you must consider how the investment affects each partner's rights and options.

It's also worth considering what would happen to the business (based on the marital regime) if you split up or if either, or both, of you dies. France's inheritance laws – see *Buying a Home in France* (Survival Books) – can cause some bizarre situations, particularly regarding the inheritance of shares in a business. If the business is one in which all owners must be qualified in the profession (e.g. lawyers, doctors, hairdressers, pharmacists), it can happen that, upon death or divorce, the non-professional spouse has the right to a financial interest in the business, but cannot legally own the interest and so must be 'bought out', which may not be easy or even possible. In a different sort of business, the surviving or divorced partner could simply take possession of his shares and live off whatever income they generate. The complications of attempting to set up a business while in the throes of a divorce don't even bear thinking about!

You can change your marital regime (and may want to consider doing so before going into business with or without your spouse) if you've been married at least two years under your current regime. To do so you must go to a *notaire*. **It takes around six to eight months to change regimes and costs at least €1,500 plus whatever property transfer fees (usually around 2 per cent of their value) and miscellaneous taxes and other costs (a further 0.5 to 0.75 per cent) apply.** You should take professional advice before changing marital regimes.

Status

The role or status of a spouse in a business is another thing that needs to be considered carefully. As usual, you should take professional advice before deciding which status to allocate to a spouse. There are essentially four types of status, as described below.

Conjoint Associé

This is where the spouse is a shareholder, either in his own name or by virtue of having acquired his spouse's shareholding (except in an *SAS*). A *conjoint associé* must 'invest' in the company – which may be merely in terms of working for it – but has limited liability. A *conjoint associé* can also be an employee of the business and/or can be named as *dirigeant*, *gérant* or *PDG*, depending on the type of company. In some forms of company, a *conjoint associé* can function with his spouse as a co-director or as one of the directors of an *SAS* and is eligible for the same social insurance cover as an unpaid director in that form of business.

Conjoint Bénévole

If the spouse works for the company with no pay and no formal recognition (the most common circumstance in small companies in France), he's considered to have no profession (*sans profession*) and receives health benefits through his spouse's contributions and may be eligible for a reversionary pension after his retired spouse dies. In the case of divorce, he may be able to claim compensation for half of his spouse's investment in the company (assuming they were married under one of the communal regimes). If one partner dies, the other inherits his portion of the shares held in the company, along with his children. However, if the business has debts and the deceased partner had unlimited liability as manager, all the communal assets are at risk under a communal regime, whereas under a separation contract, only the deceased's property can be used to pay off the debts of the business.

The government is considering establishing some sort of recognition for *conjoints bénévoles*, at least as far as transfer of a company is concerned (i.e. the spouse could take it over on the death of his partner if he wished). Until then, this is the most risky status for the spouse.

Conjoint Collaborateur

A spouse who's unpaid but makes a significant and regular contribution to the business can register as a *conjoint collaborateur* (collaborating spouse). This status applies only to certain *travailleurs indépendents* (i.e. *commerçants, artisans* and under certain circumstances those in the *professions libérales*). A *conjoint collaborateur* must be declared (using *an attestation sur l'honneur*) to the social security *caisses* with which the business owner is registered, and health and maternity coverage are provided at no additional charge.

A *conjoint collaborateur* has no rights to state disability or unemployment benefits. He may, however, voluntarily make contributions to his spouse's *caisse* for a retirement pension in his own name. The level of social security contributions required depends on the type of business and its turnover, but contributions are usually paid by the business and can be deducted from taxable income, up to specified limits. If you're in one of the *profession libérales*, your *conjoint collaborateur* may be eligible for a particular type of social insurance, which is essentially an extension of your cover.

A *conjoint collaborateur* is entitled to act on your behalf (e.g. in your absence or incapacity). On the death of the business owner, if the *conjoint collaborateur* has been active in the business for at least ten years without being a shareholder or an employee, he's entitled to a special payment from the capital of the business (in addition to his inheritance rights as surviving spouse) equal to three times the annual minimum wage (*SMIC*) at the time of the death and not exceeding 25 per cent of the value of the net assets of the business.

The main benefit of this status is that the spouse can build up pension entitlements in his own right, making voluntary (and tax deductible) contributions, and the pension entitlement of the business owner, if he dies, reverts to the spouse. However, a *conjoint collaborateur* mustn't work in other paid employment for more than 75 hours per month.

Conjoint Salarié

As a *conjoint salarié*, the spouse works as a salaried employee in the business, is paid a salary and makes contributions to the general social security funds (i.e. URSSAF, ASSEDIC and the main retirement funds). The only restrictions are that the employee must be doing a genuine job within the company (e.g. not merely paper pushing) and his salary 'must not be excessive for the work performed.' (No one cares if you're seriously underpaid!)

One small catch is that for companies subject to personal rather than corporate income tax (i.e. where the managing director declares the net results of the business as personal income instead of as business profit), the spouse's salary is fully tax deductible only for spouses married under a separation regime. For couples married under one of the communal regimes, there's now a limit of €13,800 for the deduction unless the company is a member of a *centre de gestion agréé* (*CGA* – see page 198). (The limit was raised from around €2,600 on 1st January 2005!) If the company is liable for corporation tax, the whole salary of the *conjoint salarié* is tax deductible.

REGISTRATION

Before undertaking any business transactions in France, it's important to obtain legal advice to ensure that you're operating within the law. **There are severe penalties for anyone who ignores the regulations and legal requirements regarding business registration.** Working illegally (see page 33) simply isn't an option in France (or anywhere else) and, although registering your business means having to pay taxes and social security contributions, it also gives you access to healthcare, pension rights, family allowances and, for lower earners, various other means-tested benefits.

When to Register

Don't be in too much of a hurry to register your business, as from the date of registration you must pay hefty social security, pension and health insurance payments, and are also liable for income tax and VAT (see **Chapter 5**). However, you should never be tempted to start work before you're registered, as there are harsh penalties that may include a large fine (e.g. €15,000), confiscation of machinery or tools, and even deportation and a three-year ban from entering France.

Your local *centre de formalités des entreprises* (CFE – see page 137) is a good source of information regarding when you must register, which varies according to your activity and whether you're considered an employee of your business or not.

Trading Name & Trademarks

If your business is to have a trading name, it's a good idea to check whether or not your chosen name is already in use, and, in the case of original names, to ensure that it isn't a registered trademark. For a quick check, go to ▨ www.icimarques.com and click on '*Marque*' or ▨ www.euridile.inpi.fr, where you can search the database of the Registre National du Commerce et des Sociétés (click on '*Accès Visiteur*'). For a more detailed check, you must contact the Institut National de la Propriété Industrielle (INPI, 26bis rue de Saint Petersbourg 75800 Paris Cedex 8, ☎ 08 25 83 85 87, ▨ www.inpi.fr). A search among a particular type of business costs €38; a search among all businesses in France costs €760.

You may then want to register the name yourself. This is done at the RNCS, costs a minimum €215 (for exclusivity in just your area of business; more if you want to prevent people in other types of business using the same name) and is valid for ten years at a time. Your company name must be preceded or followed by the letters indicating the type of business, e.g. *SARL Bloggs* or *Bloggs SA*.

You can check and register internet domain names at the Association Française pour le Nommage Internet en Coopération (AFNIC, Immeuble International, 78181 St Quentin-en-Yvelines Cedex, ☎ 01 39 30 83 00, ▨ www.afnic.fr), or with commercial domain registration companies that handle French domain names. For a list of approved domain name registrars (in France and other countries), go to ▨ www.icann.org/registrars/accredited-list.html. You aren't required to use a .fr domain for a French company, although there have been challenges to French-based commercial websites that aren't available in French. On the other hand, if you want a French domain name, you must have a company registered in France, your site must be in French (other languages are optional) and you must pay around €300 for the name.

If you wish to establish a trademark in France, you must contact the Institut National de la Propriété Industrielle (INPI, 26bis rue de Saint Pétersbourg, 75800 Paris Cedex 08, ☎ 01 53 04 53 04, 🖳 www.inpi.fr), which issues registration forms, as well as any relevant European or international organisations.

Announcement

Notice of the company's formation must be published within two weeks in an official column in the local newspaper or specialist journal (known as the *journal d'annonces légales*); the *centre de formalités des entreprises* (*CFE* – see page 137) will supply details of appropriate journals. It must also appear in the *Bulletin Officiel des Annonces Civiles et Commerciales* (*BODACC*). This is done by the Greffe du Tribunal de Commerce after you register with the *CFE*.

Centres de Formalités des Entreprises

Registration is administered by local *centres de formalités des entreprises* (*CFE*), which checks your application and submits details to the relevant agencies (for a small fee). The *CFE* you should use depends on your activity; in fact, the term *CFE* is used to denote any of several organisations responsible for registering business activities, which include the following, and there's no such thing as a *centre de formalités des entreprises*! Local addresses of the relevant organisations can be found in the telephone directory.

- **Chambre d'Agriculture** – if your business involves farming;
- **Chambre de Commerce et d'Industrie** – if your business involves trading, retailing or industry, i.e. you're a *commerçant* (equivalent to a chamber of commerce in the UK);
- **Chambre des Métiers** – for manual trades, including arts and crafts (equivalent to a chamber of guilds);
- **Greffe du Tribunal de Commerce** – for agents and *sociétés civiles* (e.g. *SCIs*);
- **Tax Collection Office** (Centre des Impôts or Hôtel des Impôts) – for other categories of self-employment, e.g. artists and writers;
- **Tribunal de Commerce** (equivalent to the Commercial Court Clerk's Office in the UK) – if you want to act as a sales representative.

You can obtain the address of the relevant *CFE* from your local town hall. For information about French chambers of commerce contact the Assemblée des Chambres Françaises de Commerces et d'Industrie (APCFCI), 45 avenue d'Iéna, Paris 75016 (☎ 01 53 57 17 00, 🖳 www.acfci.cci.fr – available in English). For information about the appropriate Chambre de Métiers for your profession, contact the Assemblée Permanente de Chambres de Métiers, 12 avenue Marceau 75008 Paris (☎ 01 44 43 10 00, 🖳 www.apcm.com).

The *CFE* will provide you with a form M0, which is for the creation of a company. Among other things, form M0 asks you to list the intended activity or activities of your company, from which information the authorities will allocate to it the financial regimes under which it must operate (see **Financial Regimes** on page 192). **It's essential to take professional advice (e.g. from an accountant) and to make sure you know the implications of your choice of activity before completing form M0.** You have three months in which to change your mind (by notifying your tax office); thereafter you're stuck with your nominated regimes until the end of the year that follows your year of registration.

Form M0 also requires you to state your marriage regime (see page 133) and the social security status of your spouse, i.e. whether he's covered under his own employment, whether he's a shareholder in the company, whether he will be employed by the company, etc.

Documentation

In order to register your company with the *CFE*, you require the following documentation:

- A copy of the announcement of company formation from the appropriate journal (see above) or a copy of the request for publication made to the journal, along with its confirmation of acceptance;

- At least two copies of the articles of incorporation, which **must** be in French, if you're setting up a limited company (see page 141);

- Written nomination of the managing director (MD), if it isn't part of the articles of incorporation;

- A signed declaration by the MD that he has no criminal convictions (*attestation sur l'honneur de non-condamnation*);

- A copy of the MD's identity card or passport;

- *Carte de commerçant* for a non-EU citizen (see page 30);

- Proof of the company's address (e.g. a copy of a lease or recent utility bill);

- A statement from the MD if the company is to be set up in his residence for the first two years, and proof of his residence.

Staff at the *CFE* will help you with the paperwork for a small fee. They charge €40 simply to review the *dossier* and make sure everything is complete and correct before they file and distribute it. For €60 you can have a personalised consultation regarding your project and its registration. Consultants can advise you about your various options regarding VAT and other financial regimes (see **Financial Regimes** on page 192) and will give you a list of the cheques and other supporting documents you must prepare and submit with your registration form (see below). These services are excellent value, as they ensure that your registration is done properly (and that *CFE* takes the blame if it isn't!).

When the CFE receives your completed dossier and form M0, it issues you with a receipt (*récépissé de dépôt du dossier de création d'entreprise*). This may take the form of a computerised printout of your M0 form and should include a dossier number to quote if you need to contact the CFE concerning your application. **The receipt itself doesn't mean that you're registered and doesn't allow you to begin trading.** However, it does allow you to set up utility accounts in the name of your business, to take an entry in the telephone book, and to notify the post office of your business address.

The CFE sends your details to the following organisations:

● The Institut National de la Statistique et des Etudes Economiques (INSEE), France's national statistics office, which enters your company on the national register of businesses and issues your SIREN, SIRET and NAF code (see below);

● The tax authorities;

● The social security agencies – URSSAF (for family allowances), the CAM (for medical cover) and the relevant *caisse de retraite* (for pensions) – which will send you demands for contributions (see page 210);

● The Greffe du Tribunal de Commerce (applies only to businesses classed as commercial or industrial), which enters your business on the Registre National du Commerce et des Sociétés (RNCS);

● The Répertoire des Métiers if you're an artisan;

● The relevant social security and labour inspection organisations if you have employees.

Cost

Registration costs between around €200 and €350 depending on the body you must register with (see page 136): registration with the Greffe du Tribunal du Commerce costs €60, with Registre National du Commerce et des Sociétés (RNCS) €110, and with the Répertoire des Métiers between €90 and €200. Publishing the required legal announcement for the creation of a company costs an additional €150. There's also a small charge by the CFE for processing and reviewing your paperwork (see page 137).

Certification

When your company has been entered in the appropriate register, you receive confirmation, which takes the form of a certificate issued by the relevant authority. For commercial and industrial activities, entry on the RNCS is confirmed by an *extrait Kbis* (literally 'extract KB'), issued by the Greffe du Tribunal de Commerce. Tradesmen receive an *extrait d'immatriculation* from the Répertoire des Métiers. Those in *professions libérales* receive a certificate from INSEE (*certificat d'identification au Répertoire National des Entreprises*).

You need copies of your certificate to establish credit with suppliers, as well as to get the bank to release your blocked funds (see **Creating a Limited Company** on page 141) and to set up a company bank account.

SIREN & SIRET

SIREN and *SIRET* (pronounced 'seeren' and 'seeret' with the N and T sounded) are the official numbers that prove that a business is legally registered in France. A business or supplier with no *SIREN* or *SIRET* is likely to be operating on the black market. **It's illegal for anyone to pay invoices from companies or individuals who are based in France, but don't provide (or don't have) a *SIREN* or *SIRET*.**

Your *SIREN* or *SIRET* must be quoted, in full, on your business stationery. This includes invoices, orders, tariff cards, marketing documents, receipts and any correspondence. In addition, all documents (including letterhead and invoices) must include the type of company (e.g. *SARL*, *SNC*, *SAS*), the stated capital and your *NAF* code (see below). You may also be required to state your intra-European VAT number, which is based on your *SIREN/SIRET*, but can be different.

SIREN

A *SIREN* is a unique identification number given to each business and used by all public administrative bodies. It's issued by INSEE when a business is entered on the Répertoire National des Entreprises et des Etablissements (RNE). It has nine digits, which derive simply from the order in which registrations are entered. Alongside the *SIREN* goes information about the body with which a business is registered. For example, a shop registered with the RNCS in Paris might be identified as RNCS PARIS B 123 456 789 (the letter B denotes a company; individuals are designated A). A business registered on the Répertoire des Métiers might have the number 123 456 789 RM 012 (RM is for Répertoire des Métiers; the number identifies the local Chambre des Métiers).

SIRET

The *SIRET* identifies individual establishments within a company and is composed of 14 digits, namely the nine digits of the *SIREN* followed by a five-digit establishment-specific number called the *NIC*. It's demanded only by certain administrations, such as the social security and tax authorities. It must be quoted on employees' pay slips, for example.

NAF

In addition to a *SIREN* or *SIRET*, your business is allocated a code relating to the *nomenclature d'activité française* (*NAF*), which is sometimes referred to as an *APE* code. Like the *SIREN* and *SIRET*, the *NAF* is issued by the national statistical office, INSEE, and it defines your main activity (your *métier*). The mind-numbingly complex classification system gives rise to a code with three numbers and a letter, e.g. 72.2Z, which is assigned based on the activities you list on your M0 (see page 138). A list of codes is included on the website of the Greffe du Tribunal de Commerce in Paris (💻 www.greffe-tc-paris.fr/code_NAF.htm).

Your *NAF* code determines which social security regime you fall under (see **Regimes** on page 192), whether or not you must charge VAT (see **VAT** on page 208), and your insurance premiums, which is why you should take professional advice when completing your M0 form. The *NAF* code also determines which union contract your employees will fall under (if the contract for the industry has been 'nationalised', which many of them have) and what continuing education taxes you must pay (as some industries impose a special tax in addition to the standard one). Some vendors sell or extend credit only to customers with certain *NAF* codes.

The code must be printed on business documents along with your *SIREN* or *SIRET*. Fortunately, changing *NAF* codes isn't difficult. You write to INSEE requesting a change in code (it's usually safest to tell them which one you want) and they will ask you for documents backing up your description of your business activities.

CREATING A LIMITED COMPANY

Creating a company involves the completion of formalities in addition to those listed above. These are outlined below, but you're strongly recommended to seek professional advice.

- If the partners or associates are contributing initial capital to the company in any form other than cash (i.e. assets) and if **either** the value of the assets contributed is over €7,500 **or** the assets make up more than half the company's capital, these must be valued by an assessor called a *commissaire aux apports*.

- Monetary capital used to set up the company must be deposited in a blocked account, with a bank or *notaire*, until the company registration is complete. A receipt for the blocked funds must be added to the list of documents required for company registration (see page 136).

- Articles of incorporation (*statuts*) must be drafted. This is an important step and can have legal and financial consequences. It also influences the social security status of the director(s). It's therefore advisable to have the articles drawn up by a lawyer, *notaire* or accountant. This is particularly important if you want anything unusual in your articles, or if you're using one of the more flexible business forms (e.g. an *SAS*). Many forms of business don't allow for much 'creativity', and if you include terms in your articles that are contrary to the relevant regulations, they will be considered null and void. For example, certain types of decision must be approved unanimously, irrespective of what's stated in your articles. However, standard articles are available from specialist bookshops, and online (e.g. 🖳 www.lentreprise.com/creation or 🖳 www.netpme.fr).

- You must designate one or more directors. They can be named in the articles of incorporation or in a separate document. (The latter option obviates having to redraft the articles if there's a change of director – see below.) The designation should specify the directors' term of office, the extent of their powers and remuneration, and preferably the process by which they're to be appointed and can be replaced or dismissed.

- You must deposit four signed, dated copies of the articles of incorporation at your local tax office within a month of their signature.

Until a company's registration is complete, it has no legal existence and cannot therefore enter into contracts or make purchases. However, the future directors may need to make advance purchases (of equipment or materials), and sign rental or leasing contracts. To enable these costs to be charged to the company, directors should sign payments with the following wording: *'au nom et pour le compte de la société* [company name] *en cours de formation'*. The relevant bills and contracts should be appended to the company's articles of incorporation. When the company comes into being, it then assumes responsibility for the costs and obligations. However, it's sometimes possible in the articles of incorporation to give authority to the managing director-to-be to conduct business in the name of the company in advance of registration, which eliminates the need to append the initial expenditures to the articles of incorporation later on.

All changes to the articles cost additional registration fees and you must sometimes also have the changes stamped and approved at the tax office – for a per-page fee.

TAKING OVER A BUSINESS

Your decision whether to start a new business or take over an existing one may be partly determined by the premises you intend to run the business from, which may be available only with an existing business infrastructure or with a lease that restricts the activity you may carry out (see **Premises** on page 148). It's more common for French people to take over an existing business than it is for Britons to do so in the UK, for example, and in some ways (not least the paperwork involved), it's much easier to take over a business than to start from scratch and it may be less of a risk, although there are possible disadvantages as well. The French aren't in a habit of selling successful businesses – even to make a profit – and businesses are usually passed down from generation to generation; if a business is for sale, it may be because it has been unsuccessful or, worse, has liabilities or debts.

If you plan to buy a business, you should therefore obtain an independent valuation (or two) and seek unbiased professional advice, e.g. from a local bank manager or accountant, particularly regarding your rights and obligations on taking over the business.

If you're taking over an existing and operating company, French labour law compels you to respect existing employment contracts (which isn't a bad thing if you require help, as experienced staff are priceless). However, you may not be compelled to employ them if you cannot afford it. (The decision may depend on the level of unemployment in the area.)

If you want to own a licensed business (e.g. butcher's, hairdresser's or pharmacy), you must, of course, hold a qualification in the profession (see **Qualifications** on page 34).

Fonds de Commerce & Cession de Bail

When a business is for sale in France, there are often separate prices for the intangible assets of the business, such as the clientele, contracts, trademarks and patents, and leasehold rights, which are called the *fonds de commerce* (or simply *fonds*) and the property or 'walls' (*murs*), e.g. the building housing a hotel or restaurant business, which may be bought or rented (see **Costs** on page 139). Other tangible assets of a business, such as equipment and tools, stock and work in progress, are usually excluded from a sale or subject to separate purchase.

The sale of a business is, in general, a transfer of assets but not liabilities, although you're free to negotiate the liquidation of liabilities with the vendor. The seller is legally bound to disclose all liabilities, but he isn't required to provide any guarantees or warranties to the purchaser. Certain contracts, e.g. employment contracts (and therefore existing staff), insurance policies and lease agreements, are automatically transferred with the sale of *fonds*, whereas others, e.g. franchises, licences and supply agreements, aren't.

Assessing the value of a *fonds de commerce* is a difficult process, often involving more art than science, but it's **essential** to obtain at least one professional valuation and to check the value yourself. (French property agents may be able to give you a more accurate idea of the value of a *fonds* than a foreign agent.) As with business purchases anywhere in the world, the key is thorough research.

Whereas the value of the building is usually easily comparable with other buildings in the area, the value of the business may be impossible to relate to anything and you must make your own assessment of whether it's reasonable or not. If not, it may be worth negotiating rather than simply looking elsewhere. A guide to assessing the value of a business can be found on the website of the magazine *ICF l'Argus des Commerces* (🖳 www.cession-commerce.fr). Click on '*Calculez la valeur de votre commerce*' and answer the questions.

Premises may be let without a *fonds de commerce*, but with a lease (*bail*), which allows you to operate a certain type or types of business. (This is common with retail premises, such as shops.) The lease is said to be 'yielded' to you (*cédé*); advertisements often state '*cession de bail*', indicating that the lease is for sale. Buying a lease is usually cheaper than a *fonds de commerce*, as the premises (known in this case as a *local*) usually contains no equipment or stock and there may be no existing or even recent clientele. The value of a *bail* is therefore even more difficult to assess than that of a *fonds de commerce*, but the same basic 'rules' apply. (See also **Checks** on page 144.)

Taxes

The vendor of a business is liable for certain transfer taxes and other costs (*droits de mutation*), and he may 'include' these in the selling price. Check not only what taxes and fees he has added but whether these are indeed payable, as there are exemptions for certain types of transfer (see **Costs** on page 174).

Finding a Business

There are many ways of finding businesses for sale, including the following:

- **Association des Cédants et Repreneurs d'Affaires** – This association, consisting of around 20 'regional' delegations and 100 vounteers, aims to find people to take over businesses that would otherwise cease trading and organises courses and training in business take-over and management; contact the association at 18 rue de Turbigo, 75002 Paris (☎ 01 40 26 74 16, 💻 www.cra.asso.fr).

- **Chambers of Commerce** – Local and regional *chambres de commerce et d'industrie* (*CCI*) are excellent sources of information and operate a regional network called Bureaux de Rapprochement d'Entreprise (BRE) to bring together sellers and prospective buyers. You can find the address and contact numbers for your local chamber by contacting the Assemblée des Chambres Françaises de Commerce et d'Industrie (ACFCI, 45 avenue d'Iéna, 75116 Paris (☎ 01 40 69 37 00) or by looking under '*Annuaire*' on the ACFCI website (💻 www.acfci.fr). The ACFCI also publishes newsletters listing the various opportunities. Local *chambres des métiers* also have lists of businesses to take over.

- **Estate Agents** – Estate agents often handle business premises, and some agents offer a property search service. Look for agents calling themselves *agents commerciaux* or *spécialistes de fonds de commerce*, who generally handle rentals rather than sales, as few *agents immobiliers* sell commercial premises.

- **Fieldwork** – As property owners generally like to avoid incurring agency fees and even paying for advertisements, many businesses are 'advertised' by means of signs reading '*A Vendre*' or '*Bail à Céder*'.

- **Internet** – You can search for business for sale under *bails à céder* (if you're looking to buy a lease), *commerces* or *entreprises à vendre*, *fonds de commerce*, *immobiliers commerciaux* or *d'entreprise* or similar phrases, adding such words as *affaire* (business), *acquisition* (purchase) and *vente* (sale).

- **Networking** – As with finding a job, your best resource is the people you know – or at least local people, whom you should ask about businesses and premises for sale.

- **Notaires** – Many *notaires* have details of businesses for sale in their area. This is because many small businesses have to be sold when the owner dies and none of his children or other heirs are qualified, able or willing to take it over, although they may inherit the business premises.

- **Publications** – Advertisements for businesses can be found in specialist property publications such as *Bureaux & Commerces* (published monthly by De Particulier à Particulier, 40 rue du Docteur-Roux, 75724 Paris Cedex 15 (☎ 01 40 56 35 35, 💻 www.bureaux-commerces.com or 💻 www.pap.fr), which costs around €3; the relevant business journal; many French newspapers and magazines, particularly *La Centrale des Particuliers*, *Défis*, *ICF l'Argus des Commerces*, *L'Indicateur de l'Entreprise* and local papers; English-language publications such as *French Property News* and *Living France* (see **Appendix B**). A few French businesses are advertised for sale in British publications such as *Dalton's Weekly* and *Exchange & Mart*. The Agence Pour la Création d'Entreprises (APCE, 142 rue du Bac, 75007 Paris, ☎ 01 42 18 58 80, 💻 www.apce.com) publishes a bimonthly bulletin, listing business opportunities.

Checks

In addition to the usual checks you should make before buying or renting a property (detailed in **Buying a Home in France** by Survival Books – see page 419), there are certain things you should check (or preferably have checked by a lawyer experienced in commercial property transactions) before buying (or even renting) a business premises.

You can start by checking the published information on the company's finances (turnover, profit, etc.), which can be done online. Go to the information site of Les Greffes des Tribunaux de Commerce (🖥 www.infogreffe.fr) and enter the company's details (name or *SIREN*). You must study the articles of incorporation as well as the financial statements and all the books and records of the company you're interested in buying. You should ask to see a current business certificate (see **Certification** on page 34) and any other relevant authorisations. Verify turnover figures and talk to clients, customers, suppliers, bankers, landlords and other local people to make sure you know as much as you can about the business and its financial situation as well as the professional and personal relationships on which its success depends.

Check that no one is objecting to the sale of the business. Just as anyone may object to an application for planning permission, anyone may object to the sale or transfer of a business. Objections can be lodged at any time from the moment a business is offered for sale until ten days after the signing of the sale contract. Your lawyer should find out whether there are any legitimate objections, e.g. by a family member who should have inherited all or part of the business or its premises or by a supplier who's owed money.

Make sure the business you're buying is debt-free, including outstanding taxes or social security contributions and outstanding payments for equipment or stock. You can check whether any equipment or installation is subject to a lien (*nantissement*) or other debts (*endettement*) on the Greffes des Tribunaux site (see above).

You must also check that there are no 'hidden vices' (*vice caché*), which could compromise your use of the premises. For example, you may be restricted as to exterior renovation or alteration to a building, particularly if it's a listed building (*monument historique*), even to the extent of painting it a different colour or putting up a new sign.

Procedure

The procedure for buying a business is essentially the same as for starting a business (see page 136), coupled with that for buying or renting property (covered in *Buying a Home in France* by Survival Books – see page 419). There are, however, a few steps that are different, and these partly depend upon the type of business, its legal form and how the parties involved in the purchase want to handle the business.

If the business is owned by more than one person, the sale must be carried out in accordance with the procedure outlined in the articles of incorporation. In some forms of business, the shareholders or partners must approve (often unanimously) the sale of any ownership interest to an outsider and this, of course, must be documented (usually through the minutes of a special shareholders' meeting).

Once any necessary agreement has been obtained, a sale document must be drawn up. This can be done by a *notaire* (who charges a fee, usually calculated as a percentage of the selling price) or can be done by the parties involved, with or without the assistance of lawyer or accountant. (There are sample sale documents in many of the business books and publications aimed at small businesses.)

If you're buying a lease rather than the freehold, the sale contract may be called a *compromis de cession* rather than a *compromis de vente*; what you're actually buying is the right to the lease (*droit au bail*). As with all property purchase contracts, there is a deadline by which you must pay the full agreed price; if you don't, the *fonds de commerce* may revert to the seller.

You may wish to have clauses included in the contract forbidding the vendor (and his immediate relatives) from starting or investing in a similar business in the area or from using or selling the business's database, for example. **As a *notaire*'s function is merely to ensure that the government gets the taxes due to it and not to protect the interests of the buyer or the seller, you should have a contract checked by a legal expert before signing anything.**

The sale must then be registered with the tax office, which involves the payment of transfer tax on the shares – normally 2 to 4 per cent depending on the nature of the shares and how long the seller has held them.

The appropriate changes to the articles of incorporation must be drafted and approved by the new owner(s) and the revised articles registered with the RNCS, along with the change of management, which also must be published in one of the official newspapers and the *BODACC* (see **Announcement** on page 137), at the purchaser's expense. Any other changes occasioned by the sale (e.g. change of company name or address, change of *statut* of the director) should be registered at the same time, as everything can usually be done for a single fee (around €200).

The relevant *CFE* (see page 137) is a good source of information about the details of transferring business ownership and can often help in securing and filing the forms – provided you've paid your 'help' fee!

OTHER REQUIREMENTS

Before you can start trading, you may need to fulfil other requirements or undertake other procedures, such as the following. In addition to those detailed below, non-EU nationals require a licence (*carte de commerçant étranger*) to start a business in France (see page 30), and no commitments should be made until permission has been granted.

Management Courses

In addition to compulsory management courses for entrepreneurs (see page 106), optional courses are available for creators of commercial and industrial businesses. Both *CGAs* (see page 198) and the relevant *CFE* offer courses, seminars and booklets on running a company. Local business associations connected with the town, region or department hold meetings and seminars for reasonable costs. Employers' organisations and some unions also run training courses – particularly on accounting and payroll matters. If you're in an industry covered by a compulsory employee agreement, the training might be free. The Mouvement des Entreprises de France (MEDEF, ▣ www.medef.fr) publishes a directory of professional organisations. On the website, highlight '*Le réseau*' and click on '*MEDEF territoriaux*' for a list of offices where you can consult the directory.

Accounting

You shouldn't start a business until you have the accounting infrastructure in place, including an accountant and banking facilities. There are strict laws regarding accounting records, which, along with all marketing material, must be in French (mostly for the convenience of VAT auditors), so it's important to employ a French-qualified accountant (*expert comptable*) to do your books, although you shouldn't expect him to be interested in reducing your social security charges and you should question costs that appear too high. See **Accounting** on page 221.

You're also highly recommended to join a *centre de gestion agréé* (*CGA* – see page 198), which for a small annual membership fee will ensure that your accounts are *comme il faut*. Members qualify for tax credits and there are accountants who offer their services to *CGA* members for somewhat reduced fees.

Health & Safety

Employers are required to abide by certain regulations designed to ensure the health and safety of their staff, most of which are included in the *Code du Travail* (see page 153) or the relevant collective agreements. Businesses with over nine employees (and, from 1st January 2006 all other businesses) must develop a risk assessment plan, i.e. an evaluation of the risks to employees in the business, and programmes covering relevant procedures, such as the training of staff in the use of equipment and safety procedures, the regular inspection, maintenance and upgrading of equipment, and the installation of safety systems such as sprinklers and alarms. This information must be submitted to the company doctor (see below) once a year, and he must draw up the assessment, which must be sent to your insurer. The assessment can affect not only your insurance premiums, but also the likelihood of the insurance company honouring claims! **If you file a claim that relates to a risk you haven't disclosed, an insurance company can refuse payment.**

Company Doctor

Most businesses must have a company doctor (*médecin du travail*), who may in fact work for a number of companies. The company doctor, who's supposed to be specially trained to deal with work-related health matters, conducts pre-employment and biannual medical examinations (see below).

Medical Examinations

Most French employers require prospective employees to have a pre-employment medical examination performed by the company doctor (see above), who's certified to evaluate his fitness for the job for which he's to be hired. An offer of employment is usually subject to a prospective employee being given a clean bill of health. However, you may decide that this is required only for employees over a certain age (e.g. 40) or for employees in certain jobs, e.g. where good health is of paramount importance for safety reasons.

In addition to requiring employees to undergo a medical examination before taking up employment, you may insist that they be examined by the company doctor every two years (annual examinations are no longer required) to confirm their continued fitness for the job; you may also request an examination at any time if there's a doubt about an employee's physical condition. Examinations normally take only around 15 minutes.

Special examinations are scheduled for employees returning to work after certain types of leave (e.g. maternity leave or following an accident or illness) to assess their fitness to return to work.

PREMISES

Your business premises can be part of your home or a separate property, which you may rent or own.

Your Home

If you start a business, you're legally entitled to run it from your home for the first two years. If you're in rented accommodation or a community property, you must notify your landlord and/or syndicate, but they cannot prevent you from running a business unless it involves a public safety or nuisance factor (e.g. you must have regular deliveries or hordes of customers visiting your home – particularly in an area with little or no parking).

After the first two years, you must have a commercial lease for the business. If you wish to continue running it from your home, you must have the space you're using for the business declared 'business property' by the *préfecture*, which involves drawing up a commercial lease with yourself and paying yourself rent. This payment is deductible from your business profit, but must be declared on your personal income tax return. In proportion to the size of the 'business property', you will also pay less *taxe foncière*, but must pay *taxe professionelle* (see page 204). Oddly, there's no stipulation as to how much rent you must pay, so you should take advice as to whether it's to your advantage to pay a small or large amount.

Rent or Buy?

If possible, it's best to purchase a business with the building, particularly if you need to raise a loan. However, it's rare to find business premises for sale or rent 'empty' (*local vide* or *locaux vides*), i.e. without an existing business activity or 'going concern' (*fonds de commerce* – see page 142) or, in the case of rented premises, without a lease specifying the type of business that may be run. **Even if you do find 'empty' premises, there may be restrictions on the type of business you can set up – for example, restaurants, cafes and fast food outlets are generally unpopular with landlords and town councils – so you should always check whether you will be allowed to run your intended business before entering negotiations to purchase or rent empty premises.** Premises in which you may (theoretically) run any business may be advertised with the words *'toute activité possible'* or *'sans cession de bail'* (or simply *'sans cession'*) or *'sans pas de porte'*, but you must still check whether there really are no restrictions.

If a business is advertised for sale, the premises may also be for sale or they may only be to let. If they're for sale, the advertisement may say *'fonds et murs'* or *'toute propriété'* or there may be two prices, one for the *fonds* and one for the *murs*. The purchase of the premises may be optional, in which case there may be a purchase price and a monthly rental price, or a rental price and a phrase such as *'possibilité achat des murs'*, in which case the purchase price is likely to be negotiable (which it is anyway, of course!).

If the premises are for rent, you must usually buy a lease (*bail*), which may cost almost as much as the freehold and usually restricts the business activity you may undertake there. The first thing you should check before purchasing a lease is that the lease permits you to start a new business, even in a related field, as this isn't always the case. You should also check what use the owner intends to put the rest of the building to. In the case of a shop, for example, there may be a flat above or behind it, which may continue to be occupied by the previous owner or a relative – a potential nightmare!

In addition to the cost of the lease or *fonds de commerce*, you must pay rent (*loyer*). In advertisements, a monthly rental price may be stated. In many cases, however, the rental price isn't stated: an advertisement may state simply *'faible loyer'* or *'loyer raisonnable'* (low or reasonable rent). In other cases, there's no mention of a rental price at all. This doesn't mean that the premises are rent-free, as there's **always** a rent to be paid, but you must contact the vendor or the agent to find out how much it is.

Renting

It's possible to rent business premises, although you may not have the same legal protection as a private lessor and it's essential to seek expert legal advice before signing an agreement or lease, which must contain a right to rent clause to ensure the future value of the business.

Renting business premises is normally done on a nine-year lease, with negotiable changes at three-year intervals. Standard commercial leases are available from many stationery shops; you simply fill in the blanks. These are particularly handy when drawing up a lease with yourself (see **Your Home** above), but also useful for finding out what to expect when renting premises.

Buying

You can obtain a mortgage of up to 80 per cent on a commercial property, but you must fund the business yourself. The procedure for buying business premises is essentially the same as for buying private property in France. This is generally a straightforward process, although there are certain precautions to be taken and regulations to be observed. For details of buying property in France, obtain a copy of the latest edition of *Buying a Home in France* (see page 419).

Commercial property in France is generally handed down from generation to generation, as it's a popular investment for people approaching retirement age, being seen as a fairly secure source of income. This means that commercial property for sale may be scarce (see also **Costs** on page 139).

Société Civile Immobilière

It's fairly common practice for a business to create a *société civile immobilière (SCI)* for its property holdings, which means that the building appears on its books as an 'investment' in a company (the *SCI*) at the net of the value of the building less any outstanding financing, and the business is in effect leasing the building from the *SCI*. The business then deducts nominal 'rent' payments for use of the building, and any mortgage payments are handled through the *SCI*.

Alternatively, the business owner may set up the *SCI* himself so that he can keep the building when he sells the business. Or a group of small businesses can get together to buy a building and form an *SCI* to deal with the funding. A *notaire* can set up an *SCI* for you.

Finding Premises

Sources of business premises are generally the same as those for businesses themselves (see **Finding a Business** on page 143), as it's unusual to find empty commercial property.

Costs

As will be seen from the figures below, the cost of business premises varies enormously, not only according to whether you're buying or renting only the premises, whether you're buying an existing business plus the premises or buying a business and renting the premises, or buying the right to a lease and renting a premises, but also according to the size, condition and (above all) location of the premises. The different purchase options are explained above (see **Fonds de Commerce & Cession de Bail** on page 142).

Premises Only

Commercial premises are rarely sold 'empty' (*local vide*), although you may find premises to let, which usually cost between €2 and €10 per m^2 per month.

Premises & Lease

The cost of a lease (*bail*) can be between €500 and €2,000 (€650–4,000 or more in Paris) per m^2. In addition, you must then pay a monthly rental (*loyer*) for the use of the premises, which can be from €4 to €25 per m^2 (€10–30 in Paris).

Premises & Business

The cost of a business or 'going concern' (*fonds de commerce*) varies between around
€300 and €2,000 per m² (€650–3,500 in Paris and up to €6,500 per m² in the most
salubrious areas) according to a number of factors (see **Fonds de Commerce &
Cession de Bail** on page 142). Sometimes the building itself (*murs*) is included in the
price, although rarely in Paris. Otherwise, you must rent the premises, which can
cost between €5 and €150 per m² per month (€25–400 in Paris).

Equipment & Stock

Business equipment (*matériel*) and stock (*marchandises*) are usually sold separately
and aren't included in the price of the premises or the *fonds de commerce*.

INSURANCE

It's essential that your business is properly insured. This section covers the
compulsory insurances for various types of business, and also looks at other
insurances relevant to businesses and the self-employed.

Insurers have networks of branch offices in every town, and arranging insurance
is easier face to face than by telephone, even if your French is fluent. You can also
arrange insurance over the internet. Many insurers offer 'multi-risk' (*multirisques*)
policies aimed at various types of business (e.g. shops, restaurants) which cover all
the relevant risks. Insurance premiums are generally reasonable, but, as always, it
pays to shop around.

In order to establish the insurance your business needs, take an 'inventory' of the
risks to which it's exposed, which usually fall into the following categories:

● Loss of or damage to physical possessions (e.g. fire, breakage or theft);
● Liability due to the responsibilities of the business for its activities (e.g. products
  sold or work done by the business);
● Risks related to employees (e.g. illness, accidents and death);
● Bankruptcy or other cessation of business.

Then evaluate each type of risk for all possible financial consequences and not only
ensure that you're insured against them, but also set up policies within the company
to prevent losses or limit damage (see **Health & Safety** on page 147).

Premises

If you operate business premises, you should insure both the building and its
contents, although neither is obligatory. It's preferable to choose a multi-risk policy
that also covers injury or damage to property sustained by third parties whilst on
your premises. Premises insurance is known as *assurance des locaux*. If you work from
home, make sure your household insurer is notified and that the policy has sufficient

cover for your computers, etc. Often the same company or insurance agent who handles your home insurance can offer premises cover for your business, whether or not it's located in your home.

Public Liability

Everyone living in France must be insured for public liability (*responsabilité civile*). This is often included in household insurance policies, but if you're running a business from home, you must insure your business activity separately, as business activities aren't covered by personal policies.

Director's Liability

The managing director of most companies is responsible for any breaches of corporate responsibility and can have his personal assets seized even if his business is a limited liability company. This, of course, is also the case in an unlimited liability business. A policy covering *responsabilité personnelle du dirigeant* (director's personal responsibility) protects you from ruin if you're sued personally for mistakes made by your company or business or if it doesn't fulfil its legal obligations in any way.

Car Insurance

Make sure your car insurance covers business use if you will be using your car for business purposes and that you have separate cover for any vehicles owned by the business. Basic car insurance is, of course, compulsory.

Other Insurance

Other compulsory insurance includes a ten-year guarantee (*garantie décennale*) on all building work for companies involved in construction or renovation. Other optional insurance includes the following:

- Policies called *assurance de matériel professionnel* are available to cover tools and machinery.

- *Assurance perte d'exploitation* covers your business if you're prevented from operating, for example by a fire or an equipment breakdown. It will pay your employees' salaries and other fixed costs.

- *Protection juridique* covers legal costs.

- Although your social security contributions cover you for treatment in the case of illness or accident, they won't normally compensate you for loss of earnings resulting from these. There are various policies that will do so; any insurance broker will be pleased to explain the options to you. You may also wish to take out life assurance or insurance.

See also **Pensions** on page 218.

EMPLOYING STAFF

Hiring employees shouldn't be taken lightly in France and must be taken into account before starting a business. There are around 1.4 million companies in France without employees – and not without reason, as many successful small businesses become less so as soon as they start to recruit!

You must enter into a contract under French labour law and employees enjoy extensive rights. It's also very expensive to hire employees: in addition to salaries, you must pay a 13th month's salary (see page 158), five weeks' paid annual holiday (see page 166) and 40 to 60 per cent in social security contributions (see page 210), although there are reductions for hiring certain categories of unemployed people (see **Incentives** on page 155).

There are tax 'holidays' for limited periods for newly formed companies, particularly regarding the first employee. During their first two years' trading, most new businesses are required to pay only around 10 per cent of their first employee's wages in social security contributions. Note, however, that the managing director's spouse doesn't count as a first employee! Neither does a shareholder in the company (or the spouse of a shareholder).

Regulations & Employee Rights

General rules and regulations governing the employment of staff are set out in the French Labour Code (*Code du Travail*) as well as collective agreements (*conventions collectives de travail*); specific rules are contained in an individual employee's contract (*contrat de travail*) and the employer's in-house rules and regulations (*règlements intérieurs/règlements de travail*).

Employees have extensive rights under the French Labour Code. The Code details the minimum conditions of employment, including working hours, overtime payments, holidays, trial and notice periods, dismissal conditions, health and safety regulations, and trade union rights. The French Labour Code is described in detail in a number of books, including the *Code du Travail* (VO Editions), and is available online at the Legifrance website (🖳 www.legifrance.gouv.fr).

Collective agreements (*conventions collectives*) are negotiated between industry associations (*syndicats*) and employers' associations in many industries. These specify the rights and obligations of employees and employers in a particular industry or occupation and cover around 75 per cent of the workforce. Agreements specify minimum wage levels for each employment category in a particular industry or company. If an employer doesn't abide by the laws or the regulations in a particular industry, employees can report him to the works council or work syndicates (see **Employee Representation** on page 159). Where there's no works council or employee delegation, the case is heard before an industrial tribunal (*conseil de prud'hommes*) comprising employer and syndicate representatives (elected by the workforce). When an employee is wrongfully dismissed, he's awarded damages based on his length of service – and you must pay them!

Employment courts, trade unions and employee representatives jointly ensure that employment laws are respected, and regulations are supervised by local work inspectors (*inspecteur du travail*) and the Direction Départmentale du Travail et de l'Emploi et de la Formation Professionnelle (DDTEFP). Inspectors aren't merely bloodhounds who check up on you and impose fines for breaches of the law, they're also consultants and can provide information and advice on employer (and employee) rights and obligations; they can be contacted via the DDTEFP. (One of your obligations is to display the name and contact number of your *inspecteur*!)

Employment laws cannot be altered or nullified by private agreements. In general, French law forbids discrimination by employers on the basis of sex, religion, race, age, sexual preference, physical appearance or name, and there are specific rules regarding equal job opportunities for men and women. In 2002, a law was introduced forbidding 'moral harassment'.

It's some consolation for employers that French courts are hesitant to interfere with hiring practices. It's virtually impossible to bring a discrimination action against an employer for not hiring someone. Although discrimination on the job is severely dealt with in the courts, the courts won't normally interfere with the employer's free choice of candidates.

Salaried foreigners are employed under the same working conditions as French citizens, although there are different rules for certain categories of employee, e.g. directors, managers and factory workers. Part-time employees are entitled to the same rights and benefits (on a pro rata basis) as full-time employees.

Recruiting

You're required to notify the government employment service, the Agence Nationale Pour l'Emploi (ANPE, 19 boulevard Gambetta, 92136 Issy-les-Moulineaux, ☎ 01 46 45 64 85 or 08 10 80 58 05, 🖳 www.anpe.fr), which has some 600 offices throughout France, of all job vacancies, but you're generally free to recruit staff as you wish. You can, of course, make use of the services of ANPE or you can place job advertisements in newspapers, on the internet and even on television and radio. (There's a cable/satellite channel, *Demain*, devoted to career information and job opportunities.) But most recruiting in France is done on a personal 'word-of-mouth' basis, so local networking should be an essential part of your early business plan. Whichever method you use, you must be **absolutely sure** you're engaging the right person, as firing employees is difficult and normally expensive (see **Dismissal & Redundancy** on page 170). The hiring process (*embauche*) in France can take several months from initial application to job offer and may involve several repeat visits for interviews, testing, etc. You should take full advantage of this practice and not attempt to short-cut the system, which could be a costly error.

A recruit must be declared to URSSAF (see page 211) using a *document unique d'embauche* (*DUE*), which must be submitted not more than a week before the employee is due to start work. This is known as the *déclaration préalable à l'embauche* (*DPAE*), which must be acknowledged by URSSAF before employment can start. URSSAF pass the *DUE* on to the organisations responsible for registering the employee with social security (health, unemployment and pension benefits, for which you will be told which fund you must contribute to on behalf of your new employee – see **Pensions** on page 218) and for health and safety (see **Medical**

Examinations on page 147). The only time you might need to contact any of these organisations directly is if there's a change in status of one of your employees, e.g. you promote him from 'rank and file' to management, in which case his state pension, for example, would be administered by AGIRC instead of ARRCO (see **Pensions** on page 218). Details of the *DUE* can be found on URSSAF's dedicated website (🖳 www1.due.urssaf.fr).

Incentives

There are various incentives for employing certain categories of people, including those listed below. Categories and incentives vary from area to area, the latter being most generous in regeneration zones (*zones de redynamisation*). Details of those that apply in your area are available from local offices of ANPE or the Direction Départementale du Travail, de l'Emploi et de la Formation Professionnelle (DDTEFP). Further general information about recruitment incentives can be found on the government website 🖳 www.travail.gouv.fr.

- **Trainees** – People between 16 and 25 who are studying for a vocational qualification. You must give them a contract for between one and three years (subject to a two-month trial period) and pay them between 25 and 78 per cent of the minimum wage (depending on their age and the number of years they've worked for you). You receive an annual payment of between €1,000 and €5,000 (depending on the location of your business) and you don't need to pay the trainee's social security contributions. The trainee must obviously be allowed time off for studying. This is known as a *contrat d'apprentissage*.

- **Long-term Unemployed** – People over 25 who have been unemployed for at least 18 months (12 months if they're over 50). You may give them a fixed term or indefinite contract (see **Contracts** on page 162) and pay them at least the minimum wage. You receive a payment of €330 per month for the first one or two years of employment (€500 per month for up to five years in the case of the over 50s), and the employee may be entitled to continue claiming unemployment benefit. This is known as a *contrat initiative emploi* (*CIE*) and is currently available only to certain types of business, including associations.

- **Young People** – Unemployed people between 16 and 23 who haven't passed their *baccalauréat*. You must give them an indefinite contract, although this can be for part-time work, and pay them at least the minimum wage. You receive a payment of between around €250 and €300 (depending on the employee's salary) per month for the first two years of employment and half of this for the third year. This is known as a *contrat jeunes en entreprise* (*CJE*).

Stagiaires

Many French employers 'hire' students on training courses (*stagiaires*). Nearly all training programmes, including those at university level, involve several periods of 'employment' – usually for a period of three to six weeks, but sometimes as long as six months. In the vast majority of cases, these short-term 'employees' aren't allowed to accept payment (or only a limited amount, e.g. the statutory minimum wage) and their social charges are covered by the school or university (or their parents). This is therefore a cheap (and legal) way of engaging staff for what amounts to a trial period, and many *stagiaires* are highly trained.

At certain times of the year, most small businesses receive telephone calls, letters and even emails from students who must arrange a course (*stage*) related to their study programme. It's up to the *stagiaire* to contact employers and to negotiate the functions they should do to fulfil the requirements of their school or university. Some schools and local governments send out appeals to small businesses to offer internships, summer jobs and other types of employment to various categories of young people.

There are some tax benefits to hiring *stagiaires* or apprentices (*apprentis*). Businesses often re-engage the same *stagiaire* for the whole of their training/school career and then make them an offer of permanent employment when they finish school. By the time they graduate, they know your business reasonably well and can start doing some 'real' work the moment you have to start paying them 'real' money!

Titre Emploi Entreprise

A new recruitment system called *Titre Emploi Entreprise* was pioneered in the catering trade and has recently been extended to other sectors, including butchery, car repairs, estate agency, hairdressing and other services. The system offers employers a simplified recruiting procedure for employees on a short-term (less than 100 days in a year) contract, known as *occasionnels*. Pay slips and social security contributions are handled by a centralised office, which provides a standard contract. Further information on this service can be obtained by telephone (☎ 08 10 12 38 33).

Representatives

Sales or distribution representatives may be engaged under a normal fixed or indefinite term contract or they may have the status of *voyageurs représentants placiers*, who have particular rights and obligations. If you intend to set up a sales or distribution network, you should take expert advice regarding the recruitment of representatives and consider alternatives, such as using intermediaries, brokers, commercial and commission agents, and franchisees.

Letters & CVs

For all recruitment, candidates submit a CV or résumé (the French use the same two terms), which often includes a photograph of the candidate. French CVs are relatively conservative, without the hype and hard-sell commonly found on American résumés, although the format is much the same. (Normally no more than one to two pages, reverse chronological order, but only a very brief description of job responsibilities if the job title doesn't make them obvious.) If your business is listed in any sort of local guide or even just in the yellow pages you will receive unsolicited applications from would-be *stagiaires* (see above) and from those looking for permanent employment. You don't need to respond to these, but a candidate might be just the person you're looking for. In France, most covering letters asking for employment (*lettres de motivation*) are handwritten (so that the employer can use a graphologist to determine the candidate's personal traits, as many do).

Salaries & Minimum Wages

For general information about salaries in France, see **Earnings** on page 22. It isn't common practice to specify a salary in a job advertisement and you should negotiate with a prospective candidate according to what you think he's worth! There has been a statutory minimum wage (*salaire minimum interprofessionnel de croissance*, known as *le SMIC*) since 1950. The cost of living index is reviewed annually and, when it rises by 2 per cent or more, the minimum wage is increased. (In practice, the minimum wage rises every year, usually in July and especially when elections are coming up!) The minimum wage is currently €7.61 per hour, equal to gross pay of €1,153.73 per month for 151.67 hours (the new standard under terms of the 35-hour working week), which equates to €859.29 net. In fact five different 'guaranteed monthly remunerations' (*garanties mensuelle de rémunération*) were created in 2003 as a result of the complex 35-hour-week legislation, but these are to be adjusted so that by 1st July 2005 there will be a *SMIC unique*.

The *SMIC* is lower for juveniles, those on special job-creation schemes and disabled employees. Unskilled workers (particularly women) are usually employed at or near the minimum wage, semi-skilled workers are usually paid 10 to 20 per cent more, and skilled workers 30 to 40 per cent more (often shown in job advertisements as '*SMIC + 10, 20, 30, 40%*'). Details of the legislation relating to minimum wages can be found on the INSEE website (🖥 www.insee.fr/fr/indicateur/smic.htm).

Although many employers pay certain employees, particularly seasonal workers in the farming and tourist industries, below the minimum wage, the French government is increasingly clamping down on this practice and penalties can be severe.

Salaries in many industries are decided by collective bargaining between employers and unions, regionally or nationally. When there's a collective agreement, employers must offer at least the minimum wage agreed. Agreements specify minimum wage levels for each position within main employment categories in a particular industry or company and often require bonus payments related to the age or qualifications of the employee or the length of time he has been with the company (*prime d'ancienneté*). This means that wage levels are effectively fixed. Cost of living increases for salaries above the *SMIC* aren't regulated by the government, although the collective agreement may provide for annual increases based on cost of living figures.

Unless you're paying the minimum wage, it may be advantageous to 'pay' part of your employees' salaries in kind, i.e. in the form of benefits and perks such as lunch and holiday vouchers, inexpensive or interest-free home and other loans, rent-free accommodation, travelling expenses (see **Expenses** on page 159), a non-contributory company pension, and a top-up health insurance policy, which may qualify you for tax deductions or allowances and mean that you have to pay less in social charges. The legalities of doing so are complicated and you should take expert advice on the subject.

An employee's salary (*salaire*) must be stated in his employment contract, and salary reviews, planned increases, cost of living rises (etc.) may also be included. Salaries may be stated in gross (*brut*) or net (*net*) terms and are usually paid monthly (see **Payment** below), although they may be quoted in contracts as hourly, monthly or annually. If a bonus is paid, such as a 13th or 14th month's salary (see below), this must also be stated employment contract. General points, such as the payment of a salary into a bank or post office account and the date of salary payments, are usually included in a separate list of employment conditions (*règlement intérieur*), which must be drawn up by any company with 20 or more employees.

Salaries in France must be reviewed once a year (usually at the end of the year), although employers aren't required by law to increase salaries that are above the minimum wage, even when the cost of living has increased. Salary increases usually take effect on 1st January.

Payment

Salaries above €3,000 per month must be paid by cheque or direct transfer (not cash), although it's never wise to pay salaries in cash, as it makes you subject to scrutiny by the tax authorities! You must issue employees with a pay slip (*bulletin de paie*) itemising their salary and deductions.

Computerised payroll programs are widely available, usually as part of a 'management software' package (*logiciel de gestion*), including accounting, payroll, and *gestion commerciale*, which combines purchasing, inventory, and accounts receivable and payable. Among the cheapest are *Ciel* and *ESB*, which can even be bought in hypermarkets; one of the most popular programs is *Sage* (not to be confused with the English software package of the same name, which is incompatible with French accounting practice!).

Payroll software in France must be capable of producing the electronic version of the approved year-end reporting forms (known as *DADS*). In fact, businesses with more than five employees are strongly encouraged to submit their year-end report electronically, which means you must keep your payroll software up to date. There are specific requirements as to what must be printed on a pay slip (including the collective agreement that applies, the employee's social security number and the number of hours worked, plus his holiday entitlement).

It's possible to use a payroll service, such as ADP (🖥 www.adp.com), which will take care of all this for you: prepare pay slips and make the bank transfers, then send you a report with totals for the various compulsory insurances and withholdings (see **Chapter 5**). Ciel also offers online payroll services (🖥 www.ciel.com) for around €15 per pay slip (cheaper if you agree to sign up for a year at a time): you enter the data and Ciel produces a printable pay slip and will direct transfer the pay into your employees' accounts.

13th Month's Salary & Bonuses

Most employers in France pay their employees a bonus month's salary in December, known as the 13th month's salary (*13ème mois*). A 13th month's salary isn't mandatory unless part of a collective agreement or when it's granted regularly in a particular sector, and it should be stated in your employees' contracts. In practice, however, its payment is almost universal and it's often taken for granted. In the first and last years of employment, an employee's 13th month's salary and other bonuses should be paid pro rata if he doesn't work a full calendar year.

Some companies also pay a 14th month's salary, usually in July before the summer holiday period, although this isn't recommended until you're earning millions! Where applicable, extra months' salary are guaranteed bonuses and aren't pegged to the company's performance (as with profit-sharing). In some cases, they're paid monthly rather than in a lump sum at the end or in the middle of the year. Senior and middle managers are often paid additional bonuses, perhaps linked to profits, equal to around 10 to 20 per cent of their annual salary.

Employees of many French companies are also entitled to participate in bonus schemes (some tied to productivity) and profit-sharing schemes (*participation des salariés aux résultats de l'entreprise* or *système d'intéressement aux bénéfices*), which must be provided by any company with over 50 employees. Companies are obliged to contribute a minimum amount of their total payroll towards training (see **Taxe d'Apprentissage & Formation Professionnelle** on page 205). Some employers also operate optional investment plans (*plan d'épargne d'entreprise*), where the company holds a portfolio of securities on behalf of its employees, and share option schemes (*options sur actions*). Employees on a term contract for a fixed period are normally paid an end-of-contract bonus (*indemnité de fin de contrat*) equal to 10 per cent of their salary, in addition to other bonuses.

Expenses

Expenses (*frais*) paid to employees may include travel costs from their home to work, usually consisting of a second-class rail season ticket or the equivalent amount in cash (paid monthly with their salary). In the Paris area, most employers pay 50 per cent of the cost of an employee's *carte orange*, a monthly public transport pass for the Paris underground, buses and suburban trains. Travelling expenses to and from a place of work are tax deductible. Companies without a restaurant or canteen may pay a lunch allowance or provide lunch vouchers (*chèques* or *tickets restaurant*) for use in local restaurants and some food shops.

Permitted expenses should be listed in your employment conditions. Expenses paid for travel on company business or for training and education may also be detailed in your employment conditions or listed in a separate document.

Employee Representation

All businesses with more than 11 employees must have a works council or a labour management committee comprising employee delegates (*délégués du personnel*), elected by staff for a two-year term, whose role is to act as liaison officers between individual employees and management, although employees are entitled to approach managers directly with problems or complaints. The number of delegates increases in proportion to the number of employees, up to a maximum of 50.

Delegates represent employees when they have questions or complaints for management concerning, for example, working conditions, job classification, wages, and the application of labour laws and regulations.

In companies with more than 50 employees, employee delegates must be elected to the board of directors and a works council or labour management committee (*comité d'entreprise/CE*) must be formed, comprising employees elected for two years by staff and union representatives. The committee must be consulted before any major decision concerning the company's management or organisation, although managers aren't obliged to take any notice of the committee's views! The company must pay an amount equal to 1 per cent of its payroll into the committee's fund, to be used at the discretion of the employees to provide benefits such as private day-care, holidays, theatre discounts, holiday gifts and a staff Christmas party. The committee must be provided with a room in which to meet. Some companies allocate extra funds to their *comité d'entreprise* as a means of attracting employees.

Companies with at least 50 employees must also set up a health, safety and working conditions committee (*comité d'hygiène, de sécurité et des conditions de travail/CHSCT*), which must be consulted in advance of any major decisions affecting these issues.

Companies with separate locations (e.g. factories or offices) employing over 50 employees must have a local labour management committee (*comité d'établissement*), with representatives of this committee sitting on a central labour management committee (*comité central d'entreprise*).

Taxes

Employees pay their own tax, as France has no pay-as-you-earn (PAYE) system. There has been periodic debate on the introduction of a PAYE system, but the idea has had little support, especially from employers, who are reluctant to 'do the government's work for it', and tax authority employees, who don't want to give the government any excuse for thinning their ranks! It's even unpopular with employees, who consider it a violation of their private lives for their employer to calculate how much tax should be withheld from their pay.

As an employer, you must of course declare and pay your own income tax (see page 196).

Social Security

As an employer, you must pay a significant portion of your employees' social security contributions, which can add up to 40 per cent or more of their salaries (see **Employers** on page 212).

Employees are entitled to sickness and maternity, work injury and invalidity, family allowance, unemployment, and old age, widow(er)'s and death benefits, most of which an employer must contribute to. However, employees must earn a minimum salary to qualify for certain benefits. For further details of employee entitlements, obtain a copy of *Living and Working in France* (Survival Books – see page 419). Employers normally continue to pay employees who are off sick for short periods, after which they become entitled to social security sickness benefit (see **Sick Leave** on page 168 and **Salary Insurance** below).

Employers are required to have various forms that must be completed in the event of an accident or injury. These can be obtained from your local URSSAF office (some are available on the URSSAF website, 🖳 www.urssaf.fr, but these may be for reference only and not for submitting claims). You must report a work accident to URSSAF within 48 hours. **Not having the relevant form isn't considered a valid excuse for not reporting an accident within the time limit.**

Supplementary Health Insurance

Many industries and professions have their own supplementary health insurance schemes (*assurance complémentaire maladie*, commonly known as a *mutuelle*) that pay the portion of medical bills not covered by social security (usually 20 or 30 per cent). Membership may be obligatory and contributions may be paid wholly by the employer or split in some proportion between you and your employees.

A medical examination may be necessary as a condition of membership of a company health, pension or life insurance scheme. Some companies insist on certain employees having regular health screening, particularly executives and senior managers.

Salary Insurance

Salary insurance (*assurance salaire*) pays employees' salaries during periods of sickness (*congé maladie*) or after accidents until state benefits take over (see **Sick Leave** on page 168). Some employers opt to pay their employees' full salaries for a limited period in cases of extended disability or illness, state benefits being paid to the employer rather than to the employee. A leaflet explaining state sickness benefits is available from CPAM offices (listed on 🖳 www.ameli.fr). Information is also available on the Service Public website (🖳 www.service-public.fr).

Supplementary Pensions

In many industries, supplementary pension schemes (known as *institutions de réparation*) are provided for employees earning above a certain salary, e.g. €1,800 per month. Almost every trade or occupation has its own scheme and in many companies it's obligatory for employees to join. For example, executives and managerial staff must contribute to a supplementary pension scheme called a *caisse de retraite des cadres ou des cadres supérieurs*. In addition to providing a supplementary pension, most schemes are allied to a complementary health insurance fund (see **Supplementary Health Insurance** above). Few French employers (other than large international companies) offer optional retirement schemes.

Managing directors (only) are entitled to buy a separate retirement plan – usually offered through an insurance company. It works rather like life insurance in that you make regular payments of a set amount, which accumulates in an investment account. When you retire, the balance accumulated is converted into a monthly retirement payment for your life and the life of your spouse. The payment is guaranteed for a certain number of years (usually 10 or 20) so that if you and your spouse die before the fund has paid out the guaranteed minimum, the balance goes to your heirs. Payments made into this retirement plan can be set against the company's revenue just like any of the required social security contributions. But, because this is an optional insurance (and you set the amount you pay in order to obtain the benefit you think you need), all payments are added to your revenue for the purpose of calculating the mandatory contributions (to URSSAF, etc.).

For further information about pensions, see page 218.

Life Insurance

French social security pays only around three months' salary or a maximum of around €6,000 to a widow or dependants. Many French companies provide free life insurance as an employment benefit, although it may be accident life insurance only (i.e. if you die as the result of an accident at work).

There's a difference between life insurance, called 'death insurance' in France (*assurance décès*), and life assurance (*assurance vie*). A life assurance policy is valid until you die and is essentially the same as a pension scheme, whereas a life insurance policy pays out only when you die. A life assurance policy benefits you, whereas a life insurance policy benefits your survivors.

New tax rules are removing many of the tax exemptions previously accorded to life insurance policies. In certain cases, however, premiums are tax-deductible and income from a life assurance policy may be exempt from tax provided the policy is allowed to mature for at least eight years and the fund is redeemed as a lump sum.

Many employers offer (it isn't obligatory) what's called a *prévoyance*. This covers death and incapacity (temporary and long-term). It's a standard coverage and the rate is set as a percentage of pay, just like social security contributions. For 2005, it's 2.138 per cent of the first *tranche* and 2.886 per cent of the second *tranche* (see page 210), split between employer and employee, the slightly larger part paid by the employer. As long as the *prévoyance* meets the set standards, it's fully deductible from the company's income and employees can deduct their portion from their taxable income.

Managing directors can buy *prévoyance* coverage under more or less the same conditions that apply to the extra retirement savings plan (see above). Rates vary according to how much coverage you buy (usually a certain 'salary' level) and the business pays the premiums and deducts them as running costs. The premiums paid are added to the MD's pay to determine the income on which his social security contributions are based.

Contracts

Legally, an offer of employment in France constitutes an employment contract (*contrat de travail/d'emploi*), although it's safer to offer a formal contract. Employers usually issue a formal contract stating such details as job title, position, salary, working hours, benefits, duties and responsibilities, and the duration of employment. Employment contracts usually contain a paragraph stating the date from which they take effect and to whom they apply. **Contracts must be carefully worded and you should take expert advice before drafting them.** For example, whether or not an employee can be required to work at a different location than the one he was hired for or to move if the company moves depends on the wording of his contract.

All employment contracts are subject to French labour law (see page 153), and references may be made to other regulations such as collective agreements. In some sectors, e.g. the catering trade, you must use a standard contract. Anything in contracts contrary to statutory provisions and unfavourable to an employee may be deemed null and void and any exclusion clauses must be 'clear and comprehensible'. All contracts must be written in French.

There are three main types of employment contract in France: a temporary contract, a fixed term contract and an indefinite term contract.

Temporary Contracts

A temporary contract (*contrat de travail temporaire*, also known as an *intérim*), which has no minimum or maximum duration, can be issued in specific circumstances only, as follows:

- For someone who's replacing a staff member who's temporarily absent (except if striking) and whose function is essential to the running of the business;

- For someone who's filling a post on an interim basis until a permanent staff member takes over;

- In the case of a temporary, unforeseen and otherwise unmanageable increase in the workload of existing staff;

- If the business is seasonal and requires additional workers at specific times of year (e.g. in agriculture for harvesting or in catering for peak periods);

- For workers in specific sectors (e.g. the theatre), where the use of temporary contracts is habitual.

Any other type of short-term contract is regarded as a fixed term contract (see below). A worker engaged on a temporary contract is known as a *salarié intérimaire* or simply *intérimaire*. Details of the obligations of employer and employee can be found on the website of the Monster Company (🖳 www.jobpilot.fr/content/service/channel/interim/pratique/contrat.html).

Fixed Term Contracts

A fixed term contract (*contrat à durée déterminée/CDD*) is, as the name suggests, a contract for a limited term. This is normally a maximum of 18 months, although it's limited to nine months if a post is due to be filled permanently and can be extended to two years if the post is due to be suppressed (there's no minimum term). A contract for longer than two years comes under the rules for indefinite term contracts, particularly regarding the dismissal of employees. A term contract must be in writing and for a fixed term or, in the case of temporary employment, for a specific purpose that must be stated in the contract. A term contract ends on the date specified, although it can be renewed twice for a term no longer than the original contract, provided it doesn't exceed two years in total.

A *CDD* can also be for replacement of a specific employee (usually someone on maternity leave) or a general replacement over the summer (to pick up the slack while various employees are off on holiday).

*CDD*s are strictly regulated, mainly because they're considered a contributing factor to the ever-increasing 'precariousness' of employment (*précarité d'emploi*). For example, the salary of an employee hired on a fixed term contract mustn't be less than that paid to a similarly qualified person employed in a permanent job. The employee has the right to an end of contract bonus (*indemnité de fin de contrat*) equal to 10 per cent of his salary, in addition to other agreed bonuses, although this doesn't always apply to seasonal employees.

Contracts for seasonal and temporary workers fall under the same rules as for a *CDD* contract. A *CDD* can be issued when a permanent employee is on leave (including maternity or sick leave), if there's a temporary increase in business, or at any time in the construction industry or for youth employment schemes.

Indefinite Term Contracts

An indefinite term contract (*contrat à durée indéterminée/CDI*) is the standard employment contract for permanent employees. Surprisingly, it isn't necessary for it to be in writing (unlike a term contract), although it's in your interests as well as the employee's to provide a written contract. A *CDI* often includes a trial period of one to three months (three months is usual), depending on collective agreements, before it becomes legal and binding on both parties.

The trial period doesn't really affect the binding nature of the other terms of the contract, just the initial period of time during which either side can terminate the contract without the severance benefits and notice periods taking effect. There can also be a lower rate of pay during the trial period, but the hours and other terms must be in force.

Working Hours

In 2000, France introduced a mandatory 35-hour working week for all large employers, and on 1st January 2002 this became effective for all employers, although the original legislation has since been subject to various amendments, which have 'softened' the obligations of employers and the limitations on employees to exceed a 35-hour week.

The objective of the 35-hour week scheme, referred to as the 'working hours reduction' programme (*réduction du temps de travail* or *RTT*), was to dramatically reduce unemployment by spreading the existing amount of work across more workers. Companies were encouraged to negotiate with their employees to find flexible ways to distribute the reduced working hours – including a seven-hour day, a four-and-a-half day week or even varying weeks within the same month. Some industries were allowed to recognise seasonal workload variations by granting extra time off during the off-season to compensate employees for longer hours necessary during peak times of year.

All these plans were considered somewhat radical disruptions of hard-won job security rights and privileges, and there was initially considerable employee discontent and numerous strikes and demonstrations. The government offered employers financial incentives such as a reduction in social security contributions and annual payments for new jobs created under this scheme.

Since the introduction of the 35-hour week, time keeping requirements have become much more complex and nearly all employees must be tracked to ensure that weekly, monthly and annual hours and days worked don't exceed the legal limits. For example, employers can establish mandatory break periods (*heures de repos*) to adapt working schedules to the new *RTT* rules. However, drinks or (if allowed) cigarettes can usually be taken at an employee's workplace at any time.

Flexi-time

Flexi-time (*horaire mobile/horaire flexible*) isn't common in French companies. A flexi-time system requires employees to be present between certain hours, known as the block time (*temps bloqué/heures de présence obligatoire*). For example from 08.30 to 11.30 and from 13.30 to 16.00. Employees may make up their required working hours by starting earlier than the required block time, reducing their lunch break or by working later. Smaller companies may allow employees to work as late as they like, provided they don't exceed the maximum permitted daily working hours.

Overtime

In principle, if an employee works more than 35 hours per week, he must be paid overtime or be given time off in lieu. Employees can be asked to do overtime, but cannot be compelled to do more than 130 hours per year, although this can be altered by collective agreements. The total hours worked per week mustn't exceed an average of 44 over 12 consecutive weeks or an absolute maximum of 48 hours per week.

The minimum legal pay for overtime is the normal rate plus 25 per cent for the first eight hours above the standard 35-hour week (i.e. up to 43) and plus 50 per cent for additional hours (i.e. above 43). Employees can be granted time off in lieu at overtime rates (i.e. 1.25 hours for each hour of overtime worked) instead of being paid. The working week for round-the-clock shift workers is limited to 25 hours, and night work and shift working is usually paid at higher rates as specified in collective agreements. Employees cannot be obliged to work on Sundays unless collective agreements state otherwise. If an employee agrees to work on a Sunday, normal overtime rates apply.

Salaried employees, particularly executives (*dirigeants*) and managers (cadres), aren't generally paid overtime, although this depends on their employment contracts. Most categories of manager are subject to *RTT* and maximum work time regulations, even though their work time may not be tracked on an hourly basis. For most managers, working time is measured in days per year and many managers have been accorded additional holiday time to meet *RTT* requirements.

Holidays & Leave

The French enjoy generous holiday and leave entitlements compared with employees in most other countries (and especially the US).

Annual Holidays

Under French labour law, an employee is entitled to 2.5 days' paid annual holiday (*congé/vacances*) for each full month he works. Annual holiday entitlement is calculated assuming that Saturdays are work days, a legacy of the time when the usual working week consisted of six days. After working for a full year, an employee is entitled to 30 days off (12 months x 2.5 days per month), which equals five weeks (including Saturdays).

Legally, holiday entitlement is earned over the course of a year that runs from 1st May to 30th April. So, if an employee starts work in January, by 1st May he will have earned ten days of holiday, which he can take during the subsequent year (i.e. starting 1st May). By the next 1st May, he should have accrued a full five weeks of holiday, which is available to him over the next 12 months.

Employers cannot include official French public holidays (see below) as annual holidays. Some collective agreements grant extra days off (usually from one to three) for long service, and many *RTT* agreements grant additional days off in lieu of overtime or to meet 35-hour working week regulations.

French employees are legally entitled to take up to four weeks' paid holiday in a single block between 1st May and 31st October (known as the *période légale*), unless business needs dictate otherwise (although other agreements are possible). However, if you oblige employees to take more than two days off outside the *période légale*, they're entitled to additional holiday: an extra day for three to six days outside the *période légale*; an extra two days for six or more days outside. Traditionally August was the sole month for summer holidays, many businesses closing for the whole month. However, the government has been trying to encourage companies to stagger their employees' holidays throughout the summer, and it's becoming more common for employees to take their main summer holiday in July. Almost half of French companies, particularly small businesses and local shops, close for the entire month of July or August. Even if you don't wish to close for such a long period, you may be obliged to – if, for example, your suppliers shut during this period and you cannot carry large enough stocks to keep your business going. If you do close during the summer, your employees are obliged to take their holiday at that time.

It's becoming increasingly popular for employees (and businesses) to take their summer holiday from 15th July to 15th August, which fits neatly between two national holidays (see below).

Many small businesses experience cash flow problems during July and August, when they may be unable to process incoming payments due to accounting staff holidays. On the other hand, this can give you a good reason for delaying payments to your creditors!

Before taking on staff, check what holidays they've booked or planned. If these fall within their trial period, you aren't obliged to allow them.

Public Holidays

Since 2004, there have been ten public holidays in France, which are listed below. Surprisingly, the only public holiday an employer in France is legally obliged to grant with pay is 1st May (irrespective of which day of the week it falls on). Nevertheless, most collective agreements allow paid holidays on several public holidays and it's usual for employers to grant all of them.

Officially, after the heatwave of 2003, which supposedly killed tens of thousands of people, Pentecost Monday was 'sacrificed' to save money to pay for . . . (it wasn't clear what). In typical French style, however, employers were offered a compromise: if you don't want to do away with the Pentecost holiday (e.g. because your business is too busy at that time), you can cancel any of the other holidays (except 1st May) instead.

Date	Holiday
1st January	New Year's Day (*Nouvel An/Jour de l'An*)
March or April	Easter Monday (*Lundi de Pâques*)
1st May	Labour Day (*Fête du Travail*)
8th May	VE Day (*Fête de la Libération/Victoire 1945/Anniversaire 1945*)
May	Ascension Day (*Ascension*) – the sixth Thursday after Easter
14th July	Bastille Day (*Fête Nationale*)
15th August	Assumption (*Fête de l'Assomption*)
1st November	All Saints' Day (*Toussaint*)
11th November	Armistice Day (*Fête de l'Armistice*)
25th December	Christmas Day (*Noël*)

When a public holiday falls on a Saturday or Sunday, you aren't obliged to offer another day (e.g. the previous Friday or following Monday) as a holiday instead. However, when a public holiday falls on a Tuesday or Thursday, you must decide whether to allow the day before or the day after (i.e. Monday or Friday respectively) as a holiday. This practice is called 'making a bridge' (*faire le pont*) and you may make yourself unpopular with your employees if you don't allow them to do so. (Some even expect to be allowed to bridge from a Wednesday to the previous or following weekend!) Depending on how the public holidays fall, you can gain or lose a significant number of days' work (e.g. in 2003, five holidays fell on a Tuesday or Thursday and only one at a weekend, creating a possible total of 13 days, including bridges, whereas in 2005 there's just one possible bridge and five days fall at weekends, making a total of only six – if you have ten staff, that's a difference of 70 days!).

Sick Leave

Employees in France don't receive a quota of sick days as in some countries (e.g. the US), and there's no limit to the amount of time an employee may take off work due to sickness or accidents, although they're entitled to social security benefits for long-term illnesses or disabilities. For this reason, many French employers take out salary insurance (see page 161).

An employee is normally required to notify you immediately of sickness or an accident that prevents him from working. He must also obtain a doctor's certificate (*arrêt de travail*) on the first day of his sickness; otherwise it counts as a day's holiday. If an employee is off sick, he may leave home only between 10.00 and 12.00 and between 16.00 and 18.00 (these restrictions are apparently to prevent moonlighting), and you're entitled to check that the employee is at home during the appropriate hours. You can also insist that an employee consult the work doctor (see page 147) to verify an illness.

Parental Leave

Female employees are entitled to extensive benefits with regard to pregnancy (*grossesse*) and confinement (couches) – and in most cases benefits extend to their partners. Maternity leave (*congé maternité*) is guaranteed for all women irrespective of their length of employment. The permitted leave period is 16 weeks, six weeks before birth (*congé prénatal*) and ten weeks after (*congé postnatal*); leave is extended for the third and subsequent children as well as for multiple births or caesarean section or other complications. A doctor may authorise additional time off for an employee, before or after the birth, in which case you must continue to pay her salary.

New fathers are entitled to paternity leave (*congé de paternité*) in addition to the three days off normally granted on the birth of a child (*congé de naissance* – see **Compassionate & Special Leave** below), provided they've been making health insurance contributions for at least ten months. The permitted leave period is 11 days for a single birth and 18 days for a multiple birth, which must be taken in a continuous period during the four months following the birth. An employee must notify you at least a month in advance of the days he wishes to take. Employees are entitled to continue to receive their normal salary (less social security contributions) up to a maximum of €2,353. Fathers are entitled to a further three months' unpaid paternity leave.

A mother and her husband have the right to an additional year of unpaid parental leave (*congé parental*), which applies equally to parents of adopted children, and employees also have the right to take paid time off work to care for a sick child. The regulations allow 12 days a year for each child, although a doctor's certificate (*fiche médicale pour enfant*) must be provided.

Provided an employee doesn't extend his leave beyond the permitted period, you're obliged to allow him to return to the same job at the same (or a higher) salary, taking into account general increases in wages and the cost of living. An employee's parental leave also counts towards his employment period for retirement purposes.

Compassionate & Special Leave

It's usual, and in many cases compulsory, to allow employees days off for 'family events' (*congé pour événements familiaux*). Compulsory leave includes marriage of the employee (four days), marriage of a child (one day), birth or adoption of a child (three days – see **Parental Leave** above), death of a spouse or child (two days), death of parents, in-laws, brother or sister (one day). These must be paid days off unless they take place during a holiday or other normal absence from work. Paid leave for other events (*congé pour convenance personnelle*), e.g. moving house, attending a family wedding, isn't compulsory. Grounds for compassionate or special leave are usually defined in collective agreements and may include leave to care for a seriously ill or disabled child (*congé de présence parentale*). A recent law entitled employees to up to three months' unpaid leave to care for a family member who's terminally ill, their employer being obliged to keep their position for them.

Employees who have worked for a company for at least three years are entitled to take a year's sabbatical, but you don't have to pay them!

Education & Training

Employee training (*formation* or *éducation continue*) is taken seriously in France, whether it's conducted in their own office or factory or elsewhere, and employers with ten or more employees must allocate a percentage of their gross payroll for employee education and training. If you want to attract the best employees, particularly those engaged in high-tech fields, you may need to allocate extra funds and provide superior training schemes (large companies often spend an amount equal to around 10 per cent of their payroll on training).

You must pay a training tax, which is calculated as a percentage of your total payroll. This is normally 1.5 per cent, but in some industries you must pay 2 or 2.3 per cent. Businesses with at least ten employees can claim some or all of the money they spend on training against this tax. If your business comes under a collective agreement, you can usually obtain training programmes and material cheaply from the relevant industry body. (These are theoretically what they charge you the tax for!)

Employees are normally entitled to paid vocational training after two years with a company employing over ten people or three years with a company with fewer than ten staff; they should apply at least two months in advance (four months if the training is to last more than six months). Staff are also entitled to unpaid time off for training (*congé individuel de formation*), although you may postpone this for up to nine months.

If your company has a works council (see page 159), you must present a training plan for its approval at the beginning of each year, outlining the types of training you intend to provide, who's eligible, and the amount of money to be spent. Training may include management seminars, special technical courses, language lessons or any other form of continuing education. Time spent on training must be counted as working hours for purposes of the 35-hour working week rules.

Dismissal & Redundancy

The rules governing dismissal (*licenciement*) and redundancy or severance pay (*indemnité de licenciement*) depend on the size of a company, the employee's length of service, the reason for dismissal (e.g. misconduct or redundancy), and whether the employee has a protected status, such as that enjoyed by union and employee representatives, who can be dismissed only for 'gross misconduct'.

The two main reasons for dismissal are personal (*motif personnel*) and economic (*motif économique*), i.e. when a company is experiencing serious financial problems. An employee can be dismissed at any time during his trial period, usually the first one to three months, without notice or compensation. Thereafter, you can dismiss an employee for personal reasons only in the case of a 'valid and serious offence' (*cause réelle et sérieuse*), e.g. stealing from an employer. In fact, there are three kinds of offence (*faute*):

- **Faute simple** – This means that the employee is unable to fulfil the role (i.e. is incompetent), although the onus is on you to prove this, which is seldom easy. If you dismiss an employee for *faute simple*, you must make him a redundancy payment of 10 per cent of his month's salary for each year of employment (e.g. an employee earning €2,000 per month who had been working for you for four years would be entitled to €800). You must also give him a month's notice (two months if he has been employed for more than two years).

- **Faute lourde** – This means that an employee has intentionally harmed the interests of the company, e.g. by laziness or persistent lateness, and you're entitled to dismiss him without notice.

- **Faute grave** – This includes offences that make an employee liable to prosecution, such as theft, violence and sexual harassment, and you're entitled to dismiss him without notice.

It's difficult for an employer to dismiss an employee unless he has blatantly proved his total incompetence or is guilty of some form of gross misconduct and even then a strict procedure must be followed.

Before you can dismiss anyone, you must give him two warnings: the first is called an *avertissement*, the second *blâme*; you may then suspend him (*mettre à pied*) for a short period, e.g. two weeks. During that time, you must summon him by registered letter to attend a formal preliminary hearing with you, during which the alleged misconduct is discussed. He has the right to bring another person to the interview – a colleague or an employee representative (whose name must appear on an official list). If dismissal could result, you must mention this as a possibility during the hearing. If you decide that the offence warrants dismissal, there's usually a cooling off period before you can effect the dismissal. The grounds for dismissal must be stated in the dismissal letter, which must also be sent by registered post to the employee's home address.

A dismissed employee is entitled to accrued holiday pay, severance pay if he has at least two years' service, and compensation in lieu of notice when a notice period cannot be observed. Payment must also be made in lieu of any outstanding paid holiday (*indemnité compensatrice de congés payés*) up to the end of the notice period (i.e.

for earned holiday not yet used in the current year). Severance pay must equal at least 20 per cent of his average monthly salary for each year of service (i.e. 100 per cent if he has been employed for five years). Collective agreements may provide for increased severance pay. Severance pay may not be payable when an employee is dismissed for a serious breach of conduct – usually a criminal act.

An employee dismissed for misconduct can appeal against the decision to a union or labour court. If you didn't abide by the law or the regulations in a particular industry, the employee can have his case heard by his union or syndicate. If there's no union, the case is heard before an industrial tribunal (*conseil des prud'hommes*) comprising employer and syndicate representatives (elected by the workforce), for which both sides require legal representation. If the employee wins the case, he's entitled to severance pay and compensation (e.g. six months' salary or more) for breach of his labour contract, but he may not be reinstated. In order to avoid the expense and publicity of legal proceedings, most employers come to an out-of-court settlement.

A fixed term contract can be terminated before the end of its period only in specific circumstances (see **Trial & Notice Periods** below).

When an employee is dismissed for economic reasons, i.e. made redundant, the procedures are strictly regulated. As a result of several high-profile mass redundancies in recent years (notably Marks & Spencer, Danone and Moulinex) which prompted a number of demonstrations and strikes, legislation has been passed to tighten up legal requirements in an attempt to discourage further plant closures and redundancies. (Unfortunately, these measures also tend to discourage businesses from taking on new employees.) Companies intending to fire at least ten workers within a 30-day period or at least 18 workers in a year must consult the relevant administrative authorities as well as the works council or employee delegates before any steps are taken.

This also applies in the case of any planned reorganisation or the sale or transfer of ownership of any portion of the company. Under rules which came into effect in 2002, a company considering redundancies is obliged to table an 'employment protection plan' (*plan de sauvegarde de l'emploi*) disclosing its reorganisation and restructuring plans and their expected impact on employees. Employers must propose specific actions to try to avoid redundancies, including reducing working hours, retraining and redistributing workers within the company, and offering training programmes to permit workers to find new jobs outside the company. There must also be an explicit plan for calling back workers laid off if and when the economic situation turns around or new jobs are created within the restructured organisation.

You must also justify any hiring you do during a period of up to two years after a major redundancy, unless you're recalling laid-off workers (i.e. to prove that this really is a new position that none of the laid-off workers could have filled).

If you're thinking of employing a full-time, part-time or temporary employee, you should ask him to sign a written statement agreeing to the terms of the termination of employment, or you could be sued for unfair dismissal. At termination, it's customary to ask the employee to sign a receipt for amounts due (*reçu de solde de tous comptes*), although it has recently been ruled that this document doesn't limit the ex-employee's rights to claim further payments from you.

Unions

There are numerous trade unions in France, many grouped into confederations, although French unions aren't as highly organised as those in many other western countries and their power and influence has been reduced considerably since the late '70s, when labour disputes and strikes were common. Since then, union membership has declined dramatically, membership of the Confédération Générale du Travail (CGT) dropping from over 2.5 million to around 1 million today. (Other major unions are the Confédération Française des Travailleurs Chrétiens, the Confédération Française de l'Encadrement/Confédération Générale des Cadres, the Confédération Française Démocratique du Travail and the Force Ouvrière.)

Union membership includes only around a fifth of the total workforce and less than 9 per cent of the private sector workforce – the lowest proportion in the EU. Unions are strongest in traditional industries such as mining, railways and automobile manufacturing and have had little success in new high-tech industries. However, they're still capable of causing widespread disruption, as has been demonstrated in recent years.

Despite their meagre membership, unions are considered one of the three 'social partners' when changes in laws or work rules are negotiated. Unlike in the US and UK, where unions negotiate directly with employers, in France there are three-way negotiations: between the government, the union and employers (represented by their 'union', MEDEF).

Under French law, unions are allowed to organise on any company's premises, but 'closed shops' are banned. With the exception of some public sector employees, e.g. the police, employees have the right to strike and cannot be dismissed for striking. Even where workers don't belong to a union, their rights are protected by labour laws. See also **Employee Representation** on page 159.

Trial & Notice Periods

For most jobs in France there's a trial period (*période d'essai*) of one to three months, depending on the type of work and the employer (three months is usual). The trial period isn't required by law, although there's no law forbidding it. The length of a trial period is usually stated in collective agreements. During the trial period, either party may terminate the employment contract without notice or any financial penalty, unless otherwise stated in a collective agreement.

If, at the end of the trial period, you haven't decided whether you wish to employ someone permanently, you may repeat the trial period, but only once and only to the maximum period allowed by the collective agreement for the industry. After this period, if you don't officially dismiss the person, you're deemed to have hired him permanently, irrespective of whether an employment contract exists.

Notice periods are governed by law and collective agreements and usually vary with length of service. The minimum notice period is usually a month for clerical and manual workers, two months for foremen and supervisors, and three months for managerial and senior technical staff. The minimum notice period for employees with over two years' service is two months.

Although many employers prefer employees to leave immediately after giving notice, employees have the right to work their notice period. However, both parties can agree that the employee receives payment in lieu (*indemnité compensatrice de préavis*) of notice. Compensation must also be made for any outstanding paid annual holidays (*indemnité compensatrice de congés payés*) up to the end of the notice period, and all dismissed employees receive a redundancy payment (*indemnité de licenciement*) of some sort (see also **Dismissal & Redundancy** on page 170).

A term contract can be terminated before the end of its period only in specific circumstances, i.e. when the employer or employee has committed a serious offence (*faute grave*), in the case of an event beyond the control of both parties (*force majeure*), or with the agreement of both parties. Under recently passed regulations designed to modernise labour law in France, an employee may terminate a temporary contract without penalty if he accepts a job with an indefinite contract. If the employer commits a serious offence or illegally dismisses the employee before the end of his contract, the employee is entitled to be paid in full for the remaining period of the contract, plus 10 per cent of his salary and bonuses. If the employee commits a serious offence or unilaterally breaks the contract other than to accept a permanent job, he may need to pay damages and loses his right to any bonuses. No compensation is payable if termination is due to *force majeure*.

Changing Jobs & Confidentiality

Companies in a high-tech or highly confidential business often have restrictions on employees moving to a competitor in France or within Europe (*clause de non-concurrence*), although strictly these aren't legal unless the employer offers employees a financial incentive not to change jobs. This is a complicated subject and disputes must often be resolved by a court of law. French laws regarding industrial secrets and general employment confidentiality are strict, however, and if an employee breaches this confidentiality, you may dismiss him.

SELLING A BUSINESS

Although this book is primarily concerned with acquiring and running a business in France, it may be useful to add a few words about selling a business – hopefully when it's worth millions! Selling a property is dealt with in *Buying a Home in France* (Survival Books – see page 419), and this section covers only additional information relevant to selling a business.

Selling a business is rather like buying a business (see **Taking Over a Business** on page 142), and the way to go about it depends largely on what you're selling (e.g. stock, shares, premises, equipment or a combination of these). Sales of shares, for example, can usually be negotiated directly between buyer and seller, whereas selling premises inevitably involves the services of a *notaire* (see **Costs** below).

The sale of a business (i.e. the *fonds de commerce*) is known as a *cession de fonds de commerce* (meaning 'ceding' rather than 'cessation'). You should have the business valued by a professional, although you can work out an approximate value by using the website of the magazine *ICF l'Argus des Commerces* (💻 www. cession-commerce.fr). Click on '*Calculez la valeur de votre commerce*' and answer the questions; this will tell you whether a valuer is grossly under or overvaluing your business. You must pay for a valuation unless it's done by the estate agent you've appointed to handle the sale, but he won't necessarily provide an objective valuation, which is recommended – even if it costs you money. Valuers are listed in the yellow pages under *Experts en estimation immobilière, industrielle et fonds de commerce*.

As soon as you decide to sell a business, you must inform the authority with which it's registered (see **Registration** on page 136) and the tax office, to which you must submit a final tax declaration within two months. Depending on the type of company and how the articles of incorporation are set up, it may be necessary to hold a shareholders' meeting to approve the selling of part or all of the shares, especially if they're to be sold to an 'outsider.'

With a commercial property, which is theoretically earning its owner money every day, the buyer normally pays a deposit, which will be used, in the event that the sale falls through between signing the preliminary sale agreement (usually a *compromis de vente*) and the date of completion (usually one to three months later), as 'compensation' for the fact that the seller has been unable to use it during this period. This deposit, known as an *indemnité d'immobilisation*, is usually around 10 per cent of the sale price and should be paid into an escrow account (e.g. the *notaire*'s or estate agent's). If the sale goes through as planned, the deposit is returned (or deducted from the sale price); if not, it's paid to the seller.

Once the sale has been completed, you and the buyer must inform the RNCS (see page 138) and complete a form called *Mutation de Fonds de Commerce ou de Clientèle*. You must also publish details of the sale in the appropriate newspaper or journal (see **Announcement** on page 137), although this is normally arranged and paid for by the buyer.

If your business hasn't made millions and you're selling it with debts, your creditors have ten days from the publication of the sale announcement in which to claim a proportion of the sale price. If a claim is more than the selling price, the business must be auctioned and you must accept the highest bid, which may be from the creditor. For six months after the sale, you remain jointly liable with the buyer for any debts subsequently claimed or taxes due.

Costs

Using a *notaire* usually involves paying a fee that can amount to up to 20 per cent of the value of the business being sold, depending on the type of property and whether it includes equipment or stock (on which there's a 15 per cent charge for transfer of ownership). There's also a 4 per cent transfer tax on shares. The sales agreement (one copy for each party to the agreement) must be 'certified' by the tax office when the tax is paid, and there's a per page charge (around €1 to €1.50) for certifying the documents.

Depending on who you're selling to and what the terms of the sale are, you may have to pay for formal appraisals, e.g. an audit or review of your accounting records to convince the buyer they're correct, or other incidental fees. You may also be liable for various taxes on the sale of a business property, including the following.

Capital Gains Tax

You may be liable for capital gains tax on any increase in the value of your business (not only its premises but also its assets and the value of the business as a going concern) since you purchased or started it although this is unlikely unless the business is subject to corporation tax (see **Capital Gains Tax** on page 207). Rates vary between 0 and 11.4 per cent according to the tax regime of the business. There are exemptions for certain transfers (e.g. transfers as part of an inheritance, businesses worth less than €300,000 sold before 31st December 2005, businesses in a development zone and all businesses in communes with fewer than 5,000 inhabitants – ask about the latest regulations). Obviously, you can avoid paying CGT by selling the business for the same price as you bought it (or less) but, if the selling price is significantly below its current market value, as assessed by a professional valuer, you can be liable for fines.

Value Added Tax

If your business premises are less than five years old and haven't previously been sold, you must pay VAT (*TVA*) on the sale price of the building (*murs*), i.e. excluding the value of the *fonds de commerce*, unless you had the building constructed and have already paid VAT on it, in which case you pay VAT only on the difference between the price you paid and the sale price.

5.

MONEY MATTERS

If you're going to make a living in France, in whatever capacity, you must familiarise yourself with all kinds of financial matters so that you remain firmly in control of your new working life. This chapter covers financing your business, banking, taxation, social security contributions, pensions and accounting. There's also a summary of the financial considerations to be made when selling a business – hopefully worth millions!

FINANCING YOUR BUSINESS

Running a business in France, whether you're self-employed or the owner of a company, can – and should – be enjoyable and rewarding, but at the end of the day, business is business and you must at least break even to survive; if you want to enjoy the fruits of your labour as well as the labour itself, you must make a profit. Money may not buy happiness, but it's certainly a lot easier to have fun if you aren't worrying about how you're going to pay the next bill.

The most common mistake people make when they arrive in France with plans for a new life is to be unrealistic about what they can achieve and overoptimistic in their financial projections. It's highly unlikely that your business will make substantial amounts of money from day one. At this early stage, make sure that your financial projections are pessimistic rather than optimistic. If the bug has bitten you hard, it may be tempting to brush aside those nagging little potential problem areas, hoping they will go away. If you don't want your dream to turn into a nightmare, don't be tempted to do this! Make sure that your business plan allows plenty of money to survive on until you can earn some of your own.

Some people suggest having resources to last a year, others as much as two or even three years. Many foreigners find that the worst point for them comes at around 18 months to two years after their arrival. The novelty has well and truly worn off, business is slow, money is running out fast, and they don't feel they can stomach any more French bureaucracy. At this point it's very tempting to give it all up and go home, especially if you have a family with you. It only takes one of them to be homesick or unhappy and your business problems seem to be magnified a thousand times. Make sure you haven't burnt all your bridges and sold all your assets in your home country. If your finances run to it, keep a small property there so that you can go back and 'regroup' if you need to.

As a foreigner, you will find it doubly hard to make a success of your business – and not just because of the language barrier. Unfortunately, it's all too common to hear of foreigners whose big ideas have turned to dust and who have disappeared overnight, in some cases owing money right, left and centre. However genuine the reasons for this, it doesn't engender trust from customers, suppliers and other businesses. Understandably, French people and other foreigners alike have a healthy suspicion of new arrivals. It's often the reason you're given a wide berth until you've proved that you're here to stay. Part of the long hard road to success depends on your ability to

demonstrate that you have staying power and commitment within the business community in France. Only you can decide whether it's better financially (and for your sanity!) to cut your losses and go home or to stick it out. Much depends on how good a start you get with your business and much of that depends on finances.

Budgeting

Before setting up a business in France (or anywhere else) you will, of course, draw up a detailed budget, including the amount of capital and other assets you require to start the business, expected running costs and a (pessimistic) estimate of income. The Agence Pour la Création d'Entreprises (APCE) recommends that a business budget comprises the following, depending, of course, on the type of business:

- Business registration fees (see page 139);
- Initial capital, if required, which must be paid by the owners into a holding account before the company registration will be accepted for processing (see **Business Entities** on page 123). Once the company is established, the shareholders or partners may have up to five years to make up any deficiencies in their quoted share, depending on the form of the company.
- Fees for legal advice or assistance;
- Patent or copyright fees or advice (see page 136);
- Funds for initial publicity (advertising, marketing material, etc.);
- Purchase, rental or construction of business premises (see **Premises** on page 148);
- Installation fees, e.g. shopfitting (see page 294);
- Utilities, e.g. electricity and water;
- Acquisition of machinery, material, vehicles and computers;
- Acquisition of stock, samples or demonstration merchandise;
- Purchase of leasing rights (if taking over an existing business – see page 142);
- Deposits, e.g. for rented premises and equipment;
- Insurance premiums (see page 151);
- Staff wages, including social security contributions (see pages 160 and 213).

All this constitutes your start-up funds or working capital (*besoin en fonds de roulement/BFR*), i.e. the amount of money you need to get the business operating until the first sales are made and payment collected (not always the same thing!). **Start-up funds are ALWAYS higher than you anticipate, so you should add a generous contingency to allow for everything you haven't thought of!**

When you've reached the appropriate stage in your research, you should put together a business plan and take it along to a professional who's familiar with the economic trends in the area you're interested in and can advise you about the local business environment and any opportunities for obtaining financial support for your venture. There are legal firms that offer a service in your home country and in France and specialise in advising on business ideas and financial plans. They can speak your language, they know France and its legal system and can help you to present your business plan in a form acceptable to France banks and financial institutions. You will find advertisements for legal advisers who offer this type of service in the French lifestyle magazines (see **Appendix B**). These are packed with useful information, articles and relevant advertisements, some of which also appear on their websites.

Cash Flow

Once you've drawn up an initial budget, you should produce a cash flow forecast (*prévision financière*), which you must present to a bank or investor if you need to raise capital. In fact, you're advised to make three forecasts: your projected cash flow if everything goes according to plan; the cash flow you can reasonably hope for; and what will happen if things go badly. It's this last projection that needs to be pinned above your computer screen, as this will remind you of what you must do to survive! **More businesses fail as a result of poor cash flow or poor cash management than to lack of profits, and it's possible for a business to go bust even when, on paper, it's profitable.**

Avoiding cash flow problems in France is a fine art, as social charges and taxes must be paid on time (to avoid an automatic 10 per cent penalty for late payment, not to mention possible fines), but the French don't have the world's best record for prompt payment of bills. Getting customers to pay can be one of the more 'challenging' aspects of running a new (or even an established) business. Although the European Union (EU) has proclaimed 30 days as the default payment term between businesses, many French businesses are used to paying after 45 or 60 days. Add to this the four or five-week summer holiday period, when it's common to be told "Oh, our bookkeeper is on holiday and we cannot pay any bills until her return" and you begin to see the potential problems.

It's possible to charge a late payment fee (which must be at least 1.5 times the official interest rate), and most vendors put a warning to this effect on their bills, although few implement it and you won't earn a favourable reputation if you do.

Another way round the problem is to provide incentives (i.e. discounts) to customers who pay by direct debit (*prélèvement*). If you make payments (e.g. tax and social security contributions) by direct debit, you must of course ensure that there are sufficient funds in your account to cover them on the due date.

There are various arrangements you can make with your bank to help your cash flow, including an overdraft facility (*découvert*). (French bank statements may not show a cumulative balance, except at the end of the month, making it difficult to check that you haven't overdrawn your account at any point.)

It's also possible to buy receivables insurance from certain insurance companies; you pay a set premium each month or quarter based on the evaluation of the 'riskiness' of your business – usually calculated as the balance outstanding for each of your customers and the assessment of the individual and overall risk of not being paid. Note, however, that receivables insurance pays out only when a customer goes bankrupt and not in cases where a customer simply delays payment for months on end. In some businesses, where customers are particularly at risk of business failure, receivables insurance can be a good investment, but normally it's easier (and cheaper) to work directly with the customers to encourage payment – by requiring progress payments, direct debits or deposits or issuing regular dunning letters.

Raising Capital

Unless you're fortunate enough to have sufficient 'cash' to finance the set-up of your business, you must raise the necessary capital. The standard sources of financing a new business are discussed below. As well as investigating the opportunities for raising capital in France, you should consider the options for doing so in your home country or previous country of residence, as it may be advantageous to do so. **If you wish (or need) to borrow money for a business venture in France, you should carefully consider where and in what currency to raise finance.**

If you need to import funds from abroad, there are no limits to this. However, if you receive any amount above €1,500 by post, it must be declared to customs. Similarly if you enter France with €8,000 or more in French or foreign banknotes or securities (e.g. travellers' cheques, letters of credit, bills of exchange, bearer bonds, giro cheques, stock and share certificates, bullion, and gold or silver coins quoted on the official exchange), you must declare it to French customs. **If you exceed the €8,000 limit and are found out, you can be fined €1,500 or more.** For details of importing (and exporting) money, refer to *Living and Working in France* (Survival Books – see page 419).

A number of possible sources of start-up capital – and of further information – are listed below. A general source of information is your regional Direction Régionale de l'Industrie, de la Recherche et de l'Environnement (DRIRE, 🖳 www. drire.gouv.fr), operated by the French Ministry of the Environment and Sustainable Development; contact details are listed on the website.

If you don't have time to seek sources of capital yourself and have the resources to use an agency to do so on your behalf, there are a number of specialist companies that will investigate all possible grants, loans and subsidies for you, including Subsidies in France, AFS Management, 91 rue du Faubourg Saint Honoré, 75008 Paris (☎ 01 44 71 36 41, 🖳 wwwsubsidies-in-france.com).

⚠ If you require capital to set up your business (see Business Entities on page 123), French law forbids you from carrying forward losses indefinitely. When your losses (accumulated or suffered in a single tax year) equal or exceed half of your stated capital, you must call a shareholders' meeting to determine whether you want to continue with the company. If the shareholders decide to go ahead and try to make up the loss, you then have two years to restore the capital to the stated value. If you fail to do so, you must call another shareholders' meeting to disband the company or recapitalise it (by putting in more funds or reducing the stated capital level). Recapitalising involves submitting forms to the chamber of commerce – and the fact that you've lost half your capital is included on your *Kbis* until you recapitalise or restore the funds, which in turn can interfere with your ability to arrange credit with banks or suppliers. The cost of recapitalising is low (around

€50), but the paperwork is involved, which is a good reason not to set up a company with capital of only €1 or some other token amount.

Dossier Financier

Whatever type of funding you require, you must produce a financial 'dossier' to present to potential investors, banks and other interested parties. This should include the results of your market research (see **Research** on page 116), a three-year cash flow forecast and a statement of the start-up funding available and required and how this will be used over the first three years. You should attach a copy of your business plan (see page 122) to the dossier. If sums aren't your strong point, you can generate financial forecasts from your expected figures using the Opticrea website (🖳 www.opticrea.com).

Personal Savings

This includes the savings of the creator of the company (i.e. you) and the shareholders or partners. You may not wish to invest personal savings in a business venture, but it's important that you do so, as it demonstrates your commitment to the business. It's particularly important if your business needs credit, from banks or from suppliers, as personal trust is an essential part of doing business in France.

Some banks offer would-be entrepreneurs a special business savings account (*livret épargne entreprise/LEE*), in which they can accumulate the necessary funds (up to €45,800) tax-free over a period of at least two years. This account entitles you to a business loan at preferred rates and terms once the business has been established. Note, however, that banks aren't usually keen to offer you these accounts (which is a sure sign that they're worth having!) and they may be difficult to find, or you may have to ask about them.

It's also possible to use funds in a personal 'share saving' account (*plan d'épargne en actions/PEA*) to finance the start-up of a small business under certain circumstances. With a *PEA* you're allowed to invest in non-quoted companies and there are tax advantages according to how long the *PEA* has been in existence. In some cases, an *épargne logement* account can be used to finance business or professional premises.

Loans

Generally, French financial institutions are wary of lending money to entrepreneurs, particularly foreigners and (sad to say) women. French banks won't usually loan more than 70 per cent of the pre-tax value of any asset put up as collateral, and the term of the loan is limited to the expected economic life of the asset. Most banks also limit their commitment to the amount the business owner has committed of his own funds (see above) and require a guarantee that the money will be repaid (see below). Regional and local banks are often parochial in their outlook and their managements insufficiently autonomous to deal with untypical cases. Banks can also impose high interest rates on loans they consider to be 'high risk'.

It's therefore advisable to deal with financial consultants who are familiar with banking practices rather than directly with individual banks. The APCE recommends a number of agencies, including l'Association pour le Droit à l'Initiative Economique (ADIE, 💻 www.adie.org), France Active (💻 www.franceactive.org) France Initiative Réseau (💻 www.fir.asso.fr – see also below) and le Réseau Entreprendre (💻 www.reseau-entreprendre.org). Some banks have agreements with organisations dedicated to supporting new businesses, including clubs for business creation, *boutiques de gestions* and local economic development organisations. Members of the organisations may be eligible for unsecured loans at reduced rates of interest (or occasionally even at zero interest).

Providing a personal guarantee for a bank or other loan is a risky undertaking. Fortunately, there are a number of funds that offer loan guarantees (*fonds de garantie*), including the following. Banks may be able to put you in touch with funds that they deal with regularly. Note, however, that guarantees normally cover only 70 per cent of a loan and that there's a charge (in the form of a 'contribution' to the fund – usually of between 0.5 and 4 per cent of the amount guaranteed).

- **Fonds France Active** – Contact Fonds France Active, 37 rue Bergère, 75009 Paris (☎ 01 53 24 26 26).

- **Fonds de Garantie pour la Création à l'Initiative des Femmes** – For businesses started by women; contact FGIF, 10–12 rue des Trois Fontanot, 92000 Nanterre (☎ 01 55 23 07 13).

- **Garantie Entreprendre en France** – Entreprendre en France, 50 rue de la Rochefoucauld, 75009 Paris (☎ 01 48 74 54 97, 💻 www.entreprendre-en-france.fr).

- **Société de Caution Mutuelle** – Contact SCM, 24 avenue de la Grande Armée, 75854 Paris Cedex 17 (☎ 01 53 81 51 51, 💻 www.asf-france.com).

- **Société Française de Garantie de Financement des PME** – Contact SOFARIS, 27 avenue du Général Leclerc, 94710 Maisons-Alfort (☎ 01 41 79 80 00, 💻 www. sofaris.com).

There are also regional and departmental guarantee funds; for details contact the relevant Conseil Régional or departmental chambre of commerce.

A number of interest-free, low-interest and other loans are available from central, regional, departmental and local government and other organisations, including the following:

- **Prêt à la Création d'Entreprise** – A government business start-up loan (*prêt à la création d'entreprise/PCE*) of between €3,000 and €8,000 over five years is available under certain conditions, e.g. that your start-up capital doesn't exceed €45,000 and that the money isn't spent on fixed assets. No guarantee is required. Contact the Banque du Développement des Petites et Moyennes Entreprises (BDPME, ☎ 08 25 30 12 30, 💻 www.bdpme.fr) for details.

- **Prêts d'Honneur** – Regional and departmental administrations often make 'trust loans' (*prêts d'honneur*) – meaning that no guarantees are required. These may be interest-free, but must be repaid within a certain period (e.g. five years), are usually up to a maximum of around €40,000 and may be limited to certain types of business (see below). A nationwide organisation offering trust loans is Réseau

Entreprendre, a federation of business owners (over 2,500 of them in 31 'regional' groups) who, on average, lend around €24,000 to business starters; addresses of all 31 groups can be found on ▣ www.reseau-entreprendre.org. Trust loans of up to €15,000 are offered to innovative entrepreneurs by the Fondation Jean Guyomarc'h, Pépinière Pentaparc, BP 43602, 56006 Vannes Cedex Paris (☎ 02 97 68 91 99).

- **Aquitaine** – The Caisse Sociale de Développement Local, 29 rue du Mirail, 33000 Bordeaux (☎ 05 56 33 37 97, ▣ www.csdl.asso.fr) offers loans of up to €12,000, repayable over five years, to entrepreneurs in the Bordeaux area who are unable to obtain other funding.

- **Auvergne** – Cantal Expansion, 16–18 rue Paul Doumer, 15015 Aurillac Cedex (▣ www.cybercantal.org) offers zero-interest *prêts d'honneur* over four years to anyone wanting to set up in the department; it supports around 50 new businesses each year.

- **Burgundy** – The Association Régionale pour le Développement de l'Artisanat en Bourgogne (ANDAB, 19 rue Colson, 21000 Dijon, ☎ 03 80 50 11 44) offers zero-interest loans of up to 50 per cent of investment capital to businesses in certain trades. Information is also available from local *chambres des métiers*.

- **Franche-Comté** – Cré-Entreprendre, ZA les Prs de Vaux, 25000 Besanon (☎ 03 81 65 37 65) offers loans of between €1,500 and €15,000 to businesses setting up in Doubs. Vivre en Bresse, Grande Rue de la Bresse, 39230 Chaumergy (☎ 03 84 48 62 56) offers zero-interest loans up to €7,500 to businesses setting up in the Bresse Comtoise area.

- **Ile-de-France** – In the Paris area, Paris Initiatives Entreprises (☎ 01 53 04 02 62, ▣ www.parinitiativentreprise.com) offers entrepreneurs interest-free loans of up to €30,000.

- **Limousin** – The Fondation Crédit Mutuel Loire-Atlantique et Centre-Ouest, 46 rue du Port-Boyer (☎ 02 40 68 14 94) offers between 50 and 70 zero-interest *prêts d'honneur* to innovative businesses in Limousin, Loire-Atlantique and northern Deux-Sèvres.

- **Nord-Pas-de-Calais** – The Caisse Solidaire du Nord-Pas-de-Calais, 3 contour Saint-Martin, 59100 Roubaix (☎ 03 20 81 99 70, ▣ www.caisse-solidaire.org) is a cooperative offering loans totalling around €3 million per year to small businesses. Nord-Entreprendre, 50 boulevard du Général de Gaulle, 59100 Roubaix (☎ 03 20 66 14 60) is an association that offers zero-interest *prêts d'honneur* over three years to industrial product or service businesses likely to employ between 10 and 15 people.

- **Pays-de-la-Loire & Poitou-Charentes** – The Fondation Crédit Mutuel Océan, 34 rue Léandre-Merlet, 85000 La roche-sur-Yon (☎ 02 51 47 54 75) offers around ten zero-interest *prêts d'honneur* of €7,600 over five years to innovative businesses in Charente-Maritime, Deux-Sèvres and Vendée. (See also **Limousin** above.)

- **Rhône-Alpes** – Rhône-Alpes Entreprendre, 1 rue Fleming, 69007 Lyon (☎ 04 78 61 51 03) is an association offering around 20 zero-interest *prêts d'honneur* of between €7,500 and €30,000 (repayable only if the business is successful!) per year to manufacturing and service businesses.

- **Prêts Bonifiés & Prêts Conventionnés** – A number of organisations, including departmental Chambres de Commerce et d'Industrie (CCI), offer low-interest loans (*prêts bonifiés*), although these are generally limited to the agricultural and trades sectors. Loans are usually for up to 80 per cent of the required capital, up to a maximum amount (e.g. €45,000), and attract around 4 per cent interest. A *prêt conventionné* may be unlimited, but repayable at a slightly higher interest rate (e.g. 6 per cent). A nationwide organisation offering low-interest loans is the Réseau d'Accompagnement des Créations et des Initiatives pour une Nouvelle Epargne de Solidarité (RACINES, 8 square de la Dordogne, 75017 Paris, ☎ 01 45 66 08 19, ⌨ www.racines-clefe.com). *Prêts bonifiés* are also offered by a number of large companies, including Péchiney, 7 place du Chancelier Adenauer, 75218 Paris Cedex 16 (☎ 01 56 28 20 00), Sofra-Elf Aquitaine, Centre d'Affaires Activa.XX, allée Concordet, 64000 Pau (☎ 05 59 02 01 97) and Usinor Sacilor, 127 avenue Charles de Gaulle, 92202 Neuilly-sur-Seine Cedex (☎ 01 46 40 97 97); other companies offer financial support of various kinds (see page 116).

- **Nouvelle Economie Fraternelle** – NEF is an organisation offering loans to new businesses in the health and personal services, environment and ecology, education, art and culture sectors. Loans are of up to €10,000, repayable over two to seven years, but must be guaranteed. Contact the Délégation de Paris, 35 rue de Lyon, 75012 Paris (☎ 08 11 90 11 90, ⌨ www.lanef.com).

- **Association des Banques Populaires pour la Création d'Entreprise** – The ABPCE supports 30 to 45 new businesses in the industrial sector every year with zero-interest loans of between €15,000 and €75,000 and, occasionally, grants. Businesses must be innovative and have the potential to achieve a turnover of at least €750,000 within three years. Contact the Chambre Syndicale des Banques Populaires, 5 rue Leblanc, 75015 Paris (☎ 01 40 39 60 00, ⌨ www. banquepopulaire.fr).

- **Female Entrepreneurs** – The French Ministry for Equality has a guarantee fund (*Fonds de Garantie pour la Création, la Reprise ou le Développement d'Entreprises à l'Initiative des Femmes/FGIF*) for loans of up to €38,000 made to female entrepreneurs. You must repay it within seven years and standard interest rates apply. Details can be obtained from the *Droits des Femmes* service at your local *préfecture* or on the Ministry website (⌨ www.droitsdesfemmes.org/ entreprises.htm). Low-interest loans are also available through Clubs d'Epargne Solidaire pour les Femmes qui Entreprennent (CLEFE, 8 square de la Dordogne, 75017 Paris, ☎ 01 45 66 08 19, ⌨ www.racines-clefe.com).

- **Disabled Entrepreneurs** – The AGEFIPH (⌨ www.agefiph.asso.fr) offers loans to disabled entrepreneurs via its 19 regional offices (listed on the website).

Further information about loans is available from France Initiative Réseau, 14 rue Delambre, 75014 Paris (☎ 01 40 64 10 20, ⌨ www.fir.asso.fr), a part state and part private funded organisation that runs over 200 local 'initiative platforms' (*plates-formes d'initiative locale/PFIL*); the website has a search facility to enable you to find the one nearest you. If your business is likely to employ 'disadvantaged' people, you may obtain a loan via a government organisation called France Active, which operates on a regional basis; contact details can be found on ▣ www.france active.org. Lists of organisations offering business loans are available from Finansol, 133 rue Saint-Maur, 75011 Paris (☎ 01 53 36 80 60, ▣ wwwlfinansol.org).

The European Union (EU) offers both direct and indirect assistance (usually in the form of start-up loans) to new businesses. Direct assistance is usually limited to businesses that operate in at least three EU countries. Indirect assistance is usually confined to regions in need of development; there are various funds, including FEDER, FEOGA and FSE. Information about all EU schemes can be obtained from your nearest Euro Info Centre; for a list of centres contact the CCIP, 27 avenue de Friedland, 75008 Paris (☎ 01 55 65 73 13, ▣ www.ccip.fr/eic).

Grants & Subsidies

There are over 250 different grants and subsidies (often referred to as 'incentives', although strictly these are financial benefits – see page 190) available to individuals for starting up a personal enterprise or small business in France, particularly in rural areas. These include EU subsidies, central government grants, regional development grants, redeployment grants, and grants from departments and local communities. Grants may take the form of assistance to buy buildings and equipment (or the provision of low-cost business premises), subsidies for job creation, or tax incentives.

Most government subsidies are intended to provide support for small businesses already up and running, but there are occasionally specific subsidies available for new businesses, particularly for individuals who have been unemployed for a long period. Some regional governments offer subsidies to new businesses, particularly if local jobs are assured or local skills put to good use. Most grants apply only to the creation of a first business. **Even if you're eligible for a grant and it has been approved, you shouldn't bank on receiving it, as it can take months or even years to materialise.** Schemes include the following (in order of scope, from Europe-wide to local):

- **European Union Grants & Subsidies** – Information about EU grants and subsidies available in France can be obtained from Euro-Info Centres, a list of which can be found on ▣ www.info-europe.fr/document.dir/fich.dir/QR000737.htm.

- **Encouragement au Développement d'Entreprises Nouvelles** – This national programme (*EDEN*) was originally established to work with young people and those in 'precarious situations' (i.e. working on fixed-term contracts), but in 2004, the programme was opened up to include people over 50 who have been unemployed for some time. Information about available subsidy programmes can be obtained from the APCE (see above) or through your local *centre de formalités des entreprises* (see pages 103 and 137).

- **Primes d'Aménagement du Territoire** – The French Ministry of Equipment, Transport and Tourism, through its agency DATAR, offers a *prime d'aménagement du territoire*, which is an incentive scheme for businesses setting up in 'special development' zones – geographical areas declared to be in need of development, including urban areas (*zones de redynamisation urbaine/ZRU*), rural areas (*zones de revitalisation rurale/ZRR*) and other regions. The local chamber of commerce or Chambre des Métiers can indicate what zones exist in your region or department, or you can consult a map of the eligible areas on the DATAR website (🖥 www. datar.gouv.fr – click on '*Aide aux entreprises*'). Incentives generally involve tax breaks rather than direct funding for new businesses, e.g. a partial exoneration from business taxes over the first five to seven years of the company's existence. The exoneration decreases over time: in the case of the five year scheme, for example, there's 100 per cent exoneration for the first two years, 75 per cent in the third year, 50 per cent in year four and 25 per cent in year five.

- **Fonds de Revitalisation Economique** – This fund is aimed at small and medium-size businesses (with no more than five employees) setting up in development zones (see above). Grants are of around €3,000 and must be claimed within the first year of operation. For details, contact your local chamber of commerce.

- **Fonds d'Intervention pour les Services, l'Artisanat et le Commerce** – This is a central government initiative administered by regional Délégations au Commerce et à l'Artisanat (DRCA) and local chambers of commerce and guilds to support the creation of businesses (other than pharmacies and anything connected with tourism) in villages and towns with fewer than 2,000 inhabitants.

- **Dotation de Développement Rural** – This is a national scheme designed to revitalise rural areas by offering grants and incentives for the construction of business premises or the renovation of existing premises for business use; although grants aren't made directly to businesses, it's worth finding out whether such a scheme is in operation, as the resulting premises can be sold or rented at low cost.

- **Primes Régionales à la Création d'Entreprise** – Regional councils give grants to new businesses creating at least two permanent jobs; grants are worth up to €4,000 per employee.

- **Primes Régionales à l'Emploi** – Another regional council grants, for those setting up or taking over businesses employing local people.

- **Fonds Régionaux d'Aide au Transfert de Technologie** – A regional grant for small and medium-size businesses needing to undertake research or training.

- **Fonds Régionaux d'Aide aux Conseils** – Regional chambers of commerce offer grants to cover part of the cost of professional advice to entrepreneurs, up to certain limits.

- **Fonds Départementaux de Développement Economique** – Each department has a fund which is to be used to encourage the construction of business premises; although this isn't a direct grant to businesses, it's worth finding out whether such a scheme is in operation, as the resulting premises can be sold or rented at low cost.

Foundations: A number of 'charitable' foundations offer grants and other support to specific types of entrepreneur, including the following:

- **Fondation Aventis** – Ten grants of around €31,000 each, plus other support, to entrepreneurs under 35 setting up a science-based business in the healthcare sector; contact the Fondation Aventis-institut de France, 46 quai de la Rapée, 75601 Paris Cedex 12 (☎ 01 55 71 09 94, 🖳 www.fondation-aventis.org).

- **Fondation des Brasseries Kronenbourg** – Fifteen grants of between around €3,000 and €23,000 to people starting businesses in food processing, catering and related sectors; contact the foundation at BP 13, 67037 Strasbourg Cedex 02 (☎ 03 88 27 48 54, 🖳 www.brasseries-kronenbourg.com).

- **Fondation Jean Guyomarc'h** – Around 10 to 15 grants of around €1,500 each year to entrepreneurs with innovative business ideas; contact the foundation at Pépinière Pentaparc, BP 43602, 56006 Vannes Cedex Paris (☎ 02 97 68 91 99).

- **Fondation Macif** – Around 100 grants of between €750 and €45,000 annually to businesses that employ people on indefinite term contracts; contact the foundation at Carré Haussmann, 22–28 rue Joubert, 75435 Paris Cedex 09 (☎ 01 55 31 63 15, 🖳 www.macif.fr).

- **Fondation Marcel Bleustein-Blanchet** – Around 20 grants of around €7,700 each year to entrepreneurs aged between 18 and 30 who have innovative business ideas; contact the foundation at 60 avenue Victor-Hugo, 75016 Paris (☎ 01 45 01 29 28, 🖳 http://fondationvocation.org).

- **Fondation Schneider Electric** – Three to ten grants of between €10,000 and €30,000 annually to entrepreneurs aged under 35 with business ideas related to Schneider's own; contact the Fondation Schneider Electric pour l'Insertion des Jeunes, 89 boulevard Franklin Roosevelt/BP 323, 92506 Rueil-Malmaison (☎ 01 41 29 52 97, 🖳 www.schneider-electric.com).

Competitions: In addition to the above, there are many competitions (*concours* or *prix*), at national, regional and departmental level, which can take the form of financial or other benefits. These include the following (national competitions are listed first, followed by regional and then departmental competitions):

- **Bourses Défi-Jeunes** – Prizes worth up to €8,500 each, for entrepreneurs aged 18 to 28 in certain sectors; contact Défi-Jeune, 62 rue de Saint-Lazare, 75009 Paris (☎ 01 40 82 97 97, 🖳 www.defijeunes.fr).

- **Concours National d'Aide à la Création d'Entreprises de Technologies Innovantes** – Grants of up to €45,000 to innovative entrepreneurs in the technology sector; contact the Ministère de la Jeunesse, de l'Education Nationale et de la Recherche, 1 rue Descartes, 75231 Paris Cedex 05 (🖳 www. recherche.gouv.fr).

- **Talents-Parcours des Nouveaux Entrepreneurs** – Ten national prizes and four prizes in each region per year worth €8,000 each, for businesses that have been established for a year; contact the Comité de Liaison des Boutiques de Gestion, France Active, 38 rue Bergère, 75009 Paris (☎ 01 53 24 26 22, 🖳 www.concours-talents.com).

- **Trophées de la Création d'Entreprise** – Three prizes per year worth up to €45,750 each, for young entrepreneurs; contact Le Revenu Français, 1bis avenue de la République, 75011 Paris (☎ 01 49 29 30 93, 🖳 www.lerevenu.com).

- **Alsace** – Les Trophées Espoirs de l'Economie du Sud Alsace offer free advertising to new businesses setting up in southern Alsace; contact the CCI Sud Alsace, 8 rue du 17 Novembre, 68000 Mulhouse (☎ 03 89 66 78 19, 🖥 www.mulhouse.cci.fr).

- **Auvergne** – Seventeen 'Réussissez Votre Création d'Entreprise en Auvergne' prizes for young non-agricultural businesses in the region; contact the Mission Régionale pour la Création d'Entreprise, 43 rue Wailly, 63000 Clermont-Ferrand (☎ 04 73 34 84 80).

- **Poitou-Charentes** – Twelve 'Entreprendre et Innover en Poitou-Charentes' prizes worth up to €15,245 for innovative new businesses in the region; contact Poitou-Charentes Création/Transmission, Pôle Technologique Régional, 8 rue Raoul-Follereau, 86000 Poitiers (☎ 05 49 44 76 20, 🖥 www.creation-transmission.com).

- **Bouches-du-Rhône** – Thirteen 'Créatreize' prizes worth up to €13,720 for young non-commercial businesses in this department; contact the Conseil Général des Bouches-du-Rhône, 52 avenue Saint-Just, 13556 Marseille (☎ 04 91 21 22 52, 🖥 www.cg13.fr).

- **Finistère** – Seven 'Challenge Espoirs de l'Economie' prizes worth €3,000 each every two years (2006, 2008, etc.) for new industrial, commercial and service businesses in the department; contact the CCI du Finistère, place du 19e RI, BP 126, 29268 Brest (☎ 02 98 44 43 77).

- **Hauts-de-Seine** – Five 'Trophée des Espoirs de l'Economie des Hauts-de-Seine' prizes worth up to €3,000 for young businesses in the department; contact the CCI des Hauts-de-Seine, 6–8 rue des Trois Fontanot, 92000 Nanterre (☎ 01 46 14 26 63, 🖥 www.ccip92.com).

- **Indre** – One 'Impulsion Indre' prize worth €38,500 plus other benefits to a new service or industrial business in the department; contact the Agence de Développement Economique de l'Indre, place Marcel-Dassault, Zone Aéroporuaire/BP 59, 36130 Déols (☎ 02 54 35 50 60, 🖥 www.objectifindre.com).

- **Isère** – Five or six prizes worth up to €2,300 in the biennial Concours Jeunes Entreprises for new industrial or service businesses in the department; contact the CCI de l'Isère, Espace Entreprendre, place André Malraux, 38016 Grenoble (☎ 04 76 28 27 83, 🖥 www.grenoble.cci.fr).

- **Loire-Atlantique** – Twenty-one 'Challenge Entrepreprises' prizes worth up to €40,000 for new businesses in the department; contact the Conseil Général de Loire-Atlantique, Service de Développement Economique, 44000 Nantes (☎ 02 40 99 17 12, 🖥 www.cg44.fr).

- **Nord** – Thirteen prizes worth up to €15,250 in the Concours Départemental à la Création d'Entreprise for new businesses in the department; contact the Conseil Général du Nord, 51 rue Gustave Delory, 59000 Lille (☎ 03 20 63 57 42, 🖥 www.cg59.fr).

- **Seine-et-Marne** – Three 'Prix Départemental de la Création d'Entreprise' ptizes of €10,000 to new businesses in the department; contact Seine-et-Marne Développement, Hôtel du Département, 77010 Melun (☎ 01 64 14 19 22, 🖥 www. seine-et-marne-invest.com).

Further Information: To find out about possible grants, incentives and competitions, start by contacting your local town hall or *mairie*, the relevant *ccentre de formalités des entreprises* (see page 103 & 137) and the departmental chamber of commerce. For further information about grants and incentives, contact Invest in France (AFII), which has offices in Belgium, Germany, Italy, the Netherlands, Spain, Switzerland, the UK, the US (four offices) and in various Asian countries. Its head office is AFII, 2 avenue de Vélasquez, 75008 Paris (☎ 01 40 74 74 40, 🖷 www.afii.fr).

Financial Benefits

The French government offers new businesses a number of financial benefits or incentives, including those listed below. Note, however, that the nature and value of these are subject to sudden change with a change of government or financial policy and you should check with your local tax office before including any incentives in your financial calculations.

- Income tax reductions and exemptions for companies setting up in 'special development' zones (see **Grants & Subsidies** on page 186);

- Delayed payment of first four corporate tax instalments for businesses not in special development zones;

- Exemption from *IFA* (see page 204) for the first three years for certain types of company;

- Twenty per cent corporate or income tax reduction plus €915 tax reduction for businesses belonging to a *centre de gestion* (*CGA* – see page 198);

- Reduction in corporate tax to 15.45 per cent on profits up to €38,120 under certain conditions;

- Exemption from *taxe professionnelle*, property tax and other local taxes for the first two years;

- Tax benefits for businesses investing at least 15 per cent of their turnover in research and development;

- Other financial incentives for limited and public companies.

Lease Financing

Lease financing (*crédit-bail*) is another way to secure property and machinery for a new business, and the advantage is that it's possible to finance 100 per cent of the buying price without the debt showing up on the balance sheet. However, lease financing is rather more expensive than an ordinary bank loan and may involve a hefty deposit or the payment of the first month's rent in advance.

Venture Capital

Generally, venture capital is available only to new businesses in certain types of industry, usually technology or research related. It involves a venture capitalist or organisation taking a minority share in the company for a limited period in exchange for the capital gain on the sale of their interest once the business is up and running. The requirements are usually very strict and you must usually have considerable experience in the industry. The principal companies looking to invest in new businesses include the following:

- Atlas Venture (☎ 01 45 23 41 20, ⌨ www.atlasventure.com) – IT and 'life sciences';

- Banexi Ventures (☎ 01 40 14 26 63, ⌨ www.banexiventures.com) – electronics and 'life sciences';

- CDC-Innovation (☎ 01 40 64 22 00, ⌨ www.cdcinnov.com) – High-technology;

- Innovacom (☎ 01 44 94 15 00, ⌨ www.innovacom.com) – IT;

- Partech International (☎ 01 53 65 65 53, ⌨ www.partechintl.com) – IT and communications;

If you're setting up a small business (or one in a 'low-tech' field), it's unlikely that you will be able to secure investment from any of the above. However, there are small organisations that may be able to help – on a smaller scale. These include the following:

- Autonomie et Solidarité (81B, rue Gantois, 59000 Lille, ☎ 03 20 30 97 25) – Looks to invest in companies intending to employ around eight or ten 'disadvantaged' people.

- Club d'Investisseurs pour une Gestion Alternative et Locale d'Epargne (Cigales, 61 rue Victor-Hugo, 93500 Pantin, ☎ 01 49 91 90 91, ⌨ www.cigales.asso.fr) – A network of 'investors' clubs', comprising five to ten individuals looking to invest in new businesses, especially those considered to be 'socially beneficial'. The average investment is between around €1,500 and €4,500 and you're normally expected to buy back the shares after five years.

- Fonds France Active (FFA, ⌨ www.franceactive.org) – Supports businesses started by (or employing) people who are 'threatened with social exclusion'.

- Love Money Federation, 10 rue de Montyo, 75009 Paris (☎ 01 48 00 03 35) – A group of around 20 associations investing in SAs (see page 125).

There are a number of 'fundraising' companies that try to match business projects with suitable venture capitalists (known as 'business angels'). Among the largest are Association France Angels (⌨ www.franceangels.org), Business Angels (⌨ www.businessangels.com), Chausson Finance (⌨ www.chaussonfinance.com), Leonardo (⌨ www.leaonardofinance.com), MGT (⌨ www.mgt.fr) and Proxicap Invest (⌨ www.proxicap.com). They will help you prepare your business plan for presentation and they receive a fee based on the amount of funds provided by the venture capitalist. There are also fairs and seminars run by various groups, such as Finance et Technologie, 9 rue Lincoln, 75008 (☎ 01 58 36 10 30, ⌨ www.fftgroup.com) and Mar-Tech et Finance, Centre Nautique Paris-Boulogne, face au 36 quai Le Gallo, 92100 Boulogne Billancourt (☎ 01 41 31 62 62, ⌨ www.altexie.com/martech) that are intended to bring interesting business projects and proposals to the attention of investors. The events are advertised in trade journals and business publications.

Local Chambres de Commerce et d'Industrie (CCI) and Chambres des Métiers sometimes can help in matching businesses with potential private investors, and private investment clubs are permitted to invest some of their funds in small, unquoted businesses. The Association Française des Investissuers en Captial (AFIC, 14 rue de Berri, 75008 Paris, ☎ 01 47 20 99 09, 🖥 www.afic.asso.fr) is an independent organisation whose 200 members are seeking to invest in new business. The Union Nationale des Investisseurs en Capital pour les Entreprises Régionales (UNICER, 🖥 www.unicer.asso.fr) is a grouping of potential investors in each region of France. If your business is of an environmental or sociological nature, you should contact the Société Coopérative des Finances Solidaire (NEF, 🖥 www.lanef.com), which is supported by the Banque de France and links entrepreneurs in these fields with investors, as well as offering loans (see page 182).

More generally, the APCE recommends calling on friends and family as investors, as the initial investments in small businesses can earn them a credit on their income taxes equal to 25 per cent of the amount invested (as can later increases in capital). The business must be subject to business taxation (see page 203) and the investment must be made in the form of funds (i.e. not contributed equipment or labour). There's a €20,000 limit for individuals (€40,000 for couples) on the tax credit in any one year, but the unused credit can be carried forward for the next three tax years.

Commercial Mortgages

Commercial mortgages in France are generally regarded as long-term loans (see **Loans** on page 182). Most banks won't lend more than 70 per cent of the pre-tax cost of a building and may expect the business owner to have at least as much invested personally in the business as the amount of the loan.

Selling Shares

Unless a business is being set up in one of the forms that permits listing on the stock exchange (e.g. an *SA* or *SAS* – see **Business Entities** on page 123), all the shareholders must be listed in the articles of incorporation. If shares change hands at a later stage, you must follow an elaborate procedure for documenting the sale, having it validated by the tax authorities (once the tax on the transaction has been paid) and then amending the articles (by holding a special shareholders' meeting) to reflect the changes in ownership.

Most types business (other than *SAS* and *SA*) must include something in their statutes regarding the sale of shares to outsiders (i.e. those not originally investing in the company), and some forms of incorporation require a unanimous decision by the existing shareholders approving the sale or transfer (e.g. via inheritance) of shares to an outsider.

Financial Regimes

French financial practices are defined in terms of 'regimes' (*régimes*), and in everything to do with the finances of your business you are allocated or must choose a regime. **If you have a choice of regime, it's essential to take professional advice as to which option is to your advantage (particularly as their nomenclature is confusing and often inconsistent across the various financial authorities), as this can save you thousands of euros per year.** The various regimes you may need to choose between include the following:

- **Marital Regimes** – If you're married (obviously!), you may have a choice of how ownership of your possessions is divided between you, which can affect the inheritance of a business (see **Marital Regimes** on page 133).

- **Income Tax Regimes** – There are income tax regimes for small businesses, which may be to your advantage (see **Income Tax Regimes** on page 197).

- **Corporate Tax Regimes** – There are also different regimes for corporate tax (see **Corporate Tax** on page 203).

- **VAT Regimes** – Not only may you be able to choose whether or not to register for value added tax (VAT), but you may have a choice of VAT regimes (see **Value Added Tax** on page 208).

- **Social Security Regimes** – If you're self-employed or running a small business, you may be entitled to make reduced social security contributions (see **Micro Regimes** on page 214).

BANKING

Details of the French banking system, types of bank and account, charges, bank cards and other facilities and services are provided in *Living and Working in France* (Survival Books – see page 419), and this section deals only with aspects of banking that apply specifically to businesses.

Opening an Account

You can open a bank account whether you're resident or non-resident (see below). It's best to open a bank account in person, rather than by correspondence from abroad. Ask your friends, neighbours or colleagues for their recommendations and make an appointment at the bank of your choice. You must be at least 18 and provide proof of identity, e.g. a passport (be prepared to produce other forms of identification), and of your address in France, if applicable (an electricity bill usually suffices). If you're resident in France, you must also provide payslips (usually for the last three months) or, if you're self-employed, bank statements and other evidence of your earnings.

If you wish to open an account with a French bank while you're abroad, you must first obtain an application form, available from overseas branches of French banks (e.g. the Crédit Lyonnais in London, ☎ 020-7758 4000, 💻 www.creditlyonnais.fr). You must select a branch from the list provided, which should be close to where you will be living in France. If you open an account by correspondence, you must provide a reference from your current bank, including a certificate of signature or a signature witnessed by a solicitor. You also need a photocopy of the relevant pages of your passport and a euro draft to open the account.

Any account holder can create a joint account by giving his spouse (or anyone else) signatory authority. A joint account can be for two or more people. If applicable, you must state that cheques or withdrawal slips can be signed by any partner and don't require all signatures. Note that in the event of the death of a partner, a joint account is blocked until the will has been proven.

Non-residents

If you're non-resident (i.e. spend at least six months per year outside France), you're only entitled to open a non-resident account (*compte non-résident*). A non-resident account previously had many restrictions, including limiting account holders to making deposits from outside France only, but this is no longer the case. There's now little difference between non-resident and resident accounts and you can deposit and withdraw funds in any currency without limit, although there may be limits on the amount you can transfer between accounts (an anti-money-laundering measure). Non-resident accounts have a ban on ordinary overdrafts (*découverts*), although loans for a car or property purchase are possible.

French banks are imposing increasing minimum deposits on non-resident accounts; these can be up to €3,000, although it isn't usually necessary to maintain this balance once an account is open. Shop around for the best deal. To open a non-resident account, you must usually produce two pieces of identity, two proofs of address no more than three months old and a letter of recommendation from your existing bank.

Business Accounts

To open a business account, you must usually give the bank a copy of your articles of incorporation and a copy of your *Kbis*. As explained in Chapter 4, when setting up a business, you must first deposit the required capital in a holding account, then use the receipt to support your registration; when you receive your first *Kbis*, give a copy to the bank, which then unblocks the account and opens a business account in the name of the company.

Business accounts are charged 0.005 per cent of all withdrawals of funds (known as *commission de mouvement*), plus an account 'holding fee' – i.e. a charge for nothing in particular, simply to keep the bank in profit – (*commision de tenue de compte*), and charges are levied quarterly. Both fees are subject to VAT at 19.6 per cent.

It costs more to have a bank card for a business account than for a personal account, and this is generally a charge card rather than a debit card. Charges for online access to your account are usually also higher: around €20 per month instead of €4 for personal account holders.

You can make direct debits from your customers' accounts and various sorts of transfers (e.g. of payroll to employees' accounts), facilities which are available online. Most standard accounting software packages offer electronic transfer features (payroll or bill paying) – although banks generally charge for these. (Writing cheques is still free, although you must pay to post them!)

Technically, you're supposed to provide the bank with your financial statements each year, whether or not you have a loan outstanding with them, although this isn't a legal requirement.

Chèque Emploi Service

A special cheque account, called *Chèque Emploi Service*, is available for those wanting to pay casual workers who don't have accident or third party liability insurance. You must apply to your bank for a special cheque book, which usually takes two to three weeks to arrive and is accompanied by instructions for use. Before any work is done, complete the *volet social* corresponding to the cheque to be issued (it has the same number at the bottom) with the worker's details and details of the work to be done and the rate. Tick the box *base fortaitaire* for basic insurance, *salaire réel* for comprehensive insurance.

Preferably before the work is done, send the *volet social* to the Centre National de Traitement du Chèque Emploi Service, 42961 Saint-Etienne Cedex 9 (addressed envelopes should be supplied) and the relevant social security contributions will be deducted automatically from your bank account. (You receive notification of the amounts to be deducted at the beginning of the following month and the deduction be made at the end of that month.) If you're over 70, you're exempt from making contributions on behalf of casual workers, but you must complete the form at the front of the cheque book as well as the *volet social*.

A leaflet entitled *Chèque Emploi Service* providing details of the system is available from your bank or from the Union de Recouvrement des Cotisations de Sécurité Sociale et d'Allocations Familiales (URSSAF), which has 105 offices throughout France and an informative website (⌨ www.ces.urssaf.fr). **If you agree to pay casual workers in cash or by ordinary cheque and they have an accident on your premises, you can be sued for a very large sum of money.**

TAXATION

One of the two certainties in life, taxes come in various forms in France. Those that apply to running a business (including a self-employed activity) are detailed below. For further information about taxation in France, refer to *Living and Working in France* (Survival Books – see page 419).

The first thing to check, if you're leaving another country to set up a business in France, is that you have no outstanding tax liabilities there. **Make sure you confirm with your existing tax authorities that you owe no tax in your home country before leaving – and obtain a written declaration to that effect.**

Most new businesses enjoy an exemption on corporate tax and professional tax for the first two years of trading and an exoneration from the *imposition forfaitaire annuelle* (the minimum income tax on businesses) for the first three years (see page 204). Those in 'special development zones' also enjoy tax exonerations for between five and seven years (see **Grants & Subsidies** on page 186). Some departments (normally in low-employment regions) help companies recruiting staff with tax exemptions or grants. Information about the financial assistance available when creating a company (or becoming self-employed) can be found on the APCE website (⌨ www.apce.fr).

As you would expect in a country with a 'billion' bureaucrats, the French tax system is inordinately complicated and most French people don't understand it. It's difficult to obtain accurate information from the tax authorities, and errors in tax assessments are commonplace. Unless your tax affairs are simple, it's prudent to employ an accountant (*expert comptable*) to complete your tax return and ensure that you're correctly assessed. In fact, a good accountant can help you (legally) to save more in taxes than you will pay him in fees. A list of registered accountants is available from the Conseil Supérieur de l'Ordre des Experts-Comptables (☎ 01 44 15 60 00, 🖳 www.experts-comptables.fr). Details of Franco-British tax consultants are available from the French Chamber of Commerce in London (☎ 020-7304 7021). It's always best to choose an accountant who has been recommended to you.

Income Tax

In general, you must pay income tax at the same rate whether you're employed, self-employed or an employee – an instance of the French respect for *égalité*, perhaps. This is known as personal or 'physical person's' income tax (*impôt sur le revenue des personnes physiques/IRPP*, usually abbreviated to *IR*), while corporate tax is called *impôt sur la société* (*IS* – see **Corporate Tax** on page 203). Note, however, that some types of company pay *IR* rather than *IS* (see **Business Taxes** on page 203).

If your total assets are worth more than €732,000, you may also become liable for wealth tax (*impôt de la solidarité sur la fortune*/ISF), but once you reach that stage, you know that your business is a success!

French income tax rates are below average for EU countries, particularly for large families, and income tax accounts only for some 20 per cent of government revenue, and successive governments have been reducing income tax levels for the past decade.

Unlike many other countries (including most other EU countries), France doesn't operate a 'pay-as-you-earn' system, whereby employees' income tax is deducted at source by employers, and individuals are responsible for declaring and paying their own income tax.

The French have a pathological hatred of paying taxes, and tax evasion is a national sport (most French people don't consider cheating the *fisc* a crime). It's estimated that around a third of non-salaried taxpayers don't declare a substantial part of their income. Consequently, if your tax affairs are investigated, the authorities often take a hard line when they find you've been 'cheating', even if you made an 'innocent' mistake. If your perceived standard of living is higher than would be expected on your declared income, the tax authorities may suspect you of fraud, so contrive to appear poor (not difficult for struggling entrepreneurs!). In extreme circumstances, additional income tax or a higher rate of tax can be arbitrarily imposed by tax inspectors (*régime d'imposition forfaitaire*). The tax authorities maintain details of tax declarations, employers and bank accounts on computers to help them expose fraud and can now use social security numbers and access all other government computer systems to identify residents and their circumstances.

Many books are available to help you understand and save taxes, and income tax guides are published each January, including the *Guide Pratique du Contribuable* (Syndicat National Unifié des Impôts, 🖳 www.guideducontribuable.com). The Service Public website (🖳 www.service-public.fr) also has extensive tax information under '*Impôts*'. If your French isn't up to deciphering tax terminology, refer to *Taxation in France* by Charles Parkinson (PKF Publications).

Income Tax Regimes

As with all financial procedures, there are different income tax 'regimes' (*régimes*) for different types of business – some optional and some compulsory – and the names are confusing (and often used inconsistently by the tax authorities themselves!).

For example, you may see reference to a *régime normal* and a *régime option*, which are essentially the 'default' regime and any other regime (respectively). But what constitutes the *régime normal* varies according to your situation: it may be a *régime simplifié* (whereby the filing and payment procedures are simplified by 'assuming' certain expenses, etc. – usually, but not always, to the advantage of small businesses) or a *régime réel* (whereby nothing is assumed, but you declare your actual figures and pay tax on these amounts). To further complicate matters, there are specific regimes for small businesses (see below).

Micro-entreprises: If you operate a small business or are starting a business and your turnover is low, it can be to your advantage to operate as a *micro-entreprise*, which doesn't mean 'tiny business', but is a specific tax regime that can be adopted by businesses whose turnover is below certain limits. There are essentially three types of declaration for *micro-entreprises*:

- **Micro-BIC** – You come under this category if you run a 'commercial' business, i.e. selling goods; *BIC* stands for *bénéfices commerciaux*. The turnover limit is currently (2003 tax year) €76,300.

- **Micro-BNC** – This category applies to 'non-commercial' businesses, i.e. those that provide a service; *BNC* stands for *bénéfices non-commerciaux*. The turnover limit is currently (2003 tax year) €27,000.

- **Micro-BA** – This category is for agricultural businesses; *BA* stands for *bénéfices agricoles*.

Even if your turnover is below the specified limit, if you opt to register for VAT (see page 208) or if your business is registered for *impôt sur la société*, you cannot operate as a *micro-entreprise*.

If you qualify and choose to operate as a *micro-entreprise*, you don't have to keep business records (although you would be foolish not to and you must in any case prepare summaries of money received and expenses paid – see **Accounting** on page 221). You simply declare your turnover (*chiffre d'affaires*) and your taxable income (see below) is assumed to be 28 per cent of that (for merchandise businesses) or 48 per cent (for service businesses).

There's no need to register for this regime; you simply declare your turnover on the appropriate form when filing your income tax return and your tax is calculated automatically.

Registering as a *micro-entreprise* also reduces your social security contributions (see **Micro Regimes** on page 214) and can save you accountants' fees, as there's no need for complicated bookkeeping (see **Micro-entreprises** on page 197).

Taxable Income

Income tax is calculated on earned income (*impôt sur le revenu*) and unearned income (*impôt des revenus de capitaux*). Certain types of income are exempt from income tax, including payments from a complementary insurance policy or a temporary accident and illness insurance policy and allowances for obligatory training courses. Social security contributions (see page 213) **aren't** taxable (with the exception of the non-deductible part of *CSG/CRDS* – see page 211) and are deducted from gross income.

There are other allowances, such as a 'mileage' (*kilométrage*) allowance for using your car for business purposes. Contributions to a complementary health insurance fund (*mutuelle*), up to €7,131 per year, are tax deductible.

Certain losses are allowable against income tax (e.g. from agricultural and certain other investments), as are certain expenses (e.g. taxes on historic or listed buildings, subscriptions to certain cultural organisations and capital invested in a business).

The figure you arrive at after deducting all allowances is your net taxable income (*revenue net imposable*).

Self-employed

Salaried workers, including employers, qualify for two general deductions from gross salary: a 10 per cent allowance (*déduction forfaitaire*) for 'professional' or 'notional' expenses, and a further general deduction (*abattement général*) of 20 per cent. The self-employed don't qualify for either of these, which means that they must pay considerably more income tax than employees. But, as so often in France, there's a way around this problem.

If you're self-employed, you can obtain a 20 per cent reduction on your taxable income by joining a *centre de gestion* (see below). You must join before the end of March in the year for which you want to claim the 20 per cent reduction, and the joining fee is around €110. You must then pay an annual subscription of around €150 (payable at the end of the year). This means that, provided your taxable income is above around €9,000, joining is to your advantage.

Centres de Gestion

To qualify for tax reductions, businesses (whether sole traders or registered companies) can join their regional *association agréé des professions libérales* (commonly known as a *centre de gestion* or *CGA*), a government-sponsored body that regulates the income tax declarations of self-employed people and businesses.

Centres de gestion can also provide training and general advice on running a business. There's an annual membership fee, which varies between around €100 and €1,000 according to the size of the business, which must be paid by the end of March in order for you to be considered a member for tax purposes for the current financial year.

Members are supposed to use an accountant, although there are accountants who offer their services to members for somewhat reduced fees. However, membership provides you and your business with an additional safeguard in that your accounts are being checked by a government-approved agency, so that it's highly unlikely that any anomalies will slip through and come back to haunt you.

Family Quotient

Families are taxed as a single entity, and the French income tax system favours the family, as the amount of income tax paid is directly related to the number of dependent children (if you have enough children, you pay no tax at all!). French tax rates are based on a system of coefficients or 'parts' (*parts*), reflecting the family status of the taxpayer and the number of dependent children. The number of parts is known as the *quotient familial* (*QF*). Details can be found in *Living and Working in France* (Survival Books – see page 419).

Calculation

The tax year in France runs for the calendar year (i.e. from 1st January to 31st December). The income tax rates for a single person (1 part) for 2004 income (2005 tax return) are shown in the table below. Taxable income is income after the deduction of social security contributions and various allowances (see above). Your tax 'base' (*assiette fiscale*) is calculated by multiplying the taxable income within a particular bracket by the tax rate.

Taxable Income (€)	Tax Rate (%)	Tax (€)	Aggregate Tax (€)
Up to 4,262	0	0	0
4,262 – 8,382	6.83	281.40	281.40
8,382 – 14,753	19.14	1,219.41	1,500.81
14,753 – 23,888	28.26	2,581.55	4,082.36
23,888 – 38,868	37.38	5,599.52	9,681.88
38,868 – 47,932	42.62	3,863.08	13,544.96
Over 47,932	48.09		

The following table shows the amount of tax payable for selected taxable incomes from €10,000 to €50,000 (2003 income) for various family quotients:

Taxable Income (€)	Parts					
	1	1.5*	2**	2.5**	3**	3.5**
10,000	493	0	0	0	0	0
20,000	2,984	1,844–2,184	1,182	564	346	127
30,000	6,367	4,475–5,567	3,141	2,435	1,773	1,112
40,000	10,164	8,078–9,364	5,967–6,555	4,633	3,687	3,026
50,000	14,539	12,453–13,739	8,996–10,930	7,459–8,844	6,125–6,195	4,940

*   The tax due varies with the status of the child.

** Above certain thresholds married couples pay less tax than widows or unmarried partners, who pay less than single parents.

Once you've calculated your tax 'base', you may be eligible for reductions or credits to this amount (see below).

Reductions & Credits

Various reductions (*réductions*) and credits (*crédits*) can be applied to your tax 'base', according to your circumstances. (The difference between a reduction and a credit is that a credit can result in a negative amount of tax due – i.e. a refund – whereas a reduction cannot.)

Tax reductions may apply to children at school or university; the cost of registered day care for children under seven provided both parents work and earn less than a certain amount (or cannot work); contributions to a complementary health insurance scheme in accordance with the *Loi Madelin* (see page 220); dividends from a French company; purchase of forest or woodland; investment in an overseas company, a 'rural regeneration area' (*zone de revitalisation rurale*), a small or medium-size enterprise (*PME*) or an innovative job-creation project (*fonds communs de placement dans l'innovation*); management training expenses; union subscription fees.

Tax credits may apply to the following: major expenditure on home improvements; VAT on major items of domestic equipment purchased from and installed by a VAT-registered company; the purchase of an LPG-powered car or the purchase or rental of any car if you've taken a car more than ten years old off the road in exchange.

Income Tax Return

You're sent an annual tax return (*déclaration des revenus*) by the tax authorities in late February or early March of each year. If you aren't sent a form, you can obtain one from your local town hall or tax office (look in the telephone book under *Impôts, Trésor Public*). The standard return is the 2042, which everyone must complete. In addition, you may have to complete other forms, depending on your status and that of your business. Supplementary forms include those for non-commercial profits (forms 2035, 2037), property income (2044), foreign source income such as a pension or dividends (2047), capital gains on financial investments (2074), and other capital gains (2049). If your business isn't subject to business taxes, you must declare the business's income for personal income tax. In the case of a partnership or certain other forms of company, the partners or shareholders each declare their part of the income from the business.

If your earnings are below a certain limit (see **Micro-entreprises** on page 197), you should complete a *micro-entreprise* or *micro-BNC/micro-BIC* form.

There are three methods of declaring your income tax and you're obliged or entitled to opt for one or the other according to your type of business.

● **Déclaration Contrôlée** – If you're self-employed in a *profession libérale*, you must complete form 2035, which requires you to keep accounts of income and expenses, including all related receipts and documents.

● **Régime Simplifié** – Your business qualifies under the simplified regime (*régime simplifié*) if your sales of merchandise are worth between €84,000 and €763,000 or if your service revenues are between €30,500 and €230,000. As the name suggests, this regime entitles you to simplified accounting and VAT return procedures (see page 200). If your earnings are from letting unfurnished property, you can opt for the *régime simplifié de déclaration des revenus fonciers* (usually referred to as the *régime micro-foncier*); this is dealt with in **Earning Money From Your French Home** (Survival Books – see page 419).

● **Régime Réel** – If your turnover exceeds the relevant limit for the *régime simplifié* (see above), you automatically come under the *régime réel*; if it's below the limit, you can opt for the *régime réel*, but it's rarely to your advantage, as you're required to submit detailed accounts (see **Accounting** on page 221) and make quarterly VAT declarations (see **Régime Réel** on page 201).

If you're running a business jointly with your spouse or partner, both of you must sign the completed return; failure to do so means that the form will be returned to you – usually **after** the closing date, so that you must pay a 10 per cent late filing penalty.

French tax returns are complicated, despite attempts to simplify them in recent years. The language used is particularly difficult to understand for foreigners (and many French). Local tax offices (Centres des Impôts) are usually helpful and will help you complete your tax return. The Centre des Impôts also offers assistance via telephone (☎ 08 20 32 42 52 between 08.00 and 22.00 Mondays to Fridays and from 09.00 to 19.00 on Saturdays) and the internet (🖳 www.ir.dgi.minefi.gouv.fr). Tax declarations can be made online, but not the first time you make a declaration in France; once you've been issued with a taxpayer number, you can use the online facility, which is free and allows you an extension of one to three weeks on the filing deadline. Other useful websites are 🖳 www.dna.calcular.com and www.ifiscal.net. You can make an appointment for a free consultation with your local tax inspector at your town hall. However, if your French isn't excellent you must take someone with you who's fluent. Alternatively you can employ an accountant or tax advisor (*expert comptable/conseiller fiscal* – see **Accounting** on page 221). .

Changes in your tax liability may be made by the tax authorities up to three years after the end of the tax year to which the liability relates. Therefore, you should retain all records relating to the income and expenses reported in your tax returns for at least three years, even if you've left France.

Tax returns must usually be filed by late March (the exact date varies according to the date forms are sent out – invariably late!).

Although you're allowed to accidentally under-declare by up to 5 per cent, you must pay the difference, and penalties for deliberately undeclared or grossly understated income and unjustified deductions range from 40 to 80 per cent for fraud, plus interest on the amount owed. You may also make yourself liable for penalties if you display 'exterior signs of wealth' (*signes extérieurs de richesse*), so don't drive to the Centre des Impôts in your new Mercedes to deposit your tax return!

Tax Bills

Some time between August and December, you will receive a tax bill (*avis d'imposition*). There are two methods of paying your tax bill in France: in three instalments (*tiers provisionnels*) or in ten equal monthly instalments (*mensualisation*).

Three Instalments: This is the more common method of payment. The first two payments, each comprising around a third (*tiers*) of the previous year's tax liability, are provisional (*acompte provisionnel*) and are payable on 15th February and 15th May each year. For example in 2005, these payments each represent around a third of your total tax bill for 2004. The third and final instalment, the balance of your tax bill (*solde*), is payable by 15th September. The tax authorities adjust your third payment to take into account your actual income for the previous year.

To take a simple example, if you paid €18,000 in income tax in 2003, your first two payments in 2005 (for the tax year 2004) would each be for €6,000, i.e. a third of your previous bill. If your actual tax liability for 2004 was €20,000, you would then pay the balance of €8,000 (€20,000 minus the €12,000 already paid) in September 2005 as a final payment. If you pay your tax bill late, you must pay a penalty equal to 10 per cent of your annual tax bill.

During your first year in France you won't have a previous year's tax liability (in France). Therefore, the income tax computed with the information contained in the tax return filed at the end of March of the following year is payable in full by 15th September of the same year. In the following year, the normal procedure is applied. The following schedule shows the tax payment for a new arrival in France:

Year	Date	Action
1 (arrival in France)		tax payable in previous country of residence
2	end March	file tax return for first year's income
	15th September	pay entire tax bill for first year
3	15th February	pay first instalment of second year's tax
	end March	file tax return for second year's income
	15th May	pay second instalment of second year's tax
	15th September	pay final instalment of second year's tax
4	as Year 3	

You become liable for French tax as soon as you establish your principal residence in France, which normally means the day you move into your French home. Therefore, if you arrived in France in September 2004, you won't make your first tax payment until September 2005, and then only for the last three or four months of the year 2004, so you won't need to pay any significant income tax until two years after your arrival, i.e. September 2006, although you may of course also be liable for tax in your previous country of residence for the first part of the year of your move.

Monthly Instalments: You can choose to pay your tax in ten equal monthly instalments (*mensualisation*) by direct debit from a bank or post office account, in which case you must write to the collector of taxes in your tax region requesting this method of payment. If you make your request before 10th May, monthly payments begin immediately (with an adjustment for any instalments already paid); if you apply after 10th May, they won't begin until the following January. Once started, monthly payments continue automatically each year unless you cancel them in writing.

Under this system, you pay one tenth of your previous year's tax bill on the 8th of each month from January to October. If your income is less in the current year than the previous year, the tax office stops payments when it has received the full amount or sends you a refund if you've overpaid (they usually do so fairly promptly). On the other hand, if you're earning more than in the previous year, the tax office will deduct a final payment (*solde*), usually in December.

Monthly payments are a good budgeting and cash flow aid. On the other hand, the advantage of paying in three instalments is that you can invest the amount set aside for tax until each payment is due.

Business Taxes

Whether you're self-employed or have set up a company, you are liable for business taxes, but the two situations are different:

- **Self-employed** – You pay personal income tax (see above) on all your earnings plus *taxe professionnelle* (see page 204).

- **Company** – You pay no personal income tax, but instead pay company or corporation tax (*impôt sur la société/IS*), as well as *taxe professionelle* and, if your earnings are above a certain limit, the *contribution sociale de solidarité*; if you employ staff, you must also pay *taxe d'apprentissage* and a contribution to *formation professionnelle* (see below).

Some types of company have the option to pay personal income tax or corporation tax; others don't. It depends partly on the business entity (see page 123) and partly on the business statutes. For example, a *EURL* may normally choose between *IR* and *IS* and a family-run *SARL* usually pays *IR*, whereas one that employs non-family members is subject to *IS*. You should check when registering a company whether it is liable for *IR* or *IS* and, if you have a choice, which is to your advantage.

Corporate Tax

Corporate tax (*impôt sur la société/IS*) is the main tax on most types of company. In effect, instead of the business owner declaring its income on his or her personal income tax form, as with the self-employed, the company is charged income tax as an 'impersonal' entity. The tax is levied at two rates: 15.45 per cent on the first €38,120 of taxable income (i.e. profit) and 34.33 per cent on the remainder.

As with income tax and VAT, there are different corporate tax regimes (*régimes*), which may be referred to by various names (!). For example, you may have a choice between a *régime simplifié* (*d'imposition*) – whereby certain figures (e.g. expenses) are 'assumed' and the declaration and payment procedures are simplified accordingly (usually to the benefit of small businesses) – and a *régime réel* (*normal*), whereby you declare your actual figures and pay tax on those.

Either way, you should receive *IS* forms by the beginning of March and must usually submit them by 30th April (although dates can vary if there are strikes or changes to the tax law). You must declare your business results for the previous year, and make payments starting the following year, based on your declared results. So, for example, if you started a company whose first accounting period (*exercice*) ended on 31st December 2004, you must submit the *IS* forms by 30th April 2005, and begin making provisional payments in 2006 for the 2005 fiscal year, based on your 2004 results. This obviously means that your business has a tax 'holiday' of at least a year, which can be a great help in getting started.

The *IS* forms themselves consist of a standardised set of financial statements (see **Accounting** on page 221) and some supporting schedules detailing fixed assets, amortisation and any provisions included in the results, including a summary of any prior year losses being carried forward. There's no calculation of taxes due at this stage, but the declaration is used as the basis for the following year's assessment of provisional payments.

The first provisional payment (*acompte*) is due in April and includes a minimum tax based on your gross sales and service revenue or turnover (*chiffres d'affaires*), including VAT. This is a measure designed to prevent tax avoidance and is called the *imposition forfaitaire annuelle* (*IFA*) and starts at €750 for businesses with a turnover, including VAT, of less than €150,000. **This must be paid by all companies, whether or not they have profits subject to *IS* that year.** The *IFA* isn't refundable, but can be counted against the taxes due (see below). The other three quarterly payments generally consist of one third of the *IS* due on the previous year's net income, although there's a reduced rate of 25 per cent for small businesses meeting certain conditions.

In March of the following year, you receive a form on which you must declare your actual company taxable income for the previous year and calculate the taxes due for the quarterly payments, plus any surtaxes due (mostly for companies with income over around €7 million). All the provisional payments made in the previous year and the *IFA* for up to three years previously can be deducted from this figure. The company must then pay the difference or, if it has overpaid, claim a refund. If your company has made a loss, you only have to pay the *IFA* and then no further provisional amounts until you calculate your actual taxes due the following April.

If this sounds complicated, it is. But the various tax offices generally send out the forms a good four to six weeks before they're due. To add to the fun, the process for making provisional payments was recently changed: instead of paying these to the treasury office (*trésor public* or *perception*), you must now pay them to the tax office (*hôtel des impôts*). But the main declaration must still be submitted to the *trésor public*!

Taxe Professionnelle

The amount of *taxe professionelle* (professional tax) you pay, and how it's calculated, depends on whether you're self-employed or a company (see below).

Professional tax is assessed as follows: in your first year of French residence, you pay nothing; in your second year, you pay according to your earnings in Year 1 (pro rata if you moved to France part way through the year); in Year 3, your tax is again based on your Year 1 earnings, in Year 4 on your Year 2 earnings, and so on. It's normally payable by 15th December.

Self-employed: If you're self-employed, *taxe professionelle* is payable on your business premises and is levied at between around 15 and 20 per cent (the exact percentage varies with the commune) of a 'base', which is currently 8 per cent of your annual income, including VAT. For example, if you earn €30,000 per year, your tax base is €2,400; if professional tax is levied at 20 per cent in your commune, you pay €480.

If you work from home, you can claim a reduction on your property tax according to the proportion of your home that's used for business purposes (see **Property Taxes** below). Certain types of worker are exempt from professional tax, including writers and artists. You should check with an accountant.

Company: For a registered company, *taxe professionelle* is based on your turnover (*chiffres d'affaires*), including VAT, categorised by sales and service revenue, the number of business locations you have and the number of employees, including apprentices and disabled workers.

In addition to details of your turnover, business premises and employees, you must declare the value and details of any properties subject to *taxe foncière* (see **Property Taxes** below) – if you work from home, you must specify the size and nature of any part of your home that's used for the business – and the value of all fixed assets, including amortisable equipment, owned, rented or used (free of charge) by the business. The total value of each category of assets is multiplied by a set percentage. Rates are set by local governments – usually at town, regional and departmental level – and vary significantly. They're generally highest in the Ile-de-France region, where they can be as high as 25 per cent; elsewhere, they can be as low as 7 per cent.

Additional assessments may be made for the local CCI, Chambre des Métiers and/or other local agencies according to local policy. However, part of what you pay in *taxe professionnelle* can be credited against the *taxe d'apprentissage* (see below) – a very small part!

You should receive a form in early April, which must be returned by 1st May, declaring certain information about the business for the previous tax year. Your *taxe professionnelle* bill then arrives in November, to be paid by 15th December. So, for example, a business whose first accounting year ends on 31st December 2004 must submit a *taxe professionnelle* form by 1st May 2005, will receive a bill the following November and must pay by 15th December 2005. This means that the first two years of your company's existence are exempt from *taxe professionelle*.

Taxe sur les Voitures des Sociétés

This tax is levied on all vehicles (not just cars) owned by a business.

Cars: For each car rated at less than 7 'fiscal horsepower' (*chevaux fiscaux*) – not directly related to a car's power – you must pay €1,130 annually and for each car over 7CV €2,440. There are various exemptions, e.g. if a car is more than ten years old, is LPG-powered or is an integral part of the business (e.g. cars owned by a car hire or taxi company).

Vans & Lorries: Company-owned vans and lorries must pay road tax, which involves purchasing a sticker (*vignette*) for display behind the windscreen, although the first three vehicles are exempt. As with cars, the amount of tax payable depends on a vehicle's fiscal horsepower.

Taxe d'Apprentissage & Participation à la Formation Professionnelle

As their names indicate, these odd taxes cover the cost of apprenticeship and professional training subsidies and are payable by all companies that employ staff. What makes them even odder is that you must make the payments indirectly (see below); if you pay these taxes directly to the tax office, you're supposed to pay double the going rate!

The *taxe d'appentissage* and *particpation à la formation professionnelle* contribution are based on a percentage of your gross payroll for the previous year. The *taxe d'apprentissage* is 0.5 per cent, reduced by a percentage of the *taxe professionnelle* paid to the CCI (see below) and further reduced if you've employed your quota of apprentices during the year.

The *formation professionnelle* contribution starts at 0.25 per cent of your gross payroll, and a business may be subject to an additional amount if it's subject to certain national conventions (*conventions collectives*) that require employer contributions to continuing education funds. There's an additional tax on pay to those on term contracts (*CDD*). Companies that employ ten or more people can deduct amounts expended for continuing education during the year from the tax due.

Starting in late January, you receive forms for declaring your *taxe d'apprentissage* and *particpation à la formation professionelle* contribution from every local agency that has anything to do with training, and you simply choose one – and only one! – of these (it doesn't much matter which) to make your payments to. If you don't receive a form from any organisation, you can designate any school or agency in your area to receive the tax. Return your completed form with the appropriate payment to the chosen agency, which prepares the tax return, verifying that you've paid the tax through them. Normally, they send you a copy of the form they've filed, along with the official receipts for the tax paid, but occasionally they send you back two copies of the official form and ask you to send the original to the tax office yourself. (It pays to read the covering letter carefully, whatever they send you!)

Taxe sur les Salaires

This is an even more peculiar tax than the *taxe d'appentissage* and *particpation à la formation professionnelle*, as almost all companies are exempt from it! It applies only to companies that are exempt from paying VAT and is levied, as the name suggests, on payroll – but, as the only companies exempt from VAT are very small companies, which usually have no staff, hardly any companies are liable for the tax. And even if they are, there's an exemption if the total tax due is less than €840.

The tax is levied at 4.25 per cent of each employee's salary up to €6,675, at 8.5 per cent on each salary between €6,904 and €13,793, and at 13.6 per cent above this amount. There's a reduction if the total tax due is below €1,680, and there are allowances for associations and other non-profit organisations. Payment is due by 15th January annually, using form 2052.

If you're unsure whether of not your company should be paying payroll tax, contact the *taxe sur les salaires* representative at your tax office.

Taxe pour la Participation à l'Effort de la Construction

Another strange tax, which derives from the days when employers used to provide housing for their workers and 'encourages' them to continue doing so by allowing exemptions from the tax to companies that 'invest' in housing, e.g. by offering employees house-buying loans or contributing to local house-building projects. The amount of investment required to be exempt from the tax depends on a number of factors, including the area in which your business is located. If you aren't exempt, your obligatory 'participation in the construction effort' amounts to 0.45 per cent of your total payroll.

Contribution Sociale de la Solidarité

Although called a 'contribution', this is in effect a (compulsory) tax to cover losses incurred by the government through its non-salaried social security regimes and to foster employment. However, it applies only to companies with more than €760,000 in annual revenue from sales within France. (Sales exported from France can be deducted from the total sales figure.) The tax is assessed at a rate of 0.13 per cent and is due in two instalments, the first in April and the second in July. You should receive a letter reminding you of the existence of the tax and inviting you to contact Organic – the agency that collects it (see **Registration** on page 136) – if your turnover for the previous year is above the assessment level.

Capital Gains Tax

There are three types of capital gains tax (*impôt sur les plus-values*) that can affect businesses:

- **Les Plus-values Immobilières** – Commercial property, like residential property (other than a principal residence), is subject to CGT on transfer. Property worth over €15,000 (i.e. anything other than a portacabin!) is subject to CGT at 26 per cent up to 15 years after purchase. The purchase price of a property is no longer 'indexed' to increases in the cost of living, and there are certain exemptions to the above tax rates, as follows:
  - If you've owned a property for more than five years, but less than 15, you're entitled to a 10 per cent reduction in CGT for every year of ownership over five (i.e. 10 per cent for six years' ownership, 20 per cent for seven years', etc.).
  - If you've owned a property for at least five years and can produce proof of substantial expenditure on improving it (e.g. receipts for work done by professionals), you can claim a further deduction of 15 per cent of the property's purchase price against CGT (irrespective of the actual cost of the work), but you're no longer entitled to claim for work you've done yourself, nor for any materials purchased for DIY improvements.
- **Les Plus-values Mobilières** – 'Movable' property (generally, fixed assets other than buildings, but including property leases) is also subject to CGT. The calculation varies according to whether the business is liable to income tax (*IR*) or corporate tax (*IS*). In the former case, the calculation also varies according to whether property has been owned (by the business) for less than or more than two years. In both cases, the calculation also varies according to whether the value of the property can be written off over a period (e.g. an item of machinery) or not (e.g. a lease).
  Businesses subject to *IR* are exempt if their turnover is below €90,000 (for services) or €250,000 (for goods); partial exemption applies to businesses with turnovers of up to €126,000 and €350,000 respectively. If you hand over your

business to another person, however, you may be subject to tax, unless you continue to exercise a similar activity for the next five years. The tax rate depends on whether gains are considered to be short-term or long-term: short-term gains are taxed as income at normal income tax rates; long-term gains are taxed at 27 per cent.

There's no CGT exemption for businesses subject to IS, which must pay tax at 33.3 per cent, unless the gain is less than €38,120, in which case tax is levied at 15 per cent.

- **Les Plus-values Professionnelles** – This is theoretically a tax on the increase in value of the intangible aspects of a business (i.e. the *fonds de commerce*), but in practice most businesses, and particularly small and medium-size enterprises, are exempt from 'professional' capital gains tax (CGT).

  If you're selling shares in the business that have been held for at least two years, these count as part of its value and are included in any CGT calculation (shares that have been held for less than two years are liable to income or corporation tax instead).

Property Taxes

There are three types of property tax, known as 'local tax' (*impôt local*): *taxe foncière* (referred to here as property tax), *taxe d'habitation* (referred to as residential tax), and, in some areas, *taxe assimilée* (sundry tax). Taxes pay for local services, including rubbish collection, street lighting and cleaning, local schools and other community services, and include a contribution to departmental and regional expenses. You may be billed separately for rubbish collection.

All property, including commercial property, is subject to property tax, but only residential property is subject to residential tax (which therefore isn't dealt with here – for details, see *Buying a Home in France* by Survival Books). If you rent your business premises, however, you don't have to pay property tax; the owner must pay it.

If you work from home, you can claim a reduction on your property tax according to the proportion of your home that's used for business purposes. The procedure varies by department, but you may need to submit a formal request to your town hall or *mairie* that a portion of your home be declared business property. The request is sent to the *préfecture* and, once it's approved, the reclassified number of square meters is taken off your property taxes and added to the calculation of your *taxe professionelle* (see page 204). You must measure the total area of your living room, dining room, bedrooms and office (if separate). If your office occupies 10 per cent of the total area, for example, you may claim a 10 per cent reduction in *taxe foncière*. However, if you're operating a registered business from home (for up to the maximum two years – see page 109), there's no adjustment to your property taxes.

Value Added Tax

Value added tax (VAT) is called *taxe sur la valeur ajoutée* (*TVA*) and accounts for around 45 per cent of government revenue (twice as much as income tax!). As in many other countries, VAT is added to the price of most goods and services and is passed down the supply chain so that the end user (usually the consumer) must pay it and the manufacturer, wholesaler, distributor and retailer can reclaim the VAT they've paid.

Prices that include VAT are described as *toutes taxes comprises* (*TTC*); prices exclusive of tax are *hors taxes* (*HT*). France has the following rates of VAT:

Rate (%)	Application
0.0 (exempt)	Basic foodstuffs, children's clothes, medical and dental care, educational services, insurance, banking and financial services, and various transactions subject to other taxes
2.1 (super-reduced)	Medicines reimbursed by social security; newspapers and magazines
5.5 (reduced)	Certain foodstuffs (including most drinks and take-away food); agricultural products; non-reimbursed medicines; books; public transport; canteen food; cinema, theatre and concert tickets; travel agency fees; improvements to a home over two years old (until December 2005)
19.6 (standard)	All services and goods that don't come under the reduced or super-reduced rate

Your business activity may or may not be subject to (*assujetti à*) VAT, and you should check with your local Centre des Impôts, which collects VAT as well as other taxes. Generally, a business providing a service (*prestation de service*) with an annual turnover of more than €30,500 must register for VAT and charge VAT to its customers. If VAT relates to sales (*vente*), these must exceed €84,000 before registration is necessary. Note, however, that it may be in your interest to register, even if your turnover is below the relevant limit, e.g. if most of your sales are made outside France (see below).

If you're VAT registered, you should check the VAT rate that needs to be applied to your products or services, as this isn't always obvious. For example, if you run a restaurant, you now need add only 5.5 per cent to all bills; if you carry out property repair or maintenance work, you should charge only 5.5 per cent if a property is more than two years old, but must obtain a signed declaration to this effect from the owner.

If you're making or selling goods or providing services outside France, you must normally charge VAT at the appropriate rate or rates. However, VAT isn't charged to customers in the European Union if the customer provides you with his European VAT number. Similarly, by providing your VAT number on purchase orders, you won't be charged VAT on purchases imported from other EU countries. Nevertheless, you should declare all EU purchases on your year-end VAT return. Make sure you obtain and keep VAT receipts for all business-related expenditure.

VAT returns must usually be made quarterly. VAT refunds aren't paid automatically and must be applied for on certain dates.

There are essentially two types of VAT 'regime' (*régime*), which are explained below.

Régime Simplifié

Your business qualifies under the simplified regime (*régime simplifié*) if your sales of merchandise are worth between €84,000 and €763,000 or if your service revenues are between €30,500 and €230,000. Under this regime, you're required to file only one VAT declaration per year, a CA12, on which you report your sales and the VAT paid on purchases. This declaration forms the basis of your provisional VAT payments for the following year, which are due at the end of each quarter.

In the second half of the year, if your actual results to date will result in a difference of at least 10 per cent in the provisional payment due, you may request a variance and pay the higher or lower amount. The fourth quarter provisional payment is due in December and covers only two months of the quarter (pro rata) with the balance due in April with your next CA12 filing. If you've overpaid by at least €150, you can request a refund at this time, or apply the overpayment to the following year's provisional payments. If the amount due to you is under €150, you must apply it against the following year's payments.

In the first year of a business, you pay a fixed amount each quarter; after October, you can request a refund of the VAT you've paid on capital assets only.

Régime Réel

This regime is what it sounds like: you must declare your actual VAT inputs and outputs at the end of every quarter on form 3514K, and you're billed or (if you're lucky) sent a cheque for the balance once a year (in around October). Unlike in the UK, you don't make or receive a payment with each declaration. If your turnover exceeds the relevant limit for the *régime simplifié* (see above), you automatically come under the *régime réel*; if it's below the limit, you can opt for the *régime réel*, but it's rarely to your advantage.

SOCIAL SECURITY

France has a comprehensive social security (*sécurité sociale*) system covering healthcare (plus sickness and maternity), injuries at work, family allowances, unemployment insurance, and old age (pensions), invalidity and death benefits. Over 30 per cent of GDP is spent on 'welfare'; the total social security revenue is around €200 billion per year and the social security budget is higher than the Gross National Product, i.e. social security costs more than the value of what the country produces! This means that social security is expensive.

Social security contributions are one of the biggest expenses to be faced when running a business in France, whether on a self-employed basis or as the owner of a company employing staff, and you should ensure that you budget sufficiently for these, particularly at the outset, as contributions are backdated to your start date and you can receive a very large bill!

▲ Physiotherapist © Joe Laredo
(see **Chapter 12**)

▲ Bar owner © Dani Corbet
(see **Case Study 4**)

▼ Restaurant © Ewan Scutcher
(see **Case Study 1**)

▲ Wine maker © www.picturefrance.com
(see **Chapter 14**)

▼ Cafe-bar © Joe Laredo
(see **Chapter 7**)

▲ British grocer's © www.picturefrance.com
(see **Chapter 9**)

▲ Plumber © Mark Hoskins
(see **Case Study 15**)

▼ Bookshop owner © Heidi Lee
(see **Case Study 19**)

▲ Public house © www.picturefrance.com
(see **Chapter 7**)

▼ Chef © www.picturefrance.com

▲ *Hairdresser* © *Joe Laredo*

▲ *Publisher* © *Harold Mewes*
(see **Case Study 30**)

▼ *Florist* © *Joe Laredo*

▲ *Property agent* © *Susan Dixon*
(see **Case Study 7**)

▼ *Puppeteer* © *www.picturefrance.com*

▲ Farmer © Joe Laredo
(see **Chapter 14**)

▼ Property agent © www.picturefrance.com
(see **Chapter 8**)

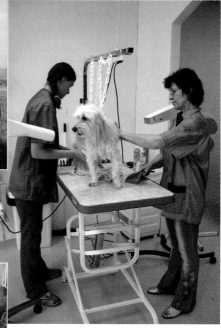

▲ Pet groomer © Joe Laredo

▼ Builder © www.picturefrance.com
(see **Chapter 8**)

▲ Fish and chip shop © www.picturefrance.com
(see **Chapter 7**)

The only good news is that the majority of social security contributions (also referred to as social charges) are tax-deductible and, with the exception of sickness benefits, social security benefits aren't taxed. Although employers are pushing to have their contributions lowered, the public has (understandably) been highly resistant to any change that might reduce benefits and the government has (understandably) taken the public's side. In 1996, in an attempt to erase some €38 billion of social security debt within 13 years (by 31st January 2009), it introduced an employee contribution towards 'the reimbursement of the social debt' (*contribution au remboursement de la dette sociale/CRDS* or *remboursement de la dette sociale/RDS*), which **all** employees must now make **in addition to** an existing employee levy, the *contribution sociale généralisée* (*CSG*) – both contributions are levied against 95 per cent of total income, including interest income, retirement pensions and investment income, and not just salary. The combined *CRDS/CSG* now amounts to 8 per cent, only 2.4 per cent of which is deductible from income taxes.

Some people have tried to get around paying the many social charges required by forming an association and paying themselves a salary (see **Associations** on page 131). **But owning or running an association exempts you from social charges, and employees of an association must pay exactly the same social charges as any other employees.**

There's little difference between social security benefits for self-employed and those for salaried employees, which are outlined in **Chapter 3** and detailed in *Living and Working in France* (see page 419). The main disadvantage of being self-employed is that there's no sick pay or unemployment benefit if you're off work due to illness, accident or lack of custom, although it's possible for the self-employed to buy a form of unemployment insurance that converts to extra retirement cover if it hasn't been used up by the time you retire.

Registration

Most business owners and self-employed people must register for social security with the Union de Recouvrement des Cotisations de Sécurité Sociale et d'Allocations Familiales (URSSAF), which has 105 offices throughout France (🖳 www.ces. urssaf.fr). You're then automatically registered with the relevant funds (*caisses*) for family allowances and pensions, each of which will send you a bill for contributions. For most activities, these are the Caisse d'Allocations Familiales/CAF (family allowances) and the Caisse Nationale d'Assurance Vieillesse/CNAV (pensions). However, some activities are covered by other funds: for example, traders (*commerçants*) are enrolled in the Caisse Nationale du Régime d'Assurance Vieillesse Invalidité Décès des Non-salariés de l'Industrie et du Commerce (bizarrely abbreviated to Organic!), tradesmen (*artisans*) in Canava, and artists (painters and performers) and authors must make pension contributions to an organisation called CIPAV. The 'standard' medical fund is the Caisse Nationale de l'Assurance Maladie (CNAM), but there may be a choice of funds, although they all offer identical benefits.

Writers and translators pay reduced contributions, provided they're registered with one of the two organisations that manage their contributions: the *Association pour la Gestion de la Sécurité Sociale des Auteurs* (Agessa) or the *Maison des Artists*.

When registering for social security, you must provide your personal details, including your full name, address, country of origin, and date and place of birth. You must also produce passports, *cartes de séjour* (if applicable) and certified birth certificates for your dependants, plus a marriage certificate (if applicable). You may need to provide copies with official translations, but check first, as translations may be unnecessary. You also need proof of residence such as a rental contract or an electricity bill.

You must also declare your business income to URSSAF using a form called a *déclaration commun des revenus* (DCR), which must be filed by 1st May of the following year.

You may then receive a letter or telephone call from the funds you've been allocated to, asking you to come in with your documents to complete your registration and to explain the payment schedules and processes – and usually to try to talk you into signing up for a direct debit from your or your company's bank account.

Self-employed

As a self-employed person, you're treated as an employer (even though you don't employ staff) and must deduct social security contributions from your own earnings and pay them directly to the relevant funds. These are, however, tax deductible, as are certain 'optional' retirement and health insurance contributions. Ask your accountant or tax adviser for details.

Employers

As an employer, you must complete the necessary formalities to ensure that your employees are covered by social security. You must report your intended engagement of an employee to URSSAF up to a week **before** he's due to start work, using a *document unique d'embauche* (see page 154), which can be faxed or submitted online. This document serves as registration for all the relevant social security funds and, if this is the employee's first job (or first job in France), it also serves as the application for a social security card and number (see **Carte Vitale** below).

Carte Vitale

When you've registered for social security, you receive a permanent registration card (*carte d'assurance maladie*, now called a *Carte Vitale*), which looks like a credit card and contains a computer chip (*puce*). The card has your name and your social security number (*no. d'immatriculation de l'assuré*) printed on the front. Social security numbers are issued by l'Institut National de la Statistique et des Etudes Economiques (INSEE). Additional information is coded into the chip, which is needed to process any claim for reimbursement or services. Contrary to some fears, there's no detailed information regarding your health or medical condition on the chip, although these may be included on the *Carte Vitale 2*, intended to supersede the *Carte Vitale* in 2005.

Along with a *Carte Vitale*, you receive a certificate (*attestation*) containing a list of those entitled to benefits on your behalf (*bénéficiaires*), i.e. your dependants, and the address of the office where you must apply for reimbursement of your medical expenses. This address is normally indicated in small type just above your name and address and is easy to miss.

If you move home, acquire or need to change or transfer beneficiaries or find any errors in the information on your *attestation*, you must inform your local social security office. If a social security official makes a regular visit to your town hall, you may be able make changes to your records and ask questions during a scheduled visit.

Contributions

Social security contributions (*cotisations sociales* or *charges sociales*) for the self-employed and those running a business are calculated as a percentage of your taxable income (i.e. the business results or their actual salary or drawings) **plus** the amount of 'optional social benefits' paid for by the business. These may include private pension plans and death and incapacity insurance plans (see **Self-employed** on page 213), as well as any complementary health insurance (see page 214). For example, if you earn €20,000 in taxable income, but pay €5,000 in optional contributions, your social security contributions are calculated based on an 'income' of €25,000. However, for certain contributions there's a maximum salary level (see **Calculation** on page 215).

Contributions start as soon as you're employed or start work in France and are backdated to this date; there's no 'grace' period, as with some taxes (but see Micro Regimes below). Contributions are paid to the relevant fund or funds, each of which has its own payment schedule (e.g. quarterly or biannually, although in most cases you can set up a monthly direct debit).

If you're the manager of a business, your contributions are assumed to be paid out of your own pocket, although there's nothing to say that the business cannot pay the contributions and deduct them as expenses when calculating your year-end figures.

If you have a limited company, you can decide the salary you pay yourself and therefore limit your social security contributions. A minority *gérant* pays social charges like a regular employee provided he has an employment contract (written or implied). If the *gérant* is a majority owner of the company (i.e. he has control over more than 50 per cent of the shares, based on his holdings and the holdings of his spouse and other household members), he's considered to be self-employed for purposes of social security charges.

Self-employed

Compulsory social security contributions for the self-employed fall into three main categories: health insurance, family allowances and pension. In addition, you must make contributions to the social security debt, known as *CRDS* and *CSG* (see page 211).

For most self-employed people, URSSAF collects family allowance and *CRDS/CSG* contributions on a quarterly basis: normally in May, August, November and February of the following year. The pension funds collect twice a year, in February and July. The health insurance funds also collect twice a year, but in April and in August. Although this may seem complex, it helps to spread the payments across the year.

In addition to the above compulsory contributions, you may make the following contributions (if you can afford them!).

- **Death & Incapacity Insurance** – Private death and incapacity insurance (*prévoyance*) for the self-employed includes provisions for paying compensation to keep a business running while the owner is unable to run it himself.

- **Complementary Health Insurance** – Commonly known as a *mutuelle*, but properly an *assurance complémentaire maladie*, this insurance covers the portion of medical bills not reimbursed by compulsory state health insurance (usually between 0 and 40 per cent depending on the treatment and your status). Contributions (up to €7,131 per year) are tax deductible.

- **Unemployment Insurance** – A form of private unemployment insurance is available to those who aren't covered by the state unemployment insurance organisation, ASSEDIC – which includes most self-employed people. This insurance pays a daily compensation when the business owner is unemployed (i.e. when the business goes bust). It's also available to *gérants* who are considered employees of the business, but who aren't eligible for unemployment benefit if they're fired (i.e. by the shareholders).

These are often referred to as *Loi Madelin* contributions, as they're regulated by the law of this name. The advantage of *Loi Madelin* benefits is that they're treated for tax purposes like the obligatory social charges, in that amounts paid by the business for the owner are deductible from the business's declared turnover and aren't added to the owner's personal taxable income.

At the end of the year, the various compulsory and optional contributions paid by the business must be reported via a *DCR* (see **Registration** on page 136). The optional contributions paid by the business are added back to the owner's net revenue to determine the base upon which the obligatory social charges are determined.

⚠️ You may receive 'demands' for contributions from organisations to which you aren't offiliated or obliged to join. Always check before paying anything whether contributions are compulsory or optional. If in doubt, consult your accountant.

For the first two years you're in business, the social security funds base their charges on an assumed salary of around €6,000 the first year and €9,000 the second year. (The figures are adjusted each year for inflation.) At the end of the first year, after you've declared your actual income, the funds calculate the actual amounts due and adjust the provisional payments for the coming year, in effect backdating contributions to your start date. **Don't be lulled into a false sense of security by low initial social security contributions: they will catch up with you in the end!**

Micro Regimes: If you're registering as a self-employed worker, you must apply to join the non-salaried social security regime (*régime social des travailleurs non-salariés* or *TNS*). However, recent legislation has provided some more than welcome respite for the newly self-employed, who, instead of making crippling social security contributions from their start-up, can now make contributions as their business generates income. If you qualify as a *micro-entreprise* (see page 197), your contributions are calculated only on a percentage of your turnover (52 per cent for commercial businesses and 28 per cent for non-commercial businesses). Contributions are payable in two lump sums on 1st April and 1st October each year.

Employers

If you employ full-time staff, you must make social security contributions for your employees (known as the *part patronale*) – see **Calculation** below. If you employ someone to undertake work for you, you should ensure that he has adequate insurance (e.g. accident and third party liability) or is registered as self-employed and, therefore, making social security contributions himself. If you pay someone to do a job on a casual basis (e.g. gardening) and he isn't registered as self-employed, you can make the necessary contributions on his behalf in order to ensure that both he and you are insured in the event of an accident. This can be done by using the *Chèque Emploi Service* system (see page 195). **If you agree to pay anyone in cash or by ordinary cheque and they have an accident on your premises, you can be sued for a very large sum of money.**

Calculation

Social security contributions are calculated in a different way for the self-employed (including business owners who don't employ staff) and for employers, as detailed below. **Calculations are VERY complicated and you should check with an accountant exactly what you must pay and when.**

Self-employed

The table below shows the percentage of gross income you must pay in social security contributions if you're self-employed, and the actual payments you will make if you earn €50,000. All percentages apply to full salary unless otherwise stated. Note that the figures below are for *artisans* in 2005; figures for traders and other types of self-employed person are currently slightly different, but within the next few years, it's intended that all self-employed people will make the same contributions.

Type of Contribution	Contribution (%)	Contribution on €50,000 (€)
Health Insurance	7	3,500
Family Allowances	5.4	2,700
Pension*	25.05	12,525
CSG (income tax deductible)	5.1	2,550
CSG/CRDS (non-deductible)	2.9	1,450
Total		**22,725**

* The pension contribution is in fact three separate contributions: 16.35 per cent for a basic state pension; 6.7 per cent for a supplementary pension; 2 per cent for death and invalidity insurance.

Employers

Employers must pay the major part of their employees' social charges (see table below), which amount to between 35 per cent and 40 per cent of their salary – in addition to their own social charges, of course. The table shows the percentage of gross income paid in social security contributions by employers and the actual payments by an employer for an employee earning an annual gross salary of €20,000. All percentages apply to full salary unless otherwise stated. Figures in brackets relate to the notes below the table.

Type of Contribution	Contribution (%) Employer	Contribution (%) Employee	Contribution on €20,000 (€)
Health Insurance	12.8	0.75	2,560
Widow's Insurance (FNAL)	0.1 (1)	0	20
Family Allowances	5.40	-	1,080
Basic Pension			
(total salary)	1.6	0.10	320
(first €30,192)	14.75	8.20	2,950
Obligatory Complementary Pension – Managers (2)			
ARRCO (first €30,192)	4.50	3.0	900
Death benefit (first €30,192)	1.50	-	300
AGFF (first €30,192)	1.20	0.80	240
AGFF (above €30,192)	1.30	0.90	-
AGIRC (above €30,192)	12.50	7.50	-
APEC (above €30,192)	0.036	0.024	-
CET	0.22	0.13	44
CSA (3)	0.3	-	60
Unemployment Insurance	4	2.4	800
Workers' Compensation	1	-	200
CSG – deductible (95% of salary)	-	5.1	-
CSG/CRDS – non-deductible (95% of salary)	-	2.4	-
AGS/FNGS	0.45	-	90
Total Employer Contributions for Employee Earning €20,000			**9,564**

1. This rate applies only to employers with fewer than ten employees. For ten or more, the rate is 0.40 per cent.
2. Contributions for non-managers are lower. Note that for employees, the basic pension (*vieillesse*) contributions are paid to URSSAF and the complementary

pension (*retraite complémentaire*) paid to a separate organisation (actually to two separate organisations!), whereas for the business owner both are paid to the same retirement fund.

3. The *contribution de solidarité pour l'autonomie* is a new charge introduced in July 2004 (supposedly to prevent a recurrence of the 'disaster' of summer 2003, when thousands of old people died during the heat wave), collected by URSSAF.

As you will see, employing staff in France is expensive! To make matters worse, employers must in effect pay their employees' portion of the social charges monthly and can reclaim them only quarterly, which can create an additional cash flow problem.

Social security contributions must be accompanied by a *Déclaration Unifiée de Cotisations Sociales* (*DUCS*), which obviates the need to send payments to several different organisations. You can calculate and make social security contributions online via an official site supported by the main social security agencies (🖳 www.net-entreprises.fr).

At the end of each year, employers are required to confirm the social security contributions made on behalf of their staff using a *Déclaration Annuelle des Données Sociales* (*DADS*), which must be submitted to the government by the end of January. Note that from January 2006, this form is to acquire the bizarre denomination *Déclaration Automisée de Déclarations Sociales Unifiée* (*DADS-U*)!

The only (legal) way to reduce the cost of employing staff is to recruit particular types of person, e.g. the young and over-50s, the long-term unemployed, those on certain types of contract (e.g. apprenticeships and certain *CDD*s) and, in some cases, women. Incentives vary from region to region and according to the business sector you're in, but most of them are limited to staff earning the minimum wage (*SMIC*) or only a little above it – in some cases even below it. Some of the options are detailed below:

Loi Fillon: The most widely used social charges reduction programme is the one relating to the *Loi Fillon* (French laws are named after the minister who introduced them), which is open to most employers whose employees are automatically registered with the unemployment insurance organisation ASSEDIC. The employer can be reimbursed up to 26 per cent of gross salary, although the more the employee is paid above the *SMIC*, the less the reimbursement; at 1.7 times the *SMIC*, the reimbursement is cancelled out.

Orientation Contracts: Employers are exonerated from all employer charges for hiring someone under 25 with certain acknowledged 'difficulties' accessing the job market. This applies only to a *CDD* of up to six or nine months. The employee is considered to be undergoing a form of continuing education and is paid only 30 to 65 per cent of the *SMIC*.

Redevelopment Zones: Employers in certain urban or rural development zones can be exonerated from the employer portion of social charges for the first 150 per cent of the *SMIC* if they create up to 50 jobs. You must work closely with URSSAF and agree to hire people on *CDI*s or *CDD*s of at least 12 months. You must not have fired anyone within the 12 months before recruiting your first employee under this programme.

Stagiaires: Although it isn't a formal programme, many employers hire *stagiaires* and apprentices, as both are usually covered for social charges by their schools or training programmes (see **Stagiaires** on page 155).

Information

For general information about social security, contact the Caisse Nationale d'Assurances Maladie des Travailleurs Salariés (CNAMTS), Centre de Documentation, 68–80 avenue du Maine, 75680 Paris Cedex 14 (☎ 01 42 79 31 80, 🖳 www.ameli.fr). Information about social security is also available via the internet, e.g. 🖳 www.service-public.fr and the CNAMTS website (🖳 www.cnamts.fr), where some information is available in English. There are a number of books (in French) about social security, including *Tous les Droits de l'Assuré Social* (VO Editions), and French consumer magazines regularly publish supplements on various aspects of social security, particularly pensions and health insurance.

PENSIONS

As in many Western countries, there's a worsening crisis in state pension funding in France, which has the largest proportion of inactive people over 55 in the EU, high unemployment, one of Europe's highest life expectancies, and over 40 per cent of 18 to 25 year olds in full-time education. The French pension system is largely unfunded, which means that the active population pays the pensions of those who are retired or otherwise inactive – known as a *régime de répartition*. As in many countries, there are plans to transfer the burden from the public to the private sector, although this is likely to create controversy and social unrest.

The state employee pension scheme – which for non-managers is administered by an organisation called La Fédération des Institutions de Retraite Complémentaire des Salariés (for some unaccountable reason abbreviated to ARRCO, 🖳 www. arrco.fr) and for executives and managers (*cadres*) by the Association Générale des Institutions de Retraite des Cadres (AGIRC, 🖳 www.agirc.fr) – comprises basic and supplementary schemes. The basic scheme covers employees in business and industry and there are special schemes for the farmers, shopkeepers, small businessmen (artisans), and the self-employed, as well as most civil servants. Contributions are paid by employers and employees and vary with income (see **Contributions** on page 218).

Basic Pension

The national retirement insurance fund is the Caisse Nationale d'Assurance Vieillesse (CNAV, 🖳 www.cnav.fr). When you first register with social security, a record is opened in your name and your payments are recorded. Your insured period is determined from your record and periods of absence from work due to sickness, work accidents, childbirth, unemployment and military service are credited for pension purposes.

To receive a full pension you must have contributed for at least 160 'terms' (meaning quarter-years), i.e. around 40 years, but there are plans to extend this to 42.5 or even 45 years. If you don't qualify for a full pension, your pension is proportional to the number of terms you've contributed for, i.e. 1/160 of the full pension multiplied by the number of terms' insurance.

A full pension is equal to 50 per cent of your average earnings in your 19 highest paid years (earnings are re-valued in line with inflation), which is progressively being increased to 25 years. The maximum pension is currently €13,255 per year (it fell by 6 per cent in 2004 and is likely to fall further in the coming years!). With at least 150 terms (37.5 years) of coverage, you're guaranteed a minimum annual pension of around €6,000 irrespective of your income level during your working life. Basic state pensions are automatically adjusted biannually in accordance with the national average wage.

Supplementary Pensions

Most employees contribute to a supplementary pension plan (*caisse complémentaire de retraite*), which may be state-funded or private, in addition to the obligatory state pension fund; almost every trade or occupation has its own scheme. If you're self-employed, however, you may wish to contribute to a personal scheme (*assurance retraite*), which operates in the same way as a life assurance policy (see page 220). This is usually more flexible than a company scheme: you can choose how much to pay in each year and may take a lump sum or an annuity when you retire. **A self-employed person must pay around €2,000 to €2,500 a year into a private pension fund for a pension that can be as low as €300 per month.** There are various specific pension savings plans, detailed below.

If you already have a private pension scheme in your home country, it may be advantageous to transfer your savings to a French scheme (e.g. the Inland Revenue in the UK allows 10 per cent of foreign pensions to be taken tax-free). Your home country may impose certain transfer conditions, however; the Inland Revenue, for example, stipulates that you must be leaving the UK permanently and entering employment in France, and that your money is transferred into a bona fide pension plan. **Before transferring a private pension to France, you should consult an expert who's familiar with pension schemes in France and your home country.**

Plan d'Epargne Retraite Populaire

A new pension savings plan is the *plan d'épargne retraite populaire* (PERP), introduced by the government in 2003. It's similar to a British approved pension scheme, whereby funds deposited are 'locked' until your retirement, when you must take an annuity, which will be liable for income tax. Ten per cent of your deposits can be deducted from your taxable income (up to a ceiling – initially €2,920). The only circumstances under which you can get your money out of the PERP before your retirement date are if you must cease your business activity due to a liquidation judgment against the business or if you suffer an invalidity that makes it impossible to exercise your profession, although in some cases it's possible to recover some or all of the amount in a *PERP* in the case of divorce, or the death or incapacity of your spouse.

It's usually possible to stop making payments for a time or to increase or reduce the payments as the situation warrants. At your retirement date, the amounts built up in the *PERP* are converted to an annuity according to the terms of the contract (e.g. it can be for a guaranteed period or made revertible to the surviving spouse).

Loi Madelin Pension Plans

The *Loi Madelin* retirement plans work in a similar way to a *PERP*. You pay in (usually a set amount) each quarter or month, and when you reach retirement (whenever you decide that this should be), the balance in your account is converted to an annuity, according to the terms of the contract you selected. Contributions up to €7,130 are tax-deductible, but annuities are taxed. Pensions can also be paid out to spouses or partners.

Life Insurance

Life insurance isn't only a method of ensuring that your dependants don't starve when you die. In France, at least, it can also be used as a means of saving for retirement. New tax rules are removing many of the tax exemptions previously accorded to life insurance policies. In certain cases, however, premiums are tax-deductible and income from a life assurance policy is taxed at a low rate provided the policy is allowed to mature for at least four years and the fund is redeemed as a lump sum: if you redeem a policy within four years, you pay income tax on the gain at 35 per cent and social taxes at 10 per cent; if you redeem it between the fifth and eighth year, taxes are at 15 and 10 per cent; and after eight years you're taxed at just 7.5 and 10 per cent.

Instead of taking a lump sum on retirement, you can opt for life annuities (*rente viagère*), whereby you're 'paid' a fixed amount each year for the rest of your life, but payments are subject to income tax (on a sliding scale according to your age – e.g. you're taxed on 40 per cent of the annuity between 60 and 70 and on 30 per cent after 70). Note also that, when you die, payments stop and your spouse cannot continue to benefit from your pension, unless you make the annuity 'reversible' (*reversible*), in which case you receive a lower annuity, but your spouse (if he or she survives you) continues to receive all, or part, of the annuity for the rest of his or her life. You may have to pay a monthly minimum (e.g. €75) into a pension plan, although some plans allow you to make a minimum payment (e.g. €100) every three or six months.

Related beneficiaries (your spouse or children) aren't liable for French gift or inheritance tax, but unrelated beneficiaries are liable for inheritance tax at 60 per cent, although they may be able to delay paying the tax until they're 70. Note, however, that the government is looking for new sources of tax revenue, and under new rules, life insurance benefits may be taxed as income or under wealth or inheritance tax laws, depending on how a policy is set up.

You can take out a life insurance or endowment policy with numerous French or foreign insurance companies, although a life insurance policy intended to take advantage of French law is best taken out in France, to ensure that it complies with the law. With all French life insurance policies you're entitled to a 30-day 'cooling off' period, during which you may cancel a policy without penalty.

Institutions de Réparation

In many industries, employers are obliged to provide supplementary pension schemes (called *institutions de réparation*) for employees earning above a certain salary, e.g. €1,800 per month (and in many companies it's obligatory for employees to join; for example, executives and managerial staff must contribute to a supplementary pension scheme called a *caisse de retraite des cadres ou des cadres supérieurs*). The cost of such schemes obviously needs to be budgeted for.

Any new company must subscribe to an employees' pension fund (*caisse de retraite complémentaire des salariés*) as soon as it's formed, whether or not there are immediate plans to employ anyone. No contributions are demanded until the first salaried employee is taken on.

Many companies also provide free life insurance as a benefit, although it may be accident life insurance only (i.e. if you die as the result of an accident).

ACCOUNTING

French accounting principles derive from the *Code de Commerce* and the *Plan Comptable Général*, which are amended and updated periodically by the Conseil National de la Comptabilité, as well as from the *Code Général Des Impôts*. The French make much of the supposed differences between 'French accounting' and what they call *la comptabilité anglo-saxonne*. In practice, however, they aren't all that different, although French accounting – in true Gallic style – involves a host of complex rules that must be observed.

First, it's a legal requirement that accounting records be in French. The principles also specify not only the names, but also the method of numbering for business accounts. Although this can be a nuisance, it simplifies many of the tax reporting requirements, as the instructions refer to the number of a particular account, making it easy to identify. The initial digit of an account number indicates the type of account, as follows:

1. Capital accounts (shareholder equity);
2. Fixed assets (property, plant and equipment);
3. Stock, including raw materials, work in progress and finished goods;
4. 'Third party accounts' (*comptes tiers*), which include all outside parties to which the business owes money or from which it's due money; separate accounts (and account numbers) are required for each social security agency and each taxing authority, a series of VAT accounts and accounts for money owed to shareholders or employees.
5. Bank and other treasury accounts.
6. Expenses.
7. Sales and other income.

There are three legally required journals: the general journal (*le livre-journal*), the inventory journal (*le livre d'inventaire*) and the general ledger (*le grand livre*). (The English terms are approximate – they don't correspond closely to the French journals.)

- **Livre-journal** – The 'general journal' is a chronological list of operations (i.e. journal entries) that track the daily sales and expenditure of the business. The French tend to divide the general journal into sub-journals, dealing with sales, purchases, treasury (i.e. the bank accounts) and 'miscellaneous operations' (*opérations diverses*).

- **Livre d'Inventaire** – The 'inventory journal' isn't strictly speaking confined to inventory or stock taking. It's more of a trial balance, a listing of each account and its balance as of a specific date. Under French accounting law, you're allowed to review the trial balance at the end of the year, and make adjustments, up and down, to those assets and liabilities that have fluctuated in value. This requirement includes the need to verify the status of your stock (of merchandise, raw materials, work in progress and finished goods) and to verify your fixed assets (property, plant and equipment). You must maintain a year-end inventory journal, documenting the final balances in each account, which serves as the basis for your balance sheet.

- **Grand Livre** – The 'general ledger' is the document where the transactions from the general journal (or from the various sub-journals) are summarised and sorted by the accounts affected.

Certain accounting requirements vary according to the type or size of business.

Micro-entreprises

Businesses qualifying as *micro-entreprises* (see page 197) are required only to keep a daily listing of receipts (sources and amounts) and expenditures. They aren't required to maintain a full set of books nor to categorise or summarise transactions by account. At the end of the year, *micro-entreprises* only need to summarise their revenues and provide a listing of their fixed assets and depreciation for the year. Those businesses with more than €18,294 in revenue must summarise their revenues, expenditures, debts, property and stocks (inventory) at the year end, but don't need to prepare formal financial statements.

Other Businesses

Registered companies, such as *SARLs*, *EURLs* and *SASs*, must usually file their financial statements with the *CCI* within 30 days of their annual meeting, which must be held within six months of the close of the fiscal year. The main purpose of the annual meeting is to allow the shareholders to approve the financial results for the year.

Financial statements (referred to collectively as the *bilan*, although *bilan* is also the term for a balance sheet) consist of the balance sheet (*bilan*), income statement (*comptes de résultat*) and accompanying notes (*annexe*). The filing for the *CCI* must also include a report from management, discussing the year's results and the coming year's prospects, and extracts from the minutes of the annual meetings, detailing all matters subjected to a vote and documenting the approval of the financial results as presented.

French standards for financial statements vary somewhat from those in English-speaking countries, mostly in the order in which the various components are presented. For example, some French companies present their expenses before their sales figures, and on the balance sheet, capital accounts appear before liabilities.

Certain types of company, e.g. *SA*, *SAS* and *SCA*, must appoint an auditor; other types must do so when they reach a certain size (in terms of turnover, assets or number of employees).

Accounting Packages

There are a number of French accounting programmes, any one of which will produce acceptable financial statements and the supporting journals and ledgers. The advantage of using a package program is that they all come with the standard accounts already set up. Most accounting packages consist of a number of modules, which transfer information and journal entries to the main accounting module.

The most common modules are those for accounting (*comptabilité* – usually shortened to *compta*), payroll (*paye* or *paie*), commercial administration (*gestion commercial* or *gescom*) – a combination of sales, inventory, purchasing and order processing – and fixed assets (*immobiliers*). Many software distributors offer bespoke versions for associations, *professions libérales* or specialised types of businesses, such as those dealing with property rental.

The most popular software packages for small businesses are EBP, Ciel and Sage (in order of increasing cost and complexity). All three of these can usually be found in computer shops and even in the software section of most hypermarkets. Other software packages are available through specialised consultants and system vendors. An online accounting service for small and medium-size companies is provided at 🖳 www.comptanoo.com.

Accountants

French accountants (*experts comptable*) vary greatly in their expertise, helpfulness and cost. Like *notaires*, they tend to view their profession as one designed to enforce the letter of the law, rather than to assist their clients. For example, there are very few (if any) accountants in private practice who do 'write-up' work for clients (i.e. where the client puts all his receipts and invoices in a shoebox and takes them to the accountant every fortnight or so for the accountant to transcribe into the relevant books). In France, you risk being charged by the invoice if you ask your accountant to do this sort of bookkeeping work for you!

You shouldn't expect much in the way of tax saving or tax planning assistance from an *expert comptable*. This is due, in part, to the fact that changes are often made to the current year's tax law as late as October or November in the year, which makes advance tax planning almost impossible. Bear in mind also that, if your accountant makes a mistake, e.g. in calculating your tax, you must pay the correct amount and he's under no obligation to compensate you for his error.

Many small businessmen complain bitterly about how expensive their accountants are, and especially how much they charge for miscellaneous tasks, such as determining which account an invoice should be charged to. (The standard joke is that they charge €60 to tell you which account a €20 invoice should go to – and you still have to book the entry yourself!) The chances are an accountant won't save you money on a day-to-day basis, but they can save you hassle with the tax authorities – if only by having the forms correctly filled out. It can also be an advantage to have accountant-prepared financial statements if you need to obtain a bank loan or credit of any kind.

If you're producing only financial statements for filing with the CCI, you may not need an accountant, provided you're capable of producing them yourself. The statements filed aren't closely reviewed, and minor errors in presentation won't keep your statements from being registered and filed. In fact, many small businesses don't bother to file at all, and only run into difficulty when they need to dissolve the business or make some other major change that highlights the fact they have no annual statements on file. (When dissolving a company, the judge can refuse to allow you to shut down until past filings are done. He can also assess a fine, but this rarely happens.) Some vendors review your filed statements when making credit decisions, but if you have a good record of paying bills, that's far more important than what your balance sheet shows.

Nevertheless, if your financial affairs are anything but simplistic (which is rarely the case – especially in France), you need an accountant – and a good one is worth his weight in gold, so you should seek recommendations (French accountants aren't allowed to advertise) before 'signing up' with a particularly *expert*.

The usual way to work with an accountant is to maintain your own financial records, preferably using some form of approved financial software. (Spouses are often enlisted to do this sort of thing, and *stagiaires* or apprentices in commercial studies are also popular and economic ways to get the bookkeeping done.) At year-end, the accounts files are sent or transmitted (most software packages are set up to facilitate this) to the accountant, who transforms the files into financial statements and may or may not complete the various tax declarations (*impôt sur le revenue/la société, taxe professionnelle, TVA*, etc.).

Some *centres de gestion* (see page 198) may require members to use an accountant for the preparation of their financial statements and tax forms. But in France, accountants normally focus on the reporting and tax requirements, not on business consultation. The *centres de gestion* offer classes, libraries and other resources on the accounting and financial aspects of running a small business and, in some areas, may even have English-speaking staff available.

French accountants are an excellent source of information on the technicalities of the law, especially tax and accounting law. They may be more knowledgeable than many lawyers when it comes to knowing the various forms of business that are possible, and can advise you about the various social security regimes. Another useful resource the 'Club Comptable' website (🖥 www.club-comptable.com), which is designed to enable accountants and businesspeople to exchange information.

6.

COMMUNICATIONS

Whichever way you plan to make a living in France, communications will be vital, especially if you want to start your own business. This chapter looks at telephone and internet services and the French postal service, as well as transport links with and within France. Information technology and internet-related businesses are discussed in **Chapter 11**.

TELEPHONE SERVICES

Anyone running a business needs access to fixed and mobile telephones, and the majority of businesses will operate more efficiently by using the internet. Broadband connection (*haut-débit*) isn't available in all areas of France (see page 230).

The telephone network is operated by France Télécom (FT), which is 55 per cent state-owned (and one of the most indebted companies in the world!), but since 2002, call services have been open to competition, which has resulted in an intense price war. Despite this 'market liberalisation', however, FT is still the only company that offers a complete service, including the installation of telephone lines, others providing only call services. Nevertheless, some other companies may offer call charge packages that suit your business needs and it's worth investigating the alternatives. There's a variety of tariffs, so make sure you thoroughly investigate the alternatives, particularly if your business will rely heavily on telephone communications.

Alternative Providers

There are currently around 20 alternative telephone service providers (i.e. not France Télécom) in France, some of which advertise in the English-language press (see **Appendix B**). If you wish to use another provider (or several providers, for different types of call), you must open a separate account with each one. You must still have an account with FT for line rental.

If you're using an alternative telephone provider for local or long-distance calls, you must normally dial a code to route your call to the appropriate telephone company. For example, to use Cégétel (*Le 7*) for long-distance calls, you replace the first zero of the area code with a 7 (e.g. 01 40 20 70 00 becomes 71 40 20 70 00) and dial 70 instead of 00 for international calls. To route local calls through Cégétel, you must dial 3695 and then the entire 10 digit phone number. Each provider has its own code or procedure for accessing its network. It's possible to have subscriptions with several different telephone providers, and each one will indicate what numbers you must dial to route your calls correctly. Alternatively, you can notify FT of your default provider and they will set up your telephone line to automatically route calls to whichever of the alternative telephone providers you prefer, without having to use the extra numbers. This facility costs around €11 and takes a week or two to set up (during which time you can use a prefix).

If you have all your calls automatically routed via another provider, it's possible to revert to the FT system by dialling 8 before the number. This service, which is useful if there's a problem with your alternative provider, must be ordered in advance from FT and it's free.

To help you find your way through the maze of alternative telephone providers, you may want to consult a service such as BudgeTelecom (🖳 www.budgetelecom. com), where you can compare the available tariffs based on your own calling pattern and review customer evaluations of the services available from each provider.

An increasing number of expatriates (and French people) make use of a 'callback' service, such as those provided by Eurotelsat (🖳 www.eurotelsat.com) and Kallback (🖳 www.kallback.com). It's no longer necessary to wait to be called back and, as with an alternative provider, you simply dial a local freephone number or a code before numbers. Calls are routed via the cheapest provider, and companies claim that you can save up to 70 per cent on international calls.

Installation & Registration

If you're planning to move into a property without an existing telephone line, you will need to have one installed. In this case, you must visit your local France Télécom agent, which you will find in the yellow pages under *Télécommunications: service*. You must prove that you're the owner or tenant of the property in question, e.g. with an electricity bill, confirmation of purchase (*attestation d'acquisition*) or a lease. You also require your passport or residence permit (*carte de séjour*).

If you buy a property in a remote area without a telephone line, it may be expensive to have a telephone installed, as you must pay for the line to your property. Contact FT for an estimate. You should have trenches dug for the telephone cable if you want a below-ground connection (you may be able to have an above-ground connection via a wire from the nearest pylon). This work can be carried out by FT, but their charges are high and it's possible to do it yourself, although you must observe certain standards. Details of the required depth of trenches and the type of conduit (*gaine*) to use, etc. can be obtained from FT.

When you go to the FT agency, you need to know what kind of telephone sockets are already installed in the property, how many telephones you want, where you want them installed and what kind of telephone you want (if you're buying from FT). If you want a number of telephone points installed, you should arrange this in advance. You may also want to upgrade a line (e.g. to ADSL – see **Broadband** below).

You will also be asked whether you want a listed or unlisted number (see **Telephone Directories** on page 234) and must inform FT where you want your bill sent and how you wish to pay it (see page 230). If you wish to pay your bill by direct debit, you must provide your account details (*relevé d'identité bancaire*). You can also request an itemised bill (see page 230) at the same time.

You may be given a telephone number on the spot, although you should wait until you receive written confirmation before giving it to anyone. It isn't possible simply to take over the telephone number of the previous occupant. You will receive a letter stating that you have a mixed line (*ligne mixte*), which is simply a line allowing both incoming and outgoing calls.

To have a line installed takes from a few days in a city, to weeks or possibly over a month in remote rural areas, although 90 per cent of new customers have a line installed within two weeks. In certain areas, there's a waiting list and you can have a line installed quickly only if you need a telephone for your safety or security, e.g. if you're an invalid, in which case a medical certificate is required. Business lines may be installed quicker than domestic lines.

When acquiring a property with a telephone line, you must have the account transferred to your name and a telephone number issued to you. **Always check that the previous occupant has closed his account before you take over the line.** FT always changes the telephone number when the ownership or tenancy of a property changes. To do this, you can simply dial 1014 or go to the FT website (🖳 www. francetelecom.com and follow the links to *l'@gence sur le net*). Some information on business services is available on the English-language section of the website. The Paris office has an English-language site (🖳 www.paris.francetelecom.fr/html/particulier/offres_dediees/englishcom/accueil.htm), and English-language assistance can be obtained via email (✉ engft.paris@francetelecom.fr).

If you move into a property where the telephone hasn't been disconnected or transferred to your name, you should ask FT for a special reading (*relevé spécial*). If you're taking over an existing line, you can usually have it connected within 48 hours.

Broadband

There are two types of broadband (*haut- débit*) connection: Asymmetric Digital Subscriber Lines (ADSL) and Integrated Services Digital Network (ISDN). France Télécom is committed to extending the availability of ADSL, but it isn't available in all areas and may even be available in one part of a village, but not another! To find out if ADSL is available in your area, go to 🖳 www.agence.francetelecom.com/eliadsl_ftbynet/html/popup_eli.html and enter your current telephone number (or a neighbour's) or the number of the department in which you live or intend to live. France Télécom expects broadband to be available throughout France by 2007.

If available, it's possible to upgrade an existing line to ADSL at no extra charge, although you must pay higher line rental charges (see page 231); if it isn't available and you aren't in a 'cabled' area, ISDN (*RNIS*, but referred to by FT as *Numéris*) is the only option. An ISDN 'line' actually provides you with three telephone numbers, but only two lines (at least, you can use only two at once!) and you must use both lines simultaneously to achieve 128kbps download speed; check whether your internet service provider allows this.

France Télécom also offers various combined telephone and internet access packages (see **Internet** on page 238). Installation of ADSL costs the same as a standard line (normally €104), but an ISDN line costs an additional €90 (for private use) or €123 (for business use).

Bills

France Télécom bills its customers every two months and allows you two weeks to pay your bill (*facture*). Bills include VAT (*TVA*) at 19.6 per cent, although an ex-VAT figure (*HT*) is shown as well as the total, including VAT (*TTC*). You can request an itemised bill (*facturation détaillée*), which lists all calls with the date and time, the number called, the duration and the charge. This service is free, but must be requested a month in advance.

Bills can be paid by post by sending a cheque to France Télécom, at a post office or at your local FT office. Simply detach the tear-off part of your bill and send or present it with payment. You can pay your telephone bill by direct debit (*prélèvement automatique*) or have the payments spread throughout the year. If you pay your bills by direct debit, your invoice specifies the date of the debit from your account, usually around 20 days after receipt of the invoice. Contact your local FT agent for information. France Télécom is trying to encourage customers to pay by direct debit, telepayment by telephone, or by *Titre Interbancaire de Paiement* (*TIP*), whereby your bank account details are pre-printed on the tear-off part of the bill, which you simply date and sign and return. Most alternative providers insist on payment by direct debit, and you may be billed monthly.

Charges

Deregulation of the telecommunications market has resulted in an intense price war, and considerable savings can be made on national as well as international calls by shopping around for the lowest rates (see **Alternative Providers** on page 228). However, as there are around 20 alternative providers, it's impossible to list all their tariffs here, and only FT's are given in detail. Comparisons between the rates offered by different service providers can be found via the internet (e.g. 💻 www. comparatel.fr and 💻 www.budgetelecom.com) or you can contact the Association Française des Utilisateurs de Télécommunications (AFUTT, BP1, 92340 Marne-la-Coquette, ☎ 01 47 41 09 11, 💻 www.afutt.org) on Mondays to Thursdays between 10.30 and 12.30. Line rental and call charges are explained below; for information about installation and registration charges, see page 229.

Line Rental

The monthly line rental or service charge (*abonnement*) varies according to the type of line, as follows:

- **Standard Line** – €14;
- **ADSL** – €26 for a 512k line or €30 for a 1,024k line unless you commit to a 12-month contract, in which case you benefit from a reduction of €18 on the former (strangely, there's no reduction on a 1,024k line!); a 2,048k line is available only on an annual contract and costs €30 per month for the first year and thereafter €35 per month;
- **ISDN Line** – €25.50 (private); €41.50 business.

If you use an alternative provider (see page 228), there may be a separate monthly fee in addition to your call charges, although most providers have dropped these.

Domestic Calls

France Télécom's tariffs depend on the destination and time of calls. Calls at peak times (*heures pleines*), which are Mondays to Fridays from 08.00 to 19.00 and

Saturdays from 08.00 to 12.00, are charged at the 'normal' rate (*tarif normal*); calls at all other times (*heures creuses*), including all day on public holidays, are charged at a reduced rate (*tarif réduit*).

Call charges are based on an initial 'connection' charge (*mise en relation* or *crédit-temps*), which pays for a minute or 39 seconds depending on whether the call is local (i.e. calls to numbers starting with the same four digits as your own) or not, plus a per-minute rate after that time. The term 'unit' (*unité*) is sometimes used for the initial charge, although you may receive different definitions of the term, even from FT staff! France Télécom's current standard charges for calls from and to fixed lines are shown below.

	Initial Charge	Peak Minute	Off-peak Minute
Local Calls	€0.09 (60 seconds)	€0.033	€0.018
Other Calls	€0.11 (39 seconds)	€0.090	€0.063

France Télécom no longer publicises these rates, however, but offers instead an array of 'all-inclusive' packages (*forfait*), of which there are currently around 20. Packages require a fixed monthly payment (e.g. between €1.50 and €10) in return for reduced price or, in some cases, 'free' calls, which makes it all but impossible to calculate what you're paying for each call or to compare rates with those of other providers. A recent comparison between rates charged by the five major providers showed a price variation between €0.13 and €0.16 for a three-minute, off-peak local call, and between €0.27 and €0.40 for a ten-minute, peak rate local call, with FT's charges – not surprisingly – generally the highest, although if you're a telephone-addict you may find their 'unlimited use' (*illimité*) packages good value.

Alternative telephone service providers (see page 228) also offer a variety of call packages, consisting of a combination of varying initial charges and lengths followed by different per-minute charges and, in some cases, a single rate for all times of day and all destinations. Cégétel, for example, charges a connection fee of €0.118 followed by a standard per-minute charge of €0.013 to all fixed lines in France, irrespective of the distance or time of the call.

Calls from fixed telephones to mobile phones are more expensive. FT, for example, currently makes an initial charge of €0.21 for 30 seconds followed by €0.21 per minute during peak times and €0.10 per minute during off-peak hours for calls to SFR or its own Orange mobile phones. Calls to a Bouygues mobile phone cost €0.25 at peak times or €0.13 during off-peak hours after a connection charge of €0.24. For details of charges for calls from mobile phones, see page 236.

International Calls

France Télécom has eight tariff levels for international calls, listed on its website. All international calls are subject to an initial charge of €0.12 (unless you're using the *Option Plus* or *Les Heures* package, in which case it's €0.11) for a period varying from 5 to 27 seconds, depending on the tariff. Calls to western Europe and North America (except Hawaii and Alaska) are charged at the cheapest tariff and cost €0.22 per minute during peak periods (see above) and €0.12 per minute off-peak. Calls to Australia and New Zealand cost €0.49/0.34 per minute.

Other telephone providers have different tariff structures for international calls. Most alternative providers also offer a variety of discount plans, such as half price on all calls to a designated 'favourite country' or to specific overseas numbers frequently called.

Using the Telephone

Using the telephone in France is simplicity itself. All French telephone numbers have ten digits, beginning with a two-digit regional code (01 for the Ile-de-France, 02 for the north-west, 03 north-east, 04 south-east and 05 south-west), and followed by another two-digit area code. If you're calling within France, you must **always** dial all ten digits, even if you're phoning your next-door neighbour.

Codes for the overseas departments (*DOM*), which have six-figure numbers, are as follows: French Guyana (05 94), Guadeloupe (05 90), Martinique (05 96), Mayotte (02 69), Réunion (02 62), Saint-Pierre-et-Miquelon (05 08). (Monaco isn't part of France and has its own country code of 377.)

Numbers beginning 06 are mobile phone numbers (see page 236), and those beginning 08 are special rate numbers.

International Calls

It's possible to make IDD (International Direct Dialling) calls to most countries from private and public telephones. A full list of country codes, plus area codes for main cities and time differences, is shown in the information pages (*les info téléphoniques*) of your yellow pages. To make an international call you must first dial 00, then the country code, the area code (**without** the first zero) and the subscriber's number.

France subscribes to a Home Direct service (called *France Direct*) that allows you to call a number giving you direct and free access to an operator in the country that you're calling, e.g. for British Telecom in the UK dial 08 00 99 00 44. The operator then connects you to the number required. This service can be used only for reverse charge (collect) calls. To obtain an operator from one of the four major US telephone companies dial ☎ 08 00 99 00 11 (AT&T), 08 00 99 00 19 (MCI), 08 00 99 00 87 (Sprint) or 08 00 99 00 13 (IDB Worldcom). (These are French 08 00 numbers, not American 0800 numbers, which aren't toll-free when dialled from abroad.)

These companies also offer long-distance calling cards that provide access to English-speaking operators, and AT&T offers a US Direct service, whereby you can call an operator in any state (except Alaska). To reach an operator in any other country from France, you must dial 12 and ask for the relevant *France Direct* number; there's no longer a list of Home Direct codes in French telephone directories. You can also use the *France Direct* service from some 50 countries to make calls to France via an FT operator.

Business users can save up to 50 per cent on international calls by using FT's Global Virtual Private Network (VPN). France Télécom publishes a useful free booklet, *Guide du Téléphone International*, containing information in French and English.

Greetings

The usual French greeting on the telephone is simply *allô* inflected as a question (*allô?*). If you're using the operator he may say, *Ne quittez pas* ('Hold the line'). 'I'm trying to connect you' is *j'essaie de vous passer l'abonné*, and 'go ahead' may be simply *parlez* (speak) or *je vous écoute* (I'm listening). The French can be abrupt to the point of rudeness on the telephone, answering and immediately asking you to hold while they finish another conversation, telling you that they 'haven't got all day' if you stumble over your words or hesitate for a fraction of a second, or even hanging up on you if you don't speak immediately.

Numbers

One of the hardest things to do in any foreign language is to understand telephone numbers given to you orally. This is particularly difficult in French, as telephone numbers are dictated in the same way as they're written, i.e. normally two digits at a time. For example 04 15 48 17 33 is *zéro quatre, quinze, quarante-huit, dix-sept, trente-trois*. It's therefore wise to practise your French numbers (particularly those from 70 to 100). Note that the French don't say 'double' when two digits are the same: for example, 22 is *vingt-deux*. Note also that some numbers aren't written in pairs, e.g. 0892 300 400; these are also spoken as written – in this case *zéro huit cent quatre-vingt douze, trois cents, quat' cents*.

Telephone Directories

When you have a telephone installed, your name and number is usually automatically included in the next issue of your local telephone directory (*annuaire*) and is included within a few weeks in internet telephone directories. Like most telephone companies, FT sells its list of subscribers to businesses, but you can choose to have an unlisted number, which saves you from the affliction of telephone marketing, although this isn't as prevalent as in some other countries. There are three options (known as *Services Vie Privée*), all of which are now free:

● **Orange List (*Liste Orange*)** – Your details aren't made available to businesses.

● **Chamois List (*Liste Chamois*)** – In addition to the above, your details aren't included in printed or electronic (e.g. online) directories.

● **Red List (*Liste Rouge*)** – In addition to the above, your number isn't given out by directory enquiries.

The chamois and red options are particularly useful if you have a telephone line reserved for a fax machine and don't want to be inundated with fax advertisements. From 2005, directories include mobile phone numbers: if you have a mobile contract, your number will automatically be listed unless you tell FT you don't want it listed; if you don't have a contract, you must ask for your number to be listed. You can also ask for your email address, postal address and profession to be included.

Telephone directories are published by department (*département*) and are numbered with the department number, e.g. 75 for Paris. Not all directories are published at the same time (the issue date for new directories is listed at the front). Some departments have more than one volume (*tome*), e.g. the Paris white pages (*Les Pages Blanches*) are in five volumes and the yellow pages (*Les Pages Jaunes*), two volumes.

Yellow pages are published for all departments and contain only business and official (e.g. government) telephone numbers. They're included with the white pages in one volume for departments with few subscribers or published in a separate volume or volumes, e.g. Paris has two volumes. When there's more than one volume, the index is included at the front of the first volume. You can obtain a copy of white or yellow pages for other departments for a fee of around €7.50 per volume (☎ 08 00 30 23 02) or refer to them in libraries or at main post offices. There are also local yellow pages (*Les Pages Jaunes Locales*) in some areas (e.g. Paris) and business to business directories (*Professionnels à Professionnels/PAP*) are published in national and regional editions as well as in a CD-ROM version available to businesses.

Telephone directories (white and yellow pages) contain a wealth of information, including emergency information and numbers, useful local numbers, FT numbers and services, tariffs, international codes and costs, how to use the telephone (in English, French, German, Italian and Spanish), public telephone information, information about bills, directories and FT products, administration numbers, and maps of the department(s) covered by the telephone book.

Subscribers are listed in the white pages under their town or *commune* (or *arrondissement* in Paris, Lyon and Marseille) and not alphabetically for the whole of a department or city. It isn't enough to know that someone lives, for example, in the department of Dordogne; you must know the town. You will receive little, or no, help from directory enquiries (who aren't always helpful at the best of times), unless you know the town or village where the subscriber is located – in which case, you might as well look up the number yourself! The online directories are more forgiving. You must specify a town or postcode, but if you've guessed wrong you can expand your search to include the surrounding area up to the entire department. The advantage of the listing system is that you can easily find the number of people in your town or village if you know their address but not their name. (A potential disadvantage is that people can easily find your number.)

When your application for a telephone line has been accepted, you're given a voucher (*bon*) for a copy of your local department telephone directory; the issuing office is usually housed in the same building as the FT agency. Annual directories are supposed to be delivered to your door or building when they're available, but in some outlying areas delivery is haphazard at best. Many people rely on the online version, which is updated on a regular basis. If you cannot obtain a directory, call ☎ 1014.

Directory Enquiries

For domestic directory enquiries, you can call 12, but note that there's a charge of €0.80 per call and you're limited to two numbers; if you want more than two, you can call 3692, but this service costs an initial €3.40 plus €1.10 every 20 seconds, so it's generally cheaper to call 12 as many times as necessary!

When the telephone is answered, you are asked for the name of the town in which you want a number (*Votre demande concerne quelle ville?*) and then the name of the company or individual whose number you require. When the operator has found the number, he asks you to hold the line (*'Patientez'*) and a recorded message tells you that you're about to be given the number and that, if you want to be connected automatically, you should say *'Oui'* (*Pour être mis en relation, dites 'Oui'*). This is a useful service if you have trouble understanding French numbers. However, if you say *'Oui'*, you are charged €0.15 (FT has underhand ways of generating revenue). If you don't want to pay, you should say *'Non'* and you will then hear the number you requested, which will be repeated. (If you say nothing, the instruction will be repeated!) If you want two numbers, you must wait until the first number has been repeated, when you are asked whether you want another number (*Voulez-vous obtenir un autre renseignement?*), to which you must say *'Oui'*. The second number may be given to you by the operator or it may be a recorded message, like the first.

For international directory enquiries dial 3212, but note that this service costs €3 per call and you may obtain only two numbers. (Unlike French numbers, foreign numbers are dictated digit by digit, which makes it much easier to write them down!) Trying to obtain foreign numbers from directory enquiries is time-consuming as well as costly, and it may be easier to call someone abroad and ask them to find the number for you. If you have internet access, it's cheaper to find an online telephone directory for the country you need. You can also find French numbers via the internet.

Mobile Telephones

After a relatively slow start in introducing mobile phones (*téléphone portable* or simply *portable*, but increasingly *mobile*), France has one of Europe's fastest growing cellular populations and it's estimated that over 60 per cent of people in France use mobiles. Mobile phones are now so widespread that some businesses (e.g. restaurants, cinemas, theatres, concert halls) ban them and some even use mobile phone jammers that can detect and jam every handset within 100m.

There are currently three mobile phone service providers: Bouygues (☎ 08 10 63 01 00, 🖥 www.bouyguestelecom.fr), France Télécom, operating under the Orange trademark (☎ 08 00 83 08 00, 🖥 www.orange.fr), and SFR (☎ 08 00 10 60 00, 🖥 www. sfr.fr). Buying a mobile phone is a minefield, as there are not only different networks to choose from, but also a wide range of tariffs covering connection fees, monthly subscriptions, insurance and call charges. To further complicate matters, all three providers have business ties to one or more of the fixed telephone services (SFR with Cégétel, for example) and offer various deals for those who combine mobile and fixed telephone services.

The major decision when buying a mobile phone is whether to take out a contract, whereby you pay a fixed monthly charge and obtain a certain amount of call time 'free', or to use a 'pay-as-you talk' system, whereby you pay only for calls using a phone card. If you take out a contract, the cost of the telephone itself is usually lower than if you use pay-as-you-talk; it may even be free. Before deciding, shop around and compare telephone prices and features, set-up and connection charges and, most importantly, call rates. If you opt for pay-as-you-talk, there's usually a time limit of one or two months on the use of each card; if you don't make many calls, you may be wasting money on cards you don't use. A telephone with an *SMS* feature is one on which you can send text messages.

The most popular contracts usually give you a set number of hours of outgoing calls (e.g. two, three or five) for a flat monthly fee. Hours included in the fee may be limited to evenings and weekends or split between peak and off-peak calling times. Fees are normally reduced if you agree to a contract of 12 months or more, or order certain packages of add-on features or services. All mobile phone bills must now include a complete list of calls made, including the exact duration and the time charged for.

If you want to use a foreign mobile in France, it's usually possible to buy a SIM card, which gives you a French mobile number and allows you to make and receive calls in France. You pay around €20 or €30 for connection to one of the French networks and can choose between a monthly contract and a 'pay-as-you-talk' card, which can be topped up (in values of €10, €20 and €35) as required. (You **must** top it up at least twice a year, or you will lose your number and have to be reconnected.)

All mobile phone numbers have the prefix 06 and there's a special (i.e. expensive) charge rate applied when you call an 06 number from a fixed telephone in France. Calls between mobile phones of the same company are generally discounted and most companies offer similar 'frequent caller' plans to those available for fixed telephone services (see page 228).

There has been a rash of mobile phone thefts, particularly in Paris, where thieves (sometimes travelling on roller skates) pluck the telephone from the hand of its owner in mid-conversation. It's possible to insure not only the telephone itself and the value of the SIM card, but also against the cost of calls made by anyone who finds or steals it, as well as against damage to the telephone if you drop it or step on it and even, in some cases, against the telephone breaking down. Insurance is offered by the three service providers – Bouygues, Orange and SFR – as well as by Darty, FNAC and The Phone House, among others.

If you lose your telephone, whether or not it's insured, you should contact your service provider immediately to report the loss and give the identification number of your telephone (which, of course, you've written down somewhere you can find it quickly!). All new telephones have an IMEI code, which appears beside the battery; if you cannot find it, dial *#06# and it appears on the display. The contact numbers are: ☎ Bouygues 08 00 29 10 00; Orange ☎ 08 25 00 57 00 or +33 6 07 62 64 64 from abroad; SFR ☎ 06 10 00 19 00 or +33 6 10 00 19 00 from abroad. You should also report the loss to your local police and, if the telephone is insured, your insurer.

In recent years there has been widespread publicity regarding a possible health risk to users from the microwave radiation emitted by mobile phones. New mobile phones must now state the amount of energy absorbed by the user (known as the *débit d'absorption spécifique* or *DAS*). This is measured in watts per kilo (W/kg), and the maximum permitted *DAS* is 2W/kg for the head and body. The French government has published a free leaflet, *Le Téléphone Mobile Santé et Sécurité*, containing guidelines for the 'safe' use of mobiles (including keeping them away from 'sensitive' body areas and not using them in poor reception areas, where they use maximum power), which are available from the Ministry of Health (☎ 01 40 56 60 00, 💻 www.sante.gouv.fr). A mobile phone should be kept at least 15cm (6in) from a pacemaker, insulin pump or other electronic implant.

INTERNET

The internet in France got off to rather a slow start due to competition from Minitel (France's pioneering telephone information service) and the market is still expanding rapidly, which has led to a proliferation of internet service providers (*fournisseur d'accès/FAI* or *serveur*), over 200 currently offering a variety of products and prices. France Télécom offers Wanadoo, a package that includes email (see below), Minitel (of course) and online shopping. AOL Compuserve France is the other major internet contender. Between them, Wanadoo and AOL have some two-thirds of the market. Contact details of some of the major French ISPs are as follows:

● AOL (☎ 08 92 02 03 04, 💻 www.aol.fr);

● Club Internet (☎ 3204, €0.15 per minute, 💻 www.club-internet.fr);

● Free (☎ 3244, €0.34 per minute, 💻 www.free.fr);

● FreeSurf (☎ 08 26 00 76 50, 💻 www.freesurf.fr);

● Tiscali (☎ 08 25 95 95 95, 💻 www.tiscali.fr);

● Wanadoo (☎ 08 90 71 99 99, 💻 www.wanadoo.fr).

For details of all the French ISPs, go to 💻 www.lesproviders.com; for a comparison of ISP services and charges, consult one of the dedicated internet magazines, such as *Internet Pratique* and *Net@scope*, or visit the Budgetelecom website (💻 www. budgetelecom.com), which carries a list of internet access providers in France, with information on current offers, customer evaluations and direct links to provider websites.

One advantage of French internet services is that junk mail is strictly controlled and therefore less of a nuisance than in many other countries. The French search engine (*moteur de recherche*) is called Voilà.

Charges

France has a number of 'free' internet access services, where you pay only for your telephone connection time, not for access to the internet provider. Alternatively, most service providers (including the free ones) offer various monthly plans which include all telephone charges for your online connections, usually at a rate that's lower than the telephone charges alone. For as little as €6 to €10 per month, you can usually have five or ten hours online. For an ordinary connection, Wanadoo offers 100 hours per month for €25 (with a reduction to €5 for the first three months). If you exceed your allotted time, you're billed a flat rate (usually around €0.05 per minute) for the excess time. AOL is currently offering 60 hours for €17 (€5 for the first three months) and Tiscali offers a *forfait illimité*, whereby you can spend as much time online as you wish for €30 per month, and FT offers a combined telephone/internet access package, including unlimited 'free' dial-up. Charges for broadband connection are around twice as high, although in Paris and other urban centres with cable television, it's often possible to have a combined television and broadband internet access package.

If you already have an AOL account with a fixed monthly fee for unlimited access, you may (or may not!) have to pay for connection time in France and you are unable simply to reregister your account in France (you must cancel your email address(es) and hope they're still available when you re-register!).

Modems

Foreign modems (*modem*) usually work in France, although they may not receive faxes (Big Dish Satellite, ✉ www.bigdishsat@aol.com, sell converters for this purpose); French modems (e.g. Elsa Mircolink and Olitec) generally work better. Note also that, if you have an ISDN line and want your computer to connect to the internet at maximum speed, you need an ISDN terminal adapter.

Email

Email is called variously *email, courier électronique, courriel* and *mél* – the 'official' word and an abbreviation of *message électronique* – other useful email vocabulary is @ (*arobase*), dot (*point*), hyphen (*tiret* or *trait d'union*) and slash (*slash*). If you don't have access to the internet, La Poste offers the facility to send and receive emails via around 1,000 post offices as well as via its website (💻 www.laposte.fr or www.laposte.net), where information about the service can be found. Messages can even be picked up via telephone (☎ 08 92 68 13 50). Note that, if you don't have a La Poste or Hotmail account, you can pick up your emails from another computer by going to 💻 www.mailstart.com and entering your email address and password, although you're unable to download attachments. This service is free once per week; if you need to use it more often, you can pay a small subscription (around €15 per year) for your own 'WebBox'. AOL users cannot use this service.

For details of registering a French internet domain name, see page 136.

POSTAL SERVICES

The French Post Office (La Poste) is a state-owned company, and post offices (*la poste* also means 'post office') in France are always staffed by post office employees, who are French civil servants (*fonctionnaires*); there are no post offices run by private businesses as in the UK, for example. Privatisation of the postal service began in 2003 and La Poste's monopoly on the handling of letters between 50 and 100g ends in 2006. There are around 17,000 post offices, 60 per cent of them in communes of fewer than 2,000 inhabitants and, as in other countries, those in the least populated areas are gradually being closed. (La Poste made a loss of millions of euros in 2001 after many years in the black.)

The identifying colour used by the French post office is yellow, and the post office logo looks like a blue paper aeroplane on a yellow background. Signs for post offices in towns vary widely and include *PTT* (the old name for the post office), *PT*, *P et T, Bureau de Poste* or simply *Poste*. Post offices are listed in the yellow pages under *Poste: Services*.

In addition to the usual post office services, a range of other services are provided, although post offices generally have fewer facilities than those in the UK, for example. These include telephone calls, telegram and fax transmissions, domestic and international cash transfers, payment of telephone and utility bills, and the distribution of mail-order catalogues. Recently, La Poste has also started offering email services on the internet, including free and permanent email addresses as well as e-commerce services for small businesses. The post office also provides financial and banking services, including cheque and savings accounts, mortgage and retirement plans, and share prices. Post offices usually have photocopy machines and telephone booths.

Main post offices usually have different counters (*guichets*) for different services, e.g. post office cheques (*CCP*), postal orders (*mandates*), *poste restante* and bulk stamps (*timbres en gros*), although some counters provide all services (*tous services/toutes operations*). Before joining a queue, make sure it's the correct one; if you join the wrong queue, you will need to start again (there are often long queues). If you need different services, you must queue a number of times if there's no window for all services. Stamps are sold at most windows and most handle letters and packages (*envoi de lettres et paquets*), except perhaps very large parcels.

The Post Office produces numerous leaflets and brochures, including the *Tarifs Courrier – Colis*, or you can obtain information on ☎ 08 20 80 80 00 for general information or 08 10 82 18 21 for information regarding international post. La Poste has a website where you can find information on all its services, although only limited information is available in English (🖳 www.laposte.fr). The site offers a search tool to help you find the address and telephone number of your nearest post office, according to the town name or postcode. The listings don't include the opening hours or the times for the last collection each day.

Note that French companies are usually slow to reply to letters and it's often necessary to follow up a letter with a telephone call.

Parcels

The post office provides a (confusing and ever-changing) range of parcel (*colis*) services, domestic and international, now collectively called *ColiPoste*. Parcel services are also provided by French railways and airlines and international courier companies such as DHL, Fedex and UPS. First-class parcels are limited to a maximum weight of 3kg, and parcels containing printed matter (e.g. books and magazines) are limited to 5kg. Parcels heavier than 5kg must be taken to a main post office. International parcels are usually limited to 30kg, although there are lower limits, e.g. 20kg, for some countries. Parcels to addresses outside the European Union (EU) must have an international green customs label (*déclaration de douane*) affixed to them. **Recent security regulations require you to present identification when sending parcels over 250g.**

Parcels posted in France must be securely packaged, and it's wise to buy padded envelopes (*à bulles*) or special cardboard boxes sold at post offices. Padded envelopes come in four sizes and are also sold in self-service machines at main post offices; the boxes also come in various sizes. The post office also sells a wide range of pre-paid (for domestic post) packaging for specific contents (*emballages Colissimo*), such as reinforced boxes for bottles (e.g. around €8.50 for a single bottle) and packaging for CDs, DVDs and video tapes (around €6.50). Boxes, padded bags and large envelopes are also sold in stationery shops.

When sending small parcels from a post office, use the window marked *paquets* (if there is one). In larger branches, there's usually an automatic coin-operated weighing machine that issues the correct postage for packages.

French railways (SNCF) also operate an express package and parcel service (*Service National des Messageries/SERNAM*) within France and to most European countries. The 'special express' service operates door-to-door and the 'direct express' service, station-to-station. Charges vary according to the speed of delivery, the distance, and whether the package is to be collected or delivered at either end. DHL and UPS also provide a domestic freight service, which guarantees airport-to-airport delivery within four hours, plus optional delivery at the receiving end.

Registered & Recorded Post

Registered post is commonly used in France when sending official documents and communications, when proof of despatch and/or receipt is required. You can send a registered letter (*lettre recommandée*) with (*avec*) or without (*sans*) proof of delivery (*avis de réception*). There are three levels of compensation (*indemnité forfaitaire*) for domestic registered letters and parcels. The sender's address must be written on the back of registered letters. You receive a receipt for a registered letter or parcel.

A domestic recorded or 'tracked' service (*courier suivi*) enables you to check the progress of your post and find out when it arrives (via the internet). It's also possible to combine the recorded service with registered post (*le prêt-à-recommander suivi*), if you need a signed receipt and also want to be able to track your letter. It's even possible to send an electronic registered letter (see ⌨ www.laposte.fr for details).

Ordinary (*ordinaire*) registered letters require a signature and proof of identity on delivery – normally of the person to whom they're addressed. If the addressee is absent when delivery is made, a notice is left and the letter must be collected from the local post office. When proof of delivery (*avis de réception*) is required, a receipt is returned to the sender.

TRANSPORT

Information about French transport networks and services can be found in *Living and Working in France* (Survival Books – see page 419), but you should consider the following points if your business is to involve regional, national or international distribution of products or travel in search of suppliers or buyers. It goes without saying that this should be done **before** you choose the location for your business.

Road

France is a **big** country – Europe's largest – and road transport is therefore slow. It's also expensive – particularly if motorways are used, as toll charges for goods vehicles are high (see 🖥 www.autoroutes.fr). If motorways are avoided, journeys can take at least twice as long. Most main roads radiate from Paris, and it can be difficult to make cross-country journeys. On the other hand, you have access to the whole of continental Europe, without the need (or expense) of crossing the sea.

Rail

France has some of the world's best and fastest rail services, which, like its roads, merge with those of neighbouring countries; it's even possible to travel right across continental Europe without changing trains. Freight (*fret*) is a major part of the national rail company (SNCF)'s business, and it offers a variety of specialised services for agricultural, automotive, chemical, consumer and other goods, including controlled temperature wagons, and transport of liquids and palleted goods. It also offers integrated rail-road transport, warehousing and other storage, stock management and IT support.

Air

All major international airlines provide scheduled services to Paris, and many also fly to other main French cities such as Bordeaux, Lyon, Marseille, Nice and Toulouse. The French state-owned national airline, Air France, is France's major international carrier, flying to over 30 French, 65 European and 120 non-European destinations in over 70 countries. Air France and its various subsidiaries (known collectively as Groupe Air France) has a fleet of over 200 aircraft and carries some 16 million passengers annually. It provides a high standard of service and, as you would expect, provides excellent in-flight cuisine.

However, Air France shares its monopoly on many international routes with just one foreign carrier and is thus able to charge high fares. The lack of competition means that international flights to and from most French airports, and French domestic flights, are among the world's most expensive. Opposition is starting to appear and high fares on some transatlantic flights have been reduced in recent years by travel agents such as Nouvelles Frontières. There are regular scheduled flights to Paris Charles de Gaulle (CDG) from many North American cities, including Atlanta, Boston, Chicago, Dallas, Detroit, Houston, Los Angeles, Miami, Montreal, Newark, New York, Philadelphia, San Diego, San Francisco, Seattle, Toronto and Washington, to Lyon from Montreal and to Nice from Montreal, New York and Toronto. There are also transatlantic charter flights to other French airports (e.g. to Toulouse from Montreal and Toronto).

In recent years, British and Irish visitors have been particularly well served by cheap flights (as well as less inexpensive services) from a number of airports – especially London Stansted – to many regional French destinations. The major budget carrier is Ryanair, but low-cost flights are also offered by a number of other

British operators. Note, however, that the low-cost airlines are notoriously fickle and frequently change services according to 'demand' (i.e. profitability), so you should check current services with the airline **and** the airport (who may well provide you with different information!). Take into account also any seasonal charter flights (e.g. to Nice in the summer and Lyon in the winter). Details of all French airports and their current services can be found on ▣ www.aeroport.fr.

7.

Bars, Restaurants
& Hotels

You certainly won't be alone if you've ever sat and dreamt of running a bar, a restaurant or a small hotel in France. This kind of business seems to hold an almost dreamlike fascination, especially for those who have spent time in the country on holiday. What better way to make a living than sitting in the sun, chatting to customers over a glass of wine?

If you think this is the kind of business you would like to run in France, you must banish those daydreams and face up to reality. **The hospitality trade, especially bars in tourist areas, is one of riskiest in France. In popular areas, bars and restaurants open and close with depressing regularity.** This is good news for the owners of the premises and the agents involved, who receive a percentage of the sale every time a bar changes hands, but it's often a personal and financial disaster for expatriates who have sunk their life savings into a dream.

The chances are that your dreams are based on holiday experiences during the summer months, when the bars and restaurants are bursting at the seams with customers, and the owners have smiles on their faces. Try sitting in those same bars during the winter months, when strong winds and rain have left the beaches and promenades empty and bar owners are desperate to lure what few holidaymakers there are away from the competition.

Of course, many foreigners make a success of running a bar, restaurant or hotel in France, but they don't do so on a whim and a prayer. This chapter looks at why those people have been successful and explores some of the pitfalls that lie in wait for the unwary and the ill prepared.

A useful source of information about cafés, restaurants and hotels in France is CHR-Link (☎ 04 72 78 58 38, 🖳 www.chr-link.fr), an independent company offering various free services to businesses in this sector.

EXPERIENCE

Relevant experience is essential, not least because working from the early hours of the morning until the early hours of the morning six days a week – hours which aren't uncommon when running a bar, restaurant or hotel – can come as more than a shock if you're used to a nine-to-five, five-days-a-week working life. **If you have no experience of working in a bar or restaurant and wouldn't consider buying such a business in your home country, don't do it in France!**

⚠ **Running a bar, restaurant or hotel – even in your home country, especially abroad – can put enormous strain on family relationships. If you've never worked with your partner for 16 to 18 hours per day, it's likely to come as something of a shock. Combine this with exhaustion and possible financial worries and you have all the ingredients for disaster in a relationship. Try to avoid this by being prepared for the worst. Think about what you will do if one of you gets ill, homesick or just needs a few days' break. If you have children to care for, especially young children, think seriously about whether it's the right thing for your family. Most people who have tried it would agree that it's almost impossible to look after a family and work the kind of hours that are needed to run a bar or restaurant successfully. If you're**

thinking along these lines, make sure your financial planning allows for the cost of employing an extra member of staff to help out.

RESEARCH

If you're serious about this kind of business and think you're strong enough to overcome the potential hurdles, make sure your market research is as thorough as possible. If you don't have any experience in the hospitality trade, find a temporary job working in a bar or restaurant in the area of France that you're interested in. There's nothing like a few long hard shifts behind a bar or waiting at tables to help you decide whether it's for you. Remember that the owner must be the first person there in the morning and the last to leave, probably in the early hours of the following morning. If your work experience doesn't put you off, you will have gained valuable experience in the industry, made some useful contacts and begun to see what's involved first hand. Get to know the busy spots in your preferred area and make sure you're realistic about the kind of competition you will be facing.

As far as location is concerned, this depends on the type of business you want to run. The Côte d'Azur is probably the most popular location for would-be bar and restaurant owners, but the big towns and cities are also seeing an increasing number of expatriate owners, and trade there is less seasonal and doesn't depend so much on the weather. Many foreigners opt for popular tourist spots, believing that the combination of tourism and a large expatriate community is a guarantee of success. Sadly, it isn't – simply because the competition is intense. In that sense, these are probably the most difficult areas in which to open a bar or restaurant. In most of the popular coastal areas, the port and seafront areas are jam-packed full of bars, cafés and restaurants and there just isn't enough trade to go round. You may have three or four months in the summer when trade is relatively brisk, but that leaves another eight or nine when custom is thin on the ground, but the bills and the rent must still be paid.

As all the contributors to this chapter would agree, it's imperative to thoroughly research the area or areas you're interested in and to allow plenty of time for finding the right premises at the right price. And, if you're buying a going concern, which is almost inevitable in the case of a bar, make sure you go through the finances of the business with a fine-tooth comb (or, even better, engage a professional to do so for you), as hoteliers and restaurant-owners are notoriously secretive about their turnover and profit figures and are likely to provide you with an 'edited' version of the truth, unless you insist on seeing their accounts.

FINANCES

Overstretching your finances is one of the biggest problems for expatriates who come to France intending to buy a bar, restaurant or hotel. Many have burnt their bridges and sold their homes to raise the money to start a new life. Steve Timewell of Fiesta Property Services warns: "If you've raised, say, €150,000 from the sale of your house, don't look at bars or restaurants at that price. Work out how much you will need to live on for a while and think hard about extra costs, then deduct that amount and a bit more and that will give you a more realistic figure." Don't forget that, once you've bought your bar, there will be stock to buy (although sometimes this is included in the price), lawyer's fees, licences to pay for, staff wages if you decide to employ others, marketing costs, and your own tax and social security payments – without forgetting rent and utility bills.

Most important of all, allow sufficient funds to live on for around a year. If you have children, research the available schools carefully, as English or international schools in France are generally fee-paying, which is an expense you may not have had at home.

PREMISES

If you're planning to buy a bar, hotel or restaurant, you should walk around the areas you like. See which bars and restaurants are the most popular, preferably in winter as well as summer, and find out why. How do they attract customers and keep them? Sit outside a few, watching the customers come and go. What type of people are they, what do they buy and which are the busiest times?

General information on finding commercial premises in France is provided on page 148. Bars and hotels for sale can be found on the website of Business Sales France (⌨ www.le-guide.com/business-sales). Bars and restaurants are usually sold as going concerns, so when you take one over, you buy the lease from the current leaseholder and pay an agreed amount for 'goodwill' (*fonds de commerce*). Thereafter, you pay the owner a monthly rent.

The 'goodwill' payment obviously varies according to a number of factors, including the position of the premises, the fixtures and fittings and whether or not there's a well established client base. **Make sure you find out whether the business you're buying has a reputation worth paying for.** Once you know the area, you can ask locally, and your professional advisers should be able to help. Have the business's accounts checked by a qualified accountant before you agree on a price and, if possible, spend some time working alongside the owner, so that you can see for yourself what trade is like on a daily basis.

Other important things that your lawyer should check include the following:

- That there are no outstanding debts on the business or the property or any social security obligations that you don't know about;

- That all the necessary licences are in place and transferred to your name once the sale is completed (see below). Reputable agencies only have legal businesses on their books, but always get your lawyer to check.

You should also consider the question of disabled access – not just through the front door, but also to the toilets, etc. – which is required in many parts of France and likely to become compulsory everywhere.

When budgeting for a bar, restaurant or hotel, don't forget to allow for regular renovation, which should be done at least every five years to prevent the premises from becoming shabby.

LICENCES & PERMISSIONS

Various licences and permissions are required to run a bar, restaurant or hotel, particularly if you plan to sell alcohol, which you almost certainly need to. Your premises must also conform to certain standards of safety, hygiene, etc., and you can be sure that there will be regular inspections. As with any business premises, your bar, restaurant or hotel must also be inspected for electrical and general safety. The requirements are outlined below.

When you've obtained the necessary permissions, you must display some or all of the following, depending on the type of establishment, on the premises:

- 'Protection of minors' (*protection des mineurs*) notice;
- Type of drinks licence obtained (see **Alcohol & Tobacco** below);
- Drinks prices;
- Opening hours (which must be approved by the *préfecture*);
- Restaurant or hotel rating.

You must also retain all the paperwork relating to licences and permissions, such as your drinks licence, and receipts for health and safety inspections, as well as a list of staff.

It's recommended to join the local Union des Métiers et des Industries de l'Hôtellerie, which can provide advice and information regarding the legislation applicable to running a bar, hotel or restaurant.

Health & Safety

A bar, hotel or restaurant must comply with general health and safety regulations (see **Health & Safety** on page 147). In addition, the premises must meet certain standards of hygiene (see **Food** below). To establish a bar or restaurant, it's also necessary to convene a *commission de sécurité* via the *Maire* of the commune. He arranges an inspection by representatives of the *sapeurs pompiers*, the *gendarmes* and the *conseil général*, who assess if any work needs doing to provide fire escapes, alarms, etc.

Separately, the Service des Vétérinaires (under the auspices of the local *préfecture*) will visit to inspect general conditions of hygiene. Each of these authorities has the power to shut down premises that don't comply with regulations. In all matters relating to local regulation, it's worthwhile getting on good terms with the *Maire*, as he's responsible for adherence to the laws in his commune.

Food

Curiously, no licence is required to sell food. Even more curiously, an alcohol licence (see below) entitles you to sell take-away food. Nevertheless, your premises must adhere to strict hygiene standards, for which you need certification. This isn't just a question of cleanliness; for example, the kitchen floor and walls must be tiled and there must be separate washbasins and chopping surfaces for meat and vegetables. The required standards and procedures can be found on the website of the Syndicat National des Hôteliers, Restaurateurs, Cafetiers et Traiteurs (Synhorcat, 4 rue de Gramont, 75002 Paris, ☎ 01 42 96 60 75, ▢ www. synhorcat.com – click on 'Hygiène').

Alcohol & Tobacco

One of the biggest expenses (apart from staff) involved in setting up a bar, restaurant or hotel is an alcohol licence. In fact, it may not even be possible to obtain a licence for a bar, as these are usually 'attached' to a business, and new licences may not be issued. A list of licensed businesses for sale can be obtained from the local *chambre de commerce et d'industrie*. Alcohol licences are strictly regulated and the system is typically complicated. There are different types of licence for bars, restaurants and hotels (described below).

Bear in mind that, in addition to the cost of a licence, you must pay the customs authorities duty on all alcoholic drinks sold in your bar, restaurant or hotel. This amounts to a 'reasonable' €1.30 per hectolitre (100 litres) for beer, €3.40 for wine but a whopping €1,450 for spirits!

Bars

There are five categories of drink licence for bars, which are essentially as follows:

- **Category 1** – Soft drinks only;
- **Category 2** – Soft drinks and beer up to 3 per cent alcohol by volume;
- **Category 3** – Soft drinks and alcoholic drinks up to 18 per cent alcohol by volume;
- **Category 4** – Soft drinks and alcoholic drinks up to 40 per cent alcohol by volume;
- **Category 5** – All alcoholic drinks.

The number of Category 2, 3, 4 and 5 licences in a town or village is limited according to the number of inhabitants (a measure designed to prevent alcoholism and drunken behaviour), and they must usually must be purchased from an existing owner. Licences can be transferred within a radius of 50km (30mi), but this involves a considerable amount of paperwork (surprise, surprise!). Needless to say, most bars require at least a Category 4 licence. The price of a Category 4 licence is typically from around €10,000, but, as with all markets, it depends on supply and demand for each location and they can cost more than €25,000. You also need the blessing of your *Maire* and no local objections before you can obtain a licence. Details are available from regional customs offices (Direction Régionale des Douanes).

Restaurants

The type of licence you require for a restaurant (including a hotel restaurant) depends on whether you intend to serve drinks only with food or also on their own (e.g. in a separate bar area). If you want a separate bar, you must apply for one of the following types of licence (*licence*):

- **Licence I** – Allows you to serve non-alcoholic drinks;
- **Licence II** – Allows you to serve the above plus wine, beer, cider and similar drinks;
- **Licence III** – Allows you to serve the above plus fortified wine, etc. up to 18 per cent alcohol;
- **Licence IV** – Allows you to serve the above plus spirits.

A *Licence I* is free; the average cost of a *Licence II* is between around €6,000 and €7,500, a *Licence III* from €8,000 to €10,000, and a *licence IV* between €18,000 and €20,000, although prices vary considerably according to supply and demand.

If you wish only to serve drinks with food, you can apply for a *petite licence restauration* (nothing to do with restoration!) or a *grande licence restauration*, which roughly correspond to a *Licence II* and *Licence IV* level (respectively) but are free! Both types of licences must be obtained from the customs authorities.

As with bar licences, there's a limit on the number of licences in each commune: one per 450 inhabitants. But, as with most things in France, there are ways around this rule. If no licence is available in the town or village where you want to set up a restaurant, it's possible to find another commune within a radius of 100km (60mi) – yes, 100km! – where a licence is available and have it 'transferred' to where you want it!

Tobacco

Although they're widely flouted, France has laws relating to smoking in bars, hotels and restaurants. Every establishment must have a non-smoking area and there must be signs indicating where customers may and may not smoke. Smoking areas must be adequately ventilated (including smoke extractors) and there's even a law specifying the minimum number of cubic metres of air that must surround each smoker! For details of the regulations, consult your local *commissariat de police*. If you want to sell tobacco products, you must obtain a licence from customs.

Music

If you want music in your bar or restaurant, whether live or recorded, you need a separate licence. If the business doesn't already have a music licence, your lawyer should check whether it's likely that one will be granted for your premises. You must obtain permission from two organisations (roughly equivalent to the Performing Right Society and the Mechanical-copyright Protection Society in the UK) and pay them royalties. Charges vary enormously according to your opening hours and whether these are seasonal, the type of drinks licence you have (see above), the size of the bar, the number of staff, your tariffs, and whether you have a dance floor, and are reduced by 33 per cent if you belong to a confederation such as the Compagnie de Promotion Immobilière et Hôtellière (CPIH, 💻 www.cpih.fr) or Synhorcat (see **Food** above). To give an example, a small, rural bar playing the radio or recorded music and having the occasional (free) live band might pay around €250 per year. For discotheques, there's a minimum fee of €460.

- **Societé pour la Perception de la Rémuneration Equitable** (SPRE, 61 rue La Fayette 75009 Paris, ☎ 01 53 20 87 00, 💻 www.spre.fr) – This organisation collects royalties on behalf of performing musicians, although payments are collected by SACEM (see below).

- **Societé des Auteurs, Compositeurs et Editeurs de Musique** (SACEM, 225 avenue Charles de Gaulle, 92528 Neuilly-sur-Seine Cedex, ☎ 01 47 15 47 15, 💻 www.sacem.fr) – This organisation collects royalties on behalf of composers who are alive or who died less than 70 years ago. (So, for example, if you wanted to play only Mozart in your bar or restaurant, you wouldn't have to pay SACEM anything, but would still have to pay royalties to the performers via the SPRE.) SACEM collects fees on behalf of the SPRE.

For further information on performing rights and the charges involved, contact your regional SACEM delegate; contact details can be found via the map on the SACEM website.

STAFF

Employing staff in France is something you should only do once you've taken advice from a specialist in labour laws (see page 153). If your establishment is a relatively small operation, it's usually possible to keep costs down by doing all the work yourselves, especially when you first start trading. It's legal to do so provided that one of you is registered as self-employed and pays tax and social security contributions on all earnings (see **Chapter 4**). That way, your dependants are covered for treatment under the French health service.

If you need to hire staff, things become **much** more complicated – if you do things legally. Bar staff are often hired on a casual, one-off, cash payment basis. Although plenty of bars and restaurants do this, it's illegal and, if you're caught, you may have to pay a heavy fine. **In popular tourist areas, inspectors make regular visits to check the contracts of the people who are working on the premises.** If the workload varies according to the season, as it usually does in the catering trade, you can legally employ someone for a short period or on a temporary contract, provided it's properly registered with the labour authorities. Be wary of issuing indefinite term contracts without a three-month trial period or training contract; once staff are 'permanent', it's very difficult to dismiss them if they do a poor job or even disappear for days or weeks at a time. Details of contracts and of your responsibilities as an employer can be found in **Chapter 4**.

Hotel, restaurant and bar staff are subject to the *Convention Collective Nationale des Hôtelliers, Cafetiers et Restaurateurs*, which can be found on the website of CHR-Link (💻 www.chr-link.fr) – all 23,600 words of it (even if you don't read it, you must have a copy of it available on the premises)! Key points to note are that you must inform the local *inspecteur de travail* (see page 153) that you're recruiting staff, make sure you're contributing to a pension fund on their behalf and that you issue them with a contract within two days of their engagement. You must also draw up a list of working hours, including rest periods, for staff and a *registre des pourboires* detailing the amount of tips received. Staff must have a bank account, as they must be paid by cheque, accompanied by a pay slip (*bulletin de paie*). If staff are from outside the European Union (EU), they must have the appropriate visa or permit (see page 26).

CUSTOMERS

You must decide what sort of customers you want to attract: families with children, young people, students, the elderly, smokers, etc. Do you want a predominantly French or foreign clientele? Even in tourist areas, you need to attract local customers as well as 'passing trade'. To do this, you must offer drink, food and ambience with which French people are familiar, although this needn't prevent you from varying the 'formula' and experimenting with, for example, foreign beers and even wines as well as international cuisine.

As with most businesses in France – and probably more than with most – your most effective 'advertising' will be word of mouth. Taking over an existing, and thriving, business will obviously make life easier than starting from scratch, where you will need to rely on advertising and promotion initially.

RESTAURANTS

To many, France is the Mecca of the gastronomic arts, and the idea of running a restaurant there as a foreigner may be daunting, to say the least. Nevertheless, many immigrants have done so successfully – and not only by offering foreign fare; many dare to take on the French at their own game and offer traditional and regional food, although often with a twist. French eating habits are changing, however, and you should be aware that many supposed traditions are now no more than myths.

One of these is that the French spend two hours every day over lunch, consuming four or five courses and gallons of wine. Even in rural areas, fewer people have even three-course lunches, and it's common for a group of diners (particularly the young) to order just one bottle of wine; often, they don't even finish it! In fact, such is the trend towards shorter lunch breaks, particularly among working people, that fast food outlets and sandwich bars are becoming increasingly popular. (One report calculated that the French eat some 765 million sandwiches a year.)

Note also that restaurant prices in France include service and that tips are virtually non-existent – except from foreigners, who often feel obliged to leave something – so don't budget for generous tips!

You must have a non-smoking area, but making the entire restaurant non-smoking will severely limit its appeal to French people, who tend to smoke throughout a meal. If you want to attract families, you must offer a children's menu (and possibly facilities such as swings and slides, games and colouring sets).

CASE STUDY 1

At one time, French people would probably have laughed at the idea of a British couple running a high quality restaurant in France, but Ewan Scutcher, who, with his wife Caroline, runs La Table du Mareyeur at Port Grimaud, along the coast from St Tropez in Var, says he has never felt any prejudice in that sense — "or at least it never came to our attention. The gastronomic reputation of England has changed dramatically over recent years and I would say that England, and even the US, are on a par with many European countries."

The Scutchers have been a long-standing and successful team, having worked together in Caroline's family's travel firm in Brighton, East Sussex, and studied together at the Lausanne Hotel Management School in Switzerland, before starting their present operation in 1989. The Lausanne course, divided equally between study on campus and practical experience in the field, led to diplomas that are widely recognised internationally. In the course of their work experience, they both spent six months working in Cannes — Caroline at the Carlton and Ewan at the Martinez — which, together with family holidays at Port Grimaud, created an attachment to the part of France where they married and have lived for the past 16 years. "Two sons and a dog later, we're still enjoying it and feel very much at home here," says Ewan.

Although their training had covered the whole spectrum of hotel activities, Ewan points out that starting and running a hotel requires a considerable initial investment: "Many ex-restaurateurs end up running chambres d'hôtes or a small hotel as a retirement scheme, although these require more dedication and experience than one imagines. Perhaps one day we will add a few rooms to the restaurant for those who have eaten too much and want to stay the night." Meanwhile, the restaurant occupies them fully enough from March to November and during the Christmas and New Year season.

The restaurant, which these days numbers politicians, film stars and royalty as well as 'ordinary' people amongst its clientele, is on the waterfront, with a terrace with its own moorings from those arriving by boat, and views over the village and canals of what is sometimes termed 'the Venice of the Riviera'. It specialises in fresh line-caught fish and seafood (mareyeur is an old word for fishmonger) supplied by local fishermen. "Although these are mainly luxury products, we try to provide value for money, efficient service and a friendly atmosphere, as opposed to the stuffiness and impersonal approach of many other gastronomic restaurants." Currently the lunch menu costs €25, including wine and coffee, and other set menus are offered at €42 and €55, the latter including foie gras and lobster. There's also, naturally enough, a range of plateaux de fruits de mer of varying contents. The Scutchers also cater for weddings, meetings, parties, conferences, etc., particularly out of season, and run a home delivery service in the area,

At the outset, the Scutchers bought an existing restaurant, with a different name and kind of business, and this had some influence on their funding. They found that French banks were cautious about lending to new businesses, even based on a solid business plan and the qualifications and knowledge of the area that went with them. "Buying an existing business gives the bank something to go on, basing the value on an average of turnover in the previous three years – although it doesn't follow that the clientele will take to the new ownership." They benefited from the advice of a *notaire* and an accountant, whose role they regard as essential, "amongst other things to help you through the administrative minefield. Word-of-mouth recommendation is a good way of finding these professionals." Language, happily, was not a problem, as both had taken their studies in French.

The Scutchers don't follow the traditional format of husband as chef and wife running the front of the house (or vice versa). "Caroline looks after the administrative side, while I deal with the front of the house and service side," explains Ewan, "and we're both very much present for our clients. Although we both had training as chefs, we confer this role to our *chef de cuisine*, Ricardo d'Elia. Our team is composed of a core of faithful staff members who have also been with us for many years. A full complement at the height of the season is 15 to 18 people. Retaining good staff in this industry isn't easy, particularly in a seasonal resort like this, and the continuity that our regulars provide helps mutual recognition between clients and staff members."

Looking back over the years, Ewan remembers "the ups and downs of running any small business: recent governmental measures concerning the 35-hour week, the transition to the euro, the prohibitive charges on salaries that make finding and employing qualified staff difficult at times. However, our ability to attract excellent, dedicated young people gives us hope for the future of our business at a time when standardisation and corporate dominance tend to overshadow the small family-run business. We're closely linked to local producers of wines and foods, and this element must be preserved: it's part of our culture and history."

For anyone contemplating following in their footsteps, Ewan emphasises that "coming on holiday or even for a longer period to a place isn't the same as living and working there. One should weigh up the pros and cons – about schools, taxes, the local culture, etc. – and get the maximum amount of information not only on the business concerned, but also on the area. Times change and a town or village that was once busy may not always be for a number of reasons. Beach concessions aren't automatically renewable on a yearly basis, for example, and one could risk losing one's business without knowledge of this and other similar laws. Seasonal work can be misleading, as turnover won't always be the same as in high season, although your fixed costs will be. The French notion of *fonds de commerce* or leasehold is not always easy for foreign potential buyers to grasp. Having made your decision, do it for the right reasons, enjoy it, don't give up, do the best you can and don't look back!"

If the idea of Britons running a fish restaurant in France is unusual, the concept of Britons running a vegetarian restaurant in France is positively outlandish. To most French people, being a vegetarian means not eating red meat; fish, poultry and even ham aren't generally regarded as meat, and supposedly vegetarian dishes are often served with chicken or *lardons* (pieces of bacon). Nevertheless, vegetarianism is becoming more popular – slowly – and offers scope for intrepid entrepreneurs.

CASE STUDY 2

Debbie and Daniel Armitage bought a vegetarian restaurant and a three-room guest house in Normandy in November 2000, just four months after staying there and discovering that it was for sale. "We didn't plan it," explains Debbie. "It was pure impulse." In that time, they closed their successful garden design business and sold their home in the UK and bought not only the restaurant and guest house building, but also a two-bedroom cottage, in which they now live, a barn and two-and-a-half acres of countryside. "It was stressful," recalls Debbie, "but not as bad as it could have been."

What made it relatively straightforward was that they were buying an existing business. "This greatly simplified the process, as the *notaire* handling the sale dealt with all the paperwork, sending relevant documents to the Chambre de Commerce, the tax office, etc." The restaurant had been running for ten years, although there was little in the way of a clientele. "The previous owners wanted to sell it simply as a property; it was the *notaire* who insisted that they add a nominal amount to the price to include the business."

Then there was the matter of licences. There are various licences for businesses offering alcoholic drinks, depending on whether you simply want to serve wine with a meal (e.g. in a B&B) or you intend to serve drinks at all times, inside and outside the premises. There's normally a limit on the number of licences permitted in a town or village, although the regulations vary from commune to commune and may have more to do with 'tradition' than any logical rules. "It's essential to clarify at an early stage whether you will be able to obtain a licence and, if so, what type of licence you need," warns Debbie. This should be done initially at the local town hall or *mairie*, although you may be referred to the departmental *préfecture*. "It turned out that the previous owners didn't have the correct licence," she says, "so this needed sorting out." The cost of licences also varies; Debbie and Daniel are fortunate that theirs costs them nothing.

As the purchase hadn't been planned, the Armitages eased their way into the business. Although competent cooks (and, of course, vegetarians themselves), they weren't confident of catering for others – particularly French people, who are renowned not only for their culinary discernment, but also for their predilection for meat. They therefore enrolled on a course at a vegetarian cookery school in Limoges, where "we learned nothing," confesses Debbie. "Everything was flavoured with Marmite." Another problem was that the previous owners had told everyone they were closing the business, so what little clientele there had been more or less disappeared. The decor was also in need of refreshment. It was as if they were starting a business from scratch, but they built it up gradually.

They placed a few advertisements in specialised magazines, such as that of The Vegetarian Society in the UK, but most of their business came by word of mouth and via the internet. "A website is absolutely imperative," states Debbie. "We only sent out two brochures last year." The guest house attracts mostly British people, but also Belgians, Dutch, Americans and other nationalities, while restaurant customers are divided equally between foreign tourists and French people – but not only locals. "People come from Paris, Honfleur, Deauville . . .".

And how do the French, notorious carnivores, take to vegetarian fare? "The French love anything different," enthuses Debbie. "We grow lots of our own vegetables and everything we grow is organic; the French love that. They're adventurous too: they will choose the more unusual things on the menu – even if they have no idea what they are."

Originally, the Armitages opened the restaurant only in the summer (from Easter to late September), although the guest house is open all year round and, of course, meals are provided for guests. Once they became established, they intended to keep the restaurant open all year as well. "Then we decided not to," says Debbie. "We wouldn't be so busy and would therefore have less revenue" and the summer season is such hard work that they need time to recuperate and do other things that need doing, "although one of the advantages of being a small business is that you can be flexible: if we want to open the restaurant at any time, we can.

"When we moved here, we thought we might have six months off every year, but that didn't work out and probably never will." This winter, after living in it for four years, they're finally getting round to refurbishing the cottage. "A lot of people coming to France think they're going to get rich and live a life of leisure. We work much harder than we thought we would and don't get as much free time. We live on half the income we had in the UK."

The Armitages have survived by diversifying their business while keeping it small. In addition to the restaurant and the rooms, they plan to open their garden, on which they've lavished their design expertise, to the public.

Being a *micro-entreprise* (see page 197), they pay little tax and low accountancy fees (around €180 per year). "Although for our own reference we keep thorough accounts," explains Debbie, "all we give our accountant is details of our income and he gives our turnover and profit figures to the taxman, who calculates our tax. We aren't VAT registered, which means we cannot claim back VAT, but we don't have the mountains of paperwork to deal with either. The previous owners were on a different tax regime whereby they declared VAT monthly and also paid around €3,000 a year in accountants' fees, despite the fact that their turnover was smaller than ours. So it's very important to look into what tax regime suits your business best. If you make the wrong choice, you're tied to it for three years, so it can be very costly."

The Armitages also don't employ staff: "We cannot afford to because of the high social charges we would have to pay [see page 210]. The only help we get is from a few students who do odd jobs for us each year in exchange for accommodation."

Debbie's advice? "Learn French." She and Daniel had only basic French when they started the business, and it hasn't improved a great deal in four years. "We don't have much of a conversation with our customers and, although we have French friends, it's hard. A lot of people plan their move for years, but don't bother to learn the language; they think they will pick it up when they get here. But it doesn't work like that.

"Before thinking about coming here, plan what you're going to do and research it properly. We don't know anyone who has survived by doing odd jobs or relying on the income from a B&B, even if they have no mortgage to pay." They've seen many other foreigners arrive thinking they're going to strike it lucky and before long they're on their way back home. "Don't do it because you think you're going to be rich; do it for the lifestyle. We were happy where we were in England; we're still happy here."

A restaurant can be an add-on (e.g. to a hotel or *gîte* complex) as well as a self-contained business. Indeed *gîtes* rarely generate sufficient income on their own to enable you to make a living, and a restaurant can be the ideal complement, as you have a 'captive' clientele who would much rather be waited on than cook for themselves!

CASE STUDY 3

Tim and Chloe Williams ran a successful marketing company in Northamptonshire with 100 employees but, when the opportunity arose to sell the business to a larger American company, they seized it to provide their children (then aged eight and six) with a bilingual upbringing and a taste of other cultures.

Linguistically, they were well prepared: Tim had a degree in French and Economics, while Chloe had both A Level and Business French qualifications. Their main business is the running of a *gîte* complex on the Dordogne/Charente border, which they took over in a rundown state and developed. Currently it consists of three *gîtes*, to which they've recently added an on-site restaurant. "Each year, business is better than the last," comments Tim, "although I sense that it's getting harder as more rental properties come onto the market." In addition, Tim manages the letting of properties in the UK and US and Chloe works part-time at a French language school in the local town.

The Williams had little trouble in making the transition in July 2001, although "the timing of sales of three homes in the UK was a challenge." Tim puts this down partly to realising that "bureaucracy is really just a matter of understanding a different culture and system. I'm sure anybody arriving in the UK for the first time would struggle similarly with council tax, road fund licences, speed cameras and the Inland Revenue. It's a surprise that émigrés to France don't expect the bureaucracy to be difficult. Difficulties come from not knowing – and you never know what you don't know!"

Opening the restaurant brought its own share of red tape: "We had to learn about live music licences, the four different kinds of drinking licence, restaurant licences and health and safety inspections by the *sapeurs pompiers* (see **Licences & Permissions** on page 249).

Tim also lectures to courses for people considering going into the *gîte* business, from which the following list of **common errors** has been adapted:

- Disregarding all the advice given;
- Not leaving sufficient financial 'cushion' for unexpected expenditure;
- Not allowing sufficient funds to live on while building the business;
- Over-extravagant advertising;
- Neglecting safety issues;
- Skimping on insurance, particularly public liability;
- Expecting the French to do things the British way – they won't!
- Making too little effort to learn/improve French;
- Struggling alone – ask for help at the *mairie* and through magazines, websites, helplines, etc;
- Forgetting to enjoy the experience!

BARS

If you want to run a bar in France, it's extremely unlikely that you will be able to buy or rent a premises and start one from scratch, as there's a limited number of bar licences in each town or village and, unless a bar closes down or there's a sudden 'baby boom', you won't be able to obtain a licence (see **Licences & Permissions** on page 249). It's therefore a question of finding an existing bar that's for sale (see **Finding Premises** on page 150).

A traditional French café/bar is unlikely to earn you a fortune, as the French aren't generally heavy drinkers and customers sit for hours over a coffee or a *pastis*. Except in big towns and cities, French people aren't in the habit of frequenting bars late in the evening, but normally stop for a drink on their way home from work, so that most bars in rural areas are shut by around 20.00. You can, of course, offer food to increase a bar's appeal (and your turnover), but again, few French people have their dinner in a bar or cafe.

A better way of widening the appeal of a bar and generating extra income may be to install 'entertainment facilities' such as a jukebox, giant television screen, pinball machine, table football, pool table or internet access. Themed bars are becoming increasingly popular in France. Much will depend, of course, on the type of clientele you wish to attract.

Although French bars are all independently owned, unlike many British pubs, for example, you can expect support from drinks suppliers in the way of glasses (it's traditional to serve each drink in an appropriately styled or branded glass), beer mats and equipment.

CASE STUDY 4

In November 2000, Guernsey-born Dani Corbet felt disillusioned with her well paid job in one of the top accountancy firms, took a crash course in cookery and became a chalet girl in the French ski resort of Tignes in Savoie. She liked the mountain lifestyle, but found the job tough and the following year applied for a more senior post. Over the next two years she had different jobs in the hospitality industry, ending up as a hotel manager, but found dealing with a remote management constricting and frustrating.

At a mid-season meeting of employees of the tour operator she worked for she found that her views were shared by two colleagues, Justine Downs and Sarah Hookes.

Over dinner to wind down after the arguments, the three discussed how much more satisfying it would be to run their own business. "Within the hour," Dani recalls, "we'd decided on the concept (a ski resort bar), the location (Tignes, where Justine had also worked) and the name (Angelbar). The next morning, the enthusiasm was still there and we spent the summer of 2003 putting the idea into action."

It wasn't, of course, simple. There were problems of finding premises, resolved at the last minute when parents of a friend leased them one with an existing Category 4 alcohol licence (enabling them to sell all drinks and open until 2am). There were problems too with raising funds: the banks refused a loan, at least partly, Dani believes, because they were female and foreign. However, they were greatly helped by the discovery of an accountant in a nearby village who spoke a reasonable amount of English. "Eric was our backbone from then on and helped us through the processes of property, analysing the financial prospects, putting us in touch with lawyers to set up the company and so on. He and his firm now handle all our accounting needs and advise us on our tax bills, the highly complex French social charges system, the health system and plans for developing the business."

Since French has virtually died out in the Channel Islands, Dani had to learn it: from tapes in her chalet period and on a six-week course in Nice while living in a French household. She still finds time for a two or three-week refresher course each spring either in Biarritz or Nice.

The Angelbar became a reality on 18th November 2003 – Dani's 29th birthday. "All our friends, seasonal workers, other business owners, French and English, even our mums descended on us. We were as disorganised, unprepared and over-excited as we possibly could have been, in retrospect. We had 250 people packed into a 70 square metre room and emerged shell-shocked, but happy at around 2am."

The three proprietors are equal partners in the French company that leases the premises, and the fact that they're all widely experienced enables them to share the responsibilities as they choose. Justine, from Nantwich, Cheshire, had worked with tour operators for more than a decade, while Sarah had managed a hotel in Nottingham, her home town, and usefully studied French at university. The bar work is divided evenly between the three and their two seasonal employees. In the first year, Dani handled the accounts, Sarah the PR and Justine stock control and ordering. The following year, Justine and Dani swapped roles "for a bit of variety".

The bar serves an extensive range of draught and bottled beers, mulled wines, cocktails, flavoured rums and vodkas and their own-label wines. "Our food menu is limited, as our kitchen is a small store cupboard, but we offer soup, nachos, panini and hot dogs, as well as selling crisps and chocolate bars. We provide English newspapers and have a table football game, a pool table and an internet connection."

Publicity includes a website, local advertising, Angelbar T-shirts and stickers "but really we rely a lot on word of mouth: we look after the English seasonal workers and in turn they recommend us to their clients," says Dani. "I also believe that if you produce a decent quality service or product, it will be talked about and generate new customers." They organise regular competitions, including a weekly snowboard raffle, which help to attract attention and create a lively atmosphere.

In the first year, Janine and Dani tried to keep the bar open during the summer, while Sarah took a job in England, but they found that the business didn't warrant the effort. This year, Sarah will go to England again and Justine is thinking of working on boats in the Mediterranean. Dani, meanwhile, has developed her own activities. Having been asked to help find an apartment for parents of a seasonal worker to buy, she discovered that there was a need for a hand-holding service – from property search to the handing over of keys (and all that goes between). Her venture, Property Angel, offers such a service on a fee basis. Alongside this is an email-based seasonal accommodation service, taking bookings and organising rentals for owners. She's currently developing a further accommodation service, Angelski, for winter holidays, which will include hotels as well as privately owned properties.

Dani clearly feels that she has made the right decisions. "I now call Tignes my permanent home and, when I look back to my office job in Guernsey, I feel no regret. I wouldn't give up my current lifestyle for anything. The last few years have certainly brought periods of uncertainty and times of surviving on very little means. When I hear people expressing a wish to open their own bar or café or to spend a season in the Alps when they retire, I want to tell them they shouldn't wait until then! Not everyone would want to take the risks and undergo the drastic lifestyle change that I have, but to those who are thinking about it I would say that, despite all the difficulties, there is always the possibility of finding a way and it's definitely worth it in the end."

HOTELS

Running a hotel anywhere is a major commitment, in terms of money and time, and France is no exception. It's generally agreed that you need at least 15 rooms to be able to make a living from a hotel, even with a restaurant attached. As with any French business, staff are expensive, so it's wise to limit yourself, at least initially, to a family concern. Indeed, with the current boom in the short break market, 25 to 50-room family-run hotels are becoming increasingly popular with operators such as the Channel ferry companies – particularly those within a few hours' drive of a port.

You need a location that offers attractions all year round, unless you want your rooms empty from October to April. Bear in mind also that hotel room rates are generally low in France, particularly compared with the UK, and you should budget accordingly.

Strangely, no licence is required to open a hotel in France, although you must inform the Commission Départementale de l'Equipement Commercial and the premises must be inspected and meet the relevant standards (see **Licences & Permissions** on page 249).

French hotels are rated according to a star system, as shown below (prices are a guide only):

Star Rating	Price Range (€)	Standard
L****	160 – 250+	*hôtel hors classe, palace* (luxury)
****	100 – 200	*hôtel très grand confort* (top class)
***	50 – 130	*hôtel de grand tourisme, grand confort* (very comfortable)
**	30 – 60	*hôtel de tourisme, bon confort* (comfortable)
*	25 – 40	*hôtel de moyen tourisme* (average comfort)
None	20 – 35	*hôtel de tourisme/simple* (basic)

If you want your hotel to be star rated, you must go to your local *préfecture* and ask for a *demande de classement*. A hotel inspector will then assess the premises and submit a recommendation to the Commission Départementale d'Actions Touristiques. If you're awarded a star rating, you will be given a minimum room charge – a system designed to prevent hoteliers from undercutting each other. Charges vary greatly according to the area. There's no charge for a rating and the procedure is relatively quick (for France!).

CASE STUDY 5

Dawn Clarke left the UK in 1979 for the Sultanate of Oman, where she acted in a PR/protocol role for the Sultan in connection with government and international meetings, etc. After ten years, she found herself missing the seasons in Europe ("rain included!") and, despite earning good money, in need of mental and physical stimulation. "Having spent ten years of my life living in five-star hotels, I knew what I did and didn't like and expected and appreciated. I love people and entertaining and had often been asked to cook for friends' dinner parties. The idea of owning and running a hotel just popped into my head, although the original concept was more of a ski chalet set-up. That idea lasted till opening day, when the harsh reality of no bookings made me reconsider. I decided to open the doors to non-skiers as well and give people two-star luxury at two-star prices."

The hotel, La Maison Anglaise, was in the village of St Robert, "perched on a hillside with a view to die for", in Corrèze, an area to which she was recommended by a work colleague. Investigating over a long weekend, Dawn found her hotel on day two and bought it on day three. After six years, for the first five of which Dawn was chef as well as proprietor, her husband walked out on her. After a messy divorce, she was able to keep the hotel and continued to run it for a further four years before a couple in the bar said that they were thinking of buying chambres d'hôtes. They asked if she would sell them the hotel – and she did.

After that, she turned to her current business as a translator/interpreter (see **Case Study 40** on page 381), but says she sometimes still regrets giving up the hotel: "I miss the lifestyle but really appreciate being able to go to bed before midnight and going out for Sunday lunch, instead of cooking and serving it."

Running a hotel business is hard work, and you need relevant experience, adequate financial resources and, if it's a family concern, strong relationships to succeed. The rewards can be substantial, but they don't come easily – in France or anywhere else.

CASE STUDY 6

In 1992, Hazel and Peter Newington and their two children sold their property in the south of England and moved to the village of Cangey in the Loire Valley with the aim of renovating a derelict 19th century farm and running a hotel.

Peter Newington had worked in the leisure industry all his life, rising through the ranks of the hotel business and "given all sorts of fancy titles". When he had reached the top of the ladder, he decided that the next step to take was running his own business. The only decision was where.

The Newingtons had lived in many parts of the world, but in the end found the decision relatively easy. "If you're thinking of setting up a business abroad, it's important to have a good working knowledge of the language," insists Peter. With a French mother, he had some knowledge of that language, and he and Hazel, therefore, chose France.

That decision made, they started to research the best areas to live and work. Never having lived in France, they had no preference for any particular region; therefore, their choice of area was made on purely business grounds. "Our research revealed that the Loire Valley is one of the most visited areas in France, on account of its chateaux, vineyards and historic towns," explains Hazel. "An added attraction for visitors is that Paris is easily accessible by motorway and high-speed train."

They settled on Cangey in Indre-et-Loire and rented a house while looking for the best location for their business and a property suitable for transformation into a hotel. Their children, Cassie and Jordan (then aged seven and nine), were enrolled at the local school and were therefore immersed in French life, soon speaking the language fluently.

Within a few months, they had found a run-down property that had been unoccupied for four years – a farm called Le Fleuray, after a local village, dating from around 1860. It had an interesting history, as Peter recalls: "During the Second World War it had been occupied by Germans, who had left some bomb casings in the vegetable garden."

The farm included a dozen or so barns in addition to the main buildings. Most of these had to be demolished, but some were suitable for renovation; an old carriage shed now functions as a conservatory. The Newingtons worked hard with local tradomen and within six months the first phase of the hotel was ready to open for business. At this stage, it consisted of six rooms and a restaurant.

"We soon found that the running costs were higher than we'd anticipated," says Peter, "so we had to expand the hotel in order to increase our income." Today, the hotel has 15 bedrooms, six of them located in one of the surviving barns and having terraces with views over gardens and swimming pool.

"We chose an English-country-manor style," says Hazel, "with striped wallpaper and floral fabrics, white wicker dressing tables and bedside cabinets."

The restaurant is also attractively decorated and serves classic French cuisine with a contemporary twist. Children have their own three-course menu. The pool is heated from spring to autumn.

The Newingtons have been successful and, with both children now grown up and participating in the running of the hotel, have achieved what they set out to create: a family business. Jordan, now 21, manages the restaurant and ensures that guests have everything they need, while Cassie, 19, takes care of bookings and much of the administration. Chris Jackson, an English expatriate chef who has been with the family for six years, runs the kitchen with Hazel, and Peter oversees the business, for which he has further plans.

8.

PROPERTY

Many expatriates aim to find work in the property market – either using experience gained in their home country or as a new venture. If you're thinking about working or setting up a business in any property-related field in France, the first thing you should do is familiarise yourself with French property market trends, which can directly or indirectly affect your business. Although the market is generally buoyant and in some areas even booming, there's intense competition in all sectors and you must, therefore, be especially enterprising, hard-working and, possibly, lucky to make a success of a property-related business in France.

This chapter looks at the ins and outs of working as an estate agent and setting up an estate agency business. There's information about relocation services (a growing market, in the private as well as the corporate sector), property maintenance, renovation and construction, as well as building trades and surveying.

This book doesn't consider running a bed and breakfast establishment (*chambres d'hôtes*) or self-catering accommodation (*gîte*) as a way of making a living in France; these activities are the subject of *Earning Money From Your French Home*, to be published by Survival Books in late 2005.

ESTATE AGENCY

Along with 'hand-holding services' (see page 379), buying and selling property has become popular with expatriates – particularly Britons – looking for a way of making money in France. Unlike estate agency in Spain, however, the practice is strictly regulated in France and you may not have the qualifications to set up an agency or even to work in an existing agency (see **Regulation** below). In fact, for most expatriates, working (legally) as an estate agent isn't an option and you're unlikely to be able to make a living solely as an *agent commercial indépendant immobilier* (see page 270). Nevertheless, it's possible to work as an *agent* in conjunction with another activity (see **Case Study 7** on page 271).

Regulation

Estate agency work is strictly regulated, and many expatriates have fallen foul of French law, as they haven't respected the regulations, which are set out below.

You cannot act as an estate agent (*agent immobilier*) in France unless you have a *carte professionnelle* (professional card) or are officially contracted to a card-holding agent. French law doesn't recognise the activity of 'intermediary' or 'property services provider'; anyone who's involved in property sales – and even rentals – is deemed to be an estate agent and requires the appropriate registration. **Saying that you're simply an intermediary between the seller and the buyer or renter is illegal; you can be fined as much as €20,000 for ignoring the legislation, and the authorities are becoming increasingly vigilant in this area.**

Carte Professionnelle

To act as an estate agent in France, you must have a 'professional card' (*carte professionnelle*); to qualify for one, you must meet certain criteria, which can vary from department to department, as the local *préfecture* issues the *cartes*, but are generally as follows:

- You have one or more of the following qualifications:

  - A *brevet d'études professionnelles* in *professions immobilières*, which usually requires two years' full-time study, although you may be able to shorten the study period if you already have relevant qualifications or experience. Note, however, that the training institutions for this qualification aren't regulated as, for example, those for lawyers and doctors are, so the quality (and cost) of training can vary considerably.

  - A recognised foreign certificate or diploma confirming that you've undertaken least two years' legal, financial or commercial studies;

  - A secondary education qualification (e.g. A Levels) plus three years of higher education and at least a year's experience of estate agency work in your home country;

  - At least two years' (and sometimes as much as ten years'!) experience of estate agency work in your home country.

- You have a reasonable level of French (e.g. A Level).

To obtain a *carte professionnelle*, you must also deposit a 'bond' of at least €120,000, although it's possible to amass this over several years, e.g. €40,000 in the first year and €20,000 per year for the next four years. **Don't think that you can get around these rules by working with a foreign-registered estate agency and paying taxes in another country. According to European Community law, taxes must be paid in the country where a property is sold.**

An estate agency must be registered as a *SARL* (see page 124) and must have the professional indemnity insurance from an accredited body such as the Fédération Nationale de l'Immobilier (🖳 www.fnaim.fr) or the SOCAF group (🖳 www.socaf.fr).

There has been a lot of abuse of the rules by people either thinking they've found a loophole or simply acting illegally, and many have got away with it for years, although there have been fines and even arrests, as the law is being tightened.

Susan Hickie, founder and director of Language in Provence (see page 315), sounds another warning. She originally bought a cottage in Brittany with her husband, after their marriage in 1979, only to find the weather too like that in Somerset where they then lived. They sold up to live in Africa and subsequently in the Far East, before returning to the UK in the '90s, when again they decided to move to France – this time to Provence. They arrived in 1992, but Susan's husband kept returning to England for his work and finally stayed there. With her children in local schools, Susan "did whatever I could to survive. I taught both French and English, did bits of translation and, almost inevitably, some estate agency work. Anyone considering this last course should be aware that, when a local agent goes into full-charm mode and invites you to do some work, you may well end up working for nothing for months on end, running round in your own car, using your own petrol, often for no result because of the problems of multiple listings with agents in France. It's a tough world."

Marchand de Biens

A number of people have tried to circumvent the above requirements by registering as a *marchand de biens*. A *marchand de biens* is someone who buys houses with his own money and then sells them, in some cases after renovating them. A *marchand de biens* is therefore different from an estate agent, who acts as an intermediary between seller and buyer and doesn't use his own money. However, a *marchand de biens* isn't allowed to sell other people's property. In fact, there's now some doubt as to whether the 'profession' of *marchand de biens* even exists in French law, so you will be risking not only your money, but also possibly your livelihood in France by registering as one.

Agent Commercial Indépendant Immobilier

A realistic option for those who don't have the qualifications to obtain a *carte professionnelle* is to act as an *agent commercial indépendant immobilier* (commonly referred to simply as an *agent commercial*), whereby you register as self-employed with the local Greffe du Tribunal de Commerce (see **Centres de Formalités des Entreprises** on page 103).

⚠ **Until May 2004, this practice was widely regarded as legal, but a test case in Calvados then revealed that it may not be, and Greffes du Tribunal de Commerce in many departments have since refused to register *agents commerciaux*, insisting that they become salaried employees of the 'parent' agency. You should therefore check local regulations before attempting to set up as an *agent commercial*.**

If registration as an *agent commercial* is allowed, you must obtain a contract with an estate agent (or preferably several) who has a *carte professionnelle* to work under his aegis. As an *agent commercial*, you're covered by the agency's guarantees and insurance and may even be authorised to sign agency agreements (*mandats*) with vendors. You're paid a commission, which can be up to 60 per cent of the agency's commission (itself between 5 and 15 per cent of a property's selling price).

Note that *agents commerciaux* are given a '*carte professionnelle*', although this isn't to be confused with a 'proper' *carte professionelle*, which are issued only to licensed estate agents. (Further confusion is caused by the fact that the *carte professionnelle* is commonly referred to as a *carte grise*, which is also the name given to a vehicle registration document!)

Contracts vary and you should check whether there are any 'catches'. Common among these is that you cannot claim commission on sales made to clients responding to the agency's advertising or who simply walk in off the street, but must find your own clients (and prove that you've found them) in order to qualify for commission.

As an *agent commercial*, you must usually cover all your costs, including telephone calls and travelling, as well as your tax and social security contributions, of course. You are usually liable for VAT at 19.6 per cent on your commission earnings. To cover all these costs and make a living as an *agent commercial*, it's estimated that you must sell at least three houses per month.

Susan Dixon, who runs Papillon Properties in the Poitou-Charentes region (see **Case Study 7** below), is an *agent commercial indépendant immobilier*, working for ICS Immobilier, a local member of the Century 21 franchise group. "I've given up hope of obtaining a *carte professionnelle*," explains Susan, "as my UK qualifications are nowhere near those demanded here."

Linda Rano and her French husband Max run Couleurs de France, an estate agency operation with a difference, in Haute-Garonne (see **Case Study 8** on page 274), but they don't sell property and don't have a *carte professionnelle*. "For this reason, we refer to ourselves as 'property agents' rather than 'estate agents'," says Linda.

CASE STUDY 7

When Susan Dixon's husband, Tony, took early retirement from the army at the age of 49, they saw at last the possibility of realising a long-held wish to settle in France. Having sold their house in Newbury, Berkshire, they spent a year living on the narrow boat they had owned for seven years and cruising the canals of the UK more extensively than had previously been possible.

That year ended when they rented a gîte for three months to search for a new home in France. "We chose the region pragmatically," says Susan, "and settled on the Poitou-Charentes, initially as a place to live, not work, although it has turned out to be an excellent choice. We wanted somewhere reasonably close to the Channel ports; south of the Loire for the better weather; north of the Dordogne to avoid the necessity of overnight stops; inland from the expensive coast; but far enough west to avoid the colder continental weather. It was an area then little known to the general public – we used to tell people it was halfway down on the left-hand side, after the Loire and before the Dordogne."

The Dixons arrived in February 1995 and spent their first two years working on the house and garden and getting to know about living in France. Susan did a little work helping with exhibitions as a thank-you to a property agency that had been helpful, although it hadn't sold them their house.

Just under two years later, Susan set up Papillon Properties, an agency designed, as she explains, "to provide clients with the service I'd like to have had when we searched for a house. Although I was happy with the agency we purchased through, I felt there was potential in offering clients a complete hand-holding service from the first point of contact for the duration of their ownership of the property. At that time, my daughter had decided to give up working and remain at home with the children, but I knew that, like me, she wouldn't find this fulfilling enough. I spoke to her and she agreed to be the UK end of the operation."

Papillon Properties is thus a family business, with four directors – Susan and Tony, daughter Samantha and her husband Ralf – running a UK-registered company and a French one handling the aftercare service.

Reviewing her experiences, Susan reckons that it took two years to establish the business financially: "I benefited from the security of Tony's income, so didn't need the money to survive and could reinvest the earnings into the company. We all underestimate the cost of setting up a new business and what our running costs will be."

As to the country, language and cultural differences: "My French was poor and required great tolerance from all exposed to it," admits Susan. "I did attend lessons for several years, but found that my desire to do things right and not to cut corners or say 'In England . . .' made it easier to work with the agency and other professionals. I quickly earned the reputation of being sérieuse, from which I took great pride. There are many rules and regulations governing estate agents in France and, unfortunately, some English people who do this type of work feel that there's no need to observe them."

ICS Immobilier had recently opened under the management of a young agent, Fabrice Michelet, who liked Susan's idea of promoting properties in the UK. Together they've developed the business. Three years ago, Fabrice bought the Century 21 franchise for the area, and his branch was the second-most successful in France.

The success of Papillon Properties has not gone unnoticed and Susan has been approached by many French agents who would like to work with the company. "For that we should need UK personnel who feel they could work in estate agency and wish to relocate to France. We're now in the process of developing Papillon as a franchise operation. We shall be able to offer a 'ready-to-roll' package, which could save them a lot of heartache in establishing a business here."

Susan believes that she has been – and is – successful "because I work hard, all the time, and have done for the past eight years. I don't think anyone should underestimate the language problem, but all it takes is courage – to make mistakes, recognise where you're going wrong and persist in communicating with what you have of the language. It's amazing how you can succeed and that gives you confidence and courage for the next time."

RELOCATION SERVICES

A related service that can be offered in conjunction with estate agency work or separately is a relocation service. Most people associate relocation services with corporate moves abroad. Big companies hire relocation consultants to handle anything and everything to ensure that their employees enjoy a smooth transition to life in a new country. In France's main cities, particularly in Paris, Lyon, Marseille, Toulouse and Bordeaux, the corporate relocation market is huge, and a few companies (e.g. Provence Welcome Services) also deal with private relocation. However, the private sector is generally poorly served and there are currently no English-speaking businesses offering such a service.

This isn't because individuals moving to France don't need help, but rather because of the bureaucracy involved in setting up as a relocation consultant. A corporate relocation service is recognised by the French administrative authorities, but a private service isn't. The nearest recognised 'professions' are estate agent and consultant, neither of which is strictly appropriate. As it's difficult to set up as an estate agent in France (see page 268), your only option is currently to register as a consultant, which means that you must join the Chambre de l'Ingénierie et du Conseil de France (☎ 01 44 30 49 48, 🖥 www.cicf.fr), which imposes a minimum hourly rate for consultants; if your service is to cover a reasonably large area (i.e. at least a department and preferably a region), you will need a network of consultants in order to be able to provide a sufficiently comprehensive service over such an area, which will be expensive.

It's possible that there will be a change in the law to allow people to register as private relocation agents; if so, with the constant flow of immigrants to France, this is almost certainly a profitable market.

Dominic Tidey of the Association of Relocation Professionals (ARP, 🖥 www.arp-relocation.com) in the UK, which promotes high standards and best practice in the industry, emphasises that, if you want to work in the relocation business, you must have extensive local knowledge: "You must have a substantial contacts file on all topics that might be useful to those coming to live and work in the area. The other recommendation is, naturally enough, that you have good language skills. All of the staff in the big corporate relocation agencies in Paris speak two or three languages, and are usually native French speakers. If you're working outside the capital, you still need languages to have the edge over any competition. Obviously English and French are the main languages, but Dutch is also a big plus, as there are still plenty of Belgian and Dutch buyers in some areas. The other thing to remember is that relocation invariably involves buying or renting a property – the client needs a home first and other services later – so it's useful to have experience in the property market."

Qualifications & Professional Standards

Qualifications and high professional standards are vital for the benefit of both clients and your business, as the relocation business is becoming more and more competitive. The ARA offers training and education for relocation providers, as does the European Academy of Relocation Professionals (EARP, 🖥 www.earp.eu.com), which is the profession's training body and provides both country-specific and general training in all aspects of relocation services. The aim of the ARA and the EARP is to ensure that the industry has a recognised qualification specific to the European industry. Dominic Tidey says that corporate users particularly look for this seal of quality in relocation agents, as they know that members are required to abide by a certain code of conduct. However, membership of the ARA is open only to UK-registered agents.

Setting Up a Relocation Business

If you're thinking of setting up your own business in this area, you must have many skills – negotiating skills, people skills, language skills – as well as extensive local knowledge and contacts. It isn't wise to try to go it alone until you've learnt the ropes working as an employee for one of the large relocation agents. Make sure you've built up an extensive network of 'local correspondents' – people who live in a particular area and can supply you with information on a one-off freelance basis should you need it. Dominic Tidey of the ARA says: "You cannot be everywhere and know everything. The big corporate suppliers in Paris use self-employed staff on an occasional basis when they need them."

CASE STUDY 8

Linda Rano met her French husband, Max, when he was working in the aerospace industry on secondment to the UK from his French company. She was an executive secretary working in London and continued doing so after their marriage, with breaks for a daughter and a son, until Max was called back to Toulouse. They left Barnet in north London, when the children were two years and six months old respectively, and moved to Haute-Garonne in 1997. After a year or two of settling in, Linda took a correspondence course with the London School of Journalism, encouraged by the possibility of combining earning with child care, and started writing for French-interest magazines and newspapers and a guidebook publisher, before working as editor for a business website.

Meanwhile, Linda and Max had been developing the concept of what was to become Couleurs de France, an estate agency operation with a difference. Tapping in on the then booming interest in French properties among UK buyers, they started by offering inclusive tour packages in which potential buyers could see properties across a wide area accompanied by the relevant estate agents and including teach-ins on the buying process in France as well as all accommodation, food and transport. This idea worked well for a time, "but we dropped it when we realised that rising costs were making this kind of package deal too expensive to be as attractive as it had been initially," explains Linda.

Since then, developing their established contacts with estate agencies in the area, they've established a property agency covering much of south-west France – all departments along the Pyrenean chain and around Toulouse – with the aim of helping English-speaking buyers to find the properties they want and to support them through the buying process. Through their website, they provide a shop window for estate agencies in their area, but they don't sell property and don't have a carte professionnelle (see page 268).

Recently, the Ranos have developed a variant on their original formula. They now offer one-day buying courses, complete with meals, usually in chateaux and other historic buildings in the area. "Allowing those attending to arrange their own travel and accommodation means that we can offer a day's crash course in the intricacies of buying French property, from finding the right place to the inevitable paperwork, plus advice on inheritance implications, buying to let, surveys, taxes and living in France, for £87 for a single person or £150 for two [2004 prices]," says Linda.

The courses are designed for small numbers – typically six to eight – and can be topped and/or tailed with visits to properties arranged with the agencies concerned. "We believe our courses to be unique for a France-based company, although others may make similar arrangements from the UK," says Linda. "We're now planning parallel courses for people interested in setting up guest houses or gîte complexes, to be held at a chambres d'hôtes operation run by a French accountant, who can advise on business plans."

Because Couleurs de France is a UK-registered company, with a trading office in London as well as the one in Toulouse, Linda and Max encountered relatively few set-up problems. With a French husband, Linda had time to develop her language skills, and she has found that her journalism (increasingly on property matters), which has required research and interviews with professionals, has kept her up to date with market trends and enabled her to share the resultant knowledge with her readers. "At the same time, the exposure this gives the company has helped reduce our reliance on conventional advertising."

She advises anyone contemplating a similar move to concentrate on "finding a good set of knowledgeable and trustworthy contacts you can do business with – not as easy in this competitive business as it might seem. You will also need to invest a lot in advertising and promotion and, above all, to work very hard: this isn't a 9-to-5 business. Buyers come out at all times, but usually during spring and summer – so forget about planning a long summer break!"

Swedes Carin Peirano and Sabine Karlberg have established themselves in the corporate relocation market on the Côte d'Azur. Like the Ranos, however, they have other strings to their bow and don't rely solely on this side of their business.

CASE STUDY 9

Carin Peirano came to France from Sweden when her French husband took a job in Sophia Antipolis, the Riviera's answer to Silicon Valley, near Antibes in September 2000. For the first year, she continued working from home for her former company, which supplies educational services for the insurance industry, and settling her two children, then aged six and three into their new environment.

She saw an opportunity for managing events in an area that frequently hosts exhibitions, conferences and seminars. Meanwhile her Franco-Swedish friend Sabine Karlberg had been providing a free service, helping other foreigners to find houses and place their children in schools, but was considering putting her expertise on a commercial basis. "We decided to join forces and founded Azurplus Relocation from scratch," explains Carin. "We both have Swedish business degrees and speak French, English, German and Swedish, so language was not among our problems."

Carin and Sabine found it necessary to employ a French accountant (expert comptable), as French financial systems are different from those they were familiar with. This had the added benefit of allowing them to concentrate on marketing and dealing with clients.

"We realised that it would take time to establish ourselves, even in such a cosmopolitan area, but, by a combination of direct marketing and advertising in hand-picked media, such as the EasyJet magazine, we've been able to build up a portfolio of corporate clients for the relocation business." The service includes searching for homes, dealing with utilities, banks and schools, registering vehicles and obtaining residence permits and insurances. The package also includes a free support service for the first two months after their clients move in.

On the event management side, Carin and Sabine have run a number of functions for corporate and private clients and, through collaboration with the Swedish Film Institute, now manage that body's magnificent sea-view apartment in Cannes, handling the rental schedule.

Carin advises anyone starting a business in France to allow at least three years before expecting profitability: "You have a lot of charges to pay, so it's essential to have a really good business plan before you start." More generally, she adds: "If you have a good idea, go for it!"

PROPERTY MAINTENANCE & CARETAKING

The continuing growth of foreign second home ownership in France means that there's a demand for property maintenance and caretaking services. Maintenance covers a host of activities, including minor construction and repair work, gardening, pool cleaning and key-holding. Caretaking a *gîte* involves cleaning, changing linen, making good minor damage and liaising with maintenance services. There's a significant market for these services, especially amongst expatriates who run *gîtes* 'remotely' (i.e. live abroad) and resident retirees who can no longer do these jobs for themselves, but – as with any business – success depends on finding a gap in the market, establishing a good reputation and working hard. If you're looking after *gîtes*, remember that 90 per cent of the work is concentrated into a single day – changeover day – so you shouldn't take on too many properties or you won't be able to bring them all up to scratch in time.

If you're thinking of providing property maintenance services or anything related to key-holding, property management or property checks, you should note that you must have the proper authority to do so from the French administration. Security is a highly regulated activity with extensive background checks made on people wishing to work in this field.

As with estate agency and relocation services, diversification is the key to a successful maintenance business – at least until you've established your reputation and learned which areas of the market are best for you to specialise in. Research is always desirable, but not always possible; sometimes, it's a case of needs must.

CASE STUDY 10

When Shaun Duckworth came to France in 2001, he was a millionaire, with a thriving business mounting prestige craft exhibitions at major centres and stately homes, dealing with royalty and owning properties in Lincolnshire, Spain and America. Things are rather different now.

The move to Normandy had been prompted by his then wife's cancer, which meant that she could not travel far and needed to have easy access to treatment in London. By the time she died later that year, Shaun's business was in difficulties to the extent that he had to sell properties to keep it going. Despite his best efforts, a bad debt of over £30,000 on the sale of his Spanish house led to the company going into voluntary administration and finally closure. Now re-married, he liquidated all his assets except the French house and a small private pension to discharge the company's liabilities.

Faced with the need to start a business, Shaun opted for a company catering to the needs of UK-based second home owners. He called it Manche Property Services.

"I arrange building work, deal with utilities, importing cars, health registration, architects and so on," Shaun explains. "I can also do gardening work, security checks on properties, key-holding, etc. and, through an associate, arrange property searches, translations and all aspects of house purchase."

This choice of direction was at least partly suggested by his own experiences as owner of a French house while still living in the UK. "When we bought the house, we hired an English building agent to organise the necessary renovation. Unfortunately, he had obviously taken on far too much work and it took months to get things done. A plumber would come for a day, then disappear and not be back for several weeks. I think whoever shouted loudest got some work done! Also some of the prices were sky high."

A continuing problem has been lack of fluency in French: "My wife and I did an intensive course, but I think it mainly showed us how much we didn't know. I now attend weekly local classes, largely made up of people like me wanting to make a go of things here. I still don't speak anywhere near well enough, but I'm trying." Happily, he had a friend to help him negotiate the bureaucracy, where he found that "all the agencies try to be very helpful."

The business doesn't justify employing anyone else, but, even so, Shaun has been surprised at how expensive running a small business in France can be: "Contributions to the health service, pensions and welfare amount to over half my income." His wife helps financially by working as project director for a large American charity on a contract basis.

Shaun's riches-to-rags story exemplifies the quality he feels anyone starting a business in France most needs: determination. "Learn the language," he advises. "Don't give up and don't expect to make your fortune. Just enjoy the good food and the lifestyle!"

Gordon Taylor found a niche market for his maintenance service – partly by chance and partly by perseverance. Like other successful entrepreneurs, however, he has taken every opportunity to diversify and to exploit opportunities as they arise.

CASE STUDY 11

Gordon Taylor had worked his way up in the insurance business to become his company's Regional Manager for the whole of South Wales and south-west England, with eight managers and 160 agents reporting to him. Then came redundancy, divorce and three years of job-hunting, during which he found that, at 50, he was over-qualified and too expensive to employ.

Things changed when a friend alerted to him to an article on 'mature' couriers working for Eurocamp, a company offering package holidays in ready-erected tents and mobile homes on campsites throughout Europe. Called for an interview, Gordon "travelled forth drowned in a wretched cold. I felt I hadn't conducted myself too well, but, to my surprise, I was accepted and asked if I had a preference for any area of Europe." Remembering holidays there, he asked for Provence.

He rented out his house in Plymouth, bought a touring caravan and, after an intensive training course, arrived at his first posting, Camping Lei Suves near Roquebrune-sur-Argens. The start wasn't propitious: "Patrick, the very Provencal campsite-owner, didn't speak to me for three months, as apparently he didn't like English people," Gordon recalls. And Patrick's wife, Catherine, wasn't impressed by his opening apology for not speaking much French. However, the Eurocamp team arrived to put up eight tents, install three mobile homes and an awning to convert his caravan into a reception office.

For the first few winters, Gordon went back to the UK, finding casual employment with various government agencies. This he recommends for anyone contemplating a life abroad: "Give it a try without 100 per cent commitment for a year or two; then, if you are happy, bite the bullet."

Meanwhile, relations with Patrick had improved, not least after Gordon had managed to interpret for some British visitors. Another useful development was that, at the end of his first season, Gordon was asked to help a sick member of the regular maintenance teams who close down the Eurocamp mobile homes. "Working with him on many sites between Antibes and Le Lavandou, I learned much about care and maintenance that has served me well since."

In the second year, Gordon was posted to a site in Tuscany, but stopped on the way back for a holiday in Lei Suves, where, by then, Patrick and Catherine had become good friends. They told him they had missed him and that there was an opening to work there for a Dutch manager of several foreign-owned units the following year. He took the offer up, but it didn't work out and, when the Dutchman sold his business, he found that the owners were happy for him to work directly for them. With Patrick and Catherine's blessing, he started the business he has run ever since.

"I charge the owners a set fee for looking after their mobile homes throughout the year, making sure the pitches are made ready for the season, kept in good condition throughout, and closed for the winter."

Establishing permanent residence and dealing with the red tape entailed in starting a business turned out to be more difficult than expected: "First I was required to attend a week's course at the local Chambre des Métiers to learn how to be self-employed. My French is fairly good nowadays, but sitting for eight hours a day listening to rapid French did nothing to add to my knowledge of procedures."

After a couple of years, Patrick and Catherine asked him to stay through the winter to look after the site for them when they were away. He sold the Plymouth house and bought his own mobile home on the site.

Now, as well as managing over 30 mobile homes belonging to British, Danish, Dutch and French owners, and 'campsite-sitting' out of season, Gordon has extended his operation to include control of all the bottled gas supplies on the site. "During the winter months, I do a lot of repair and general maintenance work. In the season, as a break from camping, I occasionally act as a tour guide for a local company running excursions to Monaco, Ventimille and the Gorges du Verdon."

RENOVATION

Many expatriates – particularly Britons – buy properties in need of renovation or restoration, with a view to using them as a holiday home, living in them permanently, letting them or reselling them at a profit (if they're lucky). Often, the work involved is beyond their capabilities – or they simply don't have time to do it – so professional help is required. Many ex-builders and property developers offer such a service, but, as with all property-related services, success depends not only on professionalism and hard work, but also on diversifying and then concentrating on the most worthwhile areas of the business.

CASE STUDY 12

David and Sharon Evans moved to Mayenne in the Pays-de-la-Loire from Hertfordshire in 2002, having bought a holiday home there three years earlier. Sharon had been teaching at a local college and David had worked as a property director for a large retail organisation. Like many expatriates, they had decided to let *gîtes*, but, unlike some, had regarded this as a source of income while settling in rather than their sole or main business. To that end, they had bought a small house in 2001, and subsequently a second, both now operated as *gîtes*. A third is currently undergoing renovation.

That apart, they concentrated initially on renovating their own house, settling themselves into the community and their eight-year-old son into the local school, where he's the only English child among 53 pupils.

Their main business, which they called Premier Property Care, started as a broadly-based building renovation and maintenance service, covering gardening, changeovers, cleaning, etc. But they found the returns on some of these operations less attractive and now concentrate primarily on renovation, including project management of properties needing complete restoration. The first year was spent sorting out business registration, accountancy methods and making contact with local tradesmen: "We work only with local registered French artisans," says David.

Careful preparation avoided most bureaucratic obstacles, but "registering our two Land Rovers, which we didn't want to sell, was a nightmare. The paper trail was unbelievable and following it took us over a year, including 23 three-hour round trips to the *préfecture*. In the end, we had to obtain a certificate to prove that the registration for both cars was in our name, even though we had produced the registration documents with our names on. This had to be obtained from another office in another town!"

Language was not the problem: Sharon had taken a degree course in French before leaving and David evening classes, although he now he finds he still has to work hard on it (particularly as, in the building world, most people want to talk to a man).

Setting up business in an area where British competitors already existed produced its own problems, as rival operators set out to establish whether the Evanses were properly registered and to assess their charges by demanding quotations for bogus projects. However, help wasn't hard to find: "When you have a child at school, you open the floodgates to contacts," explains Sharon, "as you see the parents every day and are drawn into the community." They also found a ready source of help and advice in their insurance broker, who introduced them to their "brilliant and very helpful" accountant.

In terms of general advice, David suggests that people starting businesses in France should have enough money to serve as a buffer; they should be properly registered; and they should become part of the local community rather than hide in an expatriate community. He also offers the following dos and don'ts:

- **Do**, if you have children, put them in local, rather than international, schools.
- **Do** study the language, watch French television, and speak French to the French even if their English is better than your French.
- **Do** sell your car and buy a French make and model.
- **Do** get to know your neighbours beyond the *bonjour* stage, and attend and help out at local events.
- **Do** know your limitations, budget for everything and add 100 per cent for errors.
- **Don't** mix only with expatriates or hide indoors to avoid talking to the postman.
- **Don't** think you can learn the language without hard work, but don't be afraid of making mistakes.
- **Don't** be afraid to ask for help.

Finding a gap in the market in which you can make a living is often a case of trial and error – or of making your own 'luck' by sheer hard work.

CASE STUDY 13

'Sam' Mooney (her name is derived from her initials, rather than the forenames her parents gave her, which she hates) came to France as the fulfilment of a childhood dream. The move became a possibility when she bought a house in Aude while living in Toronto, Canada, working for a corporate executive search agency and starting to design websites.

"I wanted to be in the south of France," she says, "but intuitively knew that Provence would be too expensive. I had never heard of the Languedoc, let alone Aude, but it sounded like what I wanted. I came for three weeks in 1999 and explored the area between Béziers and Carcassonne. I really liked it, came back the following spring to confirm that and the following autumn to buy. I'd assumed I'd buy in the Minervois area, but found the Corbières area better value for money. At that point, I wasn't thinking in terms of living here."

What changed her mind was her meeting with partner Mark, who was working on property repairs and renovation. Both had been through bad divorces and wanted to start a new life. They finally moved in March 2002, initially to Sam's house, but last year they sold this and moved to another, some 5km away on a wine domain 20 minutes south-east of Carcassonne. There, they started a caretaking and maintenance business for absentee owners, but that proved unappealing. They next worked for a company that offered to help find houses for buyers: "Mark registered as a translator, but the people we were working with kept changing our remuneration to the point that it wasn't worth doing," recalls Sam. "Also the services they charged for were now being offered free by estate agents."

Their focus turned progressively to one of renovation as they found it more attractive and there was demand to be filled, and they started Aude France Property. Meanwhile, Sam continued the website design business she had begun in Canada. "But the renovation projects got bigger and I started helping Mark with the administration and client contact. He ended up working with four others, all self-employed, but working together."

Now, they're in yet another transition. "Mark is 60 and finding the physical side of the work more than he can handle. He's getting a *carte professionnelle* [see page 30] and we're going to sell property, specialising in houses needing renovation. We can give an estimate of the costs, refer the buyer to Mark's former partners and earn a finder's fee."

As to the problems they faced, Sam singles out cash flow and language: "Mark already spoke French and mine is OK for coping with most situations, but I cannot really have a conversation beyond the basics. I'm not really a 'French lessons' person, but I may have to resort to them."

According to Sam, starting a business in France is like starting a business anywhere: "You have to be prepared to work incredibly hard. You're likely to be self-employed, at least to begin with; if you have no experience of that, talk to people who have or read some books so that you know what to expect. Make a business plan. Get registered right away; if your French isn't terrific, hire someone to go with you to the various offices and translate. Make sure you understand what you're signing, as it's really difficult to change anything."

BUILDING & PROPERTY DEVELOPMENT

If you plan to work or do business in construction and building services, you need a solid background in the building trade and the qualifications to prove it. Bring any qualifications you have with you and make sure they're translated into French. Many people come to France, especially to areas with large numbers of expatriates, with few qualifications and charge inflated prices on the basis that they're native English speakers – which isn't the way to establish a long-term business. Indeed, as an expatriate (particularly if you're British), you may have to overcome prejudice that results from the 'dodgy' practices of many foreign builders. Mark Powell and his partner Karen experienced the worst kind of foreign building practices before trying various enterprises and finally setting up separate businesses in Lot.

CASE STUDY 14

Mark Powell and his partner Karen came to France from the UK in 2004, at the end of a search for the right place to start a new life. They previously lived in High Wycombe, Buckinghamshire, and both worked in a film company, hating their jobs.

"One day, out of the blue, Karen said, 'I hate this country' – meaning the UK, as she had been born in South Africa," Mark remembers. "I asked where she would rather be, thinking she would say South Africa, but she said, 'Anywhere warm and away from your ex-wife.' All I wanted was somewhere accessible to my two boys." After a couple of fruitless visits to France, they were staying in a B&B, where the owners, coincidentally South African, set up a viewing of a property that had been on the market for ten years. "It was exactly what we were looking for: a small house, with just over an acre of land and a small barn."

The next step was to find work.

When Mark saw an advertisement in French Property News for skilled and unskilled personnel to work for an English building company in Périgueux, he saw it as a stepping stone to starting a business and an ideal way of acclimatising to French culture. Since the job was at some remove from their house in Gramat in Lot, the company provided accommodation.

This is where I saw the worst side of British builders. They charged over-the-top rates, treated their staff badly and expected long hours for very low pay, the owner knowing that most of them would work for him only long enough to be able to register in the system themselves.

"The advertisement had stated that contracts would be supplied and registration in the French system provided, but neither appeared in the three months I was with them. The people who had found us our house assured me that they had contacts in the French and English communities sufficient to provide me with six months' work, provided I was properly registered."

At this point, with the UK house close to being sold, Karen came out and they finally moved into their house in Gramat and set about renovating it while setting up M&K Services. They started in garden maintenance, but broadened out to include small building and renovation jobs. "Now I seem to get the jobs which are too small for established companies – putting up a shelf, digging a vegetable patch – but my biggest demand is for demolition work. There are plenty of people to do the renovation work, but none to do the demolition stuff."

Since this was outside Karen's scope, they decided to set up a separate venture for her, selling new and second-hand English books, as there was no such outlet in the area (see page 294). "We're also toying with the idea of running a small herb garden and converting the barn into a gîte," enthuses Karen. "I know everybody does this, but, if we market it well, we should be able to make a go of it even in the present economic climate."

Mark's principal obstacle in setting up a business in France was "making sure I wasn't labelled an unreliable English worker. Being registered helped in this regard. Gaining the confidence of the French community for being honest and trustworthy was our main concern and we're happy to say that we've managed this."

Although neither of them spoke French at first, they found someone through the mairie to teach them. They had intended to steer clear of British people, but found they needed British friends to help them get through such details as obtaining planning permission, medical cover and driving licences. On the other hand, they found the French "very patient and willing to help out when they hear us stumbling about with the language." Even so, officials didn't always seem to know their own protocols. "A lot of places still ask for our cartes de séjour, even though they've been done away with for European Union (EU) citizens," comments Karen.

Mark offers the following advice to newcomers planning to start a business in France: "Listen to advice, but don't necessarily take it as fact. People are willing to help, but their information may be dated. Best check with the mairie and the Chamber of Commerce. Get registered with a SIRET number – don't work on the black – but be clear how you want to be registered and, if you're running more than one operation, try to complete the whole procedure at once, which will save you trouble if not money. In our case, all we needed to set up the book shop was a modification d'activité, but if the two activities are unrelated it may not be so simple. Integrate with the community if you want work from them; work with the French and not against them."

Insurance

Not only must you be registered as a builder, but also under French law, work carried out by companies and individuals in the building trades must be guaranteed for ten years (*garantie décennale*). This means that the company or individual is required to rectify any defects arising during this period that affect the solidity of the work or that render it unsuitable for its intended use. This responsibility is covered by a compulsory insurance. **It's an offence to operate without this insurance, unless you're working as a sub-contractor, in which case you should ensure that the main contractor has the required cover.**

Insurance for the ten-year guarantee is usually coupled with public liability insurance (*assurance responsabilité civile professionnelle*). Your civil responsibility can be invoked not only while work is in progress, but also afterwards, under certain circumstances that aren't covered by the ten-year guarantee insurance. This insurance is compulsory for those in the building trades. In any case, it would be extremely unwise to leave yourself exposed to potential claims for damages by not being insured. If you're hiring sub-contractors, it's advisable to insure their work using a policy called *garantie du fait de sous-traitance*.

Construction machinery, such as diggers and cranes, must be insured for being driven on the road. It's also recommended to take out insurance covering their use as tools, as this won't be covered by the motor insurance policy.

Some foreigners have tried to get round these requirements by registering their company in their home country (e.g. the UK) and working in France. However, no British insurance company will insure work done in France and a French insurance company is equally unlikely to insure a British company. **In all matters regarding insurance, it's essential to consult an independent expert before you start trading.**

PROPERTY TRADES

For most jobs as a tradesman or artisan (*artisan*), e.g. electrician, plumber, stonemason, carpenter, surveyor, you must either be qualified (e.g. electrician, plumber) or have experience (e.g. stone cutting). Becoming a qualified electrician of plumber isn't simply a case of having your foreign qualifications translated, as French electrical and plumbing standards (*normes*) may be quite different from those in your home country, and you may have to learn a completely new *modus operandi* to work (legally) in France. For example, French electrical standards and methods differ significantly from those in the UK; the differences are explained in *Renovating & Maintaining Your French Home* (Survival Books – see page 419). Courses are run by various administrative departments, but, of course, the vast majority are in French. Like builders, you must have public liability insurance and your work must be guaranteed for ten years (see **Insurance** above).

CASE STUDY 15

SARL Apollo, based near Carcassonne, is a plumbing and heating company dealing with installations and maintenance and offering breakdown services. Its name is ironical and reflects one of the reasons that Mark and Veronica Hoskins left Wallingford, in the Thames Valley, to try their luck in France in 2003. Mark had been working as a breakdown engineer for a heating maintenance company called Midas, covering a wide territory, with long days, considerable driving between often simple jobs, and frequently having to cover for co-workers who were off sick. "There was an awful lot of stress," he recalls, "as one had little control over the management of one's days or weeks and I would often be at the sharp end, dealing with disgruntled or angry customers. There were times, when on call for out-of-hours emergencies, that I wouldn't see my children for four or five days. I never even felt valued in return." Apollo, for those unfamiliar with Greek mythology, was the god that cursed Midas . . .

An earlier attempt to start again in Spain, with which they were familiar from visits to Mark's parents' holiday home, collapsed when the sale of their UK house fell through. Later, however, the notion was revived when they visited friends in the Carcassonne area. They sold their house and moved into rented accommodation to avoid the earlier problem and, when their friends alerted them to the availability of what seemed a suitable house, they flew out at once and, after looking at alternatives, settled on it two days later.

Although they completed the purchase in December 2002, they didn't finally move until the following June. "Feeling rather shell-shocked from the stress of the move and work in the UK, and with work to be done on the house, we decided to take time out and enjoy the summer with the kids – Thomas, aged ten, and Edward, four." So it was not until January 2004 that Mark began registering with the Chambre des Métiers. SARL Apollo was officially formed that April.

There were early frustrations with bureaucrats. In order to apply for the necessary insurances, they had assembled a large dossier of all the required documentation, certificates, attestations and translations, had an hour-long interview in French and presented a cheque. Nothing happened for six months, after which the whole dossier was returned.

"The question arose over an application for public liability insurance," explains Mark. "The dossier to be sent to the company contained, as well as the cheque, the attestation from the Chambre des Métiers, my Kbis, my certificate of apprenticeship plus translation, my CORGI certificate [Council for Registered Gas Installers, essential in the UK] and translation, my ACOPS certificates [five-yearly assessment under former Approved Codes of Practice, now ACS – the nationally accredited certification scheme) and translation, plus a four-line reference from my previous company confirming that I had worked with them for five years – without a translation." The entire application was rejected because these four lines hadn't been translated into French.

There were further complications when Mark ran into a familiar Catch 22: "Registration depended on having a bank account, but to open a bank account you had to be registered; similarly, obtaining a carte de séjour required registration and registration required a *carte de séjour*." Eventually, all these problems were resolved by the sending of attestations between the various parties "but the frustrating thing was that it was as if the people concerned were doing this for the very first time and making it up as they went along." While Mark accepts that bureaucracy is a fact of life everywhere, "the sheer volume of paperwork is greater here. Everything requires a dossier and there seems to be a lot of duplication. Just when you think you have all the bases covered, they find something else they 'need'."

Because the Hoskins' came to France with very little French, they decided to target the English-speaking market for the first two years while improving their language skills. Now they find that they're gradually building up a French clientele and offering annual central heating system service contracts.

"Generally speaking, I've been surprised at how much we've been able to deal with on our own," admits Mark, "although with anything financial we've been helped by a young lady to whom we were recommended. The Chambre des Métiers, the Chambre de Commerce and the bank have all been helpful and I've joined a trade association that gives businesses all manner of training and support."

Mark's advice to anyone following in his footsteps is not to be inhibited about seeking advice from those bodies that exist to supply it, to be positive and enthusiastic, and not to skimp on preparation. On a more general note: "Enjoy the sunny days and don't forget why you're here."

Adaptability and diversification were the key to John Roberts' success – as well as not being afraid to seek local help.

CASE STUDY 16

John Roberts and his wife settled in Lot-et-Garonne when they fell in love with the area while on holiday and immediately bought a house for renovation. John had worked in barn conversion in Devon and this first purchase led to more for renovation and resale. In 1995, he formalised his operation into a company, SARL John Roberts, specialising in building, developing and, in the immediate area, plumbing and heating.

Local lessons improved his O Level French and other potential problems were eased by reading **Living & Working in France**. Otherwise he sought and found help and advice from local people: "There were, of course, other Brits around, but the French are always helpful and will invariably come to one's rescue."

He adds that the transition to France was made easier by the fact that both he and his wife, a former hairdresser, had "transportable jobs". Having lived on an estuary in Devon, they miss the sea ("Maybe we shall retire closer to the ocean in France somewhere," says John), but have no desire to return to the UK: "We're surrounded by trees, with fantastic views over a valley and our local town. One can ride for miles without going over the same tracks twice. Our daughter, one month old when we arrived, is bilingual and top of her class. France has served us very well."

SURVEYING

If you're a qualified surveyor and are thinking of working in France, there are a number of issues you should take into consideration. First, the French aren't in the habit of having a property surveyed before they buy it. There are several reasons for this. There's a tradition of trust in France, and vendors are expected (indeed required by law) to reveal any hidden defects of which they're aware before selling a property; in many cases, the buyer and seller are acquainted, so it isn't in the seller's long-term interest to conceal any problems. Secondly, there's a tacit assumption that, if there were any serious defects with a building, they would have revealed themselves; many properties are hundreds of years old and it's reckoned that, if they haven't fallen down yet, they must be good for another few decades! A French buyer may engage a builder (usually a friend or acquaintance) to look the building over, but he will rarely go to the expense of engaging a surveyor to undertake a thorough appraisal, as is the norm in the UK, for example.

Second, you will, of course, need to develop a detailed knowledge of the characteristics of French property, including traditional materials and construction techniques, methods of wiring and plumbing and other vagaries, and of the relevant specialist vocabulary. A good dictionary of building terms is the *Dictionnaire d'Architecture & de Construction/Dictionary of Architecture & Construction* by J.R. Forbes (Editions TEC & DEC) and there are numerous books on French architecture, a few of which are listed in **Renovating & Maintaining Your French Home** (see page 419).

Third, there are many types of property surveyor in France, none of which may correspond exactly to those in your home country. For example, there's no direct equivalent of a British chartered surveyor. This can make life difficult both in terms of registering your activity in France and in terms of finding French customers. French surveyors generally fall into the following categories:

- **Architect** – Architects (*architectes*) often check modern buildings for defects.

- **Expert Immobilier** – Not to be confused with an *agent immobilier* (estate agent), an *expert immobilier* generally works for banks, loss adjustors and members of the legal profession, including *notaires*, and is called upon to produce valuation and survey reports for submission to the courts (e.g. in the case of a divorce settlement or inheritance dispute or an investigation by the tax authorities). Each *expert immobilier* tends to specialise in a particular area of the property market, such as private housing, commercial property, farmland or forestry. He (most *experts* are male) is bound by the Civil Code to use 'prudence and due attention' and has professional indemnity insurance.

- **Expert en Techniques du Bâtiment** – An *expert de tecniques du bâtiment* normally carries out inspections for termites, asbestos, lead and other possible problems, such as damp.

- **Géomètre Expert** – A *géomètre expert* verifies the boundaries of a property or the area of an apartment.

- **Master Builder** – A master builder (*maître d'oeuvres*) is similar to a clerk of works in the UK and checks older (i.e. pre-1945) properties for soundness.

As every trade must be pigeon-holed in France, you may be classified as one or other of the above, depending on the region, department or commune you're working in, the administrative office you're dealing with and even the person handling your registration, although foreign-qualified surveyors are normally described as *experts en techniques du bâtiment*.

It's possible to enter into a collaborative partnership with a French-registered architect or surveyor, who simply 'signs off' work done by you, but you must ensure that in doing so you have the necessary public liability and professional indemnity insurance.

CASE STUDY 17

Martin Rushton is a chartered surveyor who lived in Cambridgeshire and had his own practice in the UK for 25 years before coming to France in February 2002. He brought with him his wife Trish, her three children (aged 13 to 22) from an earlier marriage, and their joint children (five and six). Martin had previously had contact with an architects' office in France and, given his qualifications as an architectural technologist and a good track record, found it comparatively easy to find work. Trish, meanwhile, has developed her skills as a photographer and is about to set up her own business.

Martin had always loved France, remembering marvellous holidays there with his parents when young, enjoyed the different way of life, and usefully had a good command of French. The Rushtons decided to settle in the area around Carcassonne in Aude, which offered easy access to the Mediterranean beaches, attractive countryside, the ski slopes of the Pyrenees, and Spain. Communications were another factor: the area is within reach of the TGV network and several airports with flights to the UK.

The principal problem they encountered was the paperwork associated with house-buying and taxation, for which they engaged an accountant and used a translator to ensure that they fully understood the details of what they were signing.

Martin warns anyone considering moving to France to "think very carefully about the kind of work you want to do. Technical language is a whole different kettle of fish from social or tourist language. You have to have very good French to drop into a technical occupation, even if you have many years of experience in the UK. If you don't speak the language, you will struggle, particularly if you're young and need to find work. A degree isn't enough and may not even be recognised."

On a social level, Martin recommends careful research of the region you plan to live in: "Some areas are very backward, not only in such matters as broadband telephone lines and electricity infrastructure, but also in attitudes to strangers. If you have teenage children, unless they already have very good French, they will struggle at school. If you're able, don't burn your bridges. If you come from the UK, keep a bank account there; it's really useful for sorting out presents for relatives, etc. Beware of rogue builders (both foreign and French) who work on the black: you will usually pay for it in the end. If you're starting a business, be very clear of your tax commitments before you begin."

Martin's final piece of advice to those wanting to make a living in France: "Be careful not to think you're on a permanent holiday!"

9.

RETAILING

Shopping habits in France are changing fast and, although you can still find plenty of small local traders, shopping centres and chain stores are edging their way into the lives of many French shoppers. This is partly due to the growing number of working women, who demand longer opening hours and need to be able to find everything under one roof, so that they're able to do a 'one-stop' shop on the way home. However, for the time being, small retailers and supermarkets seem to exist quite happily together, and many housewives still visit independent traders daily for their fresh produce and also enjoy a family visit to a shopping centre for all kinds of goods.

Retailing can offer a wealth of opportunities for expatriates, and an obvious avenue is to look at what your fellow countrymen might miss from home. English or international book shops have been springing up in cities and resort areas of France over the last few years, sometimes also offering greetings cards and stationery. Small supermarkets, specialising in the type of product that expatriates are familiar with, are also popular in some areas. If you're thinking along these lines, you must research your market carefully; many foreign products are far more readily available in French supermarkets than they were a few years ago, especially in areas popular with tourists and foreign residents.

You may prefer to look at the feasibility of a product which appeals to French customers and the expatriate market. The key, as with any business anywhere in the world, is to find a gap in the market, offering a product that isn't readily available in a certain location. One such is soft furnishings and decorating products, which are hard to find outside the big stores. It's even possible to infiltrate what might seem an archetypically French market: an example of this is Brake Bros, a UK bakery, whose magnolia-coloured trucks can be seen delivering part-baked bread to *boulangeries* across France!

You must also decide whether you want to buy a business that's up and running, or whether you would prefer to start with a blank canvas (see **Chapter 4**). This chapter looks at several retailing operations started by expatriates in France: a clothing company in Dordogne, book shops in Lot and Var, a grocer's in Morbihan, a shop selling books and food in Ariège, and a computer hardware and software supplier in Lot. Other possibilities include selling souvenirs and gifts (in tourist areas), selling antiques (genuine or 'junk', known as *brocante*) and running a garden centre.

RESEARCH

Whether you want to buy an existing business or start your own, your first move must be to do as much market research as possible, and this should include the level of potential competition for your business, both from other small traders and from any nearby large chain stores or supermarkets – and you should check at the town hall or *mairie* whether there are plans to build new shops in the area. If it's an area that you're unfamiliar with in commercial terms, start by spending as much time as you can in and around your intended location watching the flow of people. Look particularly carefully at those people who are likely to be your target market and make sure there are plenty of potential customers passing your way every day. Talk to as many people as you can and ask as many questions as you dare – of expatriate and of French consumers – to find out the needs and buying habits of the locals and, if relevant, tourists, in order to get a feel for the potential demand for your product or services.

The Willeys, who let *gîtes* and run a shop in Morbihan (see **Case Study 21** on page 300), stress the importance of research, both of the market potential and of the location: "Our move to France wasn't a hasty one," explains Mel. "We spent a year discussing the options available. We chose Brittany because of its education record, the quality of its healthcare, the unspoilt countryside and the fact that it's near enough to the UK for us to get home for whatever reason."

LICENCES & PERMISSIONS

It's important to be clear about your needs and to find out what the regulations are **before** you commit yourself to any particular premises. If they don't meet the requirements, it could be a complicated and expensive business to bring them up to scratch. Although no general licence is required to set up a shop or retail business, different regulations apply to different types of operation. If you intend to sell alcohol or tobacco products, for example, strict rules and procedures apply.

If you want to sell from a market stall (known as an *activité non-sédentaire*), you will need a *carte de commerçant ambulant* from your local *préfecture* as well as all the usual registration documents (see page 136). The card needs to be revalidated every two years and renewed after ten. To secure a 'pitch' in a market, you must apply to the relevant town hall for a *permis d'occupation du domaine public*. Further information about operating as a market trader can be obtained from the Fédération Nationale des Syndicats des Commerçants des Marchés de France (🖳 www.fnscmf.com).

Seek advice from a lawyer or a *notaire* about the requirements for your particular business and remember that they may vary from one region or department and even one commune to another.

Danny Lowe, who started a clothing business in 2004 (see **Case Study 18** below) was greatly helped in setting up by a company in Périgueux called Secade Conseil, which specialises in start-ups. Setting up a business in France is a complex procedure – "the paperwork is generally too complicated even for French people to cope with alone" – and Secade Conseil (8 rue Guynemer, 24000 Périgueux, ☎ 05 53 05 55 45, ✉ secade-conseil@wanadoo.fr) offered him guidance and advice on the registration process: "how to pay my taxes, how legally to avoid paying tax, where to register my brand, etc. They also continued to help me after I'd got going. They're based in Dordogne, but offer a nationwide service, and there are other companies doing similar work in other areas. I found Secade Conseil through the Chambre des Métiers, but I'm sure the chambers of commerce and similar organisations can help."

When Susan Hodge started her food and book shop in Ariège (see **Case Study 20** on page 299), she was taken by surprise by unforeseen visits by the authorities: "The DGCRF [Direction Générale de la Consommation et de la Répression des Fraudes] checked that everything on the shelves and in the window was price-marked (happily it was). Another check was whether all foodstuffs were labelled with ingredients and other relevant information in French. Unaware of this requirement, Susan found that only 5 per cent of her stock qualified and was given just three weeks to label all the rest or face closure or prosecution. While she sympathised with the need, for example, to warn of possible allergic reactions to certain foods, "I did feel that labelling the books *'en langue anglaise'* was a little extreme!"

The Willeys, who let *gîtes* and run a shop in Morbihan (see **Case Study 21** on page 300), have had little trouble with French bureaucracy: "Our *gîte* and shop businesses are registered separately. We encountered no problems with either, but a good grasp of the language is imperative," says Mel. "After your initial registration, every time you change or add a classification at the Chamber of Commerce it costs you more money to so. However, if you have a serious business plan and are determined in what you are about to embark on, there's no reason why this should be a problem. We have found them very helpful."

PREMISES

It goes without saying that location is crucial in a retailing business, and much the same precautions should be taken when choosing premises as with a bar or restaurant (see **Premises** on page 248). Heidi Lee, who started Antibes Books in 1992 (see **Case Study 19** on page 298), found suitable premises through word of mouth. Although tiny (just $12m^2$) – a major disadvantage for a book shop – it was ideally located in the centre of the charming old town of Antibes, which is frequented by tourists and favoured by English-speakers. Since then, Heidi has managed to enlarge the shop to $300m^2$ so that it's now one of the biggest retail operations of its kind in continental Europe.

When Mark Powell and his partner Karen decided to set up a retail operation selling new and second-hand English books in Gramat, Lot, they also started small. "We've been donated a lot of second-hand books by people in the area," explains Karen. "We haven't bought lots of new books and will order more as the business grows. We've also offered a mail-order service, which seems popular. Our goal is to drive Amazon out of Gramat! I would imagine that, if we were opening a large operation, the capital outlay would be enormous." Their shop, *Bonnes Pages*, opened in January 2005. "Buying stock wasn't that hard once we'd found a distributor in the UK and opened an account," adds Karen.

A rural location has disadvantages as well as advantages. James and Joy Blake started a computer retail business, GourdonNet, in 2003 (see **Case Study 23** on page 304). "The location is quite rural, but not far from the motorway," says James. "It's good for British clients, of whom there continue to be large numbers moving into the area, although there are several competitors; for sales via the internet, location doesn't really matter. However, the French client base was smaller than we'd anticipated. Being nearer to a large urban area would have provided more opportunities and where we are, a few miles out of town, we don't have broadband, which is a real frustration. We would think more carefully about location if we started again, although we love the area."

SHOPFITTERS & SUPPLIERS

You can probably get to this stage without speaking much, if any, French (provided you have your purchase or rental contract translated), especially in areas with a large number of expatriates. However, once you're past this point and are ready to fit out your premises, things begin to get more complicated in terms of language. It isn't easy to find English-speaking shopfitters in France, although the UK National Association of Shopfitters has a list of members who operate internationally on its website (🖳 www.shopfitters.org). This may be a more expensive option than using a French company or artisans, which may therefore be preferable if your French is more fluent.

However, as shopfitting isn't a recognised trade in France (there isn't even a word for it!), you may have difficulty finding a single company that can fit out your shop entirely. Instead, you may need to use several specialist tradesmen, such as a plasterer, an electrician, a plumber, a carpenter, and so on. This can work out expensive – as Heidi Lee discovered (see **Case Study 19** on page 298) – especially if you cannot be on site (or don't have good enough French) to coordinate the work yourself and need to engage an architect or *maître d'oeuvre* ('clerk of works') to do so on your behalf. As with any service in France, it's best to seek recommendations.

Where you source your stock obviously depends on the type of shop you plan to run. If you must buy abroad, e.g. in the UK, you may need to use an intermediary, such as a distributor or wholesaler, as Susan Hodge discovered (see **Case Study 20** on page 299).

INSURANCE

Insurance is a vital consideration if you don't want to lose everything you've worked for. You need buildings insurance against obvious risks such as fire and water damage. If you rent the property from a landlord, he should already have this, but you should check the details of the policy before you sign your rental contract. Then there are the contents of shop, the fixtures and fittings and your stock, which need insuring against damage and theft, including when stock is in transit. You must also ensure that you have sufficient public liability insurance, which means that should any customer injure himself in your shop and claim against you, your insurance company will pay (unless you've been negligent). If you employ others, you also need employer's liability insurance and to pay social security contributions on behalf of your staff so that they're covered for accidents, illness, etc. (see page 210). Ask around for a reliable broker or insurance agent, as there are plenty of companies offering insurance to businesses, some in specific business sectors.

MARKETING

It's natural, after all that hard work in setting up, to want news of your business to reach as many people as possible, but you must be ruthlessly selective and spend plenty of time researching the most cost-effective way of reaching the most potential customers. Indeed, you should have combined this with your market research.

As soon as you open your shop, you will find yourself bombarded by people trying to persuade you to part with your money, when what you're trying to do is make some of your own. The most persistent will be those trying to sell advertising space in publications. Many publications are free to readers and consequently only make their money through advertising. Remember that their priorities won't be the same as yours. Look carefully at **all** the publications you can, talk to other businesses that advertise in them and ask about their success rate. You can spend a large proportion of your advertising budget on a glossy magazine advertisement only to find that you get little or no custom from it.

In the early days, it may not be necessary to spend a lot of money advertising in magazines or newspapers. You could start by distributing flyers to areas where you think your customers may see them, or ask if you can display them in other relevant areas. Flyers can be printed relatively cheaply and initially they will help you to see what kind of feedback you get. Many people interviewed for this book agreed that word of mouth was the most effective, and obviously the cheapest, method of 'advertising' in France. The French in particular almost always prefer to have a recommendation and rarely contact a business 'cold' from an advertisement.

On the other hand, it isn't simply a case of waiting for the stampede of customers to your door. Before establishing his clothing business (see **Case Study 18** below), Danny Lowe tried his hand at assisting new arrivals to establish themselves in the French system: "This lasted only six months. My French partner wanted to sit back and wait for customers to find us without advertising or publicising our business. Unfortunately, life doesn't work like that, even in France and with a good idea."

Once you're a little more established, your marketing needs will become clearer and you will be able to be more discerning about how you spend your money. In this sense, running a retailing business in France is no different from running one anywhere else: you can never afford to rest on your laurels.

CLOTHING

As with any business idea, market research is essential. The French have a reputation for sartorial elegance and chic, although a visit to any French town or village (with the possible exception of Paris) will convince you that this is largely undeserved: as in most western countries, the vast majority of people wear casual clothes (jeans, trainers, sweatshirts, etc.) 90 per cent of the time (except when sleeping), and 'logo mania' is as prevalent as in the UK or US. Nevertheless, it's still true that the French value quality, and you may be more successful with an upmarket clothes shop than in many other countries, provided you choose the location carefully. Would-be shopkeepers should also note that it isn't usual to open on Sundays and most shops are also closed on Mondays. Sale periods in France are strictly limited by law (a maximum of a month in July/August and a month in January/February), so 'permanent' sales such as are common in the UK aren't allowed.

CASE STUDY 18

Danny Lowe and his wife and family left their UK Midlands village home near Ashby de la Zouch to move to south-west France in September 2002. He had spent most of his career in the garment trade and had latterly been mainly involved in organising imports from North Africa and Eastern Europe. "In retrospect," he says, "I think I had simply reached an age where, maybe unrealistically, I started to consider other opportunities. I had tried to break away from the garment trade before in the UK, but it has a remarkable way of ensnaring you once you're in."

Thus it was that, after returning to work out his notice with his previous firm – "our house purchase went through faster than expected" – he began work in late October with a partner setting up *English Yellow Pages* for south-west France. "That lasted about three months, mainly as a result of a clash of personalities. In March 2003, I set up F&GB SARL to assist new arrivals to establish themselves in the French system. This again lasted only six months – also because of a personality clash. Maybe it's me!"

After almost a year out of it, Danny found the garment trade beckoning once more. "Despite being a global operation, it's quite a small world and you can build a reputation if you're consistent and reasonably reliable. In September 2003, I started setting up Bouclier Vêtements Professionnels with a Moroccan partner who owns a garment factory. The business was registered in March 2004 and we opened the doors to our first shop, in Périgueux, the following July. We're now starting to get busy, as we offer good service in an important market. The timing was good, as the importance of good quality protective and work clothing as part of a corporate image is slowly starting to take hold in this part of France. We're planning to take the business nationwide with reps, an agency and possibly other shops."

Danny was greatly helped in setting up by a company called Secade Conseil (see above). But, although he and his family had taken group lessons before leaving the UK, the language was a problem: "Within six months, both my children were coping with school, and two years on they're completely bilingual, but French still causes me difficulties. My staff speak very little English and my level of French has forcibly improved over the last six months; I no longer have concerns about making myself understood, but I don't think I shall ever speak it well."

Danny advises other Britons thinking of starting a business to recognise that France is very different from the UK in culture, thought patterns and values. "Start out by accepting that it's going to be difficult. Carry out a good market survey, find a good French accountant and don't try to set anything up without advice. Be sure you understand things – you are allowed to ask 'stupid' questions – and don't sign anything you don't fully understand. Ever."

BOOKS

The French are avid readers and generally prefer to buy books than borrow them from libraries (France has no second-hand 'culture', and libraries are rarely found outside main towns). Nevertheless, books are expensive, there may be only one book shop in even a fairly large town. Many expatriates have set up English-language book shops, although these are necessarily restricted to areas where there's a large expatriate population or major cities (there's just one in Rouen, a city of half a million people, for example).

CASE STUDY 19

During a holiday in Nice, my husband, Brian Loughran, made the mistake of saying he thought the south of France the best place in the whole world," says Heidi Lee. "I agreed with him and decided we'd move here. He made a few anguished remarks – 'What about work?', 'We don't speak the language,' etc. – but they had no effect."

Heidi had been born and educated and worked in the UK before emigrating to Australia and New Zealand for ten years, where she divided her time between acting, writing and teaching. Brian had lived in Northern Ireland, Scotland, Belgium and London. Together they had been running a computer software company, which they moved to France in 1986, servicing their UK contracts from home. Heidi then had to go back to England to be near her terminally-ill mother. In 1992, Brian 'suggested' that Heidi might care to contribute to the family income. Examining her options, she decided it came down to teaching, which she hadn't greatly enjoyed, or selling, where the only product she could imagine was books. This marked the start of Antibes Books, aka Heidi's English Book Shop, now one of the biggest retail operations of its kind in continental Europe.

Before that could come into being, Brian had 'a wine-inspired idea'. A house that Heidi had fallen for, but they couldn't possibly afford was one of two sharing a garden. Brian thought that they should buy both and finance the deal by renting one. It worked. A French friend told them of a tiny shop available on a six-month let. They took it, drove to England, sourced a supply of second-hand books, plus some new ones, loaded the car, drove back and started the shop.

Initial problems were the high cost of shopfitting ("so we designed and made our own bookshelves"), collecting deliveries from the airport (this was before the establishment of a single European market), and accountancy. "We had several false starts: Our first French accountant was useless, the second, English, an incompetent crook. We finally found a French professional we could trust – expensive, but indispensable." Language was a smaller problem: they had both studied French to A Level and they took extra lessons before moving south – "but Racine and Balzac aren't much use when dealing with a plumber." They took more lessons, made French friends and discovered, like so many others, that "the French are very understanding if you make the effort."

Meanwhile the renting side had gone well with the notable exception of a booking by four English students, who turned out to be eight and trashed the place – so well, in fact, that they've since bought more properties and sold some, always seeking distinctive places that would attract discerning clients – "places we'd be happy to use ourselves".

Heidi's advice to those planning to start a business in France is simple, but fundamental: "Think about it, do your sums, take a deep breath and go for it!" She adds that one should never underestimate French charges and taxes: "they're seriously onerous and there's no room for negotiation. Be prepared to work hard for little or no money in the early years." On the other hand, it's essential to "like the country, the language, the food, the people, the life! Even learn to like the bureaucracy – well maybe not, but there's no point whingeing about it!"

FOOD & DRINK

Before setting up a food or drink retailing operation in France, you must study the types of food and drink outlets that are common in France. To give two obvious examples: there are few 'off-licences' in France, where most drinks are bought from supermarkets and hypermarkets or, in the case of wine, specialist wine-sellers (*caves*) or even direct from the producer; and there are few fishmongers' and virtually no greengrocers, most fruit and vegetables being bought from markets or supermarkets.

You must also make a detailed study of French eating and drinking habits – and that doesn't mean patronising every restaurant and bar within a 100km radius! – as these may be quite different from those in your home country. Again, to give two obvious examples: the French generally don't drink non-French wine, and few French people are vegetarian.

Beyond this, you must make yourself aware of current trends in eating and drinking habits. For example, the French are generally eating less 'red' meat and more 'white' meat than they used to; they're also buying more and more packaged and frozen food, so that specialist food shops are finding it harder to survive. On the other hand, 'health' and diet foods are becoming more popular, and there are, as yet, few dedicated 'health food shops' compared with the UK, for example.

Perhaps the first food retailing idea that springs to the minds of expatriates – and particularly the British – is selling foreign foods that aren't readily available in France. To be successful, such an operation obviously requires a large expatriate population, and even then it may be wise to combine the food with other products; it's unlikely that you will win many French customers.

CASE STUDY 20

One day in 1988, Susan Hodge's husband, who works all over the world, telephoned her in Lytham St Annes, near Blackpool, from Brazil to suggest they move there. Susan, who had just heard that they were expecting twins, suggested France instead. When their sons were six months old, the Hodges took a fortnight off to investigate and discovered Foix in Ariège, moving there permanently 18 months later in the summer of 1991.

Susan had been trained in hotel management, but had been working for her father-in-law's electrical contracting firm, mainly doing the paperwork. Initially in France, she gave private English lessons. But, as well as the house in which they still live, they had bought an investment property in Foix. They found the apartments easy enough to let, but had no takers for the ground floor shop. This was at the time when Marks & Spencer closed its operation in France, to the dismay of British and French alike. Owning the property and so with no rent to pay, they decided to open a shop to provide the British goods people wanted. As Susan says: "The worst scenario was that we would have to eat the stock ourselves!" She had expected to be able to collect stock direct from the UK, but found that impossible, and now works with a major wholesaler.

Susan found the Chamber of Commerce very helpful: "It was as though it was their money I was investing." They emphasised market research and Susan did much of her own "checking on existing Brit shops – thin on the ground then – and internet shopping sites, of which there were already quite a few."

Susan offers the following dos and don'ts to other foreign entrepreneurs:

- **Do** check that any relevant qualifications you have are recognised in France.

- **Do** try to think of all the questions you might need answered – although knowing what to ask is itself a problem – and, if possible, ask someone who has already done something similar.

- **Do** take the bureaucracy seriously: there are regulations here for things you might never imagine would be regulated.

- **Do** seek help and advice from everyone. If you don't understand, ask again. **Never guess.**

- **Do** introduce yourself to neighbours and local businesses as soon as possible. They know who to refer to and how to get things done. In my experience, they will be glad to help.

- **Don't** start a business on which you will rely for an income without making a business plan complete with cash-flow forecasts. Charges are incredibly high and the amounts going out each quarter are enormous.

- **Don't** employ staff unless they're essential. Each employee can cost up to double the salary.

- **Don't** be conned. Anyone who insists on an immediate signature is likely to be dodgy, particularly if you haven't approached them. Pressure to sign things can be considerable – a telephone call every ten minutes all day long isn't unheard of. If necessary, consult the police.

Like Susan Hodge, Mel and Steve Willey combined their food shop with a book service; unlike them, they decided to stock French food. They also took advantage of all opportunities that arose to expand and diversify their business, which had the highly desirable side-effect of integrating them more fully into the local community.

CASE STUDY 21

Mel and Steve Willey decided, in 2001, to leave their home and marquee hire business in Bedfordshire and live in France. With a good grasp of French, they reckoned that they would be able to integrate with local people and become a part of village life. They were lucky enough to find their new home in Morbihan, Brittany, in a single weekend: a stone house with outbuildings and three acres of land. They moved with their two sons, Simon and Fraser (then aged seven and five), that December and set to work renovating the properties with a view to letting *gîtes* the following summer.

"It was a challenge I would never wish to repeat," recalls Mel. "It meant working round the clock, day in and day out, but we made it before the first guests arrived, on 1st June 2002. We lived for a few days in each *gîte* to sort out any teething problems. The swimming pool had been tried and tested by our two boys whenever the opportunity arose. We now have four *gîtes*, with repeat guests every year."

Although their lives were largely taken up with maintenance and looking after their guests, the Willeys were ready for another challenge when a small 'English shop' in the village came up for sale. They saw the potential, bought it in December 2003, and set about researching local produce to sell alongside the English lines that were themselves expanding within the limits of the space available. A further breakthrough came with the closure of the village *boulangerie*. "The village mayor approached us with the idea that we should add a *dépot de pain* – I knew at that point that we had been completely accepted," says Mel.

This required a move to larger premises, which in turn opened up the possibility of expansion. "We now offer fresh bread and patisseries baked locally, fresh fruit and vegetables and French groceries for the local people, some of whom have no means of transport. We've been able to provide local people with their daily needs only because of the English shop, which almost totally supports the operation." The shop, called La Crème Anglaise, is now a full-time job in its own right for both Mel and Steve, who goes back to the UK every three or four weeks to replenish their stock of some 600 different British products. The business now includes a *salon de thé*, a bar and an English book exchange, which has brought people in for a pot of tea and the odd purchase while they're browsing.

With the continuing expansion of the business, the Willeys are in the process of buying even larger and more suitable premises (the previous shops were both rented). The new building has an apartment above it, which they plan to rent out to someone who will help in the shop. They're also hoping – with the help of the mayor, "who has given us 100 per cent support" – to obtain a bar licence for the new premises, since the old one has lapsed. The business has a website, which Mel hopes to develop into a mail-order service. She's also researching the possibility of moving into wholesaling: "We already supply a number of hotels and restaurants in Brittany and have people making trips of as much as two hours to buy from us."

Generally, the Willeys have had little trouble with French bureaucracy: "Our *gîte* and shop businesses are registered separately. We encountered no problems with either, but a good grasp of the language is imperative," says Mel. "After your initial registration, every time you change or add a classification at the Chamber of

Commerce it costs you more money. However, if you have a serious business plan and are determined in what you are about to embark on, there's no reason why this should be a problem. We have found them very helpful.

The main obstacle, as far as I could see, was to convince the Bretons that we wanted to integrate, and to prove to them that we weren't trying to set ourselves apart. That was quickly sorted out."

Another possible avenue is a specialist food shop, such as a butcher's, a baker's or . . . a candlestick maker's? Once again, market research is essential. To run a butcher's, a baker's or a florist's, for example, you must be an early riser. Bakers start as early as 02.00 and usually stay open most of the day, six days a week. Particular regulations may apply to each type of specialist shop. Butchers, for example, must label each cut of meat with its breed and 'origin', the premises must be kept at 12°C, and poultry, other types of meat, carcasses and packed cuts must all be stored in separate fridges. (For details of the requirements, go to the website of the Confédération Française de la Boucherie, Boucherie-Charcuterie, Traiteurs (🖳 www. boucherie-france.org).)

To be a specialist food maker in France, you must obtain a French qualification, which requires a minimum of two years' study at an apprentice training centre (*centre de formation d'apprentis*) for a *certificat d'aptitude professionnelle* (*CAP*), followed by a one or two-year apprenticeship and, if you want to run your own shop, a further two years' study for a *brevet technique des métiers* (*BTM*) and possibly another year to be able to specialise in a certain area (e.g. to run a *pâtisserie*), although you may be able to short-cut the procedure if you have a recognised foreign qualification; you can open a shop without a qualification, but must employ qualified staff.

No particular training or qualifications are required to sell wine in France, but you must obviously have a detailed knowledge of French wine (the French rarely drink anything else!).

CASE STUDY 22

Shaun and Mitch (a corruption of Margreet – her mother is Dutch) Leake came to France in 2001 after 12 years in Heidelberg, Germany, where they were both self-employed – Shaun as a golf professional and Mitch managing the pro shops they owned in two major golf clubs.

They had both long dreamed of living in France and, prompted by a press advertisement in 1995, drove 1,200km to south-west France and the following morning bought the house of their dreams, a property called Le Tuquet.

For some years, they were able to enjoy it only for brief holidays, but "the more we got to get to know our neighbours and experience the wonderful quality of life down here, the more we wanted to give up our 70-hour-a-week stressful jobs and enjoy our bit of paradise," explains Mitch. "So the idea formed to convert one of the barns into a *gîte*." The conversion took several years and finally, in November 2001, the Leakes left their businesses and moved permanently to France. "Our advertising started immediately and we had a tremendous response, with 18 weeks rented in 2002 and 2003 and mostly repeat clients in 2004."

The gîte, which they whimsically named Loco's Lodge after a late and much-loved pet dog, is designedly unconventionally. "We wanted to build a home away from home, not just a holiday house," says Mitch. It has two large bedrooms, each with its own bathroom and shower, as well as a living room complete with open fireplace equipped with an old-fashioned wind-up spit for roasting, a colonial-style terrace with hammocks, and an exclusive swimming pool (separate from the Leakes' own pool). There's also a satellite dish (guests must bring their own digibox and viewing card), a large video library and a PlayStation, and bikes are available for the more energetic.

The Leakes make a point of offering what might be called non-intrusive hospitality. Guests are treated to a barbecue supper on their arrival night and find in their gîte a generous welcome pack of wine, water, bread and fresh milk, plus long cosy dressing gowns marked with a logo of crossed champagne glasses and the slogan 'Au Tuquet ... where time stands still'. This degree of luxury sets the rental prices of €395 to €1,100 per week in context.

However, the Leakes weren't the first to discover that "renting for 18 weeks wasn't enough to pay our bills and allow us to enjoy a comfortable and easy-going lifestyle," says Mitch.

Shaun has returned to being a self-employed golf pro at a nine-hole course ten minutes down the road. As a long-standing member of the British Professional Golf Association, his qualifications are among the most respected in Europe and universally accepted. He offers lessons on the course and in the driving range, which is a converted barn.

Mitch meanwhile decided, on the strength of a long-standing passion, to find work in the wine business. She started with a three-year correspondence diploma course with the UK Wine and Spirit Education Trust. This was interrupted by a year studying full-time at Château La Tour Blanche, Sauternes, where she was fortunate to win one of only 14 hotly-contested places. The course included ten weeks' practical work, divided between harvesting, pruning and fertilising at different times of year. This she was able to arrange with a grower near home, whom she and Shaun had met taking parties of guests to his domaine.

This connection proved significant when, now qualified, Mitch sought a job. The grower had an interest in a wine shop in the nearby town of Eymet and he and his partners were looking for a replacement for their manager who was leaving. Three months later, she reopened the shop, now renamed La Cave d'Eymet, in November 2004. Initially, the arrangement was on a contract basis, but Mitch is to be made a partner and will become managing director. Already she has made changes to the stock, bringing in New World products alongside local wines and those of the Bordeaux area, and has started holding wine-tasting evenings. This in turn has spawned a Wine Club with monthly meetings on the agenda. With plans for wine tours in mind, Mitch is optimistic about turning round what had been a loss-making enterprise.

The main problems Mitch has encountered come down, as so often, to language and bureaucracy. For Mitch, improving her school French meant integrating with the locals, joining them to make pâté, pick plums, and play *pelota* and *pétanque*, supplemented by book and tape work by the pool. At Sauternes, the challenge was greater: "Conversational French is fine but, when it comes to studying oenology and viticulture, even in English I hadn't heard of half of the technical words. Both the pupils and teachers made every effort to help me and the second six months were tremendous fun. When I got my final results, finishing third in my class with a special mention, I felt it had all been worth the effort."

On the paper front, the Leakes were greatly helped by finding an English lawyer and a French accountant, as well as receiving considerable support from the local *mairie*.

I would certainly recommend anybody to make the effort if they want to start a business here," concludes Mitch. "Where there's a will, there's definitely a way. Never give up, but make an effort to learn the language – it won't work without it."

COMPUTERS

Needless to say, any business connected with computing or IT requires not only a detailed understanding of the relevant technology, but also knowledge of the specialist French terminology, although much of it is 'borrowed' from English. Although computing and telecommunications technology is more or less the same the world over, there are inevitably a certain number of French 'idiosyncrasies'. To take an obvious example, French computer keyboards have a different arrangement of keys from English-language keyboards (AZERTY instead of QWERTY).

CASE STUDY 23

James Blake worked in Hampshire as a teacher of information technology and a network manager, and one of his two grown-up sons runs an IT business in the UK, so the idea of supplying computers and support services came readily when he and his wife Joy decided to move abroad.

They had considered the possibility of moving to Canada or Australia, but having visited both to see relatives, decided they wouldn't want to live there. "This started us thinking about where we would like to live if we were to move from the UK. We decided on France, as it was easily accessible from England and provided similarly easy access to other parts of Europe. Language wouldn't be a huge barrier [see below], the climate would be better than in England, and I'd be able to continue playing rugby."

James and Joy bought a house in Gourdon, a small town in Lot near the Corrèze and Dordogne borders, in September 2002, moving finally the following January. After working on the house and preparing the ground for the new business, James started a French company, GourdonNet, in May 2003, to run alongside Euro Laptops Ltd, their UK-registered company. The UK company specialises in supplying portable computers to customers in the UK and France, "where we realised that there was a market for English-language machines, many Brits having little, if any, French and needing help to find their way through the system." The French company, which is now called Sud Ouest Informatique or SO IT, handles maintenance and internet services, runs IT courses for French and English-speaking clients and has latterly extended into relocation assistance and, with a local French colleague, language lessons.

Initially, the Blakes had thought of opening a shop and internet café, which would have given Joy a greater role, but they were put off by the high rental and set-up costs and the fact that banks weren't interested in making loans for such a purpose. That apart, they had few start-up difficulties, having studied the procedures before coming to France. "Getting into the French system as soon as possible is a good idea," says James. "It seems daunting to start with, but actually isn't too difficult, if a bit time-consuming. Costs also seem high, but aren't really excessive for the quality of the services – health, retirement, etc. – that you get in return."

Language wasn't a great problem, as James had been to school in France and spoke reasonable everyday French. Even so, he and Joy took lessons for six months before leaving England, which they found very helpful. "However, learning technical vocabulary and the language necessary for dealing with the administration in France was more of a challenge," admits James. "The regional accent and language, Occitan, provided additional interest. Another problem was the French use of abbreviations – they just reel off acronyms, expecting us to know what they mean."

James emphasises the need "to provide services for French locals and to use their services even for small things, as they will soon spread the word of your business. If you can find a French person to help with the business, so much the better. Don't work on the black; even employing someone on the black can get you into trouble. I recently had a visit from the fraud squad to impound the computer and hard drive I'd had in for repair from a British client, as he'd been imprisoned while being investigated for a variety of illegal activities. They're certainly trying to tighten things up!"

10.

TEACHING

For many expatriates, teaching in France means only one thing: teaching English as a foreign language. Although this is a popular option, and an area where there's considerable demand and opportunity, there are other teaching avenues available and this chapter looks at some of them. Teaching French to foreigners is one, and Susan Hickie explains how she set up a French-language school in Provence; others are teaching a musical instrument and running courses in an art or craft, such as cookery, as Fred Fisher does in Dordogne (see **Case Study 28** on page 323).

Information about teaching English as a foreign language and how to obtain the relevant qualifications and find a job in a language school is followed by the experiences of several expatriates who have taken things a step further and opened their own language school.

TEACHING ENGLISH & OTHER LANGUAGES

Language teaching (particularly English) is a good source of permanent, temporary or part-time work (many language schools need extra teachers in summer). This may entail teaching a foreign language at a language school or privately, or even teaching French to expatriates if your French is up to the task. Although English is the main demand, there's also a need for other languages, mainly for people whose company have moved to another country. The needs are different, as they normally affect the whole family and are more concerned with the day-to-day requirements of living in a foreign country, and this should be borne in mind if you're considering teaching a language other than English in France.

Like it or not, English has become the world's *lingua franca*, and the growth of international exchange, for business and leisure, means that English-language proficiency is now needed by millions of people in all parts of the world. Wherever people of different nationalities gather, English is almost invariably spoken. Although the French are inordinately proud of their own language, they're increasingly (albeit reluctantly) accepting the necessity of learning English and even allowing the Anglo-Saxon tongue to invade their own by using a growing number of Anglicisms. This means that English teachers generally have a certain degree of job security, at least until governments decide to teach English at a much earlier age in schools and with more efficient methods. When young adults can leave school speaking fluent English, English teachers' jobs may be in jeopardy. However, this might take a long time – especially in France, where English teaching in schools still follows a rigidly grammar and literature-based approach, with little learning of everyday phrases and structures.

Whether you're a young graduate wanting experience of another country and culture, someone planning to live and work in France long term, or a professional taking a career break who wants to try something different, teaching English can be a relatively easy way to earn a living. At the very least, it's a useful stopgap until you become more established and a great way to make contacts with English-speakers and French people when you're new to the country. What's more, teaching English is one job where you really don't need any French. In fact, one language school owner said that it was a definite advantage if you couldn't lapse into French and help your pupils out.

Advantages & Disadvantages

Unless you work in the French education system (see **Finding Work** below) or teach schoolchildren on a freelance basis, your customers will be adults. Teaching English as a foreign language, or indeed any other language or subject, to adults cannot be compared to teaching children in a school. First and foremost, the students are there for a specific (usually professional) reason. Someone (usually their employer) is paying for their course. The advantage of this is that the students are motivated – at least in theory. (There are inevitably some who regard English lessons as a 'skive' – a relaxing break from real work!) For many, success or failure could mean promotion or demotion. Most training sessions – the French generally refer to lessons as 'training' (*formation*) – are on a one-to-one basis; groups are usually small. This means that there are seldom problems of discipline and no rigid curriculum to be adhered to. On the other hand, results are expected – often in a short time – and you may be under intense pressure to achieve those results.

Teaching isn't just a question of passing on knowledge and skills to the person in front of you. It's very much an exchange of ideas, as teachers are faced with customers from many different industries and in many different professional positions. Unless you understand the nature of their jobs and situations, you cannot help students with their objectives. For example, operators and technicians increasingly need to read and understand instructions written in English. It's therefore a constant learning experience for you as well as for your customers, and can broaden your horizons and help to mould your character and personality. In many cases, you will need to be a counsellor as well as a teacher, as students will unexpectedly divulge their personal problems to you and expect you to sympathise if not provide a solution!

Teaching English is anything but routine work – and not only in terms of what and how you teach, but where and when you teach. Teachers can be required to work in the centre or away from it, as classes are as often held on company premises as in the language school itself. This can also mean a lot of travelling from company to company, so a car is almost essential. Although the actual teaching hours may not seem onerous, preparation is an important part of the work. For full-timers, the ratio is 35 hours paid for 25 hours taught, i.e. ten hours' preparation. This preparation normally includes planning the course as a whole to meet objectives, as well as preparing individual lesson plans. Travelling time isn't counted in the 35 hours, but must be taken into consideration when preparing your timetable.

Moreover, teaching adults is rarely a 9-to-5 job, which can be an advantage or a disadvantage, depending on your circumstances and attitude. Sue Burgess, who worked at a language school in La Rochelle, explains: "People want classes after work or at weekends, but don't expect to pay more – and the French want a lot for their money!" In any case, a teacher must be very flexible to accommodate students and company schedules. This can mean starting very early and finishing very late, sometimes with big gaps in the middle of the day. Most teachers admit, however, that the drawbacks are more than compensated for by the variety and interest of the job.

Contracts & Earnings

Contracts for teaching English abroad are normally short-term. In fact, as a novice you may be taken on as a *vacataire*, which means that, although technically an employee, you have no guarantee of work; you're simply called upon when there's a demand for additional teachers and ignored when there isn't. Even with a contract, there's little job security, as Sue Burgess explains: "You're never sure that you will get your hours from one year to the next. There may be a change of policy, fewer hours allocated to English or someone new rolls up and 'steals' your hours."

Although particularly in the high pay bracket, teaching is nevertheless a way of earning a reasonable living. Of course, earnings vary from company to company and also on the type of contract undertaken. As an employee of a language school or as a Greta teacher, you might earn between €10 and €15 per hour net of social security contributions (see page 210); as a freelance teacher, you can charge what the market will bear, which can be up to €50 in some areas, particularly if you have specialised knowledge (e.g. of legal or technical English).

Qualifications

Speaking English well isn't a sufficient qualification for teaching it. People use their mother tongue naturally and don't stop to think why they construct their sentences the way they do or use certain words and not others. The learner of a foreign language needs to know these things and you must be able to explain them simply and clearly. Note in particular that the French are taught grammar in school and you will be expected to name verb tenses and moods and parts of speech! Although it may come more naturally to some than others, teaching is a skill and certain techniques must be learnt. Requirements vary from centre to centre, and language schools don't always require a specific teaching qualification. A university degree and a respectable appearance may suffice (although you should take as many educational certificates with you as possible). However, most schools require a degree or its equivalent as well as language teaching certificate (see below). This doesn't mean that a person without these qualifications cannot be a good teacher, and training companies also assess your command and understanding of the language, your personality and your presentation. Some will encourage further study for a specialist qualification, and good companies will assist you financially to obtain it. If you're teaching another subject, sound experience in the relevant industry may be necessary, and technical knowledge will be as important, if not more so, than your teaching qualifications or technique, whether in the native language or in the target language.

The formal qualifications for teaching English as a foreign language are a mass of confusing initials. Most people have heard of TEFL, but there's also TESL, TESOL, TEAL and CELTA. To confuse the situation further, TEFL, TESL, TESOL and TEAL aren't in fact qualifications at all, although many people refer to them as if they were. TEFL stands for Teaching English as a Foreign Language, TESL for Teaching English as a Second Language, TESOL for Teaching English to Speakers of Other Languages, TEAL for Teaching English as an Additional Language (the latest and most 'politically correct' term). All four are in effect the same thing and refer to the profession rather than any specific qualifications.

The three most widely recognised qualifications are the Certificate in English Language Teaching to Adults (CELTA), the Trinity TESOL Certificates and the School for International Training (SIT) TESOL Certificate. To take a course, you must usually be at least 20 and have a good standard of English and of general education – at least similar to what's expected to enter higher education.

Many institutions offer a CELTA course, but the 'gold standard' is the Cambridge CELTA certificate. Cambridge courses are slightly more expensive, but it's worth paying the extra, as the certificate is highly regarded in the industry and some language schools insist on it. Cambridge CELTA courses are designed by individual centres in accordance with specifications produced by the University of Cambridge, whose website (🖳 www.cambridgeesol.org) has details of locations and a sample syllabus. Accredited Cambridge courses are available in around 40 countries worldwide, including France. CELTA courses can be done full or part-time, but they're challenging and time-consuming. A full-time course takes four to five weeks of intensive study and assessed teaching practice, while a part-time course takes from a few months to year or more depending on how much spare time you have. You must complete around 120 hours of teaching (known as 'contact hours') and a further 80 hours or more for assignments and lesson planning for both courses. Prices for 2005 are around €1,400 for full and part-time courses.

The SIT TESOL course involves 130 hours' training; for details, visit the School for International Training's website (🖳 www.sit.edu/tesolcert). There are two Trinity TESOL courses: the Trinity Certificate (known as the CertTESOL) and the Trinity Licentiate Diploma (LTCL TESOL); details can be found on the Trinity College website (🖳 www.trinitycollege.co.uk).

Information on TEFL courses in the UK can be found in the *Times Educational Supplement* and in France from the University of London Institute in Paris (formerly the British Institute in Paris), University of London Institute in Paris, 9–11 rue de Constantine, 75340 Paris Cedex 07 (☎ 01 44 11 73 73, 🖳 www.bip.lon.ac.uk). These are the official sources of information, but an internet search will reveal many more course providers. Further information about teaching English in France is available from TESOL France, 46 rue Barrault, 75634 Paris Cedex 13 (☎ 01 45 81 75 91, 🖳 www.tesol-france.org) and from the Volterre-fr website, a WebFrance International publication (🖳 www.volterre-fr.com).

Once you've obtained a basic qualification, you can undertake more specialised extension courses so that you can teach business English or English to young learners, which will make your services more marketable. Cambridge University, in association with the Royal Society of Arts, offers a job placement service to those who have obtained a CELTA certificate.

It's possible to take an online DVD-based course, such as those offered by the UK company i-to-i (🖳 www.onlinetefl.com) and the US Department of Education-approved Bridge Linguatec Language Services (🖳 www.teflonline.com), which takes just 40 hours and costs from $295. The problem with internet courses is that you cannot gain practical experience, which is a major disadvantage when it comes to getting a job. **The more practical experience you have, the better; this will tip the scales in your favour more than any certificate or qualification.**

Note also that quality requirements may not arise solely from teaching centres, but from the clients themselves, who are paying for the training and will want some guarantee that the company they choose to provide it will meet the standards they expect. Many clients insist on seeing the CVs of all the teachers, and an increasing number are demanding that the training company has ISO certification, which may be dependent on individual teachers obtaining certain recognised qualifications.

Choosing the Area

Teaching English is a more portable profession than many, as English-language skills are in increasing demand in almost every country of the world. Nevertheless, as with any kind of work, it's wise to thoroughly research an area before settling there with a view to working as a language teacher. It certainly isn't a question of choosing an area because you've spent an enjoyable holiday there or you like the climate. You must be realistic about your prospects of earning a living – not just in the immediate future, but also in the long term.

Industrial areas may not be the first you wish to consider as a place to live, but they should be high on your list for investigation for professional reasons, as the presence of a large number of businesses – particularly international companies and firms involved in overseas trade – is likely to mean demand for your services. If your aim is to set up your own language school (see page 315), you should also look at the competition. If there are several language schools in an area, but only one or two are successful, this may affect your choice. Healthy competition is a good thing and shows that there's a need for what you're offering. An absence of schools may indicate a gap in the market waiting to be exploited or simply a lack of demand. The precise location within an area is just as important and depends on the type of service or courses you plan to offer. For intensive residential courses, an attractive country property might fit the requirements and expectations of the client; for weekly two to three-hour lessons, premises within a few minutes of a main industrial area might be better. Either way, accessibility is an important factor. If you want to offer residential courses, but are reluctant (or unable) to invest in a large property, you might look for premises with a friendly and suitable hotel nearby. It's also important not to be too close to your competitors. A healthy distance could be considered a good thing by customers, who sometimes like to move from training centre to training centre.

Finding Work

New language schools open every day – some good, some bad, and some with extravagant ideas – and many close every day. There are over 500 language schools in Paris alone. The British Council in Paris (9–11 rue de Constantine, 75007 Paris, ☎ 01 49 55 73 00 and ☎ 08 92 68 44 14, 🖥 www.britishcouncil.org) keeps a list of language schools and job vacancies. The larger language schools, such as Berlitz, usually pay the lowest wages, but are the most flexible regarding qualifications. Schools can also be found via the internet or the yellow pages, and specialist training magazines and publications, such as *Vocable* and the *Educational Supplements* of *The Guardian* and *The Times* often carry advertisements from language schools.

As an alternative to a private language school, it's possible to obtain work with the government's further education organisation, Greta. Further details can be found on 🖳 www.education.gouv.fr/fp/greta, where there are details of all the Greta centres nationwide.

You can apply directly to state schools for a position as a language *assistant(e)*. The recent introduction of informal English classes into the early elementary school curriculum has created a shortage of teachers for this programme, and many schools are looking for part-time native English-speakers to teach games and songs to young children. **Full-time teachers in French state secondary schools and universities must be French citizens and possess French teaching qualifications.** Part-time language assistants are normally paid only a nominal salary – much less than that offered to a qualified French native teacher. Further information about teaching in France can be obtained from the Ministry of Education (☎ 01 55 55 10 10, 🖳 www.education. gouv.fr/personnel/enseignant/accueil.htm). The Central Bureau for International Education & Training (10 Spring Gardens, London, SW1A 2BN, UK, ☎ 020-7389 4383, 🖳 www.britishcouncil.org/education) publishes *A Year Between* and several other titles relating to teaching exchanges. You can order publications on the website, where you can also find links to several European teaching exchange programmes.

CASE STUDY 24

After teaching French, dance and music at a Manchester high school, Sue Burgess studied for a TEFL qualification before coming, in July 1989, to La Rochelle, where she stayed with a former pen-friend. "Her boyfriend ran a restaurant," explains Sue, "so I knew that, if I didn't find anything else, I could always do the washing up." In fact, she found first a temporary and then a full-time post teaching English at a language school. However, it wasn't the ideal job: "The school was run by a mad American who paid a pittance (the national minimum wage) for almost slave labour," she recalls.

Sue now teaches as a freelance in various departments of Niort University as well as teaching English privately in the department of Deux-Sèvres, 40km to the north, and translating for local companies. These activities aren't wholly secure: "Translation work in particular is unpredictable," she says, "varying from flood to famine and back."

Finding Private Students

Private students aren't usually the main target of a language school, as they can rarely afford the tariffs applied to business clients. Private students may visit a school only for courses of a few hours for a specific reason, such as preparing an interview. If you're looking for private students, you should therefore use the following resources:

- **Newspapers & Magazines** – Local newspapers and magazines may have advertisements from people wanting English lessons, or you can place an advertisement promoting your services. **However, you must be careful how you word your advertisement, as many French people think that 'English lessons' implies something quite different.**

- **Shops & Offices** – Shopkeepers in France are often willing to put a notice in their window or even on their counter free of charge, although it helps if you're a regular customer. You could also leave details with the relevant person (e.g. Human Resources manager) in local businesses.

- **Schools & Universities** – It's worth checking the notice boards in *lycées* and universities to find students (and possibly teachers) who want private lessons.

- **Clubs & Societies** – Find out about local clubs and societies (from your town hall or *mairie*) and go along, with information about your services. If you're offering French lessons, find out if there's a branch of Accueil des Villes Françaises nearby (from the Union Nationale des AVF, Relations Internationales, Secrétariat Administratif, 3 rue de Paradis, 75010 Paris (☎ 01 47 70 45 85, 🖳 www.avf.asso. fr); these usually have foreign members, who may require French lessons.

- **Networking** – Let as many people as possible know that you're offering English lessons, as French people are more likely to respond to word-of-mouth 'advertising' than to any other kind.

If you're running a language school, bear in mind that, although they're welcome (especially in periods of low activity, such as the summer holidays), private students should never form the basis of sales strategies.

Books & Material

There's a plethora of material designed to help you teach English and other languages. If you're running a language school, you will regularly receive catalogues offering you new material (books, cassettes, CDs, videos, etc.). The material is usually divided into General English and Special Subjects, and catalogues are normally further divided into three age categories: children, young adults, and adults. Books are normally accompanied by audio-material (cassette or CD) and often by a video or DVD featuring the people appearing in the book. A teacher's guide is normally provided, to help you plan your lessons. Before spending a large amount of money on published material (and some of it – particularly the audio-visual material – is very expensive), check with the school(s) you're working for what material they have. Some schools enforce particular teaching methods, although most don't and let the teachers design their own lessons. In this case, you can often put together your own teaching material using articles from magazines and material downloaded from the internet. Bear in mind, however, that French copyright laws prohibit the wholesale copying of published material without permission; the copying of cassette tapes and CD-ROMs is also illegal.

Remember also that each student responds to a different teaching method, and you shouldn't force a single method – however much you like using it – on all students, irrespective of their level, aptitude and personality. Indeed, part of the challenge and satisfaction of teaching is finding the best way of realising each student's potential. **If you aren't prepared to meet this challenge and derive little satisfaction from the achievements of your pupils, you shouldn't even consider teaching English in France (or anywhere else), which shouldn't be regarded merely as an 'easy' way of making a living abroad.**

E-learning

E-learning, as the word implies, involves learning by email, using a remote tutor to correct and mark your work. Although independent, you act as a sort of agent of the e-learning centre, which normally trains you in the techniques and methods used. You're also a salesperson for the courses, so you must be satisfied with them before you undertake any work. Although not as popular as it was once thought it would become, e-learning offers another string to a teacher's bow and another potential source of income.

Setting Up a Language School

The main activity of a language school in France is teaching business and technical English to adults in a professional environment, although general English is taught to those who need social language skills for entertaining customers or for private reasons, such as travelling and holidays. However, it's possible to expand and diversify the business in order to generate more business and, therefore, to be less vulnerable to fluctuations in demand for English lessons. Other possible activities include translation work, preparation for business trips/international meetings, residential/intensive language courses either in-house or in another country, telephone lessons (which are in increasing demand due to the growth in international tele-conferencing), and e-learning (see page 315).

CASE STUDY 25

Language in Provence is an adult training centre specialising in immersion courses in French. For Susan Hickie, its founder and director, it has brought together three salient strands in her life: teaching – "the thing I do best and love most of all" – and her enjoyment of France and its language, both dating back to her student days, working for a degree in French in Aix-en-Provence.

When she married in 1979, Susan and her husband bought a cottage in Brittany, only to find the weather too like that in Somerset where they then lived. They sold up to live in Africa and subsequently in the Far East, before returning to the UK in the '90s, when again they decided to move to France, this time to Provence.

They arrived in 1992, but Susan's husband kept returning to England for his work and finally stayed there. With her children in local schools, Susan "did whatever I could to survive. I taught both French and English, did bits of translation and, almost inevitably, some estate agency work."

In 1997, Susan returned to teach in England, where the children were taking A Levels and preparing for university entrance, renting out her house for two years and planning what she would do on her return. This was Language in Provence, which started in 2001 and had its first full year of operation in 2002.

During the research and preparatory stage of the enterprise, the *maire* of her village suggested she contact Apt Initiative, a local free service advising small businesses. As well as offering help and advice, this body made her an interest-free loan, repayable over two-and-a-half years. This wasn't given lightly, however: Susan had to make a full presentation of her research and business plan to a committee of 14 people. As she later learned from an insider, the decision almost went against her: "Although most of them liked the idea and the benefit for the region, several felt that it wasn't appropriate to lend money to a woman, who should instead approach family and friends. Southern French society is still quite 'macho' – unpalatable, but worth bearing in mind."

Since its opening, the school has expanded its business by around 30 per cent per year and, because of its way of operating, can continue to do so to meet future demand. However, Susan intends to continue as a small organisation offering a personalised service: "We are certainly not – and don't want to become – a language factory."

The sources of this flexibility are the teaching and accommodation structures. The teachers, other than Susan herself, are self-employed and charge for their time, although "they're very much part of the school and join us for lunch with the students." Courses are for a minimum of one week (with prices from €590, with 5 per cent discounts for couples or friends booking at the same time or for longer periods) and can be one-to-one or, more commonly in groups of not more than six. Those taking the immersion courses stay with people in the village in an all-inclusive package deal: "Once students arrive here, they don't need to spend another penny and their working and leisure time are both catered for."

Personnel

Most lessons are on a one-to-one basis or in small groups, so you need plenty of teachers, although you should limit the number of full-time staff – particularly in the early stages – to allow for quiet periods (e.g. summer) and slumps in business. Your personnel might include a director, a teacher manager, a receptionist and a combination of full-time and part-time teachers, plus translators if you're also offering translation work

Teaching staff must be chosen carefully. Recruitment is normally done by the director or the teaching manager, and requirements include the following:

- Native speaker of the language taught, although it's possible to use non-native speakers with a complete command of the language;

- Age at least 25, as maturity is essential;

- Appropriate qualifications (see page 34);

- Good presentation and appearance;

- Adaptability – to the needs of individual students and to the company culture;

- Reliability;

- Good communication skills;

- At least a working knowledge of French, although the frequent use of French in lessons is generally undesirable;

- A driving licence and car;

- Work experience outside the academic world;

- Experience in dealing with people in general.

Few schools need to advertise for teachers, as they receive CVs on a regular basis and the supply of teachers usually exceeds the demand. Word of mouth plays a big part in finding good teachers, as part-timers often work for several schools and their reputations usually precede them.

Running a language school isn't simply a matter of appointing teachers and matching them with clients. Your administrative team must be strong and well organised, as scheduling lessons is a complex and ever-changing task. Efficient planning and information processing are vital to ensure client satisfaction. Students constantly change, postpone and cancel appointments (or simply not turn up) to meet professional and personal obligations, and you must be able to accommodate these changes and communicate them quickly to your staff. You cannot afford to run out of rooms or teachers, as news of your inefficiency will travel fast and could jeopardise your business. You need to organise regular teacher (and other staff) meetings to discuss which material works best, and occasional brainstorming sessions to develop new ideas and teaching methods. You must also allow for the training of teachers, who may be required to test students according to a specific programme, such as the Test of English for International Communication (TOEIC, 🖥 www.toeic-europe.com), which is widely used as a barometer of English ability in France.

Infrastructure

You will need premises, even if most of your teaching is done in the offices of your clients. The more space you have, divided into suitably sized, separately accessible and preferably sound-proofed units, the more flexible and professional a service you will be able to offer. You will obviously need telephones, computers, photocopiers and other office equipment, but also video/DVD players and monitors, black or whiteboards and flip charts, overhead projectors, tape recorders and other mechanical teaching aids. A variety of equipment and material will help to generate an interesting and stimulating learning environment.

Marketing

As with most businesses, the best way to find customers it to make yourself known and to ensure a good reputation. In the world of training, word of mouth is often the way to attract customers. If the service you give is good, people will talk about it.

People are the key to the successful running of a language school, as teaching languages is all about communication and motivation – between staff and teachers and between teachers and students. It's essential that staff are motivated in order for them to motivate students. In turn, students will provide positive feedback to their company, which is your client. Customer satisfaction is paramount and the key to the success of the business. You must, therefore, be constantly thinking of improvements that will increase customer satisfaction, e.g. new teaching materials and methods and up-to-date equipment, and constantly monitor satisfaction levels by meeting clients to discuss the results of the training and assess whether their needs have been met.

Traditional methods of selling and marketing (including advertising, e.g. in the yellow pages, and setting up a website) will, of course, help, and larger schools go as far as employing sales people. As with any business, the essential thing is to offer something extra, e.g. free testing and evaluation of students, a translation service or e-learning facilities (see page 315). Language teaching, like any training, is a fickle market and, more often than not, a change of training manager in a company means a change of training company, unless you can offer something that others don't.

Legalities & Formalities

The formalities of setting up a language school are similar to those for setting up any business in France (see **Registration** on page 136). Once a training centre has been registered as a company, it must be approved by the authorities. This is done by providing them with the CV and police record of the director(s). You're then given an agreement number, without which it's illegal to operate. You must provide an annual account of all the teaching that has taken place, giving a detailed breakdown of the type of teaching, the type of students, the number of hours taught, etc. **Failure to provide this every year can have serious consequences, including the closure of the centre or the manager being banned from ever running a training centre again.** In France, training has a special status and has its own *convention collective* (see page 153), specifying the rules and regulations that apply. Because of this special status, a *convention de formation* has to be signed between the training centre and each client. This is a legal document which summarises the terms and conditions of the course (rate, duration of course, names of students, conditions of cancellation, etc.).

CASE STUDY 26

En Famille Overseas was established in the UK in 1945 to offer people the opportunity to learn languages while staying with families, for anything from a week to a year, in France, Germany, Italy or Spain. Mary-Louise Toms bought the business in 2002, but continued teaching English as a foreign language before moving to

France the following summer. Since childhood she had enjoyed holidays in France, first with her parents and latterly with her ex-husband.

The business had been very much paper-based, but Mary-Louise transformed it into one that operated principally via the internet, and it was the portability that this change allowed that enabled her to move from Colchester, Essex, to her present home in Hérault, between Carcassonne, Narbonne and Béziers. "I still have to post lots of material," she says, "but with judicious advertising and word-of-mouth publicity, I have found I have more, rather than less, success here than in England." Even so, she's still constantly looking for other things to do, but wary of the many franchise deals that demand "a lot of cash up front, with not many promises to follow, perhaps."

She found the main obstacles to working in France to be "the language and the obstinacy of the French authorities to employ anyone who isn't a native. I don't object to this, but it is a bit difficult to get round. In my experience, unless you speak first-rate French or work for an estate agent, you have to be independent, i.e. self-employed. There's therefore a tendency to form expatriate enclaves (Britons working for Britons, whether or not on the black), which reinforces the French view that we take from rather than give to their country and don't make enough effort to integrate."

Mary-Louise found help when needed particularly from her local *mairie*: "From paying bills to finding doctors, they're always there to help and, from a work point of view, can point you to the appropriate centre." That said, and although she finds "the health system brilliant, getting the appropriate paperwork sorted is a nightmare — everything in triplicate at least; and make sure you have a full-length birth certificate before you even start!"

There are no special legal requirements for running children's classes except a compulsory ratio of adults to children. This ratio can be obtained from any school or state teaching establishment. Nevertheless, you may have to negotiate local red tape in order to offer certain facilities for children, as the Rochats discovered.

CASE STUDY 27

Danielle and Claude Rochat are a Swiss couple who established La Cardère, a French language institute specialising in intensive residential courses for individuals and small groups, in 1991. Claude had been a teacher, among whose responsibilities had been a class for children with learning difficulties, while Danielle had worked for a socio-medical office mainly dealing with children and teenagers. They both felt in need of a change and settled on the Bresse area of southern Burgundy, having found it pleasant and peaceful on earlier holidays in France. It also had the benefit of being relatively close to the border and only 150km (90mi) from their families in Switzerland.

The Rochats come from the French-speaking part of Switzerland and so had no language problems, but this didn't help them in their dealings with l'administration: "When we said that we planned to arrange excursions for our students, we were told we needed special authorisation," recalls Danielle. "We made an appointment in Dijon, a considerable distance away, but arrived to find that the woman in charge had forgotten and was out. The next appointment she cancelled because it was snowing. Finally, we rang her to complain about the delay – now six months, during which we were losing money – and she said she would check our dossier if we would hang on. After five minutes, she returned to say that no special authorisation was necessary.

"Because we also thought of taking children as young as 12, we enquired of the youth and sports service if there were requirements for any special equipment. The answer was that we could build and equip our centre as we chose and then they would inspect it to see whether it met the requirements. We said it was silly to do this if it had subsequently to be dismantled, but we never received an adequate response."

Small wonder that the Rochats have a wry view of French administration and its complex procedures. "At the time of the Revolution," comments Danielle, "the French people cut off the king's head but, since then, the administration has generated many little 'kings', each of whom needs to have some power ..."

More seriously, she now thinks that, had they known what to expect, they would have started planning in detail much sooner, establishing contacts and allowing more time to ensure that they had more information: "We didn't realise how unhelpful the bureaucracy could be. Being well organised and having your dossier well prepared isn't necessarily enough."

However, in general, they found French people to be kind, welcoming and friendly. A case in point was when, a week before the school was due to open, the workmen were running behind schedule. With time running out before the first group of ten Swiss teachers was due to arrive to improve their French, the Rochats asked three local men if they could lend a hand. "They arrived with their wives on the Friday evening and worked through the weekend. The house was like a hive and it was absolutely wonderful! Afterwards, they explained that they were happy to welcome a new family to the village, especially since we were setting up a business there."

Financial Considerations

Rates: Setting rates isn't a particularly difficult task. All language schools are normally aware of the tariffs charged by the competition and there's little variation between the charges of reputable and well-established centres. Some, of course, always try to undercut and offer silly prices, but this practice isn't always well perceived by customers and, in any case, often means working at a loss, if the teachers are to receive a decent salary.

Training centres normally operate on an hourly rate basis. Rates vary according to type of teaching: groups, face to face, telephone, intensives (include lunch and sometimes dinner with students) or residential courses (include accommodation, food and sometimes evening entertainment).

Other Costs: To teachers' pay must, of course, be added social charges, which amount to almost 50 per cent (see page 210). Other costs include office equipment, such as computers, telephones and photocopiers; heating, lighting and water; office supplies; teaching equipment; and travelling expenses.

Bank Loans: After four years of teaching in a school in La Rochelle, Sue Burgess moved to another school in Niort and, over five years, worked to develop its client base from 23 to nearly 200. When the owners divorced, the school became available and Sue decided to buy it: "As I was already working in it, I knew the price that was being asked," explains Sue. "I made an offer, which in fact was the full asking price. I took advice from a lawyer and an accountant and had to produce expected figures about turnover, etc. I also needed a bank loan to buy what the French call the *fonds de commerce* – the value of the business as a going concern, which is intangible. The furniture and equipment was hardly worth anything; what you're paying for is the name and the clients, I suppose."

The bank insisted that Sue set up a *SARL* (see page 124), which meant that she needed partners. "I had to find three because of the amount of money involved. The bank also insisted that I had half the shares and put in half the money (100,000 francs at the time – €15,000) because I was classed as a salaried worker. So I had to find 50,000 francs. They also insisted that I give a personal guarantee on the bank loan." Nevertheless, owning only half the company (and not even having a majority at AGMs), she was vulnerable to her partners' decision to oust her, which is what subsequently happened. She remembers discussing the possible purchase with a client, who asked whether she had partners. "Beware of partners," he warned. When she told him one of her partners was an accountant, he said, "Beware of accountants!" "How right he was!" says Sue, who was left with a €15,000 debt hanging over her: "I'll be paying that off for some time – all my life probably."

Sue's advice to others intending to buy a business in France is: "Don't give a personal guarantee. Get lots of advice. And don't have partners who aren't themselves working in the company. She also recommends finding a sympathetic bank manager. Otherwise, "you need perseverance, determination and a lot of optimism" – especially if you're a woman.

Despite their perfect French, the Rochats had serious difficulties with banks and administrative departments in the early days. They arrived in France in August 1990 and set about renovating their house and converting it into a teaching establishment. They had previously conducted market research, prepared a business plan and, as they had 50 per cent of the capital required, were surprised to be turned down by most of the banks in Louhans, the nearest town. "Finally we found one that assured us it would be all right, but said they would have to check with their head office in Mâcon," recalls Danielle. "Suddenly they changed their minds. We had by then been eight weeks without income and were obliged to borrow from our families in order to eat. We felt it proper to advise the builders that we were having difficulties with the funding and, within an hour, they had all left."

The bank's argument was simply that the school was in the 'wrong' location, Bresse not being in the 'right' part of Burgundy – i.e. the wine-producing area. "It took another eight weeks to find a bank that would cooperate, but we kept at work decorating if only to keep up the morale of our two children, then aged 9 and 11. Finally, we found a bank in Chalon-sur-Saône, which lent us money to form the *SARL*. And it happened that the manager was in touch with a big bank in Paris that had some money to spend. So that's how we found money for the *SCI* – in fact for the house and for the land – but at a very high rate: 11 per cent."

On the subject of banks, Danielle has another cautionary tale: "In the early days of forming the institute, we had many things to organise and we couldn't find an important letter the bank had sent us with all the details of our loan (rate, dates, description, etc.), so I telephoned and asked them to send us a photocopy. They answered that they hadn't kept a copy, but had just written a few figures in the margin of our file." The Rochats' advice is either to work with a financial consultant who's well versed in the ways of French banks and tax authorities or to keep a property in your own country and use it as security for a loan.

Recognition: In 2002, the government recognised Susan Hickie's French-language school, Language in Provence, as an adult training centre, which allowed the cost of courses to be set against tax. To be recognised as an adult training centre it was necessary to demonstrate that the school met certain statutory requirements, which entailed scrutiny of all documentation (brochures, course programme and schedules, fee structure and payment arrangements, cancellation clauses, enrolment forms, etc.) as well as the CVs and qualifications of staff, and the procedures for student assessment, validation and end-of-course certificates. "We also had to supply copies of our business registration, accountants' details, etc. and each year we complete a detailed statement of student training hours over the year and our company accounts. The procedure was quite lengthy and time-consuming, but I felt it a worthwhile exercise for the school."

With the help of this recognition, the school is enjoying increasing demand from students needing French in their work, whose courses are financed by their companies; when two local restaurateurs took a 60-hour course, two-thirds of the cost was funded by their trade association. "We have also had interpreters from the EC in Brussels and Strasbourg, wanting to improve their French or to add to their bank of languages."

Susan puts at the head of her list of obstacles to starting a business in France "the old problem: never enough capital, and so having to get things going on a shoestring while supporting oneself." Next comes "the fact that the French system does not encourage the entrepreneur: social charges are very high (much higher than in the UK). It's important to choose the right vehicle for your business, so take advice before deciding. Registering as an association can avoid some expenses such as VAT. The status of *micro-entreprise* can be useful, but the income threshold isn't very high and it's expensive if you earn more than the limit."

Potential Problems

Running any business is risky, but a language school is more risky than most. When companies cut costs, language training budgets are often first to suffer, and contracts can be cancelled at short notice. Even when a contract is honoured, the following scenario is all too common: you've secured an annual contract with a major client; you organise your staffing and plan the timetable so that the teachers can cope with the workload; due to 'unforeseen circumstances', students miss lessons (meetings, sickness, problems with children and animals, etc.), but it's the client's policy that students lose training the following year if the previous year hasn't been completed, so come the autumn and students start panicking to complete their allotted number of hours; the school is then faced with too many hours and not enough teachers or teaching space and must bring in freelancers and hire rooms, incurring major additional costs through no fault of its management or staff. All that can be done is to be prepared for this every year and to allow a contingency to cover the cost.

The reverse problem is that the first few months of the year can be slow and business doesn't start rolling in until around March. Full-time teachers must be paid for doing little. Other problems are students not turning up for lessons. A last-minute cancellation is normally charged to the client, although a time limit must have been agreed with beforehand; however, if a student cancels outside the time limit, the lesson is postponed. If this happens on a regular basis and with many students, it can have a financial impact on the training centre.

Susan Hickie of Language in Provence strikes a more positive note. As well as stressing the importance of learning the language and making a well researched business plan, Susan advises: "Play to your own strengths – do something you really enjoy. If you've been brave enough to make this huge change, make sure you do something that inspires you. Don't be afraid to change your original plan. When I started the school, I expected we would be working equally in French and English. In fact, the biggest demand has been for French and I now recognise that, had I wanted to attract more French people to learn English, I would have needed to relocate to a bigger town or city and the business would be quite different." Susan also observes that "the French like to get to know you before they really want to deal with you professionally. Personal introductions count for a great deal."

OTHER TEACHING

Languages aren't the only subjects that can be taught by expatriates in France; in theory, any skill can be imparted as a way of making a living – an art or craft, singing or the playing of an instrument, technical know-how such as computing . . . or even cookery.

CASE STUDY 28

Fred Fisher reacted to the approach of his 40th birthday much as other men do. He felt restless, and saw his comfortable life as "existing, not living". After 17 years in the police force, he wanted a new challenge and thought that his self-taught expertise as a chef might provide it. Running a restaurant seemed the obvious choice, but he found it hard to find the right premises. It was in a doctor's waiting room that he saw a page of colour advertisements for houses in France at prices a fraction of those of their UK equivalents. This gave rise to the idea of running a cookery school, where students could stay while learning techniques and recipes in a beautiful rural setting. When his wife, Lucy, reacted with enthusiasm, the die was cast and, in April 2000, they, together with their then eight-year-old daughter, Jenny, took off with a caravan to start their new life.

Over the first couple of months, they saw some 50 properties without finding anything they thought suitable. Finally, an agent showed them a derelict farm. Through the drizzle they saw a crumbling establishment, unsanitary and unoccupied for a quarter of a century, but with two massive barns and seven acres of land, and decided it was perfect. Having made an offer, they were surprised to learn that acceptance would be based on an extreme form of positive vetting. Over a Sunday lunch, which led on to dinner, they were scrutinised by the owner, a local farmer, and his family and at last told that they could, indeed, buy the place.

The next 18 months passed in some discomfort, with an unreliable electricity supply and a hosepipe the only source of water, while the Fishers struggled with the bureaucracy and the casual attitudes of workmen hired to help restore the ruin and convert the first barn. "Particularly memorable was the saga of the eight 6m steel joists that had to be installed to support the barn's first floor. Everything was prepared, friends and relatives came to help (some of them from England) and we had set aside the whole day to put in 10 tonnes of steel with a fork-lift truck hired for the purpose. The steel didn't arrive and a telephone call to the supplier's wife established that he had taken on another job and couldn't do ours for another week. The same thing happened with the next appointment, when it turned out that the supplier had gone to a wedding. Neither time did anyone ring to warn us of the cancellation and there was no apology. Eventually, we cancelled the order and got another company to do the work."

Problems with bureaucracy were typified by the rigid requirement to supply information irrespective of its relevance: 'To get our carte vitale we had to supply not only our birth certificates, but also details of our parents, including their place of birth. There was no record of Lucy's mother's birth and we had the devil's own job convincing the authorities that my wife had ever had a mother. In the end they relented, but we had to wait another month before they told us we could have healthcare."

The family moved into their centrally-heated barn in late 2001. Fred comments that he didn't want another Christmas like the previous one, when at minus 15°C, he cooked the dinner wearing a ski mask, Wellington boots and a pair of Lucy's tights under his thermal underwear.

The whole period of preparing the property had been intensely busy and all idea of enjoying a normal French lifestyle had been put on hold, with a promise to find the time to do so once things quietened down. The cookery school is now up and running and had its first full year of operation in 2004, the barn now serving as a gîte. While Lucy runs the business side and Jenny has become fluent in French and has made many local friends, Fred keeps busy cooking and teaching. They've found compensation for the hard work and long hours in the "fantastic people" who have come as students and remained as friends.

Lucy also speaks excellent French, but "that often doesn't overcome the French inability to understand a description," comments Fred. "The language has a limited vocabulary, so sound effects and eyebrow movements, and even mime, play a large part in conversation. I once had an alarming case of diarrhoea and had to ask for a packet of Arret tablets in a packed chemist's. I ended up having to mime, charades-style!"

Fred's advice to newcomers is: "Follow the dream, but be aware that in a foreign country people are very different from us, often in very subtle ways, to which you must be sensitive. The French don't always welcome strangers who come to live in their country with the same warmth they show when you visit as a tourist. If you're going to run a business, get solid financial advice from an English-speaking firm that knows all the ins and outs of the French system. Make sure you have a healthy financial reserve (at least €15,000) in case anything goes wrong. Don't argue or complain: the French don't understand the concept and will merely make life more difficult for you. Smile at all times – whatever happens!"

11.

COMPUTING & PUBLISHING

The advantage of many jobs relating to computing and publishing is that they're portable: since the advent of email, and particularly broadband internet connections, you can as easily submit a web page design or an article for publication from Marseille as from Manchester or Miami. You can usually work from home, which means no office purchase or rental costs or overheads – and you can claim a percentage of your home running costs against tax (see page 205).

There are disadvantages as well: as email is 'instant', clients expect an instant response and work turned around in next to no time; everything is urgent, which can make it difficult to organise your time and plan (e.g. holidays). If your home is also your office, it's more difficult to separate work from leisure time; if your clients know you work from home, they will inevitably contact you at all hours and expect you to work evenings and weekends for the same hourly rate as during normal 'office hours'. On the other hand, deadlines permitting, you can take time off whenever you like.

Technological advances have led to the growth of 'lap-top businesses', which don't even need a fixed base and, therefore, provide scope for a new breed of entrepreneurs who don't want to be tied to one location. You may be able to enjoy the lifestyle that France has to offer you and your clients, but, thanks to the internet, keep your business registered in your home country and so avoid some of the labyrinthine French bureaucracy. Or you may choose to do this as a springboard to basing yourself in France permanently. You should take expert advice before doing so, however, in order to ensure that you're trading legally, e.g. registering your business and paying your taxes and social security contributions in the relevant country.

COMPUTING

France was generally slow to react to the information technology (IT) revolution, largely due to the inertia of the education system, which was geared to the training of engineers and took time to adapt to the production of IT specialists. For this reason, there was of a shortage of qualified IT professionals until around 2002. Even now, there's a variety of computing qualifications, many of which are limited to a range of software, e.g. Microsoft, or even a single package. However, in recent years, there has been a slowing both of the rate of IT staff recruitment and of the upgrading of hardware and software systems by companies, which are increasingly 'outsourcing' their IT work. This has created opportunities for entrepreneurs wishing to set up small computing businesses, but the increasing competition has driven down rates of pay.

The major cities dominate the IT market in France, with the exception of France's answer to California's Silicon Valley, Sophia Antipolis on the Côte d'Azur, which is the largest technology park in Europe with some 1,200 companies employing 23,000 people; a second park is under development nearby.

IT tends to be used as an umbrella term covering technical fields, such as systems management and software, and general sectors, such as internet marketing, web design and development, and web-hosting. This chapter includes the experiences of an Englishman who has set up a web design business in France.

Website Design

A website has become an essential 'shop window' for any business, and there's therefore almost endless demand for website design services. This is good news for those wanting to set up a design business in that there's no shortage of potential clients, but bad news in that there's increasing competition among those offering design services. Another negative factor is that website design software is becoming ever more sophisticated, easy to use and cheap – even free. Anyone with limited computing knowledge can design and post a simple website in a few hours for under €100.

Now that the world and his wife has internet access and many internet service providers (ISPs) offer 'free' web space as part of dial-up packages, an increasing number of individuals are wanting their own 'page' of cyberspace, but they're even less likely than businesses to be willing to pay for the services of a professional designer. Making a successful business of website design, in France or anywhere else, is therefore largely a matter of marketing: finding a niche and selling your service to the relevant people.

CASE STUDY 29

Raymond Gilbert-Griffiths's move to France took a lot longer than he had anticipated. While living in Pimlico, London, he had been working as a product manager and software designer for a British software company, based in Hounslow, Middlesex. He left for France in 1994 to live in a house he had already bought in the Loire valley with a view to starting up a gîte operation, only to be asked to return.

He had designed a piece of software, which was due to be taken to the next stage in development, and his detailed knowledge of it was indispensable. Since he had always got on very well with everyone in the company –"teaching the sales force how to sell the product and the marketing team how to position it and so on" – he agreed to go on working for them "from a converted pigsty" until late 1995. At that point, the UK company was taken over by an American firm: "Anyone technical – me included – was transferred to the Michigan HQ. I then lived and worked in the States for just over five years." In 2001, he took a job in the UK and stayed with it for just over a year before deciding to move back to France permanently in 2002.

Raymond sold the Loire house and moved to Dordogne, where he established a business creating websites for clients all over France and the UK. Although he started from scratch, he has now built up a client base in a wide range of industries, including gîte owners, tax consultants, estate agents, security companies and wine producers.

Initial problems with the bureaucracy were the familiar Catch 22, as Raymond explains: "It was necessary to have a carte de séjour in order to register with the chamber of commerce. However, I couldn't get this without proof of income – but couldn't work without the carte and therefore couldn't register . . . To get around this conundrum, I had to transfer money each month from my UK bank to prove that I was capable of supporting myself financially, backed up a letter from my UK bank to this effect. All documentation – birth certificates, bank letters, British bank statements, copy of passport, etc. – had to be translated into French and certified by a registered translator. I had to prove residence in France by way of utility bills, etc. even though, without a *carte de séjour*, I was technically living in France illegally, as I'd spent more than three months in any six here.

All this had to be presented (in triplicate) to the *mairie*, where my *dossier* was duly stamped and shipped off with my application for a *carte de séjour*, together with a fudged date of entry into the country – naughty, but necessary. I was told that the application would take up to six months, but that I would be given an official receipt stating that the application had been made and that this was good enough for the Chamber of Commerce. However, due to the high demand in Lot-et-Garonne, even the receipt would take three to four months to arrive.

Eventually, out of sheer frustration and after many phone calls with the chamber, it was agreed that if I persuaded the Maire to write a letter stating that I had, in fact, applied for my *carte de séjour*, the chamber would give me a temporary registration, which would be valid for three months. This I did and the Maire was extremely helpful, stamping my letter with the official stamp and signing it himself.

The chamber did register me, but, as indicated, only for three months. Thankfully the receipt arrived in the nick of time and I was able to send a copy off to the chamber, which accepted it pending receipt of my official *carte de séjour*. This arrived several months later. I made a copy of it and sent it to the chamber, which lost the copy and requested another. And so on . . .

Despite all this, the French government started taxing me from day one and I had to pay health charges from the same time. It seemed that the government had different ideas about my working here from the chamber of commerce." Raymond was helped through this "interesting experience" by a French friend who spoke perfect English: "I wouldn't recommend anyone to try to do this alone unless they really understand the intricacies of French bureaucracy."

Remarkably, he remains sanguine about French bureaucracy: "Although we seemed to get stuck in a loop, the system worked well once the paperwork was straight. Apart from this, running a small business in France isn't hard. Tax officers are friendly and helpful and will explain any forms to you – they even helped fill out some of the forms for me last year! There were no surprises other than having to register how much space my business takes up in the house. This information is passed on to the commune where you live and you're taxed accordingly. This is called the *taxe professionnelle* and is usually discounted by 50 per cent in your first year of business – so you have to keep in mind that it will be twice as much after that."

Raymond advises anyone contemplating setting up a business in France "to keep every scrap of paper relating to your business and all correspondence to and from the authorities, copy them three times and keep them safe – in fact, get into the habit of copying **everything**. Although French bureaucracy is slowly changing, there's still an attitude that everyone is trying to evade tax and that you're guilty until proven innocent."

His other recommendations are as follows:

- Take advice on deciding what kind of business you're going to have. As a micro-entreprise, you can automatically write off a percentage of your income as expenses, but you cannot then claim your actual outgoings back. If your real expenses are much higher, you may wish to elect to declare them – but check with your accountant first.

- Always pay an accountant to do your tax returns; don't try to do them yourself.

- Pay all your taxes and contributions before the due date: penalties for late payment are high.

- Shop around for health insurance. Once you're registered, you will be inundated with offers and other services. Read them carefully to determine the best cover for your needs.

PUBLISHING

The IT revolution has also enabled writers, editors, proofreaders and other publishing professionals to work from home anywhere in the world. There are numerous books, manuals, courses and websites on finding work in publishing, and this section provides only an overview of the opportunities and obstacles, with details of where to find further information on each topic.

If you're thinking (dreaming?) of going down this route, you must be realistic about likely earnings, especially in the early months, as it isn't easy to find work, even if you're qualified and experienced, and work isn't usually well paid.

Writing

Many expatriates try their hands at writing (for magazines, 'how to' books and autobiographical stories), largely based on their own experiences of moving to and living in France, but few manage to make a living at it. Rates of pay are generally low (around £50 per thousand words for books and newspapers, and between £100 and £150 per thousand for magazine articles, although some magazine publishers don't pay at all for 'lifestyle' articles), publishers are notoriously slow in paying (you may have to wait until several months after publication), there's a lot of competition, and writing for publication isn't as easy as most people imagine.

Countless would-be writers dream of penning the next *A Year in Provence* and then lying by the pool, rising only to fetch another bottle of wine or to collect the royalty cheques from the post box, but for every 'publishing phenomenon' there are hundreds of manuscripts consigned to editors' waste paper baskets. **The chances of your writing a best-seller at your first attempt are remote, and it may be years before you even get anything published.**

Nevertheless, France and the French remain popular subjects with many (particularly British) publishers, and with perseverance, practice and a little luck, it's possible to make money from writing in France.

There are two 'national' English-language newspapers in France, both published monthly, and half a dozen or more monthly or bimonthly magazines (published in the UK) devoted to French matters. These are all listed in **Appendix B**. Publishers of relocation guides to France include Cadogan, How To Books, Kogan Page, Vacation Work International and, of course, Survival Books, and there are numerous publishers of French guidebooks in English, e.g. Dorling Kindersley, Frommer's, Rough Guides and Time Out; look in any book shop or library for others.

Obviously, if you have specialist knowledge in a particular field – whether or not it's related to France – you should explore the possibility of writing for the relevant publications.

Writing for the internet is another possibility, although rates of pay are usually even lower than for newspapers and books – or even non-existent – and 'publishers' are harder to track down.

You may be able to persuade a publisher (or he may suggest it) to pay you royalties instead of a set fee. This is obviously an advantage if the publication sells like hot cakes, but a disadvantage if it's a lame duck. Also, instead of receiving a lump sum soon after publication, you have to content yourself with payment in dribs and drabs over a period of several years – assuming the publisher doesn't go bust in the meantime!

There's a wealth of resources available for the aspiring writer who wants to operate from his or her laptop in France. Begin your research in your home country by making sure you have up-to-date guides on all the media you might want to write for. *The Writer's Handbook* (Macmillan) and the *Writers' & Artists' Yearbook* (A & C Black), which are updated annually and cost around £15, are comprehensive guides to British and American publishers and literary agents, national and regional newspapers and magazines, useful websites and film and TV companies. There are also details of relevant professional associations and training courses. *The Guardian* newspaper publishes a *Media Guide*, which contains similar contact details. It's published by Guardian Books annually and costs around £18.

Self-publishing

Finding a publisher who's willing to print your hard-worked copy is often more difficult than writing it in the first place. Self-publishing is, therefore, a tempting – and relatively straightforward – alternative. However, self-publishing, often known as 'vanity publishing', can be a costly exercise and, without the distribution network a publisher has, selling books can be extremely hard work and virtually a full-time job in itself. There are many 'vanity publishers', some reputable, others not, so you should check an agreement carefully before signing anything and obtain competitive printing quotes.

A cheaper alternative to 'hard copy' publishing is publishing on the internet, which should be considerably cheaper and may provide you with a ready-made selling medium. Among the many companies offering a web publishing service is Publishing Internet (🖥 www.publishinginternet.com), although no details are provided on the website.

Editing & Proofreading

If you're already a qualified editor or proofreader, you may be able to operate as effectively in France as in your present country of residence, although face-to-face meetings with existing clients will obviously be less easily (and cheaply) arranged.

If you're thinking of taking up editing or proofreading in France as a way of making a living, you should bear in mind that it can take several years to obtain the relevant experience and qualifications and develop an adequate client base to ensure full-time work. As editing and proofreading are normally paid on a 'piece work' basis (e.g. by the page or the hour) and charges are more or less fixed, neither is a get-rich-quick occupation: earning more means working longer hours.

Nor can 'just anyone' be an editor or proofreader. Picking up typos in a newspaper or book is one thing: correcting proofs under pressure using the approved symbols is another matter altogether – and editing presupposes advanced proofreading skills.

Even if you're skilled, finding work isn't easy. Reputable publishers invariably use members of the SfEP (see below); small publishers often use in-house staff and, when they need freelance help, may not be willing to pay the going rate. You may send 100 speculative letters and receive one (small) job if you're lucky.

There are many publications about becoming a proofreader or editor, including *Freelance Proofreading and Copy-editing* by Trevor Horwood (ActionPrint Press), and courses are offered by a number of organisations, including the SfEP (see below). Potential clients are listed in Trevor Horwood's book as well as in *The Writer's Handbook* (Macmillan) and the *Writers' & Artists' Yearbook* (A & C Black).

To be taken seriously as an editor or proofreader, you need to join the UK's Society for Editors and Proofreaders (SfEP, Riverbank House, 1 Putney Bridge Approach, London SW6 3JD, ☎ 020-7736 3278, 💻 www.sfep.org.uk), which imposes strict standards on its members, requiring them to attend courses and complete rigorous tests, or the equivalent organisation in your present home country.

Indexing

As with editing and proofreading (see above), if you're a qualified indexer, you may be able to make a living in France just as easily as in your present home country. If you aren't and you're contemplating taking up the profession, you should contact the UK's Society of Indexers, Blades Enterprise Centre, John Street, Sheffield S2 4SU (☎ 0114-292 2350, 💻 www.indexers.org.uk), the American Society of Indexers, 10200 West 44th Avenue, Suite 304, Wheat Ridge, CO 80033 (☎ 303-463-2887, 💻 www. asindexing.org) or the equivalent organisation in your present home country for information about the training and qualifications required and, most importantly, the likelihood of finding work and rates of pay.

Setting Up a Publishing Business

Setting up a publishing business in a foreign country takes courage, determination and a certain amount of sheer nerve. It's unlikely to make you a living for several years (unless you stumble across the next *Harry Potter*) and, like the Mewes (see below), it's wise to start it as an adjunct to another, already successful, enterprise rather than to sink all your funds and energy into a highly risky business.

CASE STUDY 30

Like many, particularly British, expatriates, Wendy and Harold Mewes were attracted by the idea of hospitality in France only to think better of it later on and take a new direction. The Mewes moved from Somerset, where Harold was editor and production manager of a monthly journal and Wendy a writer, to Finistère in August 2002. That December they moved from the cottage they already owned to a four-acre farm, where they planned to run a bed and breakfast business combined with walking holidays. They did so from June to November 2003 before deciding that "having paying guests in the house and cleaning and cooking was not what we wanted, although some aspects were very enjoyable."

Instead, they decided to make use of their proven skills and set up Red Dog Books, a small publishing house, in December 2003. This was a start-from-scratch *entreprise individuelle* (*EI*), whose first title was Wendy's walking guide for their immediate area (none previously existed in English), which came out in September 2004. This was a convenient start, as it drew upon their researches for walking holidays as well as their previous experience of having published a similar book in the UK. In their first year, they also published a novel and some tourist leaflets. "After nearly a year in business, we're developing our tourist marketing services," says Wendy. "Doing what you know makes life easier in that you're confident of basic skills and methods. With the B&B, I always felt like an amateur."

The Mewes found few obstacles in setting up business in France "except the innate passivity of so much French administrative and tourist industry staff." This was demonstrated at chamber of commerce level, where help was available for form-filling, but little for developing the potential of their business; the Mewes discovered, only by chance, that there was a tourist services office in the same building. They were also unimpressed at being charged €70 to record a change of address. They found little interest at the *mairie* until they moved to another commune, where the mayor was enthusiastic enough to feature them in the local bulletin and to steer potential customers in their direction. They were also fortunate to find help and support from an accountant recommended by their *notaire*.

Initially Harold spoke good French and Wendy average, and they both worked hard on improving their skills before coming to France; they can now boast of never having spoken English in any of their business dealings.

Wendy emphasises that it's important to be businesslike about any business – "even if you're offering a single room for B&B." That means developing a detailed marketing strategy; establishing and maintaining professional standards in whatever you do; being flexible and ready to adapt and learn new skills; and keeping eyes and ears open – "many people miss openings simply by not being aware of them."

Wendy's dos and don'ts include the following:

- **Do** choose a business you know something about or have an affinity with.
- **Do** look for 'value added' features to enhance your business (as with adding walking tours to the B&B operation).
- **Do** follow up contacts and ideas – "make yourself do one new thing a week to advance the business."
- **Don't** aim solely for English-speaking clients, whatever your business.
- **Don't** expect anyone else to do things for you.

Publishing books is one thing; producing a periodical, especially a newspaper, is quite another. The establishment of a network of reliable and well informed contributors, the generation of advertising revenue as well as subscription income and the need to create a sales and distribution structure, as well as the basic task of putting the publication together require a variety of skills and experience – and sheer hard work.

CASE STUDY 31

Adam Brown came to France in 1979 from Wales, via working on oil rigs in the Persian Gulf. After a spell running the first deer farm in Dordogne, he ran an English language magazine in the same area. His partner, Miranda Neame, had come to France from Devon in 1974 and started by designing and planting gardens and painting, then trained as an electrician, worked as a builder's mate and taught English. They both had publishing in the blood: Adam's mother was a journalist and both Miranda's parents were in printing and publishing. In 1995, they took over a failing newspaper, Adam as publisher, Miranda as editor, and turned it into what is today *French News*, the country's biggest circulation English newspaper.

The project faced an initial uphill struggle with problems ranging from "lack of capital and the impossibility of any help from French banks to inaccessibility of so-called grants to help set up," comments Miranda. "However, we found, through friends, a good accountant who guided us across the minefield." A major difficulty was dealing with the differences in French business practices, including the need for *statuts de société*, the complexities of *fiches de paie* and the expense of *charges sociales*, and learning new accountancy programmes.

Today *French News* has developed into a more truly national newspaper, with correspondents in most parts of France, and has spawned regional editions for Brittany and Aquitaine, a glossy magazine, *French Times*, and a growing number of free regional guides supported by local advertisers.

Miranda's advice to newcomers is never to start anything without adequate research and "with strong nerves if you start out with inadequate capital." She offers these dos and don'ts:

- Do deal with all problems immediately; don't let them fester.

- Do deal with officials personally if you have problems: they're more likely to be sympathetic than if you write or telephone, and a face-to-face visit carries much more weight than a phone call or a letter.

- Don't assume you know the rules; there's always a new one you didn't know existed.

- Don't hope that your ignorance can be used as an excuse.

- Don't try to bend the rules: you may get an inspection that could result in your being closed down.

- Don't count on any government grant you may be promised: it usually won't be paid for a long time.

12.

HEALTH & CHILD CARE

If you're a European Union (EU) citizen and a health professional, certain EU directives ensure that the qualifications you've gained in your home country are recognised in France. However, recognition procedures can be complicated and long-winded, and certain professions that are recognised in other countries aren't in France. This chapter looks at the experiences of a chiropractor and an osteopath and also covers child care as a way of making a living in France – if only on a temporary basis. Other healthcare possibilities include acupuncture, holistic and homeopathic medicine, massage, physiotherapy and yoga teaching. There's a particular shortage of masseurs in France, where people tend to rely on physiotherapists (and, increasingly, chiropractors and osteopaths) or indulge in expensive spa treatments.

When it comes to childbirth, France has a fairly rigid system, in which home births are virtually unknown and 'natural' birthing techniques (such as water births) seldom practised. This offers scope for freelance birthing partners, maternity massage therapists and other types of doula (see **Doulas** on page 345).

There are further opportunities at the other end of the chain of life. Like most other western countries, France has an ageing population, and an increasing number of foreigners are retiring to France. Traditionally, the French look after ageing relatives and don't use professional services. However, with changing lifestyles (e.g. more women working and fewer people living near to other family members), products and services for the elderly, such as electric 'buggies' and other mobility aids, and 'third age' social and recreation groups (such as U3A in the UK), are beginning to be needed, and this market is currently underdeveloped.

LANGUAGE & CULTURE

There are a number of issues, which health professionals who are thinking of working in France should consider carefully before they attempt the practicalities of official recognition and validation of their qualifications. Not only you have a different language to contend with, but you will also encounter significant cultural differences, which may make it more difficult to practise your profession in France than in your home country. **You cannot afford to underestimate the importance of these differences, even if you're planning to work in an area with a large number of English-speaking expatriates.**

According to EU regulations, member states cannot discriminate against you on the basis of language. However, the European Commission has stated that anyone wanting to pursue their profession in another member state should "possess the linguistic knowledge necessary to do so". According to a recent article in the British Medical Journal, language barriers are one of the main reasons why more doctors don't choose to work abroad. **It's highly unlikely that English will be spoken by the majority of your French patients.**

Unless the area you want to work in has a large expatriate population, you need a fairly advanced command of the language, with the relevant specialist vocabulary. Even if you opt for an area where English is frequently spoken by your patients and colleagues, don't forget that you may still have to deal with French health professionals who may not be able to speak English – for example, if you need to refer a patient to another specialist.

RECOGNITION OF QUALIFICATIONS

Until your qualifications are officially recognised by the relevant authority, you cannot practise your profession in France. Moreover, if you wish to practise as an acupuncturist or osteopath, you must first have qualified as a general doctor. The recognition procedure can take several months, so it's best to set things in motion as soon as possible (see page 34). There are two categories of EU Directive which affect the recognition and validation process for health professionals: Sectoral and General.

Sectoral Directives

Professions regulated under the Sectoral Directive system include general doctors (*médecin généraliste*) and specialist doctors (*médecin spécialiste*), general nurses (*infirmier/infirmière*), midwives (*sage-femme*), dentists (*dentiste*) and pharmacists (*pharmaciste*). Qualifications in these professions are automatically recognised, as the required training is similar throughout the EU. Nevertheless, you must still have your qualifications validated and register with the relevant professional body (specified in each of the sections below). In theory, if your profession comes under a Sectoral Directive, the validation process should be simple and quick. In practice, experiences of validation procedures vary wildly. As in all matters connected with French bureaucracy, patience is essential.

General Directives

Professions regulated under the General Directive system include physiotherapists (*kinésiethérapeute*), opticians (*opticien*), chiropodists (*podologue*) and psychologists (*psychologue*). The full list can be found on the European Union website (🖥 http:// europa.eu.int/youreurope/nav/en/business/home.html – enter the details of the information you require). Recognition and validation under this system is more complicated than under the Sectoral Directive system, as these professions aren't automatically recognised. A European Working Party is currently trying to minimise the paperwork and duration of validation periods, so far without success.

If your profession is regulated under the General system, the competent authority examines the kind of training you've had and checks that the duration and content is as close as possible to those required for the same profession in France. Details of the documents you must provide to apply for recognition and validation under the General system are set out on page 34, but bear in mind that they vary considerably. You may have to undertake some training in France, which means that your French must be at a high level. You must also join the relevant professional body (see list under **Finding Work** below).

FINDING WORK

If you're seeking work or wanting to train in a French hospital, you should apply directly to the establishment concerned. The main teaching hospitals (Centres

Hospitaliers Universitaires/CHU) and other major and expatriate hospitals in France are listed below:

- American Hospital in Paris, 63 boulevard Victor Hugo, 92200 Neuilly (☎ 01 46 41 25 25).

- Bichat-Beaujon Hospital, 100 boulevard du Général Leclerc, 92118 Clichy-sur-Seine Cedex (☎ 01 40 87 50 00).

- CHU d'Angers, 4 rue Larrey, 49033Angers Cedex 1 (☎ 02 41 35 36 37).

- CHU de Brest, 5 avenue Foch, 29609 Brest Cedex (☎ 02 98 22 33 33).

- CHU de Grenoble, BP 127, 38043 Grenoble Cedex 9 (☎ 04 76 76 75 75).

- CHU de Nancy, 29 avenue du Maréchal de Lattré de Tassigny, 54035 Nancy Cedex (☎ 02 83 85 85 85).

- CHU de Nîmes, BP 26/5 rue Hoche, 30029 Nîmes Cedex (☎ 04 66 68 68 68).

- CHU de Reims, 23 rue des Moulins, 51092 Reims Cedex (☎ 03 26 78 78 78).

- Hertford British Hospital/Hôpital Franco-Britannique, 3 rue Barbès, 92300 Levallois-Perret (☎ 01 46 39 22 22).

- Hôpital Paris-Ouest, 2 avenue Charles de Gaulle, 92100 Boulogne-Billancourt Cedex (☎ 01 49 09 50 00).

- Hôpital Saint-Antoine, 184 rue du Faubourg St Antoine, 75012 Paris (☎ 01 49 28 20 00).

The following organisations may be able to provide information and advice on qualifications or finding work in France:

- **Chiropractic Association** – Association Française de Chiropratique (🖳 www. chiropratique.org).

- **Dental Association** – Association Dentaire Française, 7 rue Mariotte 75017 Paris (☎ 01 58 22 17 10, 🖳 www.adf.asso.fr).

- **Medical Association** – Association Médicale Française, 180 boulevard Haussmann, 74389 Paris Cedex 08 (☎ 01 53 89 32 41).

- **Medical Council** – Conseil National de l'Ordre National des Médecins, 80 boulevard Haussmann, 75008 Paris (☎ 01 53 89 32 00, 🖳 www.conseil-national.medecin.fr).

- **Midwives Council** – Ordre National des Sages-femmes, 56 rue de Vouillé, 75015 Paris (☎ 01 45 51 82 50, 🖳 www.ordre-sages-femmes.fr).

- **Nursing Association** – Association Nationale Française des Infirmières et Infirmiers Diplômés ou Etudiants (ANFIIDE), 11 boulevard Montmartre, 75002 Paris (☎ 01 47 36 34 60, 🖳 http://anfiide.infirmiers.com).

- **Occupational Therapy Association** – Association Nationale Française des Ergothérapeutes, rue Eugène Oudine, 75013 Paris (☎ 01 45 83 50 38, 🖳 www. anfe.asso.fr).

- **Physiotherapy Association** – Fédération Française des Masseurs, Kinesithérapeutes, Rééducateurs, 24 rue des Petits Hôtels 75010 Paris (☎ 01 44 83 46 00, 🖥 www.ffmkr.com).

Medics Travel is a company that was set up by a doctor, Mark Wilson, to help doctors, nurses, physiotherapists and other health professionals to arrange work opportunities overseas. Its website (🖥 www.medicstravel.co.uk) contains contact details for professional medical associations in France, as well as the main medical schools and hospitals all over the country.

CHIROPRACTIC & OSTEOPATHY

Chiropractic and osteopathy are two of the many specialised areas of healthcare that can be practised in France, but they differ not only in 'philosophy' and manipulation techniques (chiropractors look at the nervous system and the effects on it of structures such as vertebrae and the consequences for the health of the body, whereas osteopaths look more at blood flow and muscles and their effect on the nervous system), but also in the way they're regarded by the French health system.

CASE STUDY 32

Simon Pullen is a chiropractor. Practising in Dorset, he found himself "increasingly fed up with the way the UK was going. The pace of life seemed to be quickening, everyone seemed to be becoming more self-centred and it wasn't pleasant. Time for a change. It was natural for me to choose France, as I was quite well acquainted with the country and spoke some French." Simon moved in 1999, but started practising again the following year after buying and doing up a house. At that time, chiropractic was technically illegal in France, but it was legalised in 2002.

"My UK qualifications are acceptable in France. The syllabus in the UK is very similar to that followed by the French college in Paris. In fact, as there's no state registration of chiropractors as yet, a chiropractic qualification from almost anywhere would be acceptable. However, when chiropractic becomes state registered, the required qualifications will be quite specific. For example, you might not be able to obtain insurance unless you have the right qualifications. I've been a member of the French Chiropractic Association (Association Française de Chiropratique, 🖥 www.chiropratique.org) ever since being here in France and have insured myself through policies negotiated for the profession by the association."

Simon now lives and practises in Eymet, a pretty bastide town in Dordogne, which he chose because it's an area with a large British expatriate community. "I assumed that the British were more familiar with chiropractic than the French, but was surprised to find that my patient base is roughly in the ratio of three French people to one British, proportions with which I'm very happy." Although many of the

Britons are retired, he has noted a growing number of younger people living and working in the area, many of them working from home by computer and internet for UK-based companies – a trend that has been greatly helped by the development of flights from nearby Bergerac airport to Stansted, Bristol and Southampton.

Simon hasn't (yet) encountered any real obstacles in setting up his practice in France. "You always hear stories of people having a hard time getting into the system, but, to be honest, most of them haven't gone about doing things correctly. You have to appreciate that the French love their paperwork; you might just as well do your homework to establish what's required before you start."

Simon recommends getting as much advice as possible. He joined his professional association "to give me the security of being part of a recognised body" and engaged a recommended accountant: "If your French isn't very good, seek out an accountant who speaks English. When it comes to law and accounts, I believe that you should be fully aware of what's going on." His own French was based on 30-year-old O Level studies, but "I've picked up an awful lot by working mainly with French people, thus having to sink or swim – it certainly focuses the mind!"

More generally, Simon advises: "Do your homework carefully. Be sure of your market and that the location is right: don't be swayed by a particular place just because there's a nice house there. Be prepared for a long haul: it takes a long time to establish a business here, so have sufficient funds behind you to survive a slow start. Always involve the French. Don't try to be British. Put the French first and they will respect you for it. Make contact with the chamber of commerce and the mairie. Introduce yourself and explain what you want to do – normally this will help you a lot. Play by the French rules: some aren't as you might like them, but trying to defy them can cause you ongoing problems."

If chiropractic isn't officially recognised in France, osteopathy was until recently illegal unless practised by a registered doctor. This change in the law opens opportunities for qualified expatriates wishing to offer their service in France. Nevertheless, working practices can be quite different from what you're used to, as Rachael Dickens discovered.

CASE STUDY 33

Rachael Dickens is an English osteopath who, after training and working in London, came to France in October 2001 in fulfilment of a detailed three-year plan. She had previously worked for two years in Paris, spoke French and enjoyed many aspects of French life and culture. Even so, her primary aim had been to work and enjoy an outdoor lifestyle in Europe, with sun and the opportunity to ski, it didn't matter where: "My first choice was Barcelona, but I couldn't be bothered to learn Catalan," she confesses.

As part of her planning, Rachael rang six doctors working on the coast between Marseille and Menton and saw them all over a four-day visit. "One of her questions was 'Where should I work?' They all said Antibes, so on the way back to the airport I stopped off to look around. I asked the woman in the English book shop (Heidi Lee – see **Case Study 19** on page 298) if there were many English-speakers there. When I told her what I did, she held my arm and said, 'We do so need you.' Decision made."

Rachael had allowed herself a running-in period of three months to find an apartment and an accountant, set up the legal framework, deal with officials, etc. Staring on 1st January 2004 proved convenient, as it meant opening for business in a new tax year.

The timing also enabled Rachael to escape a major potential problem of which she hadn't been fully aware: "Only four days before I arrived, the French government declared osteopathy legal. They had previously recognised it as a profession, but only if performed by a doctor. There had even been a witch hunt for British osteopaths on the part of their French counterparts who didn't like the competition. One even phoned me in England to say that he would do his best to see that I was fined, and two French doctors had taken all five existing British osteopaths to court. They'd also applied sufficient pressure to close French osteopathy schools, with the result that the quality of home-bred specialists was variable. Indeed, in France anyone can call themselves an osteopath: you don't need qualifications or insurance, just a brass plaque and a white coat!"

Thanks to the change in the law, Rachael had little trouble in setting up. She even found the tax system "so easy and paper-free," a point with which many of our contributors might disagree. She has found other expatriates supportive and is on good terms with the local medical professionals. "The local doctors all invite me to their *soirées* and I've taken on the role of their petted granddaughter – it's rather sweet! And they send me patients. There are now five osteopaths in the area – four French and me – and we meet every six weeks to share information and practise techniques. We refer patients to each other and generally have a very supporting professional relationship."

"If you cannot run a business successfully in your own culture and language, it's unlikely that you will be successful in someone else's," says Rachael. With specific reference to running a business in France, she adds: "You're likely to find yourself in a small community that talks, which can be both lovely and infuriating!"

DOULAS

Under the French system of childbirth, every step of a pregnancy is monitored and overseen by a midwife (*sage-femme*) or gynaecologist (*gynécologue*) and general practitioner (*médecin généraliste*); nothing is left to chance and the idea of 'natural' birthing is alien to most French healthcare specialists. However, this attitude is changing, albeit slowly, and 'alternative' practices are increasingly being tolerated. Until recently, the concept of a doula (*doula*) - also known as a birthing partner (*accompagnante à la naissance*) - was unknown in France, but this has also changed, and there's scope for those with the necessary experience and knowledge to set up in this field.

A doula is a specialist in childbirth (in France, she must have given birth herself and breastfed) who assists the expectant mother (and father) with preparation for the birth and labour and, in most cases, also provides post-natal care for up to a few weeks. Doulas have existed since ancient times (the word derives from Greek and means 'female servant or care-giver'), but were largely sidelined by professionally trained midwives in the 17th century. They made a comeback in the US in the '70s and have since reappeared in other countries, including Hungary, Poland and the UK. In 2003, France registered its first official doula (*doula*), Vanina Goetgheluck (appropriately meaning 'good luck'!), who is now President of the French doulas' association, Accompagnement à la Naissance (ALNA, 11 chemin de la Vernique, 69160 Tassin la Demi-lune, ⌨ www.alna.fr). The association organises professional training, which takes 18 months and covers anatomy, physiology, psychology, ethics, hygiene and diet.

Doulas generally charge around €40 for a two-hour 'consultation' and between around €300 and €500 for attending a birth. General information about working as a doula can be found on ⌨ www.doula.org.uk.

CHILD CARE

There are a number of opportunities in some areas of France for expatriates who can offer good quality child care. If you're young, energetic and like children, there's no better way to learn the language than to live with a French family and work as an au pair (see below). Although this isn't strictly a way of making a living, it can provide a stepping stone to a job as a nanny or child minder (see page 350) or even to setting up your own nursery or child minding agency.

⚠ If you think you might want to work in child care in France, it's important to understand that attitudes towards children and the care of children are significantly different from those in most northern European countries, especially the UK. Generally, French children aren't put to bed early in the evening or left in the care of a babysitter while their parents go out to dinner. Children and even babies are involved in every part of French family life, and that includes taking them out to dinner and bringing them home in the early hours of the morning. Children are genuinely welcomed everywhere and the relaxed attitude towards their presence means that French parents don't have the same kind of child care needs as parents in some other countries.

Many French working mothers leave their children in the care of other family members, and the thought of paying someone to care for their child – especially someone they don't know well – is anathema. Granny is preferable to a stranger – even one with a long list of admirable qualifications – and what's more Granny doesn't charge! Those who don't have a family member they can call on usually use a nursery or day care centre.

If all this leaves you wondering whether child care in France is a possibility worth exploring, take heart. Things are changing, albeit slowly. There are opportunities in the cities and other areas, e.g. holiday resorts. There's a growing and increasingly young expatriate population, who require the kind of child care they've been used to in their home country, and French parents who need a child minder are often keen to have a native English-speaker caring for their children so that they benefit from hearing English spoken on a daily basis. There's also an increasing number of English-language nurseries and day care centres in France – especially in areas popular with expatriates – catering for children of all nationalities. Another possibility is to offer child care services in holiday resorts, e.g. ski resorts. (Snowkidz is such a business, set up by expatriate Ashanti Dickson in the French Alps, UK ☎ 0870-402 8888, 💻 www.snowkidz.com.) A list of internet sites relating to child care in France can be found at 💻 www.yakeo.com/fr/garde_d_enfant.

Even if you plan to work with an English-speaking family, you should still make sure that you can speak some French. **As an au pair, nanny or child minder, you're responsible for young children and, should there be an emergency, your French language skills could save a life.**

Fostering as a way of making a living isn't dealt with here as it's a complicated process and the French authorities are reluctant to allow foreigners to foster.

Au Pairs

The au pair system provides an excellent opportunity to travel, improve your French, and generally broaden your education by living and working in France. Single males and females aged between 18 and 27 from most countries are eligible for a position as an au pair. (Although au pair is French and the term *jeune fille au pair* is commonly used, the official French term is the 'unisex' *stagiaire aide-familiale*.) Au pairs must usually have had a high school education or the equivalent, have a good knowledge of French and must attend French classes organised for foreign students.

If you're an EU national, you need only a valid passport and aren't required to arrange a position before arriving in France, although it's usually wise. Applicants from non-EU countries need a long-stay visa (see page 26) and require an agreement (*déclaration d'engagement*) with a French family and a certificate of registration for French classes at a language school. These must be presented to your local French embassy or consulate with your passport when applying for a visa (see **Au Pairs** on page 27). You also need evidence of private health insurance, as increasing numbers of young people are obtaining au pair positions in order to obtain subsidised medical treatment in France.

Au pairs are usually contracted to work for a minimum of six and a maximum of 18 months. Most families require an au pair for at least the school year (September to June). The best time to look for an au pair position is therefore before the beginning of the school year in September. You should apply as early as possible and not later than a month before your preferred start date (at least two months if you need a visa). There are also summer au pair programmes of one to three months between 15th June and 15th September. Enrolment must usually be made before 31st March. Au pairs employed for the summer only aren't required to attend French lessons.

Au pairs are usually placed in French-speaking families with children, although non French-speaking families and families without children can also engage an au pair. An au pair's duties consist of light housework, including simple cooking for children, clothes washing (with a machine) and ironing, washing and drying dishes, making beds, dusting, vacuum cleaning and other such jobs around the home. To enjoy life as an au pair you should be used to helping around the house and like working with children. An au pair isn't a general servant or cook (although you may be treated as one) and you aren't expected to look after physically or mentally disabled children. As an au pair, you receive all meals and accommodation, usually with a study area, in lieu of a salary.

Working hours are officially limited to 30 per week, five hours per day (morning or afternoon), six days per week, plus a maximum of three evenings' baby-sitting. You should be given time off to attend French classes and (if appropriate) religious services. In some families, au pairs holiday with the family or are free to take Christmas or Easter holidays at home. Choose a wealthy family and you may be taken on exotic foreign holidays (although they may be less likely to treat you as a family member).

For your labours you're paid around €225 to €375 per month. Pay is usually higher in Paris, where you may also be given a travel card. You're required to pay your own fare from your country to Paris (and back). If you're employed in the provinces, your family pays the rail fare from Paris to their home and back to Paris at the end of your stay. In Paris, a family may provide a *carte orange*, a monthly public transport pass for the Paris *métro*, buses and suburban trains.

An au pair position can be arranged privately with a family or through an agency. There are au pair agencies in France and many other countries. Agency lists can be found via the internet (e.g. 🖥 www.europa-pages.com/au_pair). Positions can be found via newspapers and magazines (such as the British *The Lady* magazine), although you're usually better off using an agency. The better agencies vet families, make periodic checks on your welfare, help you overcome problems (personal or with your family), and may organise cultural activities (particularly in Paris).

An agency sends you an application form (questionnaire) and usually asks you to provide character (moral) and child-care references, a medical certificate and school references. Some agencies allow you to meet families in France before making a final decision, which is highly desirable, as you can interrogate the family, inspect their home and your accommodation, and meet the children who will make your life heaven or hell! Agency registration fees vary, although there are maximum fees in some countries, e.g. around £50 in the UK. You should contact a number of agencies and compare registration fees and pay, both of which may vary considerably (although the terms of employment should be similar).

Your experience as an au pair will depend entirely on your relationship with your family. If you're fortunate enough to work for a warm and friendly host family, you will have a wonderful experience, lots of free time and possibly some memorable holidays. Many au pairs grow to love their children and families and form lifelong friendships. On the other hand, **abuses of the au pair system are common in all countries, and you may be treated as a servant rather than a member of the family and be expected to work long hours and spend most** evenings baby-sitting. **Many families engage an au pair simply because it costs far less than employing a nanny.** If you have any complaints about your duties, you should refer them to the agency that found you your position (if applicable). There are many families to choose from and you shouldn't feel that you must remain with a family that treats you badly. You're usually required to give notice if you wish to go home before the end of your agreement, although this won't apply if the family has broken the contract.

Many EU countries, including France, have signed the European Agreement on Au Pair Placement, which will give you an idea of what to expect working as an au pair in Europe. There's detailed information about this on 🖳 www.europa-pages.com/aupair, along with lists of reputable au pair agencies throughout France. Experiences of people who have worked as au pairs and tips for those thinking of doing so can be found on the Au Pair Forum (🖳 www.aupair-forum.com).

Nannies

It's possible for responsible English and French-speaking young women to obtain employment as a nanny (*nurse, nanny* or *nounou*, sometimes called *garde d'enfants*) in France. Duties are basically the same as for an au pair job (see above), although a position as a nanny is a proper job with full employee rights and a real salary!

Although it's possible to find work without experience or qualifications, it's much easier if you have both. There are several ways of finding a job as a nanny: you can approach an agency in your home country or in France, look job opportunities in specialist magazines or search the internet. Nanny agencies include GreatAupair (🖳 www.greataupair.com) and Soames Paris Nannies (🖳 www.soamesparis nannies.com). Any reputable agency should insist on a qualification similar to the National Nursery Examination Board (NNEB) qualification in the UK, which includes two years' full-time training. In addition, you're expected to produce references from at least two previous employers – which will be checked.

Specialist magazines which advertise nanny jobs in France include *The Lady*, *Nursery World* and *Montessori World*, an online magazine which includes job listings (🖳 www.montessori.co.uk). In Paris, many English-speaking would-be nannies advertise in *France USA Contacts* (🖳 www.fusac.org). Internet sites that can put you in touch directly with people looking for a nanny include 🖳 www.manounou.com.

Be careful if you're applying directly for jobs, however. Families that advertise privately may not genuinely require a nanny! It's much safer to go through an agency that's a member of a recognised professional body, which polices the working practices of its members. Relevant organisations are the International Au Pair Association (IAPA, 🖳 www.iapa.org) and, in the UK, the Recruitment and Employment Confederation (REC, 🖳 www.rec.uk.com), which aims to raise standards in the child care industry. The agency should have representatives in France, so that you have an agency contact when you begin work and if you experience problems.

Salaries start at around €1,200 per month with free board and lodging and rise to around €1,500 per month for an older or more experienced nanny or one who is expected to look after more than one or two children.

Further information about working as a nanny can be found on 💻 www. assistante-maternelle.org (in French), including requirements and duties, where and how to find work, and what rates to charge.

Mother's Help

A position that is between an au pair and a nanny is a mother's help (*aide-maman*). A mother's help isn't a qualified nanny but must have experience of looking after children; duties are more onerous than those for an au pair and salaries start at around €900 per month with free board and lodging for a live-in position and around €1,200 per month with one meal per day if living out.

Child Minders

Unlike nannies, who look after children in their parents' home, child minders (*assitante maternelle*, also referred to as *gardes-enfants*) look after them in their own home. (The maximum number of children allowed at any one time is three.) There's a growing demand in France for child minding services, as there are few places available in the departmental and communal nurseries (in some places, e.g. Paris, there's a three-year wait!) and they're expensive. Previously regarded as a job for women, child minding is increasingly being done by men (largely due to the rise in unemployment), although as a man you may find it more difficult to secure a position owing to (unacknowledged) prejudice.

Like all jobs that involve working with children, child minding is heavily regulated in France. You must at first have an agreement from the *conseil municipal* (town council) and register with the Centre de Protection Maternelle et Infantile in the town where you live. There are two types of registration: 'non-permanent' (*titre non permanent*), which entitles you to look after children during the day and/or after school; and 'permanent' (*permanent*), which allows you to look after children 24 hours a day, 365 days a year. Registration is for five years but is renewable.

All prospective child minders must complete a 60-hour training course and be inspected before being registered. The first inspection is carried out by a nursery nurse or a social worker. You must answer a battery of questions and complete a number of psychological tests. The questions include your motives for being a child minder, how you will educate the children (e.g. toilet training, personal hygiene) and what sort of activities you propose. The hygiene of the premises where children are to be looked after (i.e. your home) is inspected and the surface area is calculated, as a minimum area is required for each child. There must also be a separate, isolated room where children may rest. Finally there's a visit by a medical officer to ensure that your vaccinations are up to date and, if you're lucky, you will be authorised to carry out your activity by the Direction Départementale des Affaires Sanitaires et Sociales (DDASS). You will thereafter be subject to regular checks by DDASS staff.

You must have a vocation to be a child minder, as your earnings can hardly be called generous! Depending on where you live (i.e. in a big town or in the country) the rate varies between €2.50 and €4 per child per hour. Thus you can expect to earn around €350 per month per child. The parents supply food, drinks and nappies or you can demand a daily fee to cover these expenses, and, of course, you have no travelling expenses. The income is barely enough to make a living, but it could supplement another income.

Further information can be found on 🖥 www.assistante-maternelle.org (in French), including requirements and duties, where and how to find work, and what rates to charge.

13.

LEISURE & TOURISM

France is among the world's most popular tourist destinations, receiving more visitors annually than it has citizens, and numbers are expected to increase further over the coming years. As a high percentage of these visitors are English-speakers, there's considerable opportunity for those with good or fluent English to work in or start businesses in the leisure and tourism industries.

As in many other countries, however, traditional tourism (i.e. flight and hotel accommodation) is in decline, but various kinds of 'alternative' tourism are on the increase, including 'green tourism' (le tourisme vert) – get-away-from-it all, back-to-nature detox holidays; activity holidays, e.g. walking and mountain biking; visits to theme parks; all-inclusive holidays, e.g. Center Parcs and Club Méditérannée; and themed holidays, e.g. cookery, painting or writing courses.

France's varied terrain, including hundreds of miles of coastline and river, countless lakes and half a dozen major mountain ranges, lends itself to active tourism and sports of all kinds. Another growth area is gymnasia and health clubs, which have mushroomed in recent years and can now be found in most towns. Some first class hotels also have fitness rooms, and dance, training and exercise classes are provided by sports centres and clubs throughout France. All these provide opportunities for fitness trainers, dance teachers and other exercise specialists. This chapter looks at the qualifications and experience required to become a sports instructor and dance teacher. If you plan to start a 'fishy business' in France, here are some tips on choosing, stocking and maintaining a lake for fishing.

Leisure and tourism encompasses organising holidays for foreigners or French people. You might find work as a holiday representative, although this is rarely a way or making a living long-term, a tour operator or a travel agent, or you may buy or start a campsite or colonie de vacances. This chapter also includes case studies of expatriates who have run a holiday company and a campsite. Finally, as the French are becoming increasingly keen on going to shows and exhibitions, we look at an event organising business started by two Swedish women.

Whether you're interested in sports or fitness instruction, in active or other kinds of tourism, in event organising or any other leisure-related job, the important ingredients are experience, professionalism and – as ever – finding a gap in the market. The French Government Tourist Office (FGTO) and other tourist offices are an excellent source of information about leisure and sporting activities. The French Government Tourist Office (FGTO) or Maison de la France is a mine of information and has offices in Austria, Belgium, Brazil, Canada, Denmark, Finland, Germany, Hungary, Ireland, Italy, Japan, Luxembourg, the Netherlands, Norway, Portugal, Spain, Sweden, Switzerland, the UK and the US. For details visit the FGTO website (🖳 www.francetourism.com). The FGTO publishes a free brochure, France for Active Holidays, describing many of France's sports attractions, plus a range of other sports information. Many publications promoting special sports events and listing local sports venues are available from regional and local tourist offices.

SPORTS INSTRUCTORS

As noted above, France is a sporting paradise. There's windsurfing on the west coast, rafting in the south-east, rugby in the south-west, sailing in Brittany, skiing and other winter sports in the Jura, Vosges and Massif Central, as well as in the Alps and the Pyrenees, and cycling, golf, hiking, horse riding, mountain biking, paragliding, squash and tennis in most parts of the country. If you're skilled in a sport of almost any kind and are looking to take advantage of France's climate and lifestyle, it's worth researching this increasingly popular sector.

Research

General information about sports in France can be obtained from the Direction du Temps Libre et de l'Education Populaire, Direction des Sports, 78 rue Olivier de Serres, 75739 Paris Cedex 15 (☎ 01 40 45 90 00), as well as from FGTOs (see above). The all-sports daily newspaper L'Équipe, which publishes fixtures, results and details of all sports events in France, plus major events abroad, may also be a useful source of information and contacts. Each sport has a national federation or association, all of which are listed on the website of the Ministère de la Jeunesse, des Sports et de la Vie Associative (🖳 www.jeunesse-sports.gouv.fr – click on 'Fédérations sportives' and go to the drop-down lists at the foot of the page).

Qualifications

To be a sports instructor (*éducateur sportif*) in France, you require a Brevet d'Etat d'Educateur Sportif (BEES) or an equivalent foreign qualification. No previous experience or other qualifications are required.

There's a core curriculum for all sports, dance and gym instructors, followed by specialised study for particular types of activity. The core curriculum, known as la partie commune, involves studies in biology and other sciences, sports regulation, sports psychology and communication skills, plus first aid training. Specialised study (*la partie spécifique*) covers the specific techniques, training and teaching methods, and regulations relating to a particular activity. As a guide, the following training and testing is required for ski instructors:

- 80 hours' preliminary training and a preliminary ability test;
- A 20-day initiation course;
- A technical ability test;
- Exam for the Brevet National de Secourisme;
- 160 hours' training in technique, safety procedures, teaching skills and safety;
- A safety test;
- 160 hours' training in special techniques (e.g. off-piste skiing) and foreign languages;
- A final exam.

All this can take more than two years to complete. And when you have your qualification, there's no guarantee of a good income or even of a job. If you can find freelance work with the Ecole du Ski Français (🖳 www.esf.net), for example, you can earn a reasonable living, but with the Union Nationale des Centre Sportifs de Plein Air (UCPA, 🖥 www.ucpa.com), you're more likely to be paid the minimum wage.

Training is organised on a regional basis by the Association Régionale aux Métiers du Sport et des Loisirs and locally by Organismes de Formation aux Métiers du Sport et des Loisirs. Courses cost around €1,500.

DANCE TEACHERS

There are also opportunites for instructors of indoor activities, such as gym and dance, which require similar qualifications and experience to those for sports instructors (see above). To become a dance teacher, you need a *Diplôme d'Etat (DE)* or equivalent foreign qualification. A *DE* requires 1,000 hours' training, including study of music history and performance and teaching theory and practice, which normally takes two years. You must already have a *Baccalauréat or Diplôme d'Etudes Musicales (DEM)* or equivalent foreign qualification, or a recognised dance award, and pass the *examen d'aptitude technique (EAT)* in jazz, classical or contemporary dance. Further information can be found on 🖥 www.culture.gouv.fr/culture/ infos-pratiques/formations/musique-formation.htm and 🖥 www.culture.fr/ culture/dmdts/charte_enseignement.htm.

FISHING

Fishing (especially carp fishing) is a popular leisure activity in France and, if you have relevant knowledge and experience and are seeking an outdoor lifestyle, you might consider buying a property with a lake or river frontage and selling fishing permits. Indeed, this is an increasingly popular option among foreigners seeking to settle in France and make a living there. There are estimated to be up to 30 British-owned fishing lakes within a few hours' drive of Calais, for example.

Although not particularly well known internationally, France is a paradise for fishermen, with 240,000km (150,000mi) of rivers and streams, and 120,000 hectares (300,000 acres) of lakes and ponds, in addition to its 4,800km (3,000mi) of coastline. There's excellent fishing in rivers, lakes and ponds throughout France, many of which are stocked annually with trout, grayling and pike. Fishing (*pêche*) is enjoyed regularly by around 4 million French anglers and irregularly by some 20 per cent of the population, as well as by foreign tourists and fishing fanatics.

Rivers are divided into two categories. The first category (*première catégorie* or *salmonidés dominants*) covers headwaters and rivers suitable for salmon, trout and grayling, where maggots are banned as bait. The second category (*deuxième catégorie* or *salmonidés non dominants*) usually includes the lower stretches of rivers populated mainly by coarse fish, where bait can include practically anything except fish-eggs.

Almost all inland waters, from the tiniest streams to the largest rivers and lakes, are protected fishing areas. Fishing rights may be owned by a private landowner, a fishing club or the state, but many of the best fishing waters are in private hands.

Choosing a Lake

Around two-thirds of French lakes are man made as a result of gravel works, although most are mature lakes with surrounding trees, etc. A few are purpose-built for fishing, possibly with a dam to control water levels. The first thing to establish, if you're planning to operate a fishing business, is whether a lake is public or private. If it's fed by a river, it's likely to be classified as public, in which case your business will be subject to restrictions, you will need a licence and night fishing may be prohibited, although if a lake existed before 1829 (don't ask why!) it's exempt from restrictions. If in doubt (and even if you think you're sure), you should check the status of a lake with the Service de Police de l'Eau et de la Pêche of your local Direction Départementale de l'Agriculture.

For a lake to be viable, it should cover at least 6ha (15 acres), as you need 1ha of water per fisherman and groups of six are popular. It must also be at least 1.5m (5ft) and preferably no more than 3.5m (12ft) deep. It's essential that a lake is full all year round and not only in wet periods; and ideally, it will be fed by a spring, as it's less likely to suffer if there's a drought. On the other hand, a lake that's liable to be flooded by a nearby river, with consequent loss of stock and 'contamination' (or, worse, pollution) of the water, is to be avoided. A mature, secluded lake, preferably with an island or islands, is the most desirable. Obviously, there should be no overhead cables or other hazards around a lake. If there's a dam at one end of the lake, check its condition and that sluice gates operate effectively. If a lake already has fish in it, you should check that these are compatible with the fish you intend to stock.

If you want to offer week-long holidays, you must provide some sort of accommodation or at least camping facilities (see page 361). These might consist merely of showers and a septic tank into which campers can empty toilets, but even these require electricity and mains water, which it may be costly to provide, particularly to a remote site. If there's a property on the site or you can afford (and obtain permission) to build one, you may be able to provide B&B or even gîte accommodation.

A lake that's miles from anywhere may seem the ideal spot for a tranquil fishing holiday, but remember that your customers won't be fishing 24 hours a day (not all of them, anyway) and will want to be within easy reach of shops, restaurants and other facilities.

Owing to the growing popularity of this sector, suitable lakes – particularly in northern France – are becoming scarce, although they're still available, particularly in Limousin and eastern France. Bear in mind, however, that most anglers travel by car (in order to be able to transport their equipment) and don't want to drive more than three or four hours to their destination; if you're targeting British fishermen, this restricts your target area for buying. If you choose to buy further south, you may need to provide equipment for fishermen arriving by air.

Financial Considerations

Increased demand for fishing lakes means that prices are soaring – particularly in northern France, where they're rising by some 15 per cent per year and are currently around €25,000 per hectare (2.47 acres). Add to this the cost of stocking a lake: it can cost €35,000 or more to stock a 6ha lake with good quality fish, although you should only need to stock it once, particularly if you apply a 'catch and release' policy.

You can expect to charge between around €300 and €600 per person per week, depending on the season, which is normally from March to May and from mid-August to mid-November, sometimes without a break in the summer. Obviously, you will have little, or no, income during the remaining three months of the year – especially if the lake is frozen!

On a large lake or river, particularly if it has an island or islands, you may wish to offer boats for hire, which will provide additional income. Note, however, that boats require regular maintenance, which can be time-consuming and expensive, and you may need additional public liability insurance.

You may be eligible for subsidies if you also breed fish and, therefore, classify as a fish farm, although this may involve you in a completely different set of regulations, restrictions and requirements – not to mention extra work!

Maintenance

Lakes themselves generally require little maintenance, although you may need to control water rats or coypus (*ragondin*), which can tunnel into the banks, causing them to leak or collapse. However, the surrounding land obviously needs tending, and trees will need regular pruing (*élaguer*). If there are wild animals such as deer or boar in the area, you may need to surround the lake with a fence, as they can damage trees and banks. A fence may also deter anyone wanting to fish without a permit. In fact, you're likely to have little spare time, even in winter, when you will be busy with jobs that cannot be done while fishing is in progress, e.g. chainsawing!

Information

Further information about fishing in France can be obtained from the Conseil Supérieur de la Pêche, 16 avenue Louison Bobet, 94120 Fontenay-sous-Bois Cedex (☎ 01 45 14 36 00, 💻 www.csp.ecologie.gouv.fr) and the Union Nationale pour la Pêche en France, 17 rue Bergère, 75009 Paris (☎ 01 48 24 96 00, 💻 www.unpf.fr). A brochure, Angling in France, is available from French Government Tourist Offices in a number of countries and there's a book entitled Angling in France – Pêche Française by Phil Pembroke.

A number of estate agents specialise in waterside properties and land with lakes, including Devon International (☎ 03 29 80 49 83, 💻 www.relocatefrance. com), Gascony French Properties (☎ 05 62 09 83 88, 💻 www.gascony-french-property.com), which deals in this type of property in all parts of France, and Waterside Properties International (UK ☎ 01903-850017, 💻 www.waterside properties-int.co.uk).

HOLIDAY REPRESENTATIVES

Working as a holiday representative (a 'rep') isn't often a reliable way of making a living. The work is usually seasonal, the pay is low, and by the nature of the job you're required to live and work away from home. There are permanent positions available, e.g. as resort managers, and you may be able to set up home nearby so that it becomes a 'regular' job.

One of the leading holiday companies in France is Club Méditérannée (🖥 www. clubmed.com and 🖥 www.clubmed.fr). Among its 120 worldwide resorts are two in France: at Forges-les-Eaux in Upper Normandy and at Cargèse in Corsica.

TRAVEL AGENCY

Setting up a travel agency (*agence de voyages*) in France is anything but straightforward. To become a registered travel agent (and you cannot operate without registering), you must have the appropriate qualification, which is a Brevet de Tourisme or foreign equivalent, plus at least three years' experience as a *cadre* in an agency. Note, however, that it can take years even to become a *cadre*. The only possible short-cut to setting up an agency is to buy an existing business and 'employ' the previous owner for three years, which may be possible if he's on the point of retirement. You must also pay a deposit (*caution bancaire*) of at least €99,000 in order to register the business.

If you can meet these requirements, you should obviously choose your location carefully. It's estimated that a travel agency requires a potential clientele (i.e. local population) of between 8,000 and 9,000 to be viable. Therefore, if a town of 20,000 inhabitants already has two agencies, it's unlikely that you will succeed there. The travel agency business is unstable and subject to the vagaries of the world economy and tourism trade, which can be unsettled overnight by a terrorist attack or the outbreak of a contagious disease, for example. To be successful, you must be flexible and innovative and offer other, related services, such as organising local tours (especially if you're in a popular tourist area) and handling business trips for local companies, as well as be constantly on the look-out for new markets and tourist destinations.

As with estate agency (see page 268), it's possible to work on a self-employed basis as a travel agency representative, although you must still have the appropriate qualification, but it isn't common for agencies to use reps.

The French national travel agency association, the Syndicat National des Agents de Voyages, 15 Place du Général Catroux, 75017 Paris (☎ 01 44 01 99 90, 🖥 www. snav.org), offers support and advice to members and may be able to provide information to would-be travel agents. Membership isn't obligatory.

TOUR OPERATORS

As Europe's premier holiday destination, France offers opportunities for people who want to organise tours, whether they be wine or cultural tours; canal cruises; sailing, cycling or walking holidays; painting or creative writing holidays; or any of a hundred other specialised activities. This might sound like a relaxing and enjoyable way to make a living, but, as with any business, success depends on thorough market research, expertise and hard work.

CASE STUDY 34

David and Lynne Hammond founded a London-based employee communications business – producing house newspapers and journals, organising intranet communications, conducting employee surveys and creating team-building events – developing it over 18 years to a strength of some 25 people. However, they lived in Welwyn, 25 miles north of London and increasingly felt the strain of a 90-minute commute twice a day on unreliable trains.

They had visited France extensively over 20 years, loved the quality of life and enjoyed the variety of the countryside, particularly the food and wines of Burgundy. "In France," notes David, "people don't confuse quality of life with standard of living." Lynne had excellent French, David less so, but improving. They decided that David's marketing and communications skills could combine with Lynne's passionate interest in food and wine in what their research suggested was a gap in the market: small-scale, short, personally conducted wine tours. Burgundy Discovery was launched in July 2003, around three months after their arrival in France.

The tours are typically for one or two days and for parties of up to six people, and involve visits to a variety of growers, with tasting of around 20 red and white village, regional and *premier cru* wines. So far the venture has attracted parties from 12 different countries, including France; tours are normally conducted in English, but also in French. The Hammonds have been delighted by the enthusiasm of those who have taken the tours and the local wine growers whom they visit. The latter rapport has enabled the Hammonds to develop an associated business in which the wines of these small growers, rarely available outside the immediate area, can be sold securely over the internet. David has also branched out into writing articles and participating in conferences on business start-ups in France.

"It's great to be running a business we're passionate about, in a new country and in a new language," says David. "We relish the challenge. Our commute to work is now a gentle drive through spectacular vineyards to collect our clients from Beaune, Mercurey or Meursault – a far cry from waiting on a cold wind-swept platform at Welwyn North for the late-running 7.18am to King's Cross!"

They key to starting a business in France, David believes, is to be willing to take and pay for good advice: "It's vital to seek out a good French accountant who can advise on the most appropriate business structure (see page 123) and handle the paperwork. It's a false economy to try to do the latter yourself. The chamber of commerce is a good source of advice and everyone should pay a visit to their *mairie*. The key points about running a successful business in France are to make sure that you have sufficient money to live on for twice as long as you think; to research thoroughly your chosen location and business idea; to be honest about your strengths and weaknesses; and to make sure you're having fun and making a profit."

In addition to these points, the following dos and don'ts have been adapted from check-lists that David uses in his articles and seminar presentations.

- **Do** focus on one main business idea and invest in its success.
- **Do** build a network of contacts across French and expatriate communities.
- **Do** be ready to drop a product or service if it's unlikely to produce long-term business.
- **Do** be willing to invest in marketing every year.
- **Do** speak French.
- **Don't** flit from one idea to another.
- **Don't** compromise on quality.
- **Don't** confuse income with profit – there's always an unexpected cost around the corner.
- **Don't** be tempted to cut corners or operate illegally or without the necessary permissions.
- **Do** celebrate success – if you aren't here for fun and profit, why are you here?

CAMPSITES

Camping and caravanning are extremely popular, with both the French and the many thousands of tourists who flock to France each year to spend their holidays in the open air. The French have elevated *le camping* to a high level of sophistication and chic and are the most camping-conscious nation in Europe, with over 11,500 campsites, including over 2,000 rural and farm sites. France is also Europe's largest market in camper vans (*camping-car*), with around 18,000 vehicles sold annually.

If you have appropriate experience and want an outdoor lifestyle, you may be tempted to set up or buy a campsite (*camping*). If so, you must be physically strong, as maintaining a site is hard work (and you may be faced with unruly holidaymakers), and have plenty of money to invest – or risk taking out a large loan – as campsites, particularly those with permanent 'mobile' homes, are expensive. Fluent French is, of course, almost essential, but a knowledge of other languages – particularly Dutch – is an advantage.

When choosing a location for your campsite (if you aren't buying an existing site), you must not only find out what other sites are in the vicinity but whether these are privately or publicly owned. Many French campsites are owned by the local authority, whose aim is to attract holidaymakers to the area, and are therefore non-profit-making, which may make it impossible for you to compete with their prices; and you may be highly unpopular with the authority if you try!

You must decide whether to offer tents, caravans, mobile homes or bungalows for hire, some of which may be suitable for winter accommodation, which will provide welcome additional income.

Regulations

Needless to say, there are numerous rules and regulations to be observed when setting up and operating a campsite. Unless a new site accommodates fewer than 20 people (i.e. has only around six pitches), which it must have if you're to make a living from it, you must obtain planning permission, which is arranged via the local *mairie* and granted (or not) by the departmental Direction de l'Equipement (DDE). You cannot set up a campsite anywhere: only designated land may be used, and it must obviously be reasonably flat and grassed and there must be good access for vehicles (i.e. more than a dirt track that will become a quagmire after every shower).

Each pitch (*emplacement*) must be at least 150m^2, and there must be trees not only surrounding the site, but also within it to provide shade. As well as washing facilities (*bloc sanitaire*), you must provide drinking water taps, rubbish disposal facilities and a shelter for campers if their tents are blown or washed away by a storm. They must also have access to your home, which must, therefore, be nearby. You may not be required to provide access and facilities for the disabled, but failing to do so may limit the site's appeal. If you want to attract camper van owners, you also need electricity 'hook-up' (*branchement*) points and, therefore, an electricity supply with a high power rating, which is expensive to install and maintain (annual standing charges are over €1,000).

Classification

When you apply for permission to set up a campsite, you are awarded a classification by the *préfecture* according to the facilities you plan to offer (subject, of course, to their materialising). The most basic site is classified as an *aire naturelle de camping*; anything more luxurious is a *camp de tourisme*. The latter are classified from one to four stars, as shown in the table below. The table also shows approximate costs per person per night during high season, including camping or caravan space, car parking and use of facilities, which will give you an idea of likely income.

Star Rating	Price Range (€)	Standard
****	5 – 7	*Très grand confort* (luxury)
***	4 – 6	*Grand confort* (high)
**	3 – 5	*Confort* (medium)
*	2.5 – 3	*Confort moyen* (basic)

To achieve a four-star rating, you must be able to offer a comfortable, low-density site with a range of amenities and electricity hook-ups for at least one-third of pitches. The site must have a range of indoor recreation areas, a sauna, washing machines, shops, lock-up storage for valuables, and a wide variety of sports facilities. These usually include a swimming pool (outdoor and/or indoor) and tennis courts, and may also include facilities for golf or crazy golf, volleyball, cycling, table-tennis, trampolining, canoeing, fishing and boating. A large site must usually have at least one restaurant and bar. Note that there are new regulations regarding the installation of communal swimming pools, which must be fenced or covered or fitted with alarms; details are provided in *Renovating & Maintaining Your French Home* (Survival Books – see page 419).

Three-star sites are roughly the same as four, but with slightly fewer amenities, less camping space, and fewer electricity hook-ups, e.g. just 10 per cent of spaces. Only basic amenities such as toilets, hot and cold water, public telephone and electric razor power points are provided at one and two-star sites. Note that mobile homes aren't permitted on some sites.

There's a further classification scale, which determines the length of time a site may stay open: a *camp de tourisme aire naturelle* may open six months in the year, whereas a *camp de tourisme saisonnier* must be open for no more than two months, although it can have a higher density of pitches. On a *camp de loisirs*, pitches are rented long-term, i.e. for a month or more.

Gîtes de France, La Maison des Gîtes de France et du Tourisme Vert, 59 rue Saint-Lazare, 75439 Paris Cedex 09 (☎ 01 49 70 75 75, 🖳 www.gites-de-france.fr) has its own classification system, using 'ears of corn' (*épi*) instead of stars, and there are other networks you can join, including the following:

- Airotels, Club Airotel, BP3, 64210 Bidart (☎ 05 59 41 24 64, 🖳 www.airotels.com), which has around 60 campsites in France;

- Camping Qualité, 29 rue du Patisseau, 44210 Bornic (☎ 02 40 82 57 63), which has around 220 sites throughout France;

- Sites et Paysages de France, chemin des Bosses-Orouet, 85160 Saint-Jean-de-Monts (☎ 08 20 20 46 46, 🖳 www.sites-et-paysages.com), which has around 50 members.

The most lavish campsites are listed by Castels et Camping Caravaning, CP 3751, 56037 Vannes Cedex (☎ 02 97 42 57 12, 🖳 www.les-castels.com), which has around 50 sites in the grounds of beautiful chateaux or manors or in exceptional natural settings.

If you run a farm, with a campsite attached, the site can be classified as a *camping en ferme d'accueil*, which is determined by the local Chambre d'Agriculture; details can be found on a dedicated site run by the Chambres d'Agriculture (🖳 www.bienvenue-a-la-ferme.com). However, running a campsite and a farm may be more than you can cope with.

Costs

The rates you can charge are determined largely by your star rating and the facilities you offer (see above). You can usually charge more in high season and could charge extra for the use of showers, sports facilities and other amenities, such as ironing facilities or use of a freezer, although this doesn't usually go down well with campers! It's preferable to run an on-site shop, bar or restaurant or rent canoes or bicycles, which provide a needed service for customers and generate additional income for you.

Needless to say, running a campsite is a highly seasonal business; you may even be limited as to the number of months the site can be open each year (see **Classification** above). It's generally reckoned that each pitch must be occupied for at least 30 nights per year to make a site viable.

Grants are available from certain Conseils Généraux, depending on whether tourism is encouraged in the area, and Gîtes de France (see above).

Marketing

There's a plethora of campsite guides, in which you can be listed (for a fee), including Alan Rogers' *Good Camps Guide, France* (Deneway Guides), the *Michelin Green Guide – Camping and Caravanning* (Michelin), *Caravan and Camping in France* by Frederick Tingey (Mirador), and *Camping à la Ferme* published by Gîtes de France. It's obviously worthwhile setting up a website, but the key is to have it linked with as many other sites as possible so that it comes near the top of the list when an internet search is run.

Information

Information about campsites is available from the Fédération Française de Camping et de Caravaning (FFCC), 78 rue de Rivoli, 75004 Paris (☎ 01 42 72 84 08, ☐ www.ffcc.fr), which publishes a magazine, a number of camping guides and the official regulations relating to campsites (*textes officiels*), and the Camping Club de France, 5 bis rue Maurice Rouvier, 75014 Paris (☎ 01 58 14 01 23, ☐ www.campingclub.asso.fr), as well as via the internet (e.g. ☐ www.campingfrance.com/fr). Related information (e.g. about visitor numbers to a particular area) can be obtained from the Agence Française de l'Ingénierie Touristique, 23 place de Catalogne, 75685 Paris Cedex 14 (☎ 01 70 39 94 00, ☐ www.www.afit-tourisme.fr), the Fédération Nationale de l'Hôtellerie de Plein-Air, 105 rue Lafayette, 75010 Paris (☎ 01 48 78 13 77, ☐ www.fnhpa-france.com), which publishes a journal called *L'Hôtellier de Plein Air*, and Gîtes de France (see above).

CASE STUDY 35

Mary Cox and her partner came to France on a caravan holiday in 1981. They were so taken by what they found on the Var coast that they returned the following year, having given up their jobs in a bank and lighting design/installation business in Beckenham, south London, to work for a UK-based letting agency. Two years later they started letting the first of their own mobile homes. On a visit to the Val Rose site to carry out repairs, they found it very rundown and the owner, having just seen a sale fall through, keen to unload it. Mary and her partner decided to take it on and the subsequent 16 years of hard work have been devoted to building up the facilities, adding a heated pool, restaurant, bar, shop and games areas and arranging entertainment in season, to the point that the Val Rose is now a three-star grand confort site.

"We had numerous problems that we hadn't envisaged or planned on financially," remembers Mary. "These included sewerage and water passing through the same drains and dangerous electricity installations. We still work each year on improvements."

Other early problems were school French and bureaucracy, but they found that working with French staff improved the former and getting to know people in the area and the mairie eased the latter. "We find it's better to live like the French," says Mary, who advises anyone planning to work in France to live there before selling up at home to see how easily you find it to adapt to the French system, way of life and customs.

HOLIDAY CAMPS

Like the Americans, the French are keen to pack their children off to summer holiday camp (*colonie de vacances*), where they can indulge in supervised outdoor pursuits, and these are encouraged by the government. Needless to say, however, the setting-up and running of a holiday camp are beset with rules and regulations and you must have appropriate qualifications and excellent references, even though the French are generally less paranoid about the likelihood of child molestation than, say, the British. As with campsites (see above), the land must be designated for use as a holiday camp and the necessary infrastructure must be available.

EVENT MANAGEMENT

Organising events, including conferences, exhibitions and concerts, in France obviously requires relevant experience and fluent French. Event organising is generally a precarious business, particularly in terms of cash flow, as you must usually pay a large deposit to book a venue before you're able to bank any money from delegates or exhibitors. If you're contemplating this line of business, it may therefore be wise to start it as an adjunct to another activity, as Carin Peirano and Sabine Karlberg did.

CASE STUDY 36

Carin Peirano came to France from Sweden when her French husband took a job in Sophia Antipolis near Antibes, the Riviera's answer to Silicon Valley, in September

2000. For the first year she continued working from home for her former company, which supplies educational services for the insurance industry, and settling her two children, then aged six and three into their new environment.

She saw an opportunity for managing events in an area which frequently hosts exhibitions, conferences and seminars. Meanwhile her Franco-Swedish friend Sabine Karlberg, who had been providing a free service, helping other foreigners to find houses and place their children in schools, was considering putting her expertise on a commercial basis. They decided to join forces and founded Azurplus Relocation from scratch (see page 275). They both have Swedish business degrees and speak French, English, German and Swedish, so language was not among their problems.

On the event management side, they've run a number of functions for corporate and private clients and, through collaboration with the Swedish Film Institute, now manage that body's magnificent sea-view apartment in Cannes, handling the rental schedule.

14.

OTHER JOBS

There are numerous other types of job that can be undertaken by foreigners in France, some of which are investigated in this chapter. Others include computer and software training services, satellite installation, piano tuning, hairdressing, car repairs and servicing, and running a pet parlour or a kennel or cattery. There's scope for those offering foreign luxury goods – even (or perhaps especially) in Paris and other major cities – such as furniture, boats and cars. Qualifications, requirements and procedures for setting up vary from job to job, but most situations are covered by the general information in **Part One**.

ARTS & CRAFTS

A number of people were interviewed during the preparation of this book who had tried to make a living making and selling paintings, sculpture, jewellery and other artistic products, and all of them said that they'd found it impossible. To succeed, you must be either lucky or outstandingly talented (usually both). Nevertheless, arts and crafts can be a useful (and enjoyable) sideline if you have the talent and are good at marketing, and one interviewee managed to make a living in a highly specialised area, although even this was fraught with problems (see **Case Study 37** below). Note that itinerant dealers (working in fairs or markets, etc.) must have a certificate, obtainable from the *Préfecture de Police*.

CASE STUDY 37

Barry Lester served an apprenticeship in the motor industry before finding work in sales and insurance. The skills he developed in these fields stood him in good stead when, in 1971, he turned what had started as a hobby and developed into a spare-time cottage industry into a full-scale business: the design and construction of highly-detailed scale models of the kind sought by specialist collectors and museums the world over. While most of his subjects are classic cars, he has also designed and made models of utility vehicles, trains, soldiers and many other items, either to his own designs and moulds or to those of others. His work has received international awards and he's recognised as one of the pioneers in this field. As well as producing finished models, he has designed and produced similar items in kit form that enthusiasts can assemble themselves.

It was while working in Bournemouth, Dorset, that Barry met French-born Geneviève, a fellow-divorcee then working as a French teacher and now his second wife. They both wanted to start a new life and decided to move to France. Their choice of location was governed by the fact that they needed to be able to get to and fro easily for brief spells while they were planning the details of their move. For that reason, they hit on Lanhelin, a village between St Malo and Rennes in Ille-et-Vilaine, Brittany, to which they moved in 1993.

They immediately had problems with French bureaucracy, including the familiar Catch 22 that you cannot register with the relevant chamber of commerce until you have a business bank account and you cannot have such an account until you're

---

registered. Part of the problem was that nobody concerned had any understanding of the business Barry was in and so had little or no advice or help to offer. "We met a man who claimed to have retired from a high-ranking job in a Chambre des Métiers and said he would help," recalls Barry. "He just dug an even bigger hole for us, and Geneviève then had to do even more work to get us out of the mess!" A visit from a member of the Chambre des Métiers staff sounded promising: "He was going to do wonders for us. But, of course, he was completely out of his depth and could help only bakers, plumbers, electricians and the like." To this day, Barry is baffled why he wasn't allowed to join the Chambre des Artistes, which might have had greater understanding of his needs and problems.

"In desperation, we even contacted a notaire in a neighbouring village, thinking that, as he has a Welsh wife, he might be sympathetic. He simply told us that if we didn't like the way things were, we could go back to England, and showed us the door." In contrast, Barry has nothing but praise for the officials he dealt with at the Crédit Agricole bank, who were friendly and helpful – although not with business matters.

The Lesters also had trouble registering the business, obtaining healthcare, re-registering their cars, obtaining residence for Barry and generally finding the money to pay their various dues and the time to get on with their business.

Eventually, however, it was a different problem that forced the Lesters' early retirement. Model-making of the standards of Barry's business is an international trade – he had been accustomed, through most of his working life, to dealing with orders from all over the world – and this makes it vulnerable to counterfeiting: "We would produce a new design and, within six weeks, a cheap copy made in the Far East was on the market. The authorities are keen to intercept unauthorised copies of goods by big names – Nike, Adidas, etc. – but an artisan's livelihood appears to be of no importance whatsoever."

In 1998, Barry and Geneviève closed their business and retired to Port Leucate on the Aude coast, where "we have a beach that even has a pier (unlike Bournemouth) and are within reach of Spain and Italy. Barry now has dual British/French citizenship and has no intention of returning to the UK. He concludes that the British people he knows that have been successful in France have mostly been in the building and allied trades where, like their French counterparts, they can do a lot of work on a cash basis: "You have to pick your intended business very carefully," he adds, "and model-making certainly isn't top of the list!"

FARMING

In recent years, an increasing number of foreigners have purchased farms in France. In general, farmland is cheaper in France than in any other western European country, although it varies considerably: it's prohibitively expensive in some areas (€100,000 or more per hectare in wine-growing areas – see **Vineyards** on page 374), while in others it can cost as little as €1,000 per hectare or even be practically given away with farmhouses. However, b/etween €3,000 and €6,000 per hectare should buy you reasonable land in most parts of France.

Owing to the fact that the population is drifting away from the country into urban areas, the French government encourages the purchase of farmland (see below). However, it isn't easy for foreigners to raise loans from French banks to buy farms and it's common to buy the farm buildings and rent the land.

As in all countries, farming in France is fraught with problems, particularly the vagaries of the weather (e.g. droughts, floods and late frosts), declining food prices and under-capitalisation. **If you're seriously under-capitalised, as many farmers are, your chances of success are remote.** Many foreign farmers have fled with their tails between their legs within a few years, having learnt the reality of French farming the hard way (it isn't for nothing that the French are deserting their farms in droves). **More foreigners have had their fingers burnt buying farms or farming land than any other property-based business venture in France.**

You should also be aware that there's open hostility to foreign farmers in some regions and **there have been a number of reports of foreigners being sold substandard stock and land, and some have even had their crops sabotaged!** Such problems are more likely in remote regions, where the locals are unused to foreigners and are often insular or even xenophobic.

Even if you don't experience this kind of animosity, and despite 'generous' EU subsidies, it can be difficult to make a living from running a farm and you're extremely unlikely to get rich doing so. Farming is also strictly regulated: the purchase of farmland must be approved by SAFER (see **Information** below); you must obtain permission from the Direction Départementale de l'Agriculture et de la Forêt (DDAF) to run a farm (a sample application form can be found on 🖳 www. service-public.fr/formulaires/index.html – click on '*Formulaires pour professionnels*'); and you must of course comply with regulations concerning the use of fertilisers, pesticides and other chemicals.

To register as a farmer, your *centre de formalités des entreprises* (see pages 103 and 137) is the local *chambre d'agriculture*, you must make social security contributions to the Mutuelle Sociale Agricole (MSA, 🖳 www.msa.fr) and, if yours is a small concern, you may qualify for the *micro-BA* tax regime (see **Micro-entreprises** on page 197).

Grants & Subsidies

Farmers aged betwwn 21 and 40 with recognised farming qualifications may qualify for financial incentives to buy farms in France, including government grants and low interest loans, depending on your resources and the area in which you're intending to farm. Grants are between around €8,000 and €35,000, and loans of up to around €100,000 are available. Note, however, that grants are subject to income tax!

To obtain a grant, called a *dotation d'installation aux jeunes agriculteurs* (*DJA*), you must enter into a contract called a *contrat territorial d'exploitation* with ADASEA, 🖳 www.adasea.net). You must produce a three-year financial forecast. Information about grants can be obtained from the relevant regional chamber of agriculture, ADASEA (see above) or the regional office of the Centre National pour l'Aménagement des Structures des Exploitations Agricoles (CNASEA – contact its head office, 7 rue Ernest Renan, BP 1, 92136 Issy-les-Moulineaux Cedex, ☎ 01 46 48 40 00, 🖥 www.cnasea.fr).

French farmers have traditionally been heavily subsidised, by both their own government and the European Union, but there's increasing opposition (particularly from non-EU farmers) to this policy and it's likely that subsidies will be reduced in the coming years.

Information

Information and advice on any aspect of farming can be obtained from departmental Sociétés d'Aménagement Foncier et d'Etablissement Rural (SAFER), which advise and control all transactions of agricultural land in France. For details of local offices contact the Fédération Nationale des Sociétés d'Aménagement Foncier et d'Etablissement Rural (FNSAFER), 3 rue de Turin, 75008 Paris (☎ 01 44 69 86 00, 🖥 www.safer.fr). An English-speaking organisation that helps foreigners buy and manage farms in France is Eurofarms (🖥 www.eurofarms.com). Further information can be found on the websites of the Société de Conseil pour l'Aménagement Foncier Rural (Terres d'Europe-SCAFR, 🖥 www.terresdeurope.net – in English), the French Ministry of Agriculture (🖥 www.agriculture.gouv.fr – in French) and Europe Ruris (🖥 www.europeruris.com – in French and Dutch); the last includes a price guide. The Association pour la Création d'Entreprises (🖥 www.apce.com) publishes a number of booklets about starting a farm in France. The most valuable source of local information is your departmental *chambre d'agriculture* – listed in the yellow pages (the relevant website can be found by typing www.[department name].chambagri.fr, e.g. 🖥 www.loire.chambagri.fr).

CATERING

Despite their reputation for traditionalism (to the point of dogmatism), when it comes to cuisine, the French are increasingly, although gradually, developing a taste for more exotic fare and in particular 'health' foods such as organic (*bio*) and even vegetarian (*végétarien*) and vegan (*végétalien*). **Chapter 7** contains a case history of an English couple who run a successful vegetarian restaurant in Normandy. The supply, production or importation of specialist food products is, therefore, a possible opportunity if you have knowledge and experience in this area.

Another possibility is to set up as a (general) caterer (*traiteur*), preferably with premises where parties and wedding receptions, etc. can be held. The French often use caterers, even for small dinners, and generally prefer to hire a function room or hall for large functions than to go to a restaurant or hotel.

DRINK PRODUCTION

France is obviously famous for its wine, but there are many other regional drinks which might provide an opportunity for making a living, such as armagnac and cognac in the south-west; calvados, cider, perry and *pommeau* in Normandy; *Pineau des Charentes* in Poitou-Charentes; and numerous fortified wine-based drinks, especially in the south. Nevertheless, it's probably French wine production that has the strongest fascination with foreigners wanting to work in this sector.

Running a Vineyard

Many expatriates dream of owning a vineyard and producing their own wine and an increasing number realise their dream (it's estimated that around ten vineyards are bought by British people each year in Languedoc alone) – but only a very few make a success of it. **Buying and operating a vineyard isn't something to be taken lightly, as it requires a lot of hard work and resources.** (Read *The Ripening Sun* by Patricia Atkinson if you don't believe it!) It definitely isn't for those of retirement age, as you must be strong and fit. It's essential to hire experienced staff if you're inexperienced, as it can take years to become a viticulture expert. Nevertheless, if you're successful, the financial rewards can be enormous as a number of Australian, British and Swiss owners can testify.

As with all farming, the weather is the biggest threat to your livelihood: a frost in late spring can destroy your entire grape crop overnight, and heavy rain or, worse, hail in September can ruin the wine. Even the sun can be more damaging than beneficial; the heatwave in 2003 almost cost many *vignerons* their livelihood. There are also weeds, insects, diseases and bacteria to be dealt with. There are restrictions or prohibitions on planting new vines in many areas because of over-production, so if you wish to expand production, it's essential to buy a vineyard that already has the necessary permits.

Availability & Cost

As in other farming sectors, there's a trend towards fewer, larger estates, and the number of small (successful) vineyards has dwindled in recent years. Nevertheless, there are usually vineyards for sale in most wine-producing regions and there have been a number of bargains around in recent years, although you're unlikely to find a *premier cru* Bordeaux or *grand cru* Burgundy property for sale (and, if you did, you would need a king's ransom to buy it!). White wine vineyards are generally cheaper than red wine vineyards.

Vineyard prices vary enormously, e.g. from around €10,000 per hectare for a *vin de pays* vineyard, e.g. in Languedoc, or €15,000 per hectare (2.5 acres) for an *appellation contrôlée* red wine vineyard in an average area, e.g. Bergerac in Dordogne, to over €60,000 per hectare for a good quality vineyard in a more upmarket area, right up to €400,000 per hectare for a premium plot, e.g. in Saint-Emilion in Bordeaux, where prices have trebled in the last decade. A vineyard may cover between 10 and 100 hectares, and in some areas, particularly in the south, you won't find a well-kept vineyard with a property in good condition for under €1 million. The price may include a house and winery, although not current wine stocks, which must usually be purchased separately. A commercial property is likely to be owned by a company, which is cheaper to buy in terms of transaction fees.

There are obviously many expenses to be added to the price of a property, including machinery and equipment (a grape press can cost €50,000 and steel vats €7,500 each), bottles and corks, the printing of labels and, not least, staff. Unless you're taking over a going concern, you should also take into account the delay between making the wine and being able to sell it, which, for anything other than a *primeur*, is usually at least a year and may be three or four years for a premium wine. It can, therefore, be a long time before you earn anything for your labour and a **very** long time before you make a profit, although, if you have time, there are ways of supplementing your income, such as hosting wine tours, running wine-making courses, and even offering accommodation such as bed and breakfast or self-catering apartments.

Vineyards for sale can be found via the internet, e.g. 🖳 www.le-guide.com/ business-sales/index.html. Over 150 French vineyards for sale are listed on the website of a consortium of estate agents, bankers, legal and tax consultants, insurers, land and vineyard experts, oenologists, architects and surveyors, nursery gardeners and vineyard planners called VineaTransaction.com (🖳 www.vineatransaction.com). Other specialist property dealers include the following:

- **GTI Immobilier** (🖳 www.gard-immobilier.com). Estate agent covering Languedoc and Provence, with farms and vineyards for sale.

- **Jurisvin** (🖳 www.jurisvin.fr). Network of *notaires* for vineyard owners and wine makers, including vineyards for sale.

- **Leisure and Land France** (☎ 04 67 90 27 26, 🖳 www.leisureandland.com). Consultants and search agents working on behalf of clients wishing to buy agricultural or commercial property.

- **Propriétés et Domaines** (🖳 www.proprietesetdomaines.com). Farms and vineyards for sale in Provence.

- **Vintage Investments** (☎ 05 53 80 06 94, 🖳 www.vintageinvestments.com).

- **Wine Woman World** (🖳 http://we136.lerelaisinternet.com). Everything you need to know about wine, and vineyards for sale.

Specialist exhibitions such as Bordeaux's biannual VINEXPO (🖳 www.vinexpo.fr), which takes place in June 2007, 2009, etc., and Montpellier's ViniSud (🖳 www. vinisud.org), can be good sources of information about vineyards for sale. The FNSAFER (see **Farming** on page 371) assists foreigners seeking to buy a vineyard in France.

Checks

VineaTransaction recommends that you check the following before buying a vineyard in France:

- That the vine stock form (*fiche d'encépagement*) is up-to-date and certified by the customs department. An Institut National des Appellations d'Origine (INAO) certificate will confirm the AOC classification of vines if there is one.

- The sanitary condition of the vineyard, to detect diseases, etc.;

- The local climatic risks (hail, frost, flooding, etc.);
- The quality of water if the property isn't connected to the mains;
- The condition of the buildings – in particular the presence of asbestos (e.g. in roofs), lead (e.g. in pipes) and termites;
- That planning permission has been obtained for all relevant construction;
- That no major developments are planned locally that could affect the quality of the vines, grapes and wine (e.g. a railway or main road, rubbish dump, gravel pit or wind generators);
- That all installations conform to the appropriate regulations, especially with regard to the treatment of effluent;
- That all equipment is in good condition and that copies of relevant guarantees, leasing arrangements or joint ownership contracts are available;
- That any trade names or trademarks relating to the produce of the vineyard (e.g. the name of the estate or château) are protected by law;
- That the wine that's in stock is of good quality (by professional tasting and laboratory analysis);
- That the vines are in good condition (if you have to replant, bear in mind that it takes at least three years for new vines to produce reasonable wine);
- The contracts of any staff employed on the property, which you must take over when you buy it, and that staff aren't owed any pay, leave or other benefits by the current owner or that there are any outstanding disputes between them;
- Whether the property is contracted to a cooperative and, if so, what are the terms of cancellation (in case you wish to do so);
- Whether the property is tenanted (i.e. the current owner lets land for farming) and, if so, how long the agreement has to run and what are the terms of terminating it (note that a tenant farmer may be entitled to up to 30 per cent of the value of the property in the event of its sale);
- Whether there are any pre-emptive rights to the property or rights of way across it, etc;
- How much, if any, capital gains tax would have to be paid in the event of resale.

When buying a vineyard, ensure that you have **plenty** of spare money: spend only a third of what you have on the property itself, investing another third in improvements and keeping the rest for marketing and unforeseen problems. Good marketing is essential (and some experience of this is highly desirable), and you must have a clear idea of whom you intend to sell your wine to.

A vineyard transaction in France, from the provisional sales agreement to the signature of the bill of sale, usually takes between four and six months (it can take four months just to obtain permission to farm).

Further information about buying a vineyard in France can be obtained from a company specialising in vineyard properties, Vignobles Investissement (☎ 04 67 22 55 52, ✉ adakin@vignobles-investissement.com).

CASE STUDY 38

Karen and Nick Kitchener came to France in 2004 from Cheshire, having been working respectively in software development and property, although they aren't sure what prompted them to do so. "It just seemed logical," says Karen. "We knew France relatively well from holidays there, we liked the attitude to life and the culture (plus, obviously, the wine and food). It's relatively close to England, where we still have family, and we spoke a little French. We also knew that the health service and education were good and reliable."

To that extent their rationale is common to those of many of our contributors. What makes it different was their decision to buy and run a vineyard, although neither of them had the slightest experience in that field. "We'd both been involved in service industries all our working lives," explains Karen. "We wanted to get involved in production, rather than the end of the supply chain. We felt that there would be tremendous satisfaction in producing a product – from start to finish – and knowing that we'd been there every step of the way. Very importantly, we wanted a complete change – one of the primary objectives of moving here."

Their search for a suitable property began in June 2003, following research on the web and with dozens of property agents, initially in Lot-et-Garonne and the Languedoc-Roussillon region. "Nick started making monthly trips, viewing around eight vineyards each day, mainly in the Bergerac area. On one trip, Nick was persuaded to come to Gers (a department we'd never heard of). He recognised the property, called Domaine de Lauroux, as one we'd seen on the web and discounted as too large and rather grim-looking, but was stunned by what he found there."

By July, the search had narrowed down to two properties and Karen came out to help make the final decision. "Domaine de Lauroux won hands down, primarily because the business had to stand on its own two feet – it couldn't afford to be a hobby vineyard. It's a fourth generation vineyard, whose former owner – who wanted to enjoy semi-retirement – has worked with us over the past months as we've built our experience. Nick learns very quickly and, although we've had some problems (weather, filtering, etc.), he has done a wonderful job and is acknowledged by the former owner, other vignerons and our neighbours as making excellent wine. One of his assemblages won a Paris award." As well as tending the vines, harvesting the grapes and bottling on site, the Kitcheners handle their own marketing and now sell in Belgium, Germany and the Netherlands, as well as in France.

Things have not been quite as easy as it may appear. There were timing problems in selling up in England and buying in France, eased by the vendor's willingness to let them move in before the sale was finalised. For ongoing finance, they had to sell the concept – based on a detailed business case – to a bank. "Credibility was also a problem – English people making wine in France is a bit of a joke. We overcame this by getting stuck in: Nick does all the dirty work and doesn't just sit in the office all day."

In the early stages, Karen and Nick found the estate agents very helpful and prepared to be heavily involved. "Other *vignerons* have helped too, and the French customs authorities have been very patient and helped us with the mountains of paperwork," says Karen.

"Language wasn't ever a major problem. The secret seems to be not to surround yourself with other English-speaking people – just get stuck in with the French. But people should learn French before even thinking about coming here. They should also get a good bank and ensure that they have plenty of working capital behind them."

Apart from these basic requirements, Karen suggests that having the right attitude is important: "We found that the French are very willing to help, provided people don't just turn up and behave as if they own the place. Lots of patience is needed, but help will come if you go about seeking it the right way. Don't flaunt things like driving imported cars for months without having them registered in France. Don't muck around with income taxes or customs – unless you want to end up in an overcrowded prison!"

LEGAL & FINANCIAL SERVICES

There are opportunities for qualified lawyers and solicitors to practise in France, most likely with British and English-speaking clients (e.g. house-buying and business set-up), although you must obviously have a high level of French and detailed knowledge of the French legal system, and must of course register with the appropriate authorities.

Financial services, such as tax and mortgage advice, are almost the exclusive preserve of big banks and financial institutions, and independent financial services, including insurance and mortgage brokering, are virtually unknown in France (at least 90 per cent of insurance consultants are salaried employees) and therefore – for the time being, at least – only loosely regulated. It's possible for almost anyone, for example, to buy a franchise (see page 127) to become a personal financial consultant (*courtier de crédit personnel*) or a mortgage broker (*courtier de prêt*), although you obviously need relevant experience (and excellent French) to stand a chance of being successful. If you're offering a share buying and selling service or portfolio management, you need accreditation by the Commission des Opérations de Bourse, the French Stock Exchange watchdog.

LORRY & TAXI DRIVING

To be a heavy goods vehicle (HGV) driver in France, even if you have a foreign HGV certificate, you must obtain a French *poids lourds* licence and a *formation initiale minimale obligatoire* (*FIMO*) qualification, which requires at least four weeks' training. Courses are organised by the Association Française des Transports Routiers Internationaux (AFTRI), 48 rue de la Bienfaisance, 75008 Paris (☎ 01 53 53 02 40, 🖳 www.aftri.com), whose site provides details of the *FIMO* qualification, and the

Fédération Nationale des Transports Routiers (FNTR), 6 rue Ampère, 75017 Paris (☎ 01 44 29 04 29, 🖳 www.fntr.fr); a list of regional offices can be found on the website. Further information about the *FIMO* qualification can be found on the websites of PMOIOUI (🖳 www.pmoioui.com) and Les-Permis (🖳 www.les-permis. com/savoirs/fimo.htm).

Most of the large taxi companies in the cities and large towns are short of drivers who speak foreign languages, which means that taxi driving could be an opportunity for Anglophones with a good level of French. However, there are a number of criteria that must be fulfilled. Taxi drivers are regulated at communal, departmental or national level. You must obtain a certificate proving professional capacity, administrative authorisation from the *mairie* and the *préfecture* to be able to park on public roads, a medical certificate (renewable annually), a trading card, proof of no criminal convictions and a driving licence that you've held for at least two years. You must then undertake a 300 to 400-hour training course covering the theoretical and practical sides of taxi driving.

PERSONAL ASSISTANCE

Many expatriates who aren't qualified to act as estate agents or relocation consultants (see **Chapter 8**) set up businesses offering personal assistance or 'hand-holding' services, which necessarily involve translating and interpreting (and therefore require excellent French), but can also comprise a variety of other activities – some of them quite out of the ordinary.

CASE STUDY 39

A great many foreigners come to France with one business aim in view, only to switch course later on. Often the change of heart comes with the realisation that they're not the only ones to think of converting buildings for letting. Others simply spot a different opportunity and go for it. Few have to create a business without warning. One such is Dianne Clarke-Miller. A teacher, she had been living in Nottingham while tending her mother's final stages of terminal cancer, and renting a property in order to be able to leave for France with her structural engineer husband when the time was right.

The plan had been to do up a 'habitable hovel' as the basis for starting a business based on her husband's construction skills, supported by Dianne's earnings as a teacher of English as a foreign language, in which she had qualified before leaving in England. In the event, five months after they arrived in Charente, in February 2000, they separated, her husband returned to the UK and Dianne was left with the task of earning a living and building a home alone.

She started by making a determined effort to improve her "good O Level" French: "Most people arriving in France think you can pick it up as you go along. This is true to the extent of going to the shops, ordering drinks, etc., but the only way to get a grasp on a language is to work on it." Dianne enrolled in a two-week immersion

---

course, studying all day, doing three hours' homework every evening and staying with a host family under strict instructions to speak only French. "I was forced to knock on (French) doors and tell people who I was. I went to every bingo evening, every dinner, etc. I wrote down words and looked them up frantically every moment of the day. This also involved me in French culture – the way the French really operate. It has given me an extensive vocabulary in argot – the French the French speak, which is quite unintelligible to those taught 'proper' French."

All this provided a useful grounding in what Dianne was to develop as a business: that of being a 'personal assistant' to English-speaking people in France. The work is extremely diverse and ranges from help with quite technical matters to more mundane 'hand-holding' services. "I find builders and translate estimates; I go to the bank to arrange finance for people, to notaires' to act as proxy in buying and selling property and land; I've looked after a client's dogs and taken them to the vet's; I've even introduced young children to their first French school. I may arrange a bank loan in the morning, engage in detective work chasing an artisan who has disappeared with my client's money in the afternoon, then walk a field with a construction expert to assess the boundaries of land whose purchase I'm arranging for a client, before sticking my head into a fosse septique to see if future work will conform to present legislation. I'm currently working with the owners of a number of small businesses who are trying to break into the French market.

"I started this work from scratch, having been asked for assistance, identified the need and advertised the service – also, to be honest, because I got very angry seeing people being given poor advice, ripped off or being promised the world by other intermediaries, only to be left floundering when push came to shove. I now have an international client base spread over three continents for whom I work full time."

Dianne charges all clients a €50 registration fee, which entitles them to ring her mobile phone if they need to be dug out of a hole, need a quick translation, or have urgent need of advice or help. For more detailed work, she charges €30 to €50 per hour, depending on what's required.

"The main obstacle I encountered in starting up the business is the propensity of the French civil service to throw reams of paper at you in an effort to prevent your ever getting an hour's work done in any given day. It's the unwieldiness and pettiness of the way they conduct themselves and the blinkered vision with which they do their job that's most frustrating.

"My advice to anyone tackling anything similar is to decide what you want to do, then do it. Know that you aren't going to earn a fortune doing it, enjoy what you came for – to live in France – and be very glad that you've got through a day and earned a bob.

"I would also suggest that you contact somebody who can speak French fluently and can find their way around the system. This may have a price attached, but I know from the disasters I've been called in to sort out that the price is well worth paying – even if this does sound like a good advert for myself!"

TRANSLATION

It goes without saying that, in order to be a translator, you must have an extremely high level of written French, which comes only with years of study if you aren't fortunate enough to have been brought up bilingual. If you're translating from French to English (which you will be unless you're bilingual), you should note that the majority of French people are reluctant to engage native speakers for this purpose, believing that six years of school English lessons has equipped them to write perfect English (even though they cannot string a sentence together orally). You, therefore, must be a persuasive salesman as well as a skilled translator.

CASE STUDY 40

Dawn Clarke, whom we met in **Chapter 7** (see page 262), now works as a translator, combined with acting as a consultant and intermediary for companies and individuals dealing with French counterparts or bureaucracy. She says that she "fell into the business quite naturally," having studied languages, law, accountancy and marketing. She's also an associate member of the UK Institute of Translation and Interpreting (⌨ www.iti.org.uk), a status that requires intensive study and proven ability.

However, at the time of this change in career path, she hadn't used her translating skills for some time: "When you're setting up a business, the vocabulary needed is vast: from dealing with the plumber and finding out which days rubbish is collected to meetings at the chamber of commerce, the préfecture and the bank – never mind finding where can you get your legs waxed!"

In establishing her business, she certainly felt in need of professional and other help, but didn't find it. Her solution was to work hard at understanding and meeting the requirements of the French bureaucracy and employing the four qualities she reckons are most needed by anyone starting a business here: "patience, patience, patience and determination."

Dawn's other advice is : "Don't think you can just blunder through or work on the black – integrate and learn the language. Do contact someone like me – it will save you money and stress!"

APPENDICES

APPENDIX A: USEFUL ADDRESSES

Contributors

The following is an alphabetical list of the contact details of the contributors to this book who wanted these published, with an indication of where to find their contributions.

Angelbar (☎ 04 79 06 28 76/06 18 77 80 84, 💻 www.theangelbar.com); Angel Property (✉ info@property-angel.com, 💻 www.property-angel.com); Angel Accommodation (💻 www.theangelsden.com, www.angelski.com). Dani Corbet. (See **Chapter 7**.)

Antibes Books (☎ 04 93 34 74 11, ✉ books@riviera.fr). Heidi Lee. (See **Chapter 9**.)

SARL Apollo (☎ 04 68 76 05 83, ✉ contactapollo@aol.com, 💻 www.apollo-hoskins.com). Mark Hoskins. (See **Chapter 8**.)

Aude France Property (☎ 04 68 24 02 94, ✉ sam@aude-france-property.com, 💻 www.aude-france-property.com). Mark & Sam Mooney. (See **Chapter 8**.)

Azurplus Relocation (☎ 06 23 37 01 24/06 76 08 37 19, 📠 06 15 35 00 03, ✉ azurplus@wanadoo.fr). Sabine Karlberg & Carin Peirano. (See **Chapter 8**.)

Bonnes Pages (☎ 05 65 10 87 28/06 73 54 59 40, ✉ methos02@wanadoo.fr). Karen & Mark Powell. (See **Chapter 9**.)

Bouclier Vêtements Professionnels (☎ 05 53 06 46 56, 📠 05 63 06 04 22, ✉ boucliervetpro@wanadoo.fr). Danny Lowe. (See **Chapter 9**.)

Burgundy Discovery (☎ 03 85 49 51 34, ✉ david@burgundydiscovery.com, 💻 www.burgundydiscovery.com). David & Lynne Hammond. (See **Chapter 13**.)

Camping Val Rose (☎ 04 94 66 81 36, ✉ camping-valrose@wanadoo.fr, 💻 www.campingvalrose.fr). Mary Cox. (See **Chapter 13**.)

La Cardère (☎ 03 85 74 83 11, 📠 03 85 74 82 25, ✉ la.cardere@wanadoo.fr, 💻 www.la-cardere.com). Claude & Danielle Rochat. (See **Chapter 10**.)

La Cave d'Eymet, 23 place Gambetta, 24500 Eymet. Mitch & Shaun Leake. (See **Chapter 13**.)

Dawn Clarke, ICT (☎ 05 55 25 21 66/06 08 69 55 29, 💻 dawn@worldonline.fr). Intermediary, consultant, translator. (See **Chapter 14**.)

Dianne Clarke-Miller (☎ 05 45 39 07 87, 📠 05 45 68 34 70, ✉ dianne.clarke-miller@wanadoo.fr). (See **Chapter 14**.)

Cookinfrance (☎ 05 53 30 24 05/06 22 65 57 89, ✉ cookinfrance1@yahoo.co.uk, 💻 www.cookinfrance.com). Fred Fisher. (See **Chapter 10**.)

Couleurs de France Ltd (☎ UK 0871-210 6550/France 05 61 09 54 39/06 75 56 15 93, 🖶 05 61 09 54 39, ✉ info@couleurs-de-france.com, 🖳 www.couleurs-de-france.com). Property agency. Linda & Max Rano. (See **Chapter 8**.)

Cours et Traductions (☎ 06 86 23 29 82, 🖳 burgess.susan@wanadoo.fr). Sue Burgess. (See **Chapter 10**.)

La Crème Anglaise (☎ shop 02 97 28 02 03/*gîtes* 02 97 28 04 45, ✉ LaCremeAnglaise@aol.com. 🖳 www.la-creme-anglaise.co.uk). Mel & Steve Willey. (See **Chapter 9**.)

Rachael Dickens DO MROF (🖳 www.englishosteopath.com). Osteopath. (See **Chapter 12**.)

Domaine de Lauroux (☎ 05 62 08 56 76, 🖶 05 62 08 57 44, ✉ karen@lauroux.com or nick@lauroux.com, 🖳 www.lauroux.com). Karen & Nick Kitchener. (See **Chapter 14**.)

En Famille Overseas (☎/🖶 04 68 91 49 90, ✉ Marylou.toms@wanadoo.fr, 🖳 www.enfamilleoverseas.co.uk). Mary-Louise Toms. (See **Chapter 10**.)

Le Fleuray Hotel & Restaurant (☎ 02 47 56 09 25, 🖶 02 47 56 93 97, ✉ lefleurayhotel@wanadoo.fr, 🖳 www.lefleurayhotel.com). Hazel & Peter Newington. (See **Chapter 7**.)

Gîte Courses (☎ 05 45 78 65 80, ✉ timdwilliams@wanadoo.fr, 🖳 www.gitecomplexes.co.uk). Chloe & Tim Williams. (See **Chapter 7**.)

Gîte/Golf (☎ 03 94 55 56/06 22 56 19 80, ✉ shaun.mitch@wanadoo.fr, 🖳 www.tuquet.com). Mitch & Shaun Leake. (See **Chapter 9**.)

GT Services (☎/🖶 04 94 45 43 48, ✉ GTLeiSuves@aol.com, 🖳 www.caravansatleisuves.co.uk). Property Maintenance. Gordon Taylor. (See **Chapter 8**.)

Language in Provence (☎ 04 90 75 56 47, ✉ languageinprovence@wanadoo.fr, 🖳 www.lanuageinprovence.com). Susan Hickie. (See **Chapter 10**.)

M&K Services (☎ 05 65 10 87 28/06 73 54 59 40, ✉ methos02@wanadoo.fr). Karen & Mark Powell. (See **Chapter 8**.)

La Maison du Vert, Ticheville, 61120 Vimoutiers (☎ 02 33 36 95 84, 🖳 www.maisonduvert.com). Daniel & Debbie Armitage (see **Chapter 7**).

One the Web (☎ 05 53 36 97 92, ✉ rgriffiths@onetheweb.com, 🖳 www.onetheweb.com). Raymond Gilbert-Griffiths. (See **Chapter 11**.)

Papillon Properties (☎ 05 49 87 45 47, 🖶 05 49 87 51 99, ✉ info@papillon-properties.com, 🖳 www.papillon-properties.com). Susan Dixon. (See **Chapter 8**.)

Premier Property Care (🖳 www.premierpropertycare.com/www.lamaisonronde.com). David & Sharon Evans. (See **Chapter 8**.)

Simon Pullen DC, BSc (☎ 05 53 23 32 21, ✉ chiro.pullen@wanadoo.fr). Chiropractor. (See **Chapter 12**.)

Red Dog Books (☎ 02 98 24 15 19, ✉ reddogbooks@wanadoo.fr, 💻 www. reddogbooks.com). Harold & Wendy Mewes. (See **Chapter 11**.)

SARL John Roberts (☎ 05 63 94 31 70, ✉ johnroberts@club-internet.fr). (See **Chapter 8**.)

Martin Rushton, Dip Surv, MRICS (☎ 04 68 31 76 18, 🖷 UK 0870-134 1283, ✉ martin.rushton@wanadoo.fr, 💻 msr@R-Qui-Tex.com). Surveyor. (See **Chapter 8**.)

Simply British (☎ 05 61 64 98 89, ✉ simplybritfoix@aol.com). Susan Hodge. (See **Chapter 9**.)

SO IT (Sud Ouest Informatique, ☎ 05 65 37 63 45, ✉ james@soit.fr, 💻 www.soit.fr). James & Joy Blake. (See **Chapter 9**.)

La Table du Mareyeur (☎ 04 94 56 06 77, 🖷 04 94 56 40 75, ✉ infor@ mareyeur.com, 💻 www.mareyeur.com). Caroline & Ewan Scutcher. (See **Chapter 7**.)

Estate Agents

The following agents in France and the UK deal in commercial property in the areas specified.

A Home in France, The Old Granary, Low Lane, Cuddington, Bucks HP18 0AA, UK (☎ 0870-748 6161, 💻 www.ahomeinfrance.com) & **A Home in France SARL**, 34 place de la Fontaine, 37500 Chinon (☎ 02 47 93 12 21, ✉ ahomeinfrance@wanadoo.fr). Properties with *chambres d'hôtes*/chalet potential in the Loire Valley and the Alps.

A House in France Ltd, 11 Mountview, London NW7 3HT, UK (☎ 020-8959 5182, ✉ john.hart@virgin.net, 💻 french-property-news.com/ ahif.htm). Properties include *gîte* complexes, B&Bs, bars, hotels, restaurants, studs and smallholdings. Main areas: Brittany, Normandy, Poitou-Charentes, Limousin, Languedoc, Rhône-Alpes.

Keats France, 28 Broad Street, Alresford, Hampshire, SO24 9AQ, UK (☎ 01962-734633, ✉ williamson@keatsalresford.co.uk or gakwfrance @aol.com, 💻 www.keats.biz). Mostly tourism-related and agricultural property in all areas of France.

La Résidence, St Martin's House, 17 St Martin's Street, Wallingford, Oxon OX10 0EA, UK (☎ 01491-838485, 💻 www.laresidence.co.uk). Gîte complexes and B&Bs in the north, west and south-west.

SARL PIF – Properties in France (☎ 02 41 52 02 18, 🖥 www.propertiesin france.com). Properties include *gîte* complexes, vineyards and stud farms.

Miscellaneous

Blevins Franks Tax Advisory Service, 26–34 Old Street, London EC1V 9QQ, UK (✉ jane.hayward@blevinsfranks.com).

Franco-British Chamber of Commerce & Industry, 31 rue Boissy d'Anglas, 75008 Paris (☎ 01 53 30 81 30, 🖥 www.francobritish chamber.com). Offers services to companies wishing to develop trade between the UK and France.

IBT Partners SARL, 17 rue du Colisée, 75008 Paris (☎ 01 56 88 29 00, 🖥 www.ibtpartners.com). Specialises in market entry, business development and finance and partnering services for international companies wishing to invest in France, but also offers set-up services for entrepreneurs.

IFA United Kingdom/Invest in France Agency, 21 Grosvenor Place, London SW1X 7HU, UK (🖥 020-7823 1895, 🖥 www.investinfrance.org). The French government agency for international investment.

Paris Development Agency/Paris Technopole (🖥 www.parisdevelop ment.com). Promotes the creation and development of innovative businesses that will contribute to the economic revival of the French capital.

APPENDIX B: FURTHER READING

Magazines

English-language

The publications listed below are a selection of the dozens related to France and French property. Many of these include information about working and running a business in France as well as an ordering service for books about France and the French.

The Connexion, BP25, 06480 La-Colle-sur-Loup, France (☎ 04 93 32 16 59, 💻 www.connexionfrance.com). Monthly newspaper.

Everything France Magazine, Brooklands Magazines Ltd, Medway House, Lower Road, Forest Row, East Sussex RH18 5HE, UK (☎ 01342-828700, 💻 www.everythingfrancemag.co.uk). Bi-monthly lifestyle magazine.

Focus on France, Outbound Publishing, 1 Commercial Road, Eastbourne, East Sussex BN21 3XQ, UK (☎ 01323-726040, 💻 www.outbound publishing.com). Quarterly property magazine.

France Magazine, Archant Life, Archant House, Oriel Road, Cheltenham, Gloucestershire GL50 1BB, UK (☎ 01242-216050, 💻 www.france mag.co.uk). Monthly lifestyle magazine.

France-USA Contacts, FUSAC, 26 rue Bénard, 75014 Paris, France (☎ 01 56 53 54 54, 💻 www.fusac.fr). Free bi-weekly magazine.

French Magazine, Merricks Media Ltd, Cambridge House South, Henry Street, Bath BA1 1JT, UK (☎ 01225-786840, 💻 www.french magazine.co.uk). Monthly lifestyle and property magazine.

French News, SARL Brussac, 225 route d'Angoulême, BP4042, 24004 Périgueux Cedex, France (☎ 05 53 06 84 40, 💻 www.french-news.com). Monthly newspaper.

French Property News, Archant Life, 6 Burgess Mews, London SW19 1UF, UK (☎ 020-8543 3113, 💻 www.french-property-news.com). Monthly property magazine.

The Irish Eyes Magazine, The Eyes, 2 rue des Laitières, 94300 Vincennes, France (☎ 01 41 74 93 03, 💻 www.irisheyes.fr). Monthly Paris cultural magazine.

Living France, Archant Life, Archant House, Oriel Road, Cheltenham, Gloucestershire GL50 1BB, UK (☎ 01242-216050, 💻 www.living france.com). Monthly lifestyle/property magazine.

Normandie & South of England Magazine, 330 rue Valvire, BP414, 50004 Saint-Lô, France (☎ 02 33 77 32 70, 💻 www.normandie-magazine.fr). News and current affairs about Normandy and parts of southern England, published eight times a year mainly in French but with some English articles and translations.

Paris Voice/Paris Free Voice, 7 rue Papillon, 75009 Paris, France (☎ 01 47 70 45 05, 💻 www.parisvoice.com). Free weekly newspaper.

The Riviera Reporter, 56 chemin de Provence, 06250 Mougins, France (☎ 04 93 45 77 19, 💻 www.riviera-reporter.com). Bi-monthly free magazine covering the Côte d'Azur.

The Riviera Times, 8 avenue Jean Moulin, 06340 Drap, France (☎ 04 93 27 60 00, 💻 www.rivieratimes.com). Monthly free newspaper covering the Côte d'Azur and Italian Riviera.

French

Challenges (💻 www.challenges.fr). Magazine for entrepreneurs.

Commerce Magazine. Magazine about running a commercial business in France, published nine times per year.

Courrier Cadres (💻 www.apec.fr). Magazine for executives and managers.

Défis (💻 www.entrepreneurs-fr.com). Magazine for entrepreneurs.

Entreprendre (💻 www.entreprendre.fr). Monthly magazine about running a business in France.

L'Entreprise (💻 www.lentreprise.com). Monthly magazine about running a business in France.

Franchise Magazine. Bimonthly magazine on franchising in France.

Management (💻 www.management.fr). Magazine for entrepreneurs.

L'Officiel de la Franchise (💻 www.lentreprise.com). Periodical about franchising in France, with occasional special editions.

Rebondir (💻 www.rebondir.fr). Magazine for entrepreneurs.

Repreneur: Cession Transmission d'Entreprise (💻 www.lentreprise.com). Bimonthly magazine about taking over a business in France.

L'Usine Nouvelle (💻 www.usinenouvelle.com). Magazine for entrepreneurs in manufacturing businesses.

Vente Directe Magazine (💻 www.ventedirecteline.com). Bimonthly magazine about direct selling.

Books

The Best Places to Buy a Home in France (Survival Books – see page 419)

Buying a Home in France (Survival Books – see page 419)

Comment Créer Son Entreprise (Studyrama, 🖥 www.studyrama.com)

Living & Working in France (Survival Books – see page 419)

Renovating & Maintaining Your French Home (Survival Books – see page 419)

APPENDIX C: USEFUL WEBSITES

Property Websites

Sites in English

A Vendre A Louer (🖥 www.avendrealouer.fr/en). Network for advertising all types of property for sale and rent.

Blue Homes (🖥 www.bluehomes.de/blue-en). Network of estate agents, working in five languages.

Find Your Property (🖥 www.findyourproperty.com). Global property finder.

France Magazine (🖥 www.francemag.com). English-language magazine with reviews on France and all things French.

Francophiles (🖥 www.francophiles.co.uk). UK-based property company specialising in the south-west, west, north, north-west, east and the south of France.

French Connections (🖥 www.frenchconnections.co.uk). Advertising portal for property owners and agents selling or renting in France.

French Property News (🖥 www.french-property-news.com). Containing advertisements from estate agents, solicitors, financial advisors, builders, removal companies, surveyors, etc.

Internet French Property (🖥 www.french-property.com). Property website with advertisements of properties for sale, rental and ancillary services.

Knight Frank (🖥 www.knightfrank.com/webui/france/en). Offering residential, commercial, valuation and investment services in Paris and the south of France.

Living France (🖥 www.livingfrance.com). A guide to France and French property.

Outbound Publishing (🖥 www.outboundpublishing.com). Information on emigration, jobs and property.

Salut-France (🖥 http://salut-france.com). Property search agents providing an English-language service in Brittany and Loire-Atlantique.

United Residence (🖥 www.united-residence.com/france). Network of estate agents.

General Property Websites

All sites are in French unless otherwise stated.

123 Immo (⌨ www.123immo.fr). Displays over 4,000 estate agencies' advertisements.

3d Immo (⌨ www.3d-immo.com). Portal displaying advertisements from individuals and estate agents.

Abonim (⌨ www.abonim.com). Displays advertisements from individuals and estate agents.

L'Argus du Logement (⌨ http://universimmo.servicesalacarte. wanadoo.fr/argus). Estimates of property values.

Century 21 (⌨ www.century21.fr). Estate agent with offices throughout France.

FNAIM (⌨ www.fnaim.fr). French national estate agents' organisation with advice and advertisements on buying property.

Guy Hoquet (⌨ www.guy-hoquet.com). Property company for buying or renting private or business premises.

Logic-immo (⌨ www.logic-immo.com). Monthly magazine publishing houses for sale and rent.

Nex Dom (⌨ www.nexdom.com). Advice and advertisements on buying property.

Orpi (⌨ www.orpi.com). Displays over 1,000 estate agencies' advertisements.

Panorimmo (⌨ www.panorimmo.com). Links to property websites.

Le Partenaire Européen (⌨ www.partenaire-europeen.fr). Property search agent helping buyers and sellers of property throughout France.

Propriétés de France (⌨ www.proprietesdefrance.com). Website specialising in advice and estate agents for top of the range property.

Le Site Immobilier (⌨ www.lesiteimmobilier.com). Website containing many estate agents' advertisements.

Le Tuc (⌨ www.letuc.com). Estate agent with offices throughout France.

Regional Property Websites

All sites are in French unless otherwise stated.

Acheter-louer (⌨ www.acheterlouer.fr) Estate agent specialising in the Ile-de-France.

Agence de la Bourse (⌨ www.agencedelabourse.fr). Commercial estate agent specialising in Normandy.

Bank Immo (🖳 www.bankimmo.com). Estate agent specialising in the French Riviera.

Cabinet Marcé (🖳 www.marce44.com). Commercial estate agent specialising in western France.

Commerces Bretagne (🖳 www.commerces-bretagne.com). Commercial estate agent specialising in Brittany.

Fonbail (🖳 www.fonbail.com). Commercial estate agent specialising in Paris and the surrounding area.

Immo 34 (🖳 http://immo34.ifrance.com). Estate agent specialising in Gard, Hérault and Aveyron.

L'Immobilier du Léman (🖳 www.leman-transactions.com). Commercial estate agent specialising in Savoie.

Immodumidi (🖳 www.immodumidi.com). Estate agent specialising in Languedoc-Roussillon and Aveyron.

Jouzel (🖳 www.jouzel-immobilier.com). Estate agent specialising in properties in Nantes.

Négocia (🖳 www.negocia-transactions.fr). Company specialising in commercial property in western France.

Transaffaires (🖳 www.fondscommerce.com). Commercial estate agent specialising in Provence.

Vendée Immobilier (🖳 www.vendee-immobilier.com). Commercial estate agent specialising in Vendée.

Commercial Property Websites

All sites are in French unless otherwise stated.

Acquisitions d'Entreprises (🖳 www.acquisitions-entreprises.com). Businesses for sale and advice concerning buying or setting up a business in France.

Act Contact (🖳 www.actcontact.net). Network for advice on selling or transferring a business in the south of France.

Act in Business (🖳 www.actinbusiness.com). Information regarding creating or taking over a business or franchise in France.

BNOA (🖳 www.bnoa.net). Platform for introducing those wishing to sell and those wishing to takeover a business in France.

Bureaux Commerces (🖳 www.bureaux-commerces.com). Advertisements for all types of business for sale in France.

Century 21 Enterprises et Commerces (⌨ www.century21commerce.fr). Commercial estate agent in France.

Commerces à Vendre (⌨ www.commerces-a-vendre.com). Advertisements for all types of businesses for sale in France and abroad.

CRA (⌨ www.cra.asso.fr/uk.php). Promoting the transfer of small and medium size companies, and ensuring their development through mergers or partnerships.

Croissance Affaires (⌨ http://ca.tpe-pme.com). Service for buying, transferring or selling a business in France.

ESCAP (⌨ http://escap-immo.com). Businesses for sale in northern, central and southern France.

Groupe de Karvin (⌨ www.cessionaffaires.com). Website for buying or selling a business.

ICF l'Argus des Commerces (⌨ www.cession-commerce.com). Information and advertisements for buying or selling a business.

Intercessio (⌨ www.repreneur.fr). Service dedicated to finding buyers for their clients' businesses.

La Maison Française (⌨ www.lamaisonfrancaise.fr). English-speaking estate agency.

Observatoire de la Franchise (⌨ www.observatoiredelafranchise.fr). Franchise information and opportunities.

PMI Contact (⌨ www.pmicontact.net). Advertisements for opportunities with small and medium size businesses.

Le Repreneur du Net (⌨ www.entreprises-a-vendre.fr). Advertisements for all types of business in France and abroad.

Tout Commerce (⌨ www.toutcommerce.com). Website for buying or selling a business.

Transcommerce (⌨ www.transcommerce.com). Network for the transfer of craft, trading and hotel businesses, especially in rural areas.

Vendez Votre Affaire (⌨ www.vendez-votre-affaire.com). Website for buying or selling all types of business.

Private Advertisers

L'Annonce (⌨ www.lannonce.com/immobilier/index.html). Private advertisements for property for sale or to rent.

Appel Immo (⌨ www.appelimmo.fr). Service company specialising in advertising property for sale between individuals.

La Centrale (💻 www.lacentrale.fr/home_immo.php). Private advertisements for property for sale or to rent.

E-immo (💻 www.e-immo.biz). Classified advertisements by individuals or estate agents.

Entreparticuliers (💻 www.entreparticuliers.com). Private advertisements for property for sale or to rent.

Explorimmo (💻 www.explorimmo.com). Private advertisements for property and links to other useful sites.

Immobilier-particulier (💻 www.immobilier-particulier.net). Advertisements for property to buy and rent throughout France.

Immosurcartes (💻 www.immosurcartes.com). Private advertisements for property for sale or to rent.

Immo-web (💻 www.immo-web.net). Private and estate agents' advertisements for property to buy and rent.

Le Journal des Particuliers (💻 www.journaldesparticuliers.fr). Advertisements for property for sale and holiday homes to rent throughout France.

Kitrouve (💻 www.kitrouve.com). Private advertisements for property for sale or to rent.

Mister Annonces (💻 www.misterannonces.com/FR/houses). Private advertisements for property for sale or to rent.

De Particulier à Particulier (💻 www.pap.fr). Set of magazines and services allowing private owners and buyers to complete their property transaction directly.

ParuVendu (💻 www.bonjour.fr). Classified advertisements for property for sale and rent.

Petites Annonces (💻 www.petites-annonces.fr). Private advertisements for property for sale or to rent.

French Property Magazines

France Magazine (💻 www.francemag.com). English-language magazine with reviews on France and all things French.

Franchise Magazine (💻 www.franchise-magazine.com). Information regarding all types of franchises.

ICF l'Argus des Commerces (💻 www.argus-commerce.com). Magazine of interest to all businesses.

Immobilier en France (💻 www.immobilierenfrance.com). Magazine with advertisements for property to buy and rent.

Info Presse (💻 www.info-presse.fr). Subscribe to more than 5,000 magazines, e.g. *Artisans Magazine, l'Officiel de la Franchise* and *l'Officiel des Commerciaux*.

L'Hôtellerie (💻 www.lhotellerie.fr). Magazine for those in the hotel and restaurant industry.

Living France (💻 www.livingfrance.com). English-language guide to France and French property.

Logic-immo (💻 www.logic-immo.com). Monthly magazine with advertisements for property for sale and rent.

PIC International (💻 www.pic-inter.com). Magazine for buying or selling a business.

PME Acquisitions d'Entreprises (💻 www.acquisitions-entreprises.com). Magazine for buying or selling a business.

Reprendre & Transmettre (💻 www.acquisition-cession.com). Magazine for buying or selling a business.

Repreneur (💻 www.repreneur.fr/repreneur.php). Magazine for buying or selling a business.

Development Authorities

All the following sites are in French.

Annecy (💻 www.carrefour-capital.com/annecy-alpes).

Aube (💻 www.aubedev.com, www.technopole-aube.fr).

Auvergne (💻 www.ard-auvergne.com).

Charente-Maritime (💻 www.charente-maritime.org).

Eure (💻 www.c3eure.com).

Hauts-de-Seine (💻 www.hauts-de-seine.net).

Indre (💻 www.objectifindre.com).

Le Havre (💻 www.havre-developpement.com).

Lille (💻 www.apim.com).

Limousin (💻 www.enlimousin.com).

Montpellier (💻 www.tech-montpellier.com).

Moselle (💻 www.moselle-capem.com).

Puy-de-Dôme (💻 www.business-in-europe.com/puy-de-dome/fr).

Sarthe (🖥 www.cap-creation-sarthe.com).

Toulouse (🖥 www.toulouse-emploi.com).

Financial Institutions & Insurance Companies

All sites are in French unless otherwise stated.

AFIC (🖥 www.afic.asso.fr). Investors' site.

AGIPI (🖥 www.agipi.com). Association d'Assurés pour la Prévoyance, la Dépendance et l'Epargne Retraite – pension authority.

BDPME (🖥 www.bdpme.fr). Information for small and medium-size businesses.

BNP Paribas (🖥 www.bnp.fr). Banque Nationale de Paris.

Groupe CIC (🖥 www.cic-banques.fr). Banking group.

Organic (🖥 www.organic.fr). Pensions and invalidity benefits for commercial businesses.

Job Finding Sites

Bon Job (🖥 www.bonjob.com). Site for job-seekers and employers.

Cadremploi (🖥 www.cadremploi.com). Jobs for executives and managers.

Le Comité de Liaison des Comités de Bassin d'Emploi (🖥 www.clcbe.com). Ministry of Employment site.

Emploi LR (🖥 www.emploi-lr.com). Jobs in Languedoc-Roussillon.

Emploi.com (🖥 www.emploi.com). General job site.

Journal de l'Emploi (🖥 www.journaldelemploi.com). Regional guide to employment and training.

Stepstone (🖥 www.stepstone.fr). General job site.

General Information Sites

All sites are in French unless otherwise stated.

A2C (🖥 www.a-2-c.fr). Legal information.

Acuité (🖥 www.acuite.fr). Miscellaneous information for entrepreneurs.

Agence National Pour l'Emploi/ANPE (🖥 www.anpe.fr). The national employment agency.

Agence Pour la Création d'Entreprises (🖥 www.apce.com). Official government site with information on starting a business – some in English.

AJINFO (⌨ www.ajinfo.org). Businesses in difficulty for sale.

L'Annuaire (⌨ www.annu.com). The French telephone directory online, searchable by area.

Assemblée des Chambres Françaises de Commerce et d'Industrie/ACFCI (⌨ www.acfci.cci.fr). Association of French Chambers of Commerce.

Assemblée Permanente des Chambres des Métiers (⌨ www.apcm.com). Chambers of Guilds.

Banexi Capital Partenaires (⌨ www.banexicapital.com). Information for medium-size businesses.

Bott SA (⌨ www.bott.fr). Shop window for business equipment and utility vehicles.

Car'go (⌨ www.cargo.fr). Professional vehicle hire.

Chambres des Métiers (⌨ www.artisans-de-france.com/f_chambres.html). All the Chambers of Guilds in France.

Ciel (⌨ www.ciel.com). Software for small and medium-size businesses.

La Cinquième (⌨ www.lacinquieme.fr/emploi). French TV channel with information about employment and the economy.

La Confédération Générale des PME (⌨ www.cgpme.org). The National Federation of Small and Medium-size businesses.

Demain (⌨ www.demain.fr). Site of the cable TV channel specialising in employment, training and enterprise.

EBP Informatique (⌨ www.ebp.fr). Software for small and medium-size businesses.

Éditions Francis Lefebvre (⌨ www.efl.fr). Legal and financial information.

EGEE (⌨ www.egee.asso.fr). Networking site where retired executives give the benefit of their experience.

Entreprendre en France (⌨ www.entreprendre-en-france.fr). Help and advice for those wishing to start a business.

European Union (⌨ www.europa.eu.int). General information about working in France (and other EU countries) and details of the economic situation and employment situation in each region. In English.

FEEF (⌨ www.feef.org). Site of the Fédération des Entreprises et Entrepreneurs de France, providing general information about starting a business.

Fiducial (⌨ www.fiducial.fr). Information for small businesses.

France Initiative Réseau (⌨ www.fir.asso.fr). Information about loans and other assistance for entrepreneurs.

Greffe du Tribunal de Commerce (🖥 www.greffe-tc-paris.com). Information on the formalities of setting up a company.

Groupe Revue Fiduciaire (🖥 www.GroupeRF.com). Financial and legal news.

ICF l'Argus des Commerces (🖥 www.cession-commerce.com). Information on buying a business.

Info Travail (🖥 www.infotravail.com). Government site with information on the legal aspects of employment.

Juri-Logement (🖥 www.juri-logement.org). Legal information.

La Loi (🖥 www.laloi.com). Legal information.

Métro (🖥 www.metro.fr). Wholesale information and goods.

Ministère des Equipements, des Transports et du Logement (🖥 www. logement.equipement.gouv.fr). Website for the Ministry of Housing and Urban Planning.

Ministry of Employment (🖥 www.travail.gouv.fr). Site of the Ministère de l'Emploi, du Travail et de la Cohésion Sociale.

Monter une Entreprise (🖥 www.montermonentreprise.com). Online magazine with information about starting a business.

NetPME SAS (🖥 www.netpme.fr). Information for those setting up and running companies, including model articles of incorporation.

OSEO Services (🖥 www.portailpme.fr). State-sponsored website providing general information.

Panoranet (🖥 www.panoranet.com). Mortgage and insurance information.

Paris Entreprises (🖥 www.paris-entreprises.com). Official site for information about setting up a business in the Paris area, but offers clear information relevant to all areas of France.

Le Parisien (🖥 www.leparisien.com). Site of the newspaper, *Le Parisien*, with job and property advertisements.

Perval (🖥 www.immoprix.com). General land and property prices.

Petites Affiches (🖥 www.petites-affiches.presse.fr). Legal information.

Rétif (🖥 www.retif-shop.com). Business equipment of all kinds.

SNPI (🖥 www.snpi.fr). Website of the estate agents' organisation containing advertisements and advice.

URSSAF (🖥 www.urssaf.fr). Official site of the main social security agency, with details of social security contributions.

Appendix d: Weights & Measures

France uses the metric system of measurement. Those who are more familiar with the imperial system of measurement will find the tables on the following pages useful. Some comparisons shown are only approximate, but are close enough for most everyday uses. In addition to the variety of measurement systems used, clothes sizes often vary considerably with the manufacturer. The following websites allow you to make instant conversions between different measurement systems: 💻 www.omnis. demon.co.uk and 💻 www.unit-conversion.info.

Women's Clothes

Continental	34	36	38	40	42	44	46	48	50	52
UK	8	10	12	14	16	18	20	22	24	26
US	6	8	10	12	14	16	18	20	22	24

Pullovers

	Women's						Men's					
Continental	40	42	44	46	48	50	44	46	48	50	52	54
UK	34	36	38	40	42	44	34	36	38	40	42	44
US	34	36	38	40	42	44	sm	med		lar	xl	

Men's Shirts

Continental	36	37	38	39	40	41	42	43	44	46
UK/US	14	14	15	15	16	16	17	17	18	-

Men's Underwear

Continental	5	6	7	8	9	10
UK	34	36	38	40	42	44
US	sm	med		lar	xl	

Note: sm = small, med = medium, lar = large, xl = extra large

Children's Clothes

Continental	92	104	116	128	140	152
UK	16/18	20/22	24/26	28/30	32/34	36/38
US	2	4	6	8	10	12

Children's Shoes

Continental	18 19 20 21 22 23 24 25 26 27 28 29 30 31 32
UK/US	2 3 4 4 5 6 7 7 8 9 10 11 11 12 13
Continental	33 34 35 36 37 38
UK/US	1 2 2 3 4 5

Shoes (Women's and Men's)

Continental	35	36	37	37	38	39	40	41	42	42	43	44
UK	2	3	3	4	4	5	6	7	7	8	9	9
US	4	5	5	6	6	7	8	9	9	10	10	11

Weight

Imperial	Metric	Metric	Imperial
1oz	28.35g	1g	0.035oz
1lb*	454g	100g	3.5oz
1cwt	50.8kg	250g	9oz
1 ton	1,016kg	500g	18oz
2,205lb	1 tonne	1kg	2.2lb

Length

Imperial	Metric	Metric	Imperial
1in	2.54cm	1cm	0.39in
1ft	30.48cm	1m	3ft 3.25in
1yd	91.44cm	1km	0.62mi
1mi	1.6km	8km	5mi

Capacity

Imperial	Metric	Metric	Imperial
1 UK pint	0.57 litre	1 litre	1.75 UK pints
1 US pint	0.47 litre	1 litre	2.13 US pints
1 UK gallon	4.54 litres	1 litre	0.22 UK gallon
1 US gallon	3.78 litres	1 litre	0.26 US gallon

Note: An American 'cup' = around 250ml or 0.25 litre.

Area

Imperial	Metric	Metric	Imperial
1 sq. in	0.45 sq. cm	1 sq. cm	0.15 sq. in
1 sq. ft	0.09 sq. m	1 sq. m	10.76 sq. ft
1 sq. yd	0.84 sq. m	1 sq. m	1.2 sq. yds
1 acre	0.4 hectares	1 hectare	2.47 acres
1 sq. mile	2.56 sq. km	1 sq. km	0.39 sq. mile

Temperature

°Celsius	°Fahrenheit	
0	32	(freezing point of water)
5	41	
10	50	
15	59	
20	68	
25	77	
30	86	
35	95	
40	104	
50	122	

Notes: The boiling point of water is 100°C / 212°F.

Normal body temperature (if you're alive and well) is 37°C / 98.6°F.

Temperature Conversion

Celsius to Fahrenheit: multiply by 9, divide by 5 and add 32. (For a quick and approximate conversion, double the Celsius temperature and add 30.)

Fahrenheit to Celsius: subtract 32, multiply by 5 and divide by 9. (For a quick and approximate conversion, subtract 30 from the Fahrenheit temperature and divide by 2.)

Oven Temperatures

Gas	Electric	
	°F	°C
-	225–250	110–120
1	275	140
2	300	150
3	325	160
4	350	180
5	375	190
6	400	200
7	425	220
8	450	230
9	475	240

Air Pressure

PSI	Bar
10	0.5
20	1.4
30	2
40	2.8

Power

Kilowatts	Horsepower	Horsepower	Kilowatts
1	1.34	1	0.75

APPENDIX E: MAP

The map opposite shows the 22 regions and 96 departments of France (excluding overseas territories), which are listed below. Departments 91 to 95 come under the Ile-de-France region, which also includes Ville de Paris (75), Seine-et-Marne (77) and Yvelines (78), shown in detail opposite. The island of Corsica consists of two departments, 2A and 2B.

01 Ain	32 Gers	64 Pyrénées-Atlantiques
02 Aisne	33 Gironde	65 Hautes-Pyrénées
2A Corse-du-Sud	34 Hérault	66 Pyrénées-Orientales
2B Haute Corse	35 Ille-et-Vilaine	67 Bas-Rhin
03 Allier	36 Indre	68 Haut-Rhin
04 Alpes-de-Hte-Provence	37 Indre-et-Loire	69 Rhône
05 Hautes-Alpes	38 Isère	70 Haute-Saône
06 Alpes-Maritimes	39 Jura	71 Saône-et-Loire
07 Ardèche	40 Landes	72 Sarthe
08 Ardennes	41 Loir-et-Cher	73 Savoie
09 Ariège	42 Loire	74 Haute-Savoie
10 Aube	43 Haute-Loire	75 Paris
11 Aude	44 Loire-Atlantique	76 Seine-Maritime
12 Aveyron	45 Loiret	77 Seine-et-Marne
13 Bouches-du-Rhône	46 Lot	78 Yvelines
14 Calvados	47 Lot-et-Garonne	79 Deux-Sèvres
15 Cantal	48 Lozère	80 Somme
16 Charente	49 Maine-et-Loire	81 Tarn
17 Charente-Maritime	50 Manche	82 Tarn-et-Garonne
18 Cher	51 Marne	83 Var
19 Corrèze	52 Haute-Marne	84 Vaucluse
21 Côte-d'Or	53 Mayenne	85 Vendée
22 Côte-d'Armor	54 Meurthe-et-Moselle	86 Vienne
23 Creuse	55 Meuse	87 Haute-Vienne
24 Dordogne	56 Morbihan	88 Vosges
25 Doubs	57 Moselle	89 Yonne
26 Drôme	58 Nièvre	90 Territoire de Belfort
27 Eure	59 Nord	91 Essonne
28 Eure-et-Loir	60 Oise	92 Hauts-de-Seine
29 Finistère	61 Orne	93 Seine-Saint-Denis
30 Gard	62 Pas-de-Calais	94 Val-de-Marne
31 Haute-Garonne	63 Puy-de-Dôme	95 Val-d'Oise

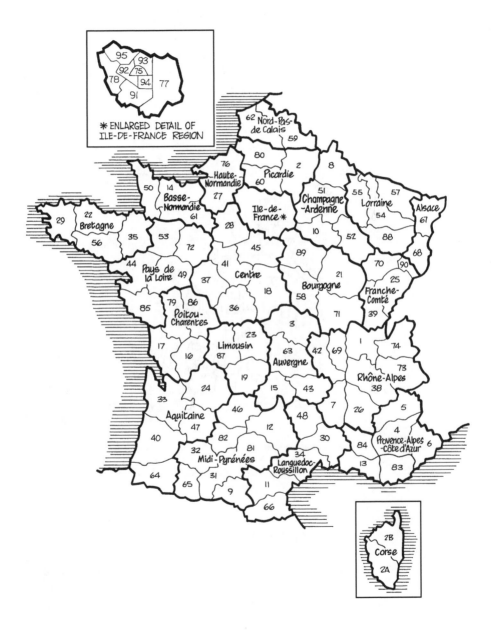

INDEX

S

LIVING AND WORKING SERIES

Living and Working books are essential reading for anyone planning to spend time abroad, including holiday-home owners, retirees, visitors, business people, migrants, students and even extra-terrestrials! They're packed with important and useful information designed to help you **avoid costly mistakes and save both time and money.** Topics covered include how to:

- Find a job with a good salary & conditions
- Obtain a residence permit
- Avoid and overcome problems
- Find your dream home
- Get the best education for your family
- Make the best use of public transport
- Endure local motoring habits
- Obtain the best health treatment
- Stretch your money further
- Make the most of your leisure time
- Enjoy the local sporting life
- Find the best shopping bargains
- Insure yourself against most eventualities
- Use post office and telephone services
- Do numerous other things not listed above

Living and Working books are the most comprehensive and up-to-date source of practical information available about everyday life abroad. They aren't, however, boring text books, but interesting and entertaining guides written in a highly readable style.

Discover what it's *really* like to live and work abroad!

Order your copies today by phone, fax, post or email from: Survival Books, PO Box 3780, YEOVIL, BA21 5WX, United Kingdom (☎/▤ +44 (0)1935-700060, ✉ sales@survivalbooks.net, ▣ www.survivalbooks.net).

BUYING A HOME SERIES

Buying a Home books, including **Buying, Selling & Letting Property**, are essential reading for anyone planning to purchase property abroad. They're packed with vital information to guide you through the property purchase jungle and help you **avoid the sort of disasters that can turn your dream home into a nightmare!** Topics covered include:

- Avoiding problems
- Choosing the region
- Finding the right home and location
- Estate agents
- Finance, mortgages and taxes
- Home security
- Utilities, heating and air-conditioning
- Moving house and settling in
- Renting and letting
- Permits and visas
- Travelling and communications
- Health and insurance
- Renting a car and driving
- Retirement and starting a business
- And much, much more!

Buying a Home books are the most comprehensive and up-to-date source of information available about buying property abroad. Whether you want a detached house, townhouse or apartment, a holiday or a permanent home, these books will help make your dreams come true.

Save yourself time, trouble and money!

Order your copies today by phone, fax, post or email from: Survival Books, PO Box 3780, YEOVIL, BA21 5WX, United Kingdom (☎/🖨 +44 (0)1935-700060, ✉ sales@survivalbooks.net, 🖥 www.survivalbooks.net).

OTHER SURVIVAL BOOKS

The Alien's Guides: *The Alien's Guides to Britain and France* provide an 'alternative' look at life in these popular countries and will help you to appreciate the peculiarities (in both senses) of the British and French.

The Best Places to Buy a Home in France/Spain: The most comprehensive homebuying guides to France or Spain, containing detailed profiles of the most popular regions, with guides to property prices, amenities and services, employment and planned developments.

Buying, Selling and Letting Property: The most comprehensive and up-to-date source of information available for those intending to buy, sell or let a property in the UK.

Foreigners in France/Spain: Triumphs & Disasters: Real-life experiences of people who have emigrated to France and Spain, recounted in their own words – warts and all!

Lifelines: Essential guides to specific regions of France and Spain, containing everything you need to know about local life. Titles in the series currently include the Costa Blanca, Costa del Sol, Dordogne/Lot, Normandy and Poitou-Charentes; Brittany Lifeline is to be published in summer 2005.

Making a Living: Essential guides to self-employment and starting a business in France and Spain.

Renovating & Maintaining Your French Home: The ultimate guide to renovating and maintaining your dream home in France: what to do and what not to do, how to do it and, most importantly, how much it will cost.

Retiring Abroad: The most comprehensive and up-to-date source of practical information available about retiring to a foreign country, containing profiles of the 20 most popular retirement destinations.

Broaden your horizons with Survival Books!

Order your copies today by phone, fax, post or email from: Survival Books, PO Box 3780, YEOVIL, BA21 5WX, United Kingdom (☎/🖨 +44 (0)1935-700060, ✉ sales@survivalbooks.net, 🖳 www.survivalbooks.net).

Qty.	Title	Price (incl. p&p)			Total
		UK	**Europe**	**World**	
	The Alien's Guide to Britain	£6.95	£8.95	£12.45	
	The Alien's Guide to France	£6.95	£8.95	£12.45	
	The Best Places to Buy a Home in France	£13.95	£15.95	£19.45	
	The Best Places to Buy a Home in Spain	£13.95	£15.95	£19.45	
	Buying a Home Abroad	£13.95	£15.95	£19.45	
	Buying a Home in Cyprus	£13.95	£15.95	£19.45	
	Buying a Home in Florida	£13.95	£15.95	£19.45	
	Buying a Home in France	£13.95	£15.95	£19.45	
	Buying a Home in Greece	£13.95	£15.95	£19.45	
	Buying a Home in Ireland	£11.95	£13.95	£17.45	
	Buying a Home in Italy	£13.95	£15.95	£19.45	
	Buying a Home in Portugal	£13.95	£15.95	£19.45	
	Buying a Home in South Africa	£13.95	£15.95	£19.45	
	Buying a Home in Spain	£13.95	£15.95	£19.45	
	Buying, Letting & Selling Property	£11.95	£13.95	£17.45	
	Foreigners in France: Triumphs & Disasters	£11.95	£13.95	£17.45	
	Foreigners in Spain: Triumphs & Disasters	£11.95	£13.95	£17.45	
	Costa Blanca Lifeline	£11.95	£13.95	£17.45	
	Costa del Sol Lifeline	£11.95	£13.95	£17.45	
	Dordogne/Lot Lifeline	£11.95	£13.95	£17.45	
	Poitou-Charentes Lifeline	£11.95	£13.95	£17.45	
	Living & Working Abroad	£14.95	£16.95	£20.45	
	Living & Working in America	£14.95	£16.95	£20.45	
	Living & Working in Australia	£14.95	£16.95	£20.45	
	Living & Working in Britain	£14.95	£16.95	£20.45	
	Living & Working in Canada	£16.95	£18.95	£22.45	
	Living & Working in the European Union	£16.95	£18.95	£22.45	
	Living & Working in the Far East	£16.95	£18.95	£22.45	
	Living & Working in France	£14.95	£16.95	£20.45	
Total carried forward (see over)					

ORDER FORM

Qty.	Title	Price (incl. p&p) UK	Europe	World	Total
			Total brought forward		
	Living & Working in Germany	£16.95	£18.95	£22.45	
	L&W in the Gulf States & Saudi Arabia	£16.95	£18.95	£22.45	
	L&W in Holland, Belgium & Luxembourg	£14.95	£16.95	£20.45	
	Living & Working in Ireland	£14.95	£16.95	£20.45	
	Living & Working in Italy	£16.95	£18.95	£22.45	
	Living & Working in London	£13.95	£15.95	£19.45	
	Living & Working in New Zealand	£14.95	£16.95	£20.45	
	Living & Working in Spain	£14.95	£16.95	£20.45	
	Living & Working in Switzerland	£16.95	£18.95	£22.45	
	Making a Living in France	£13.95	£15.95	£19.45	
	Making a Living in Spain	£13.95	£15.95	£19.45	
	Normandy Lifeline	£11.95	£13.95	£17.45	
	Renovating & Maintaining Your French Home	£16.95	£18.95	£22.45	
	Retiring Abroad	£14.95	£16.95	£20.45	
				Grand Total	

Order your copies today by phone, fax, post or email from: Survival Books, PO Box 3780, YEOVIL, BA21 5WX, United Kingdom (☎/🖷 +44 (0)1935-700060, ✉ sales@ survivalbooks.net, 🖳 www.survivalbooks.net). If you aren't entirely satisfied, simply return them to us within 14 days for a full and unconditional refund.

I enclose a cheque for the grand total/Please charge my Amex/Delta/Maestro (Switch)/MasterCard/Visa card as follows. (delete as applicable)

Card No.   _ _ _ _   _ _ _ _   _ _ _ _   _ _ _ _   Security Code*   _ _ _

Expiry date _____   Issue number (Maestro/Switch only) _____

Signature _____   Tel. No. _____

NAME _____

ADDRESS _____

_____

_____

* The security code is the last three digits on the signature strip.